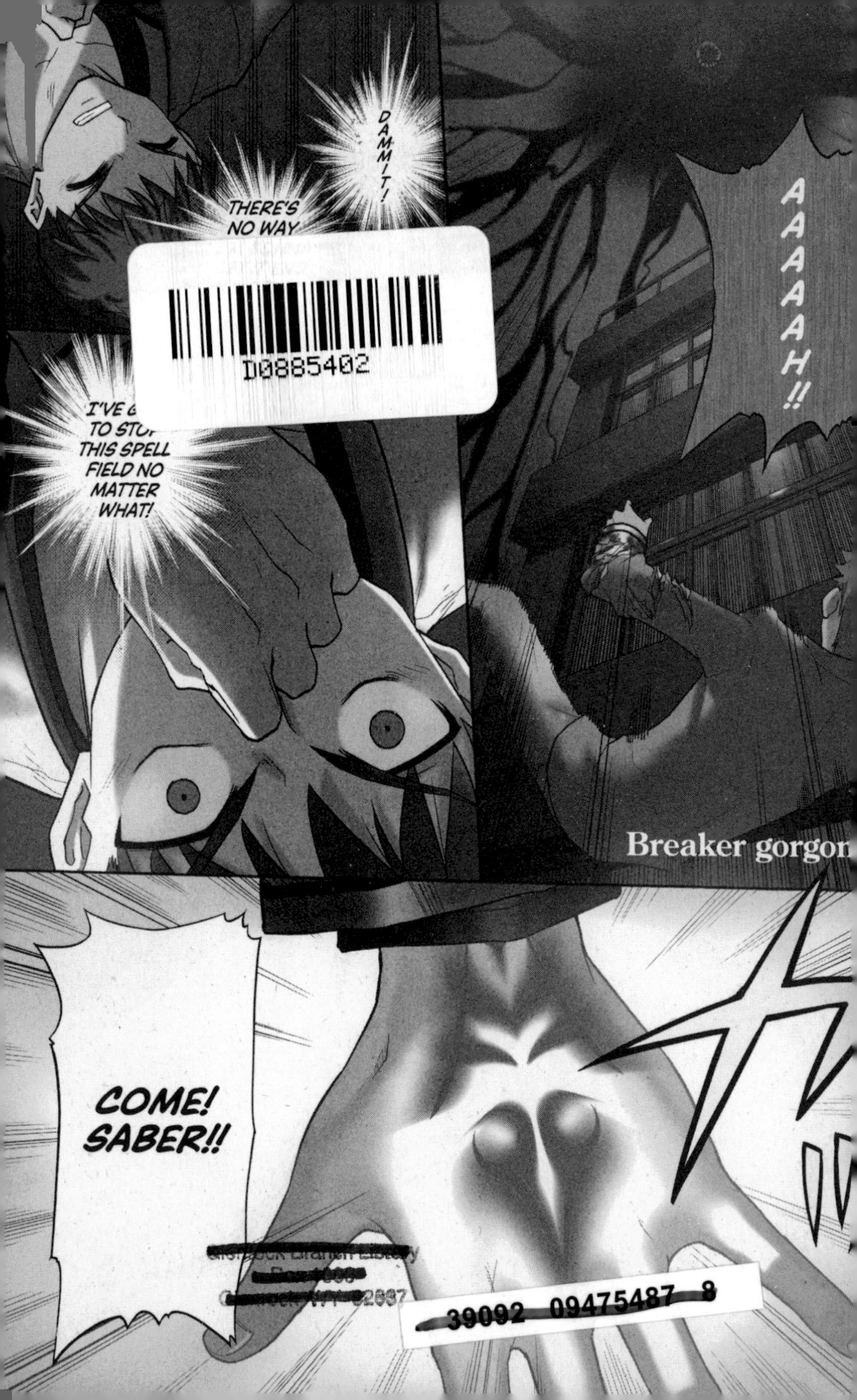
AAAAAAH!!
Breaker gorgon
DAMMIT!
THERE'S NO WAY
I'VE G
TO STO
THIS SPELL FIELD NO MATTER WHAT!
COME! SABER!!

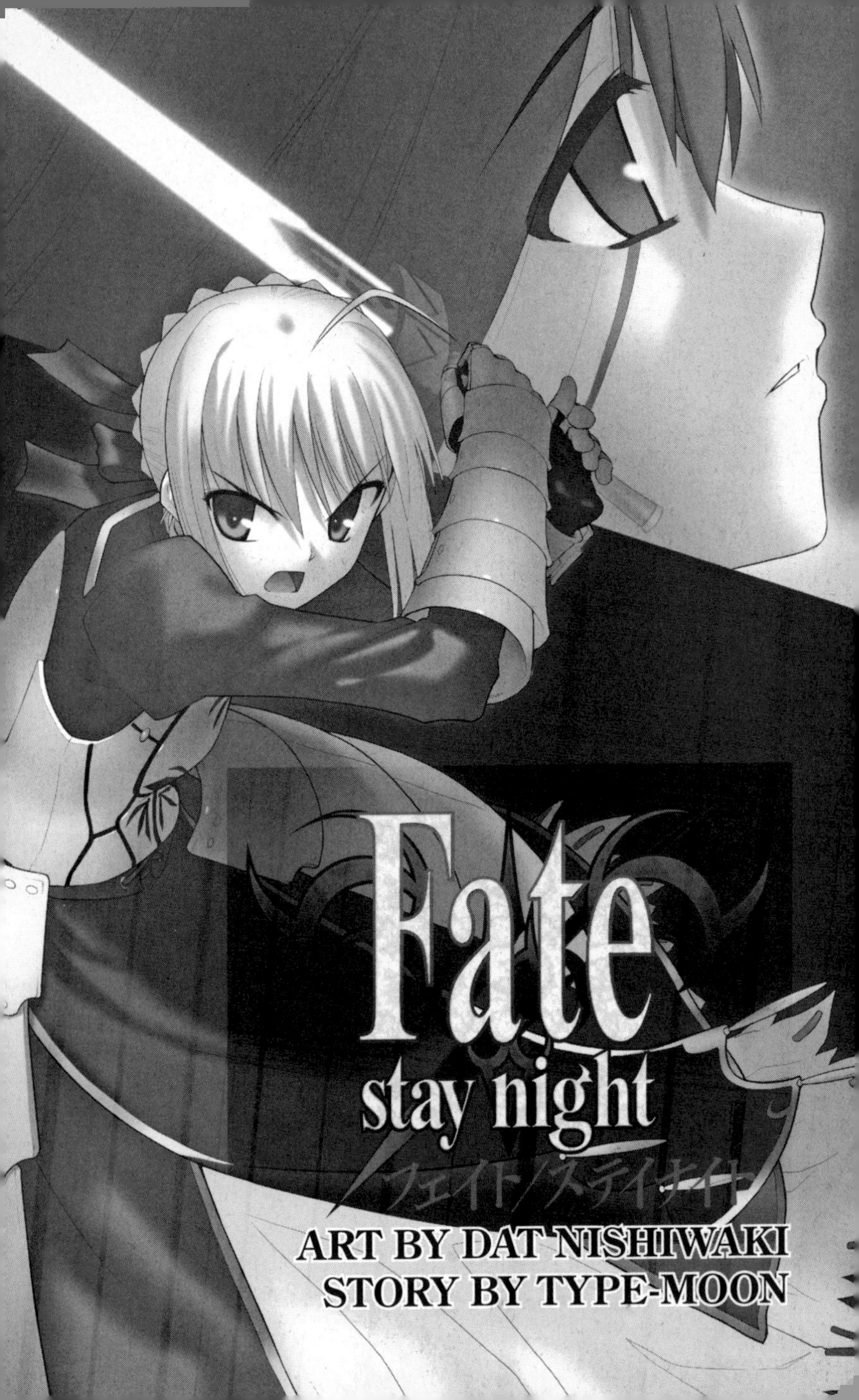
Fate
stay night
フェイト/ステイナイト
ART BY DAT NISHIWAKI
STORY BY TYPE-MOON

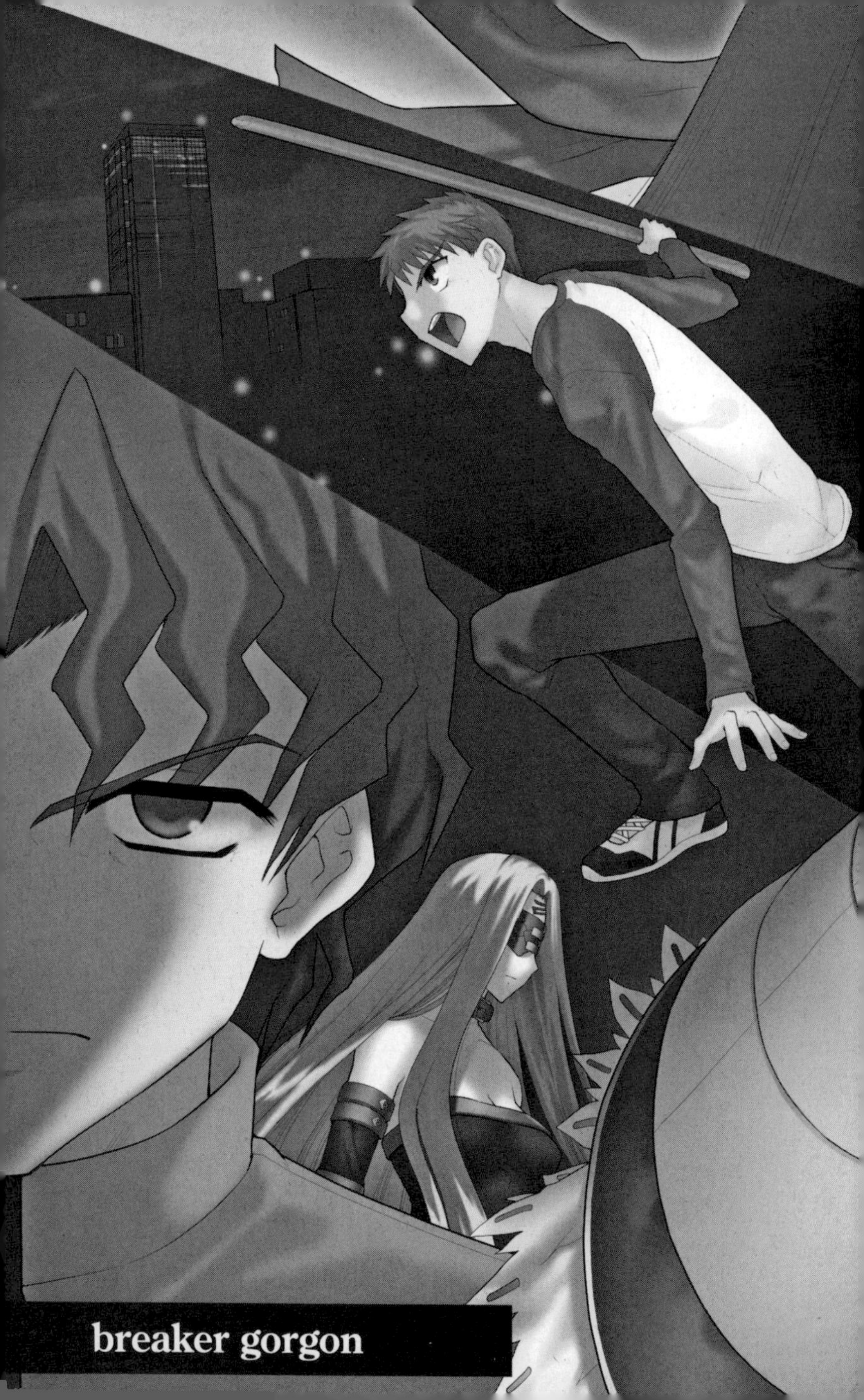
breaker gorgon

Fate
stay night ◇6◇
フェイト/ステイナイト

Fate stay night
フェイト/ステイナイト

VOLUME 6

ART BY DAT NISHIWAKI
STORY BY TYPE-MOON

HAMBURG // LONDON // LOS ANGELES // TOKYO

Fate/Stay Night Volume 6
Story by TYPE-MOON
Art By Dat Nishiwaki

Translation - Lori Riser
Copy Editor - Jill Bentley
English Adaptation - Peter Ahlstrom
Retouch and Lettering - Star Print Brokers
Production Artist - Lucas Rivera
Graphic Designer - Louis Csontos

Editor - Lillian Diaz-Przybyl
Print Production Manager - Lucas Rivera
Art Director - Al-Insan Lashley
Managing Editor - Vy Nguyen
Senior Designer - Louis Csontos
Director of Sales and Manufacturing - Allyson De Simone
Associate Publisher - Marco F. Pavia
President and C.O.O. - John Parker
C.E.O. and Chief Creative Officer - Stu Levy

A  Manga

TOKYOPOP Inc.
5900 Wilshire Blvd. Suite 2000
Los Angeles, CA 90036

E-mail: info@TOKYOPOP.com
Come visit us online at www.TOKYOPOP.com

Fate/stay night Volume 6
© 2008 Dat NISHIWAKI © TYPE-MOON
First published in Japan in 2008 by KADOKAWA SHOTEN
PUBLISHING CO., LTD., Tokyo. English translation rights
arranged with KADOKAWA SHOTEN PUBLISHING CO., LTD.,
Tokyo
English text copyright © 2010 TOKYOPOP Inc.

ISBN: 978-1-4278-1628-3

First TOKYOPOP printing: January 2010
10 9 8 7 6 5 4 3 2 1
Printed in the USA

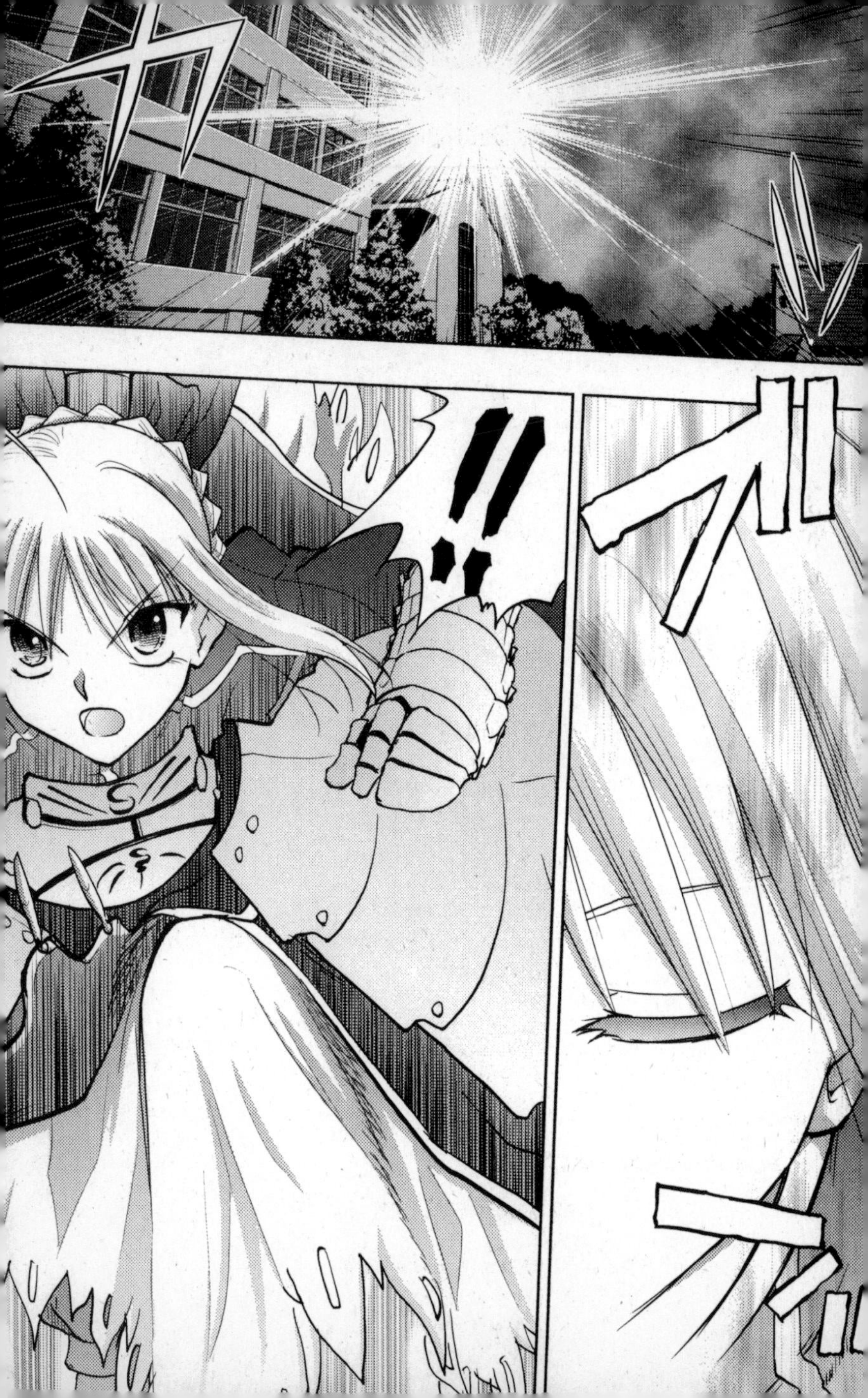
!!

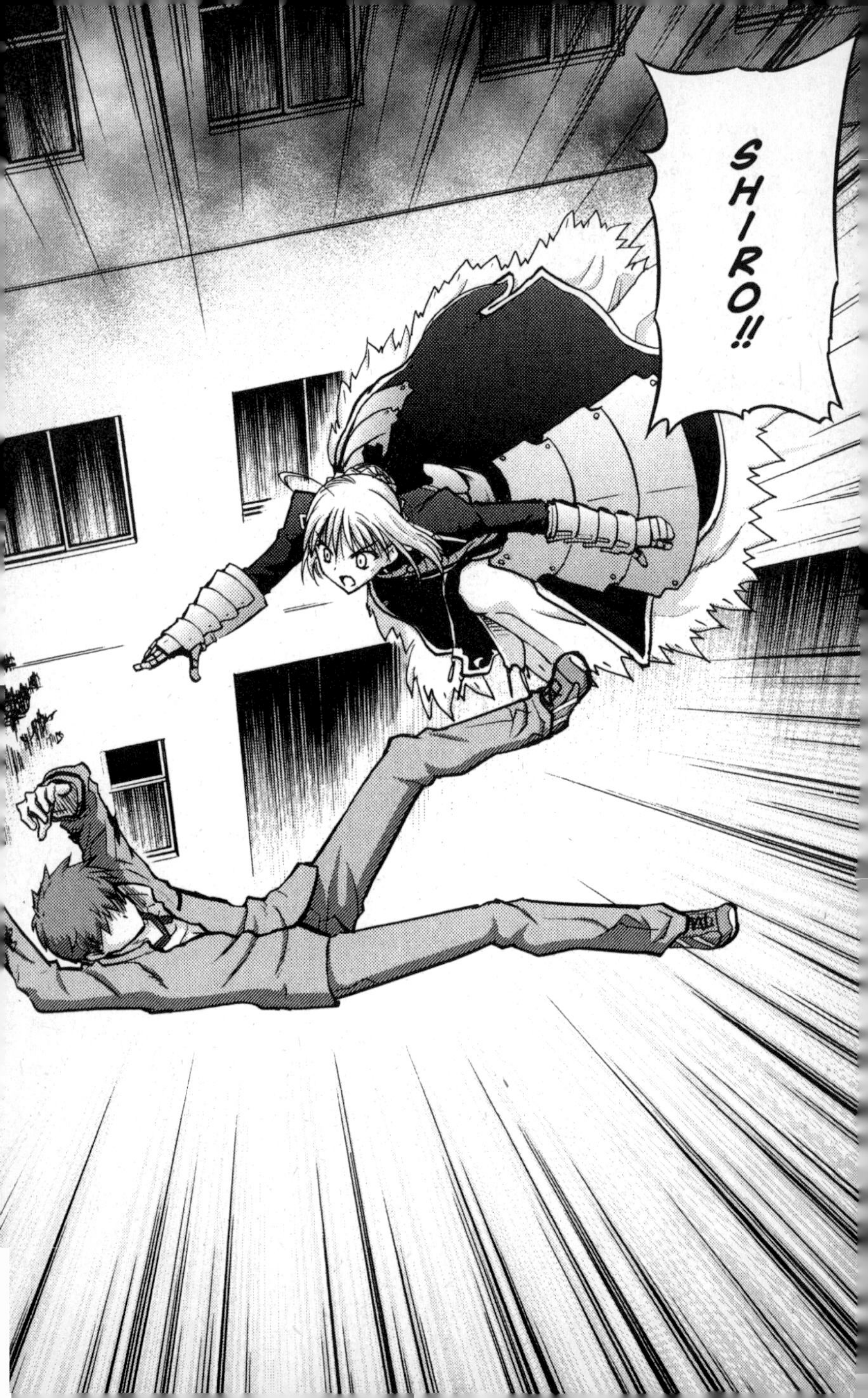
SHIRO!!

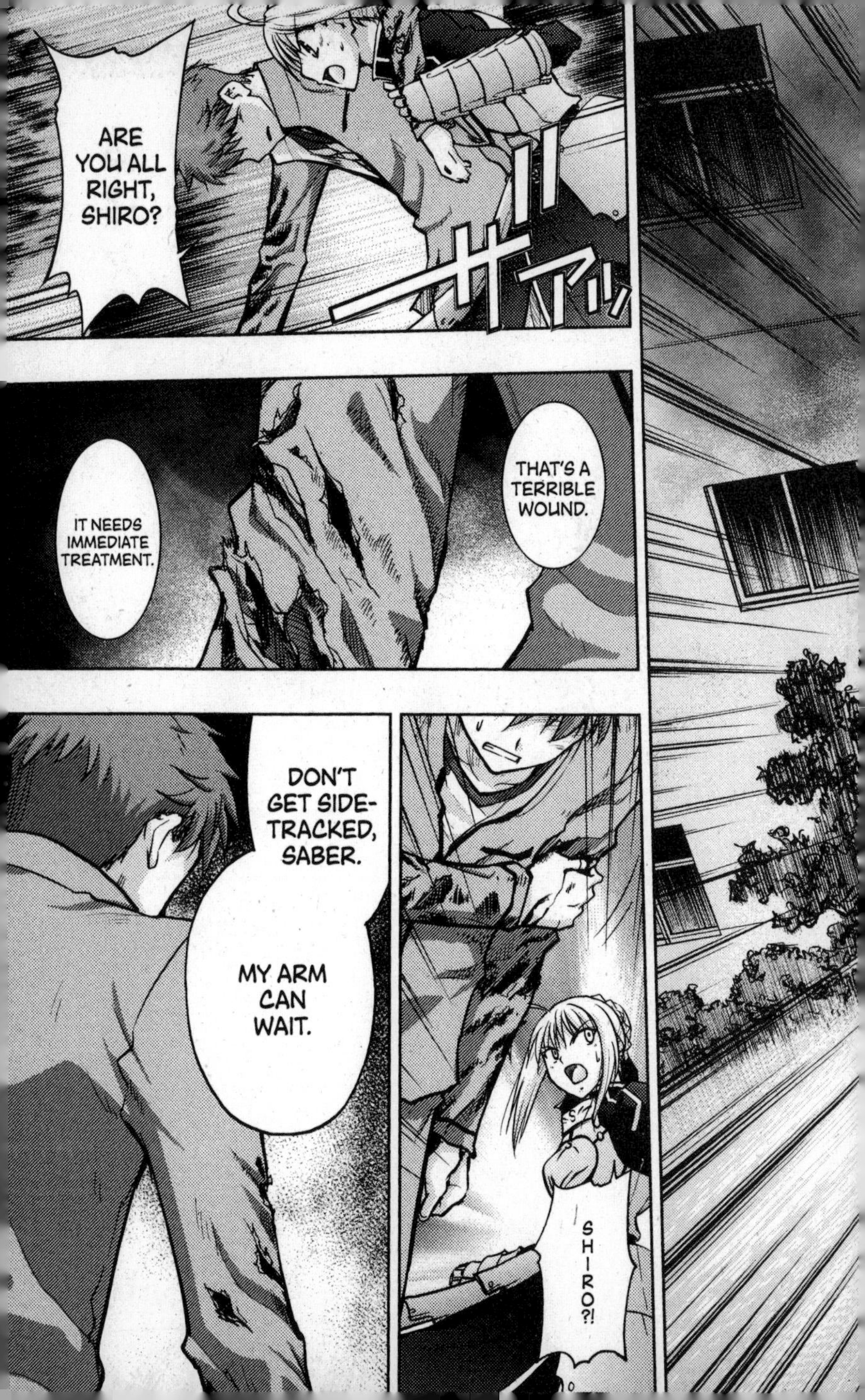
ARE YOU ALL RIGHT, SHIRO?
ザアッ
THAT'S A TERRIBLE WOUND.
IT NEEDS IMMEDIATE TREATMENT.
SHIRO?!
DON'T GET SIDE-TRACKED, SABER.
MY ARM CAN WAIT.

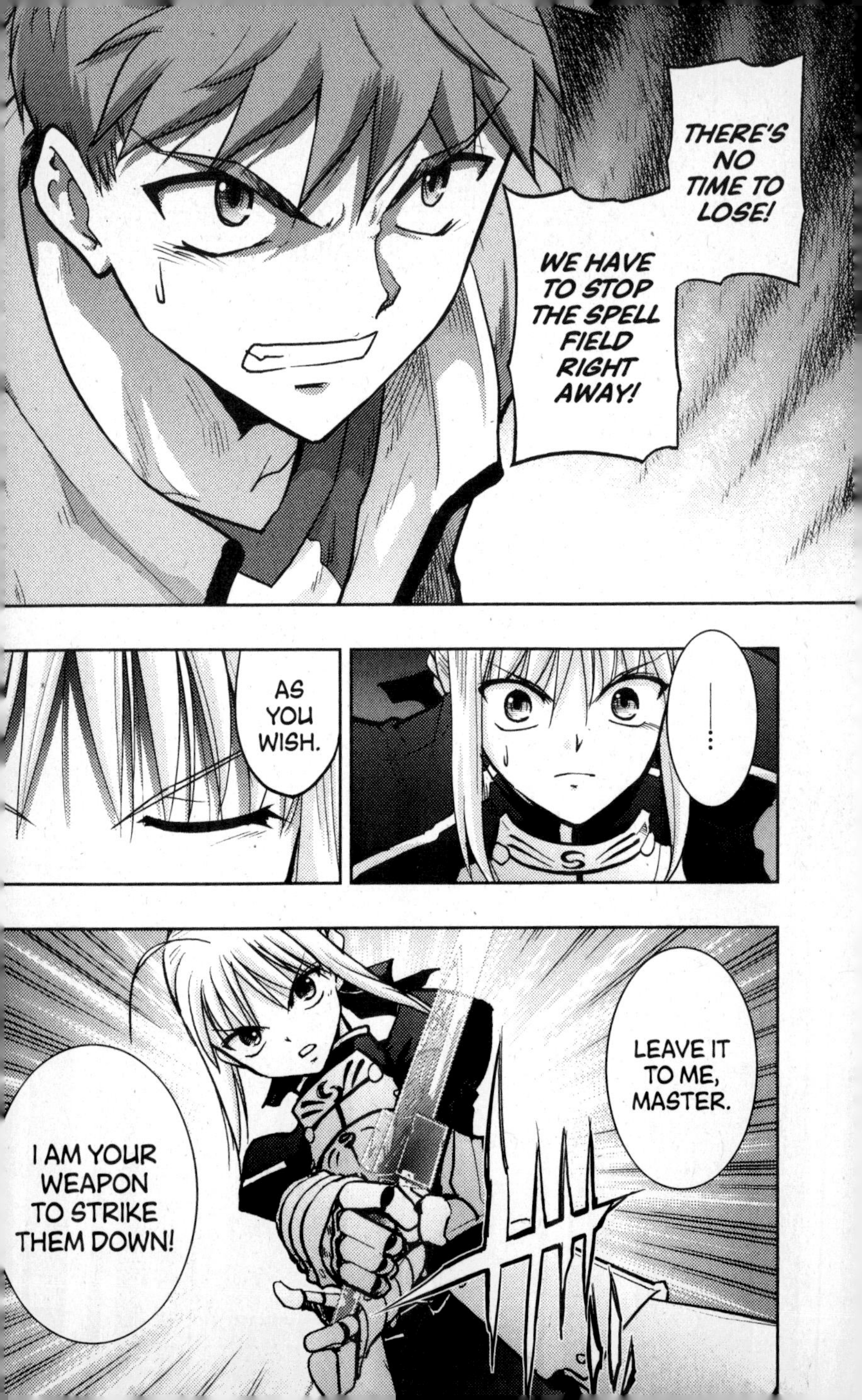
THERE'S NO TIME TO LOSE!
WE HAVE TO STOP THE SPELL FIELD RIGHT AWAY!
……
AS YOU WISH.
LEAVE IT TO ME, MASTER.
I AM YOUR WEAPON TO STRIKE THEM DOWN!

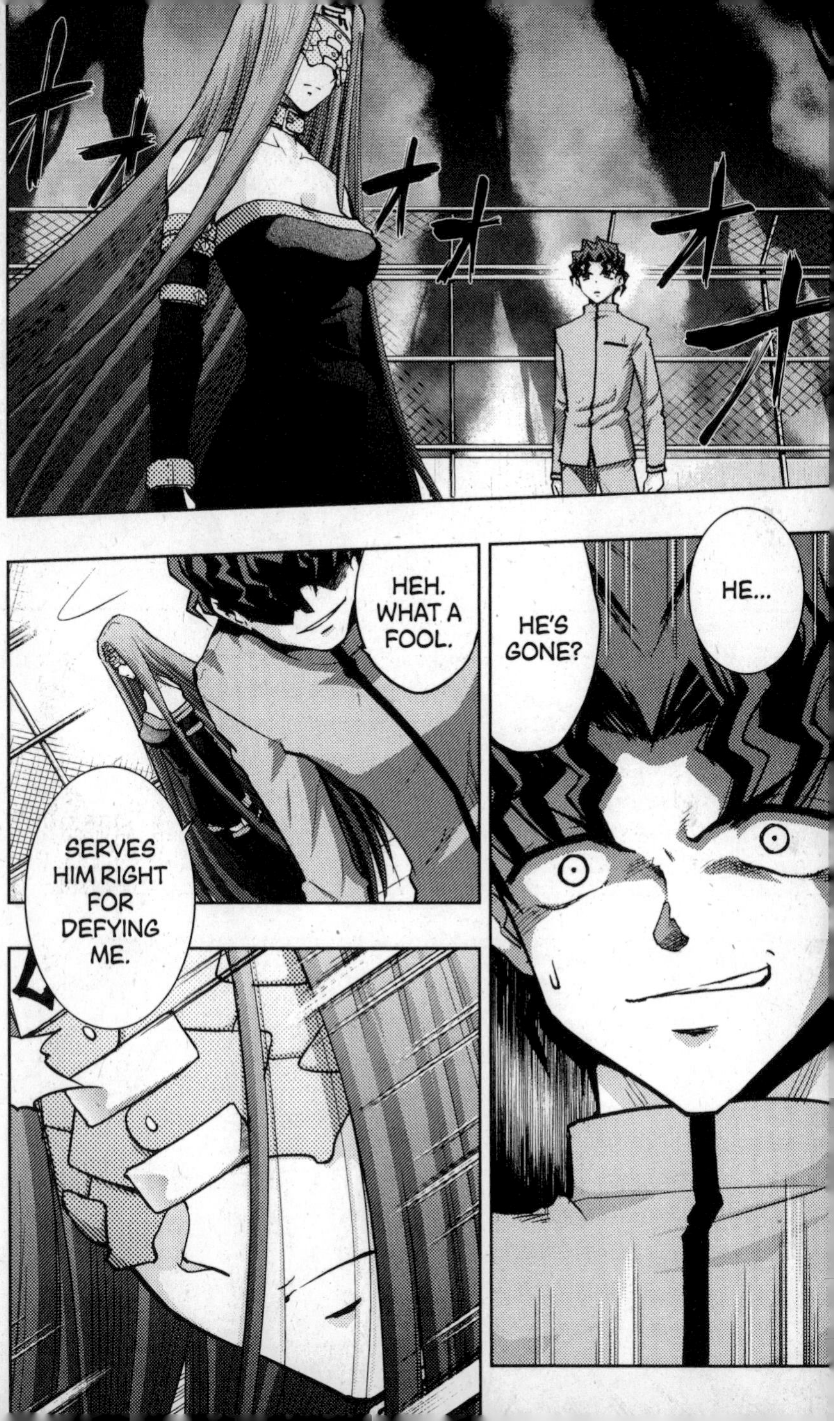
HE...
HE'S GONE?
HEH. WHAT A FOOL.
SERVES HIM RIGHT FOR DEFYING ME.

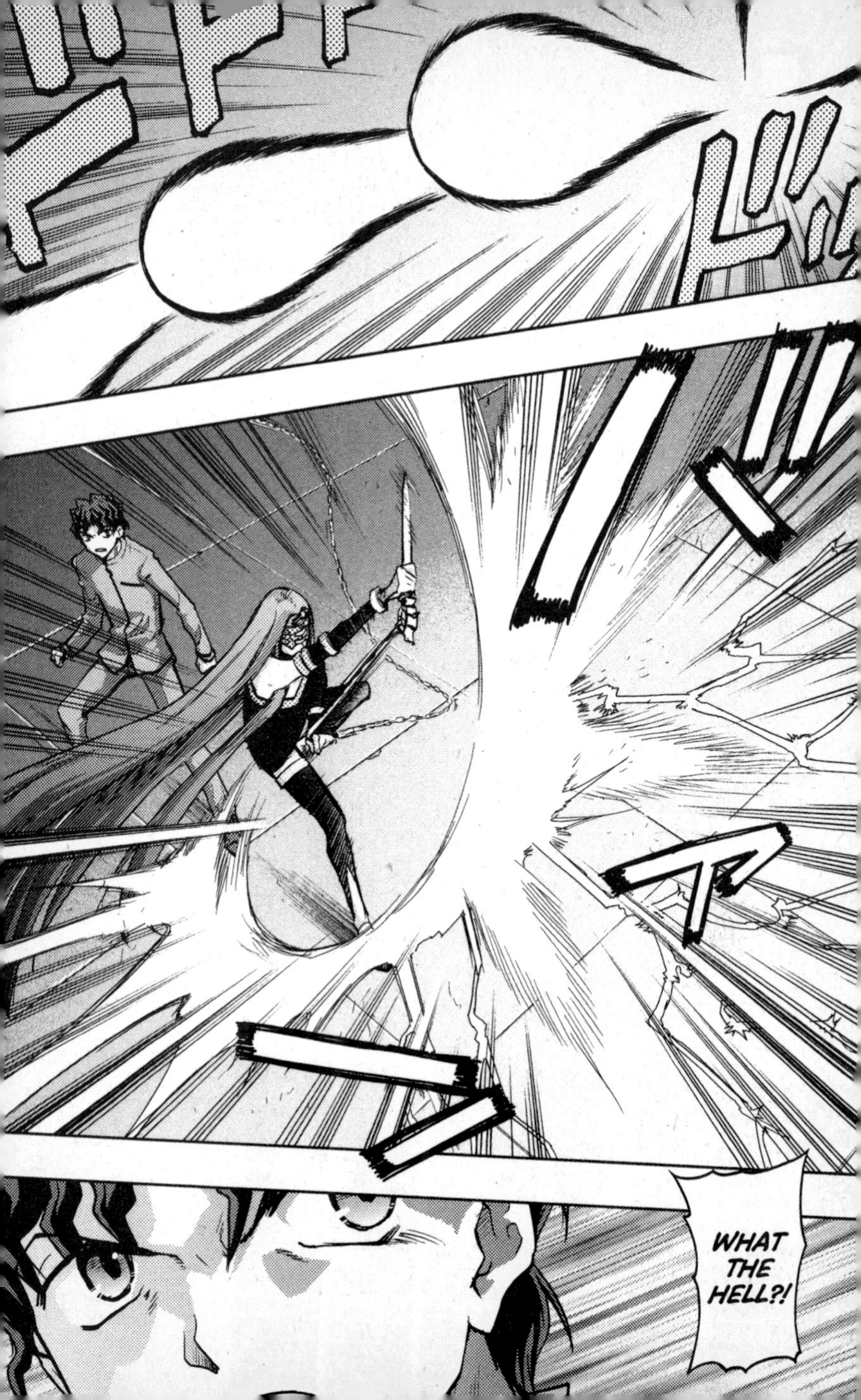
WHAT THE HELL?!

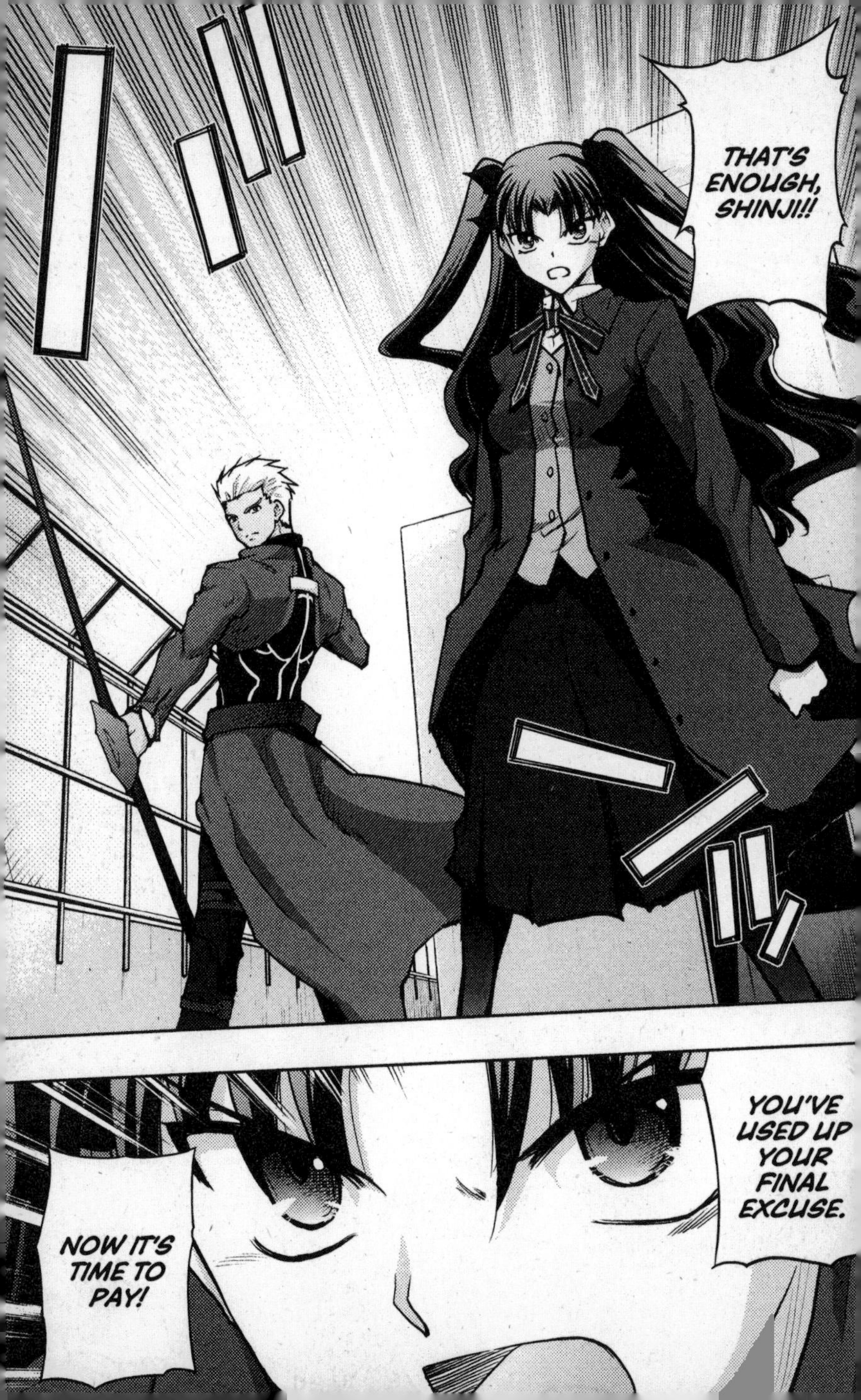
THAT'S ENOUGH, SHINJI!!
YOU'VE USED UP YOUR FINAL EXCUSE.
NOW IT'S TIME TO PAY!

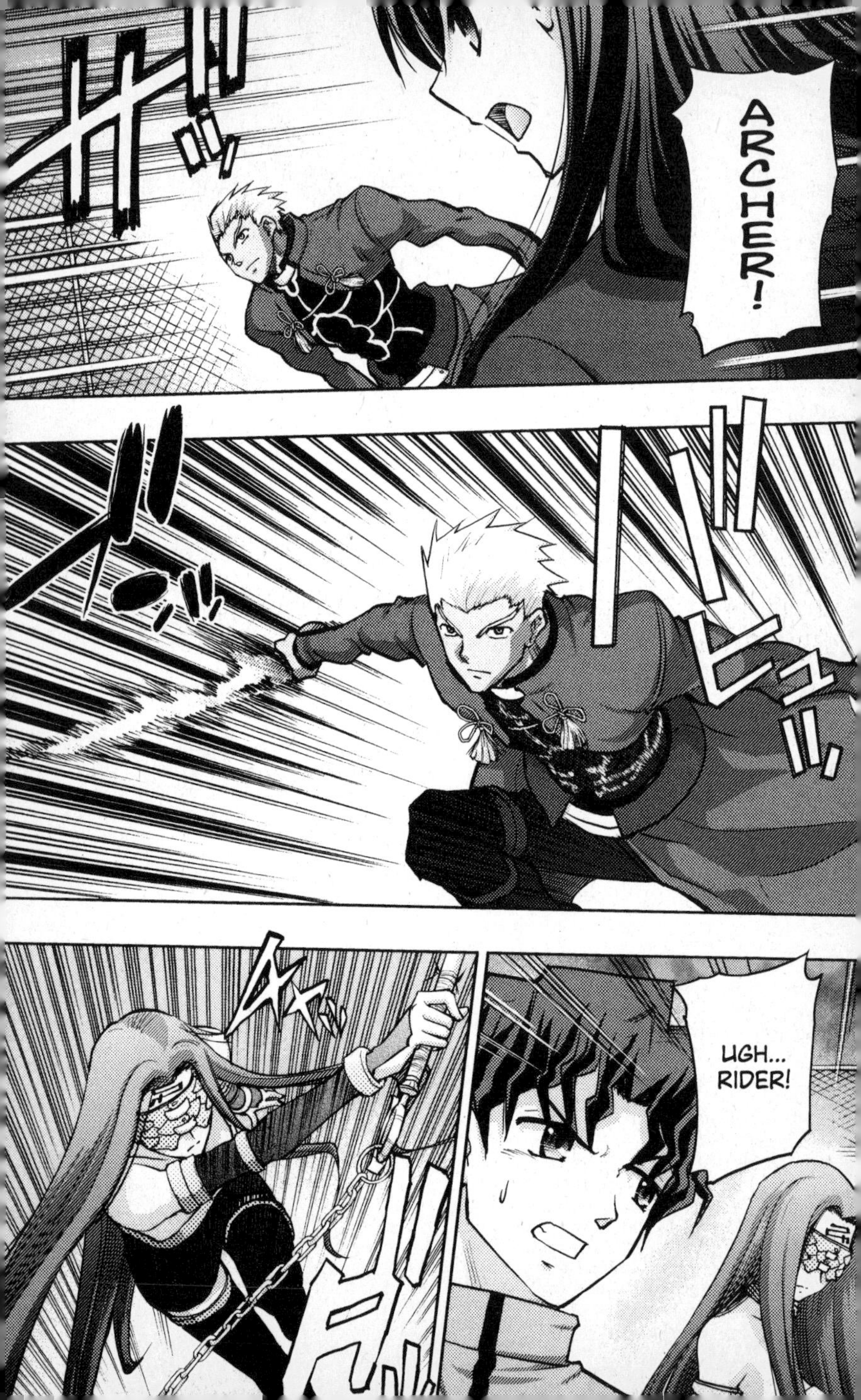
ARCHER!
UGH...
RIDER!

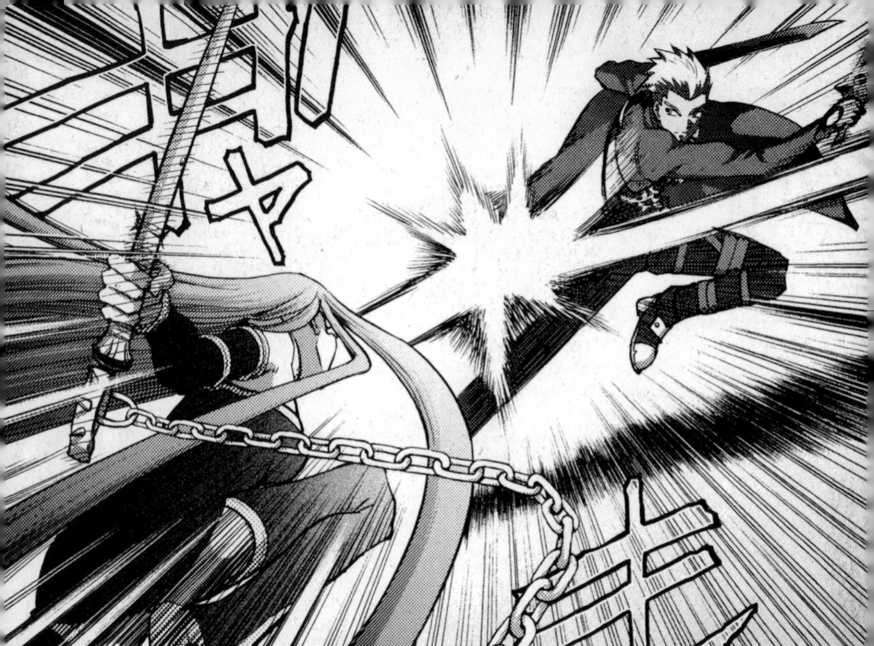
ギィィン
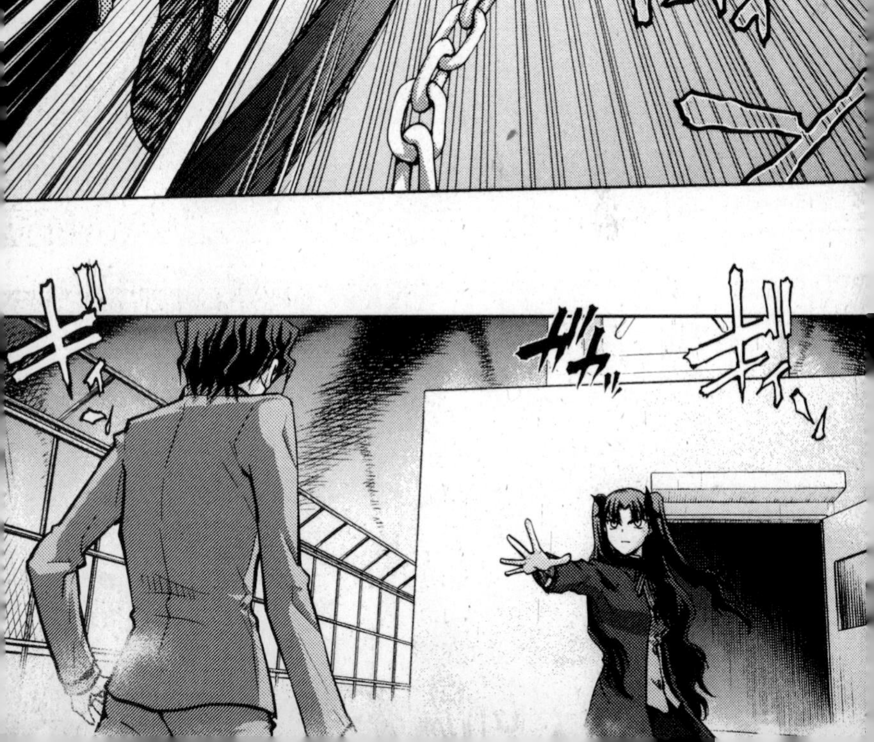
ギィィ
ザカッ
ギィ

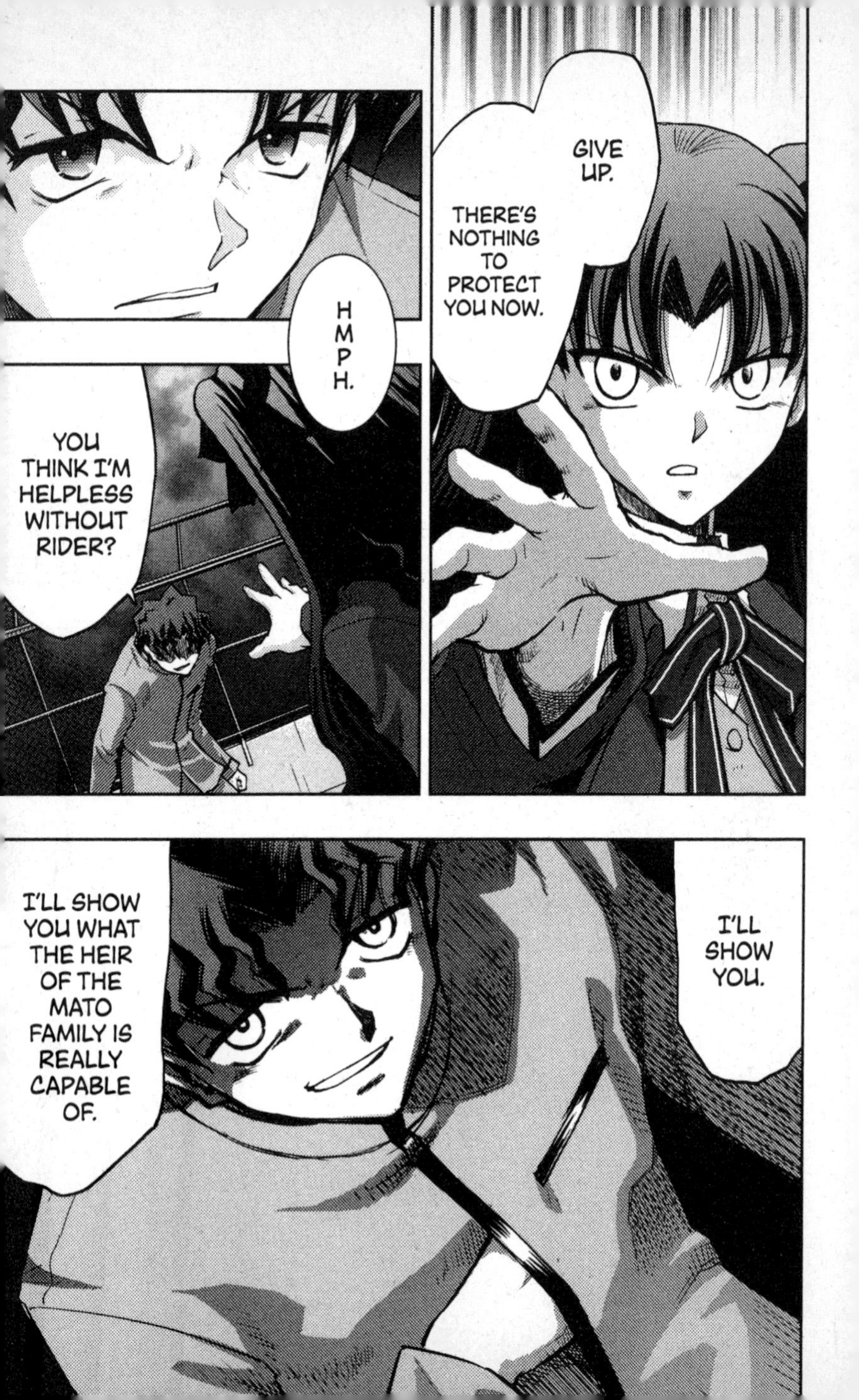
GIVE UP.
THERE'S NOTHING TO PROTECT YOU NOW.
HMPH.
YOU THINK I'M HELPLESS WITHOUT RIDER?
I'LL SHOW YOU.
I'LL SHOW YOU WHAT THE HEIR OF THE MATO FAMILY IS REALLY CAPABLE OF.

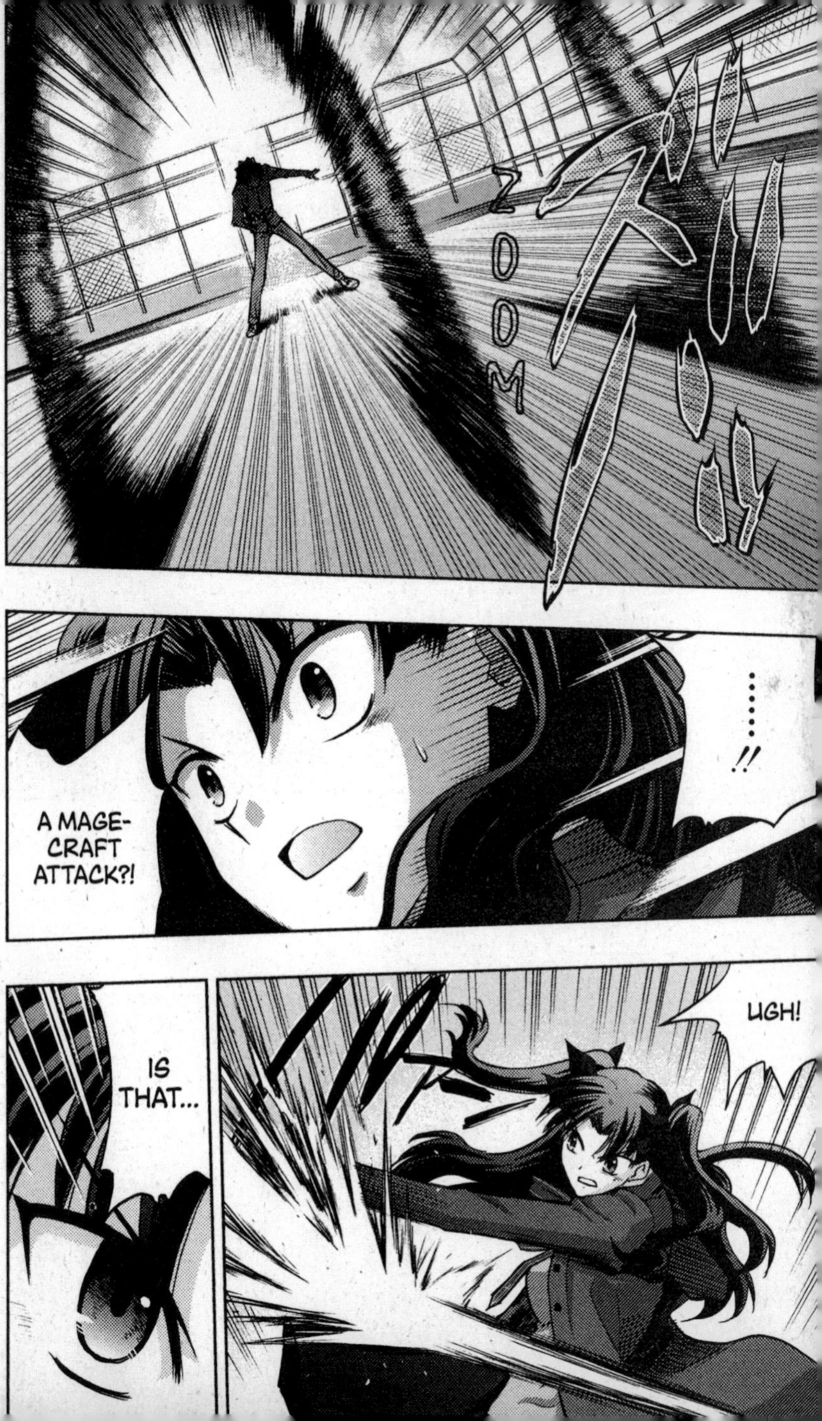
ZOOM
......!!
A MAGE-CRAFT ATTACK?!
UGH!
IS THAT...

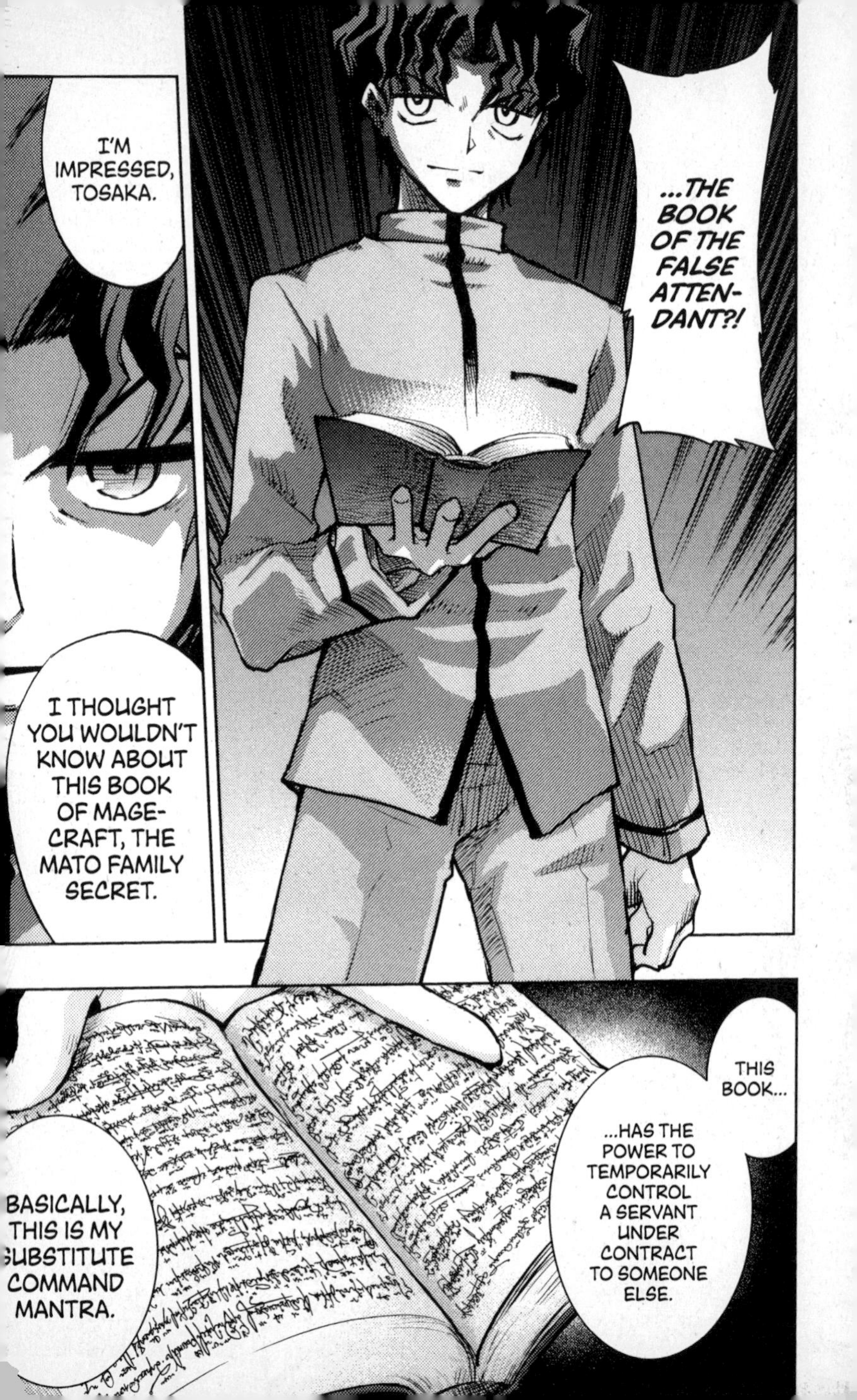
...THE BOOK OF THE FALSE ATTEN-DANT?!
I'M IMPRESSED, TOSAKA.
I THOUGHT YOU WOULDN'T KNOW ABOUT THIS BOOK OF MAGE-CRAFT, THE MATO FAMILY SECRET.
THIS BOOK...
...HAS THE POWER TO TEMPORARILY CONTROL A SERVANT UNDER CONTRACT TO SOMEONE ELSE.
BASICALLY, THIS IS MY SUBSTITUTE COMMAND MANTRA.

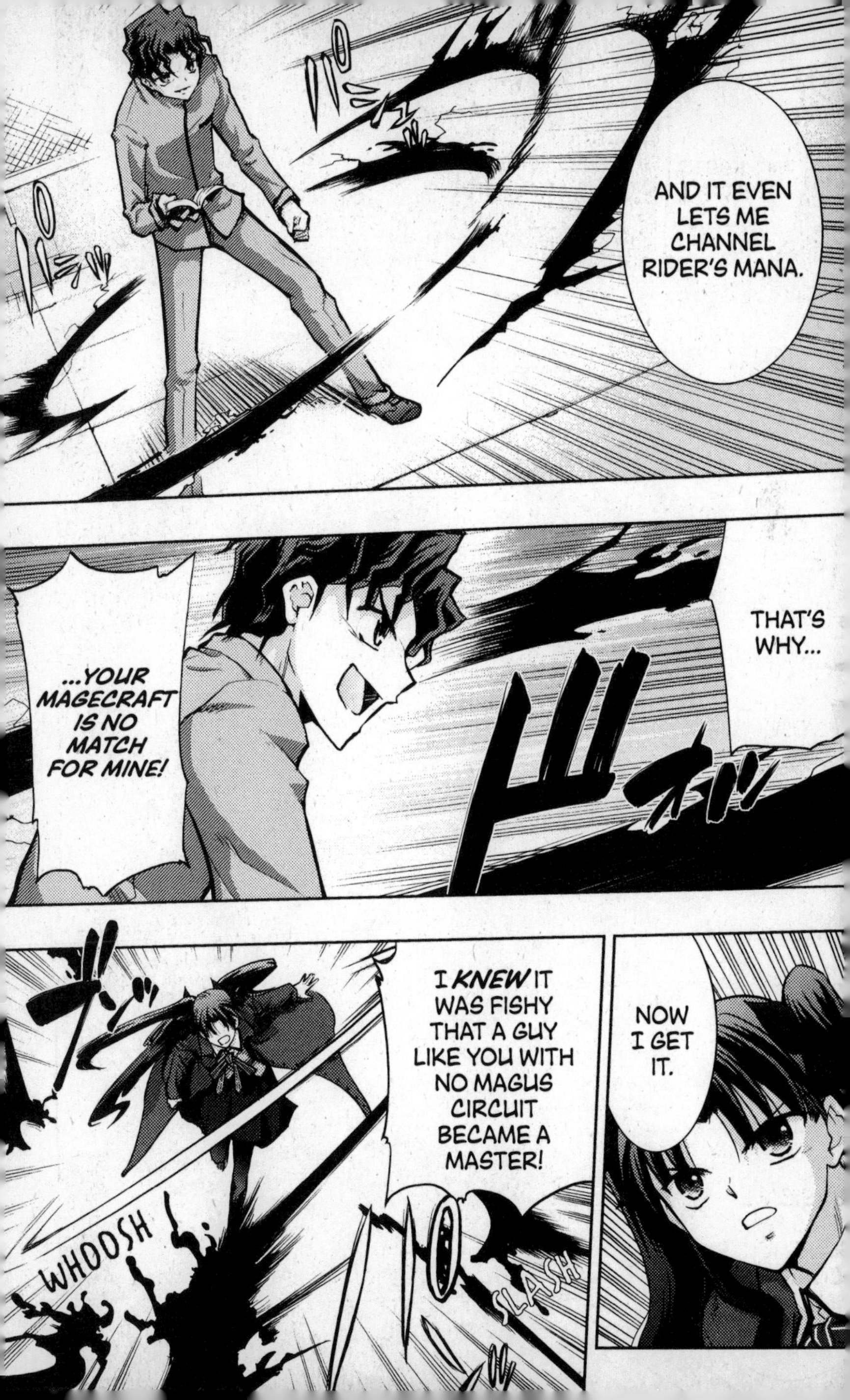
AND IT EVEN LETS ME CHANNEL RIDER'S MANA.
THAT'S WHY...
...YOUR MAGECRAFT IS NO MATCH FOR MINE!
NOW I GET IT.
I *KNEW* IT WAS FISHY THAT A GUY LIKE YOU WITH NO MAGUS CIRCUIT BECAME A MASTER!
SLASH
WHOOSH

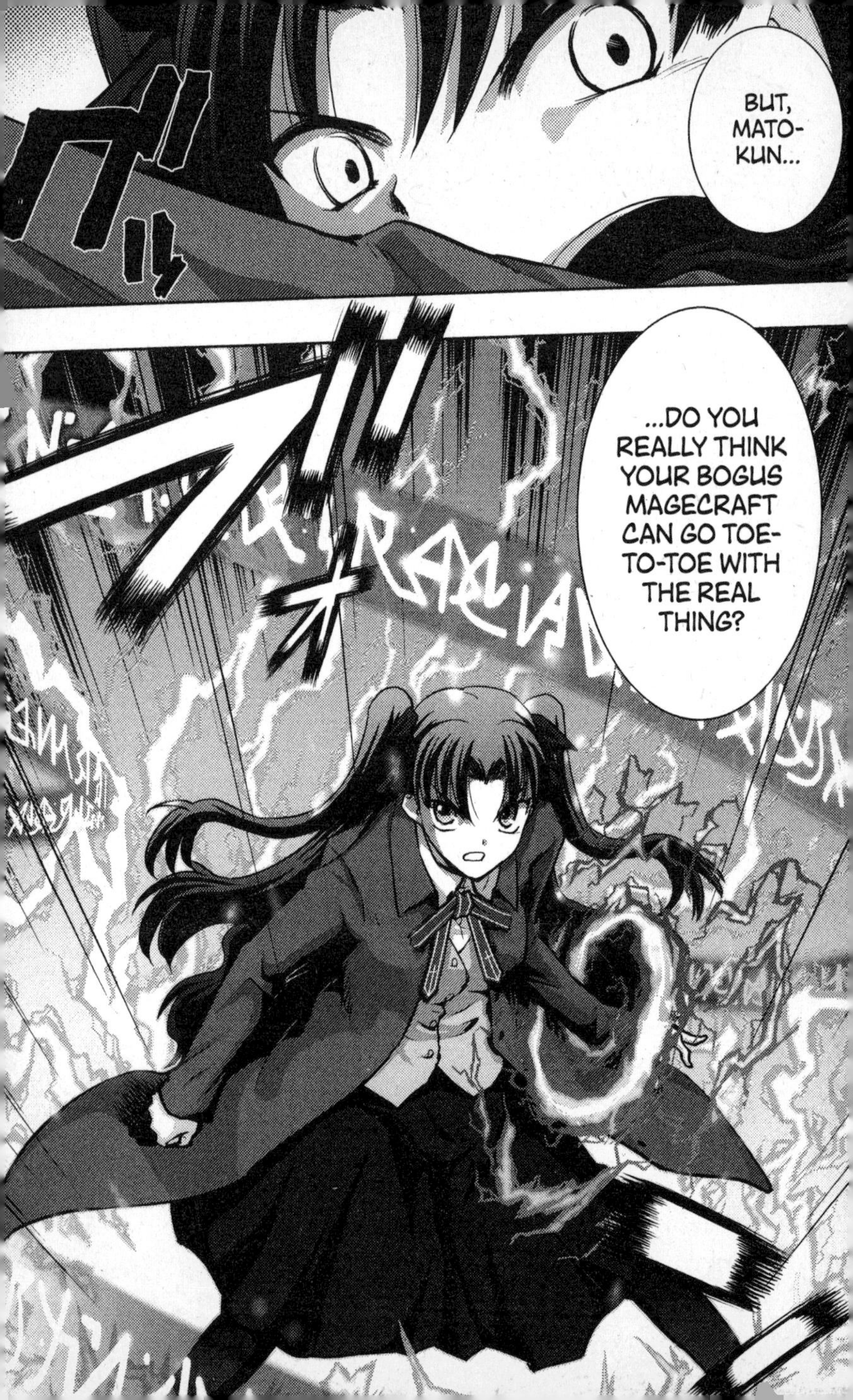
BUT, MATO-KUN...
...DO YOU REALLY THINK YOUR BOGUS MAGECRAFT CAN GO TOE-TO-TOE WITH THE REAL THING?

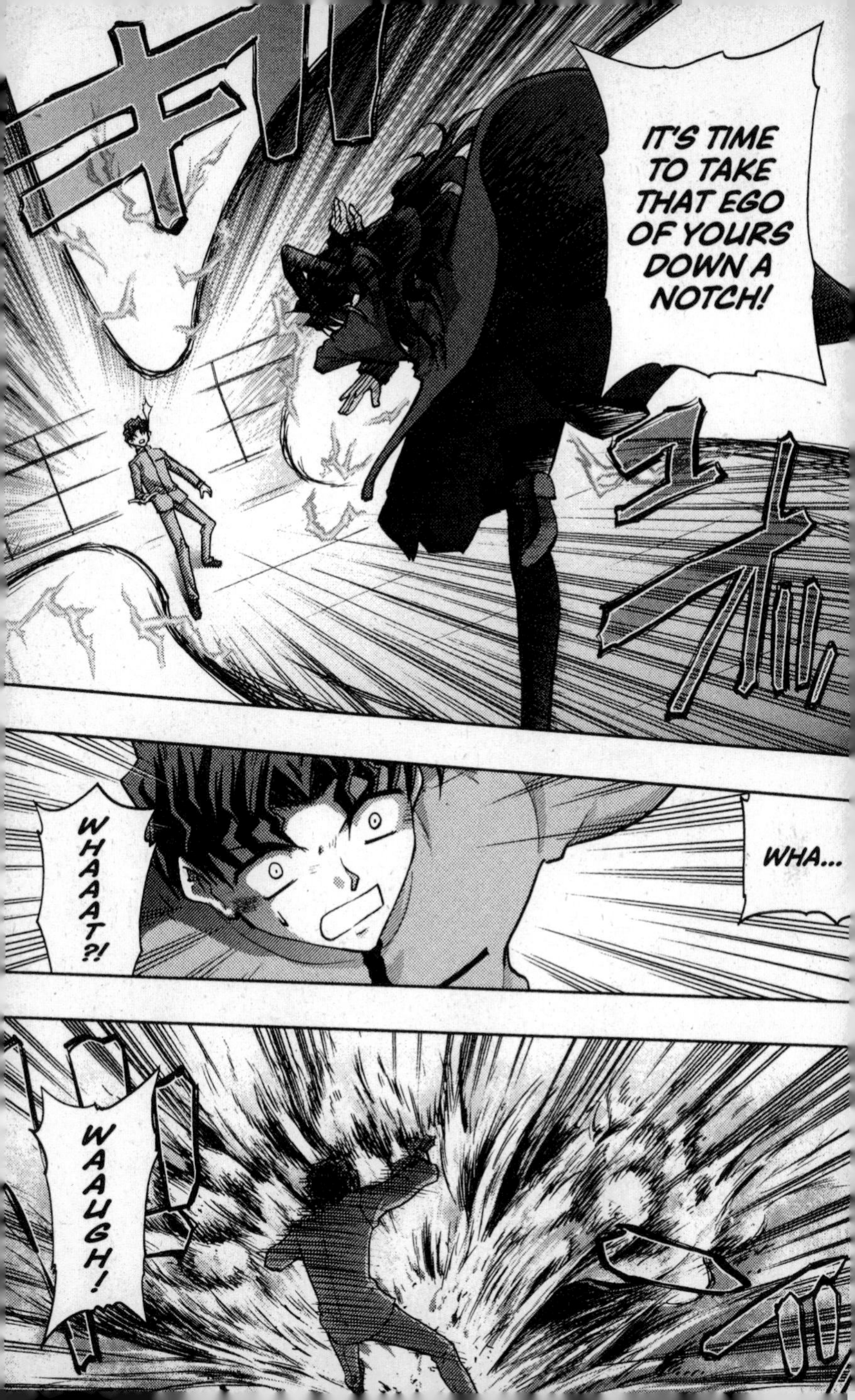
IT'S TIME TO TAKE THAT EGO OF YOURS DOWN A NOTCH!
WHA...
WHAAAAT?!
WAAAUGH!

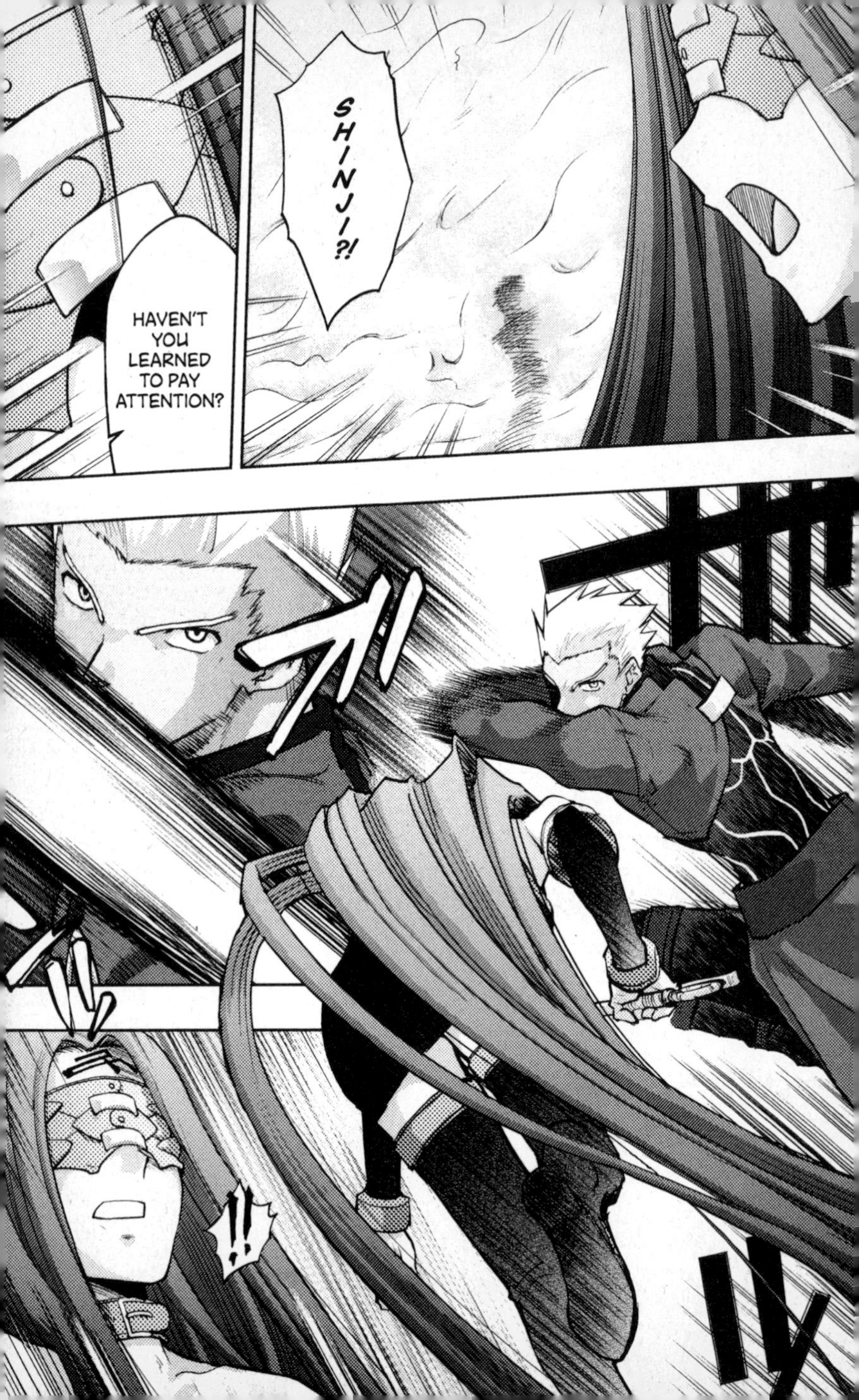
SHINJI?!
HAVEN'T YOU LEARNED TO PAY ATTENTION?
!!

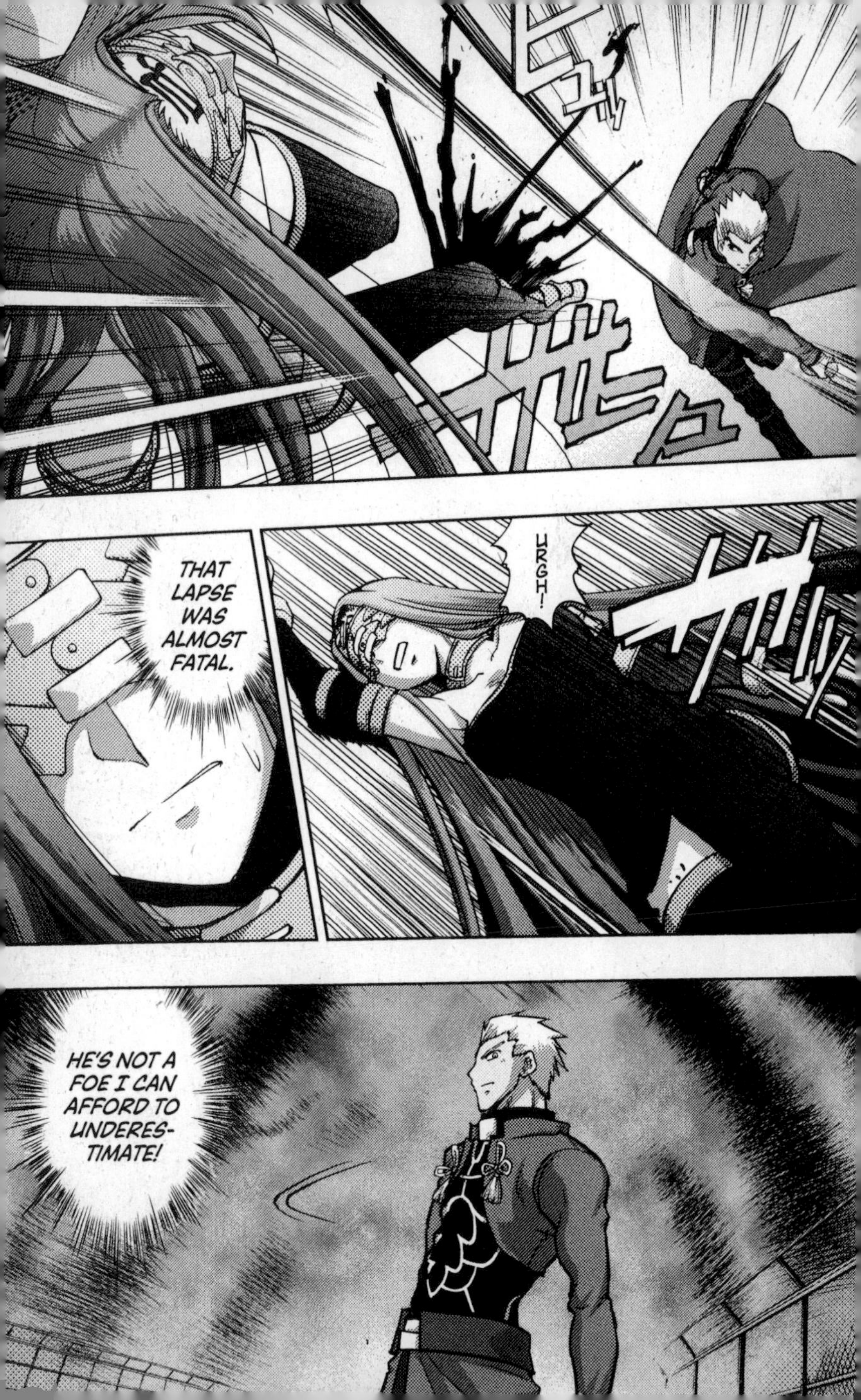
URGH!
THAT LAPSE WAS ALMOST FATAL.
HE'S NOT A FOE I CAN AFFORD TO UNDERES-TIMATE!

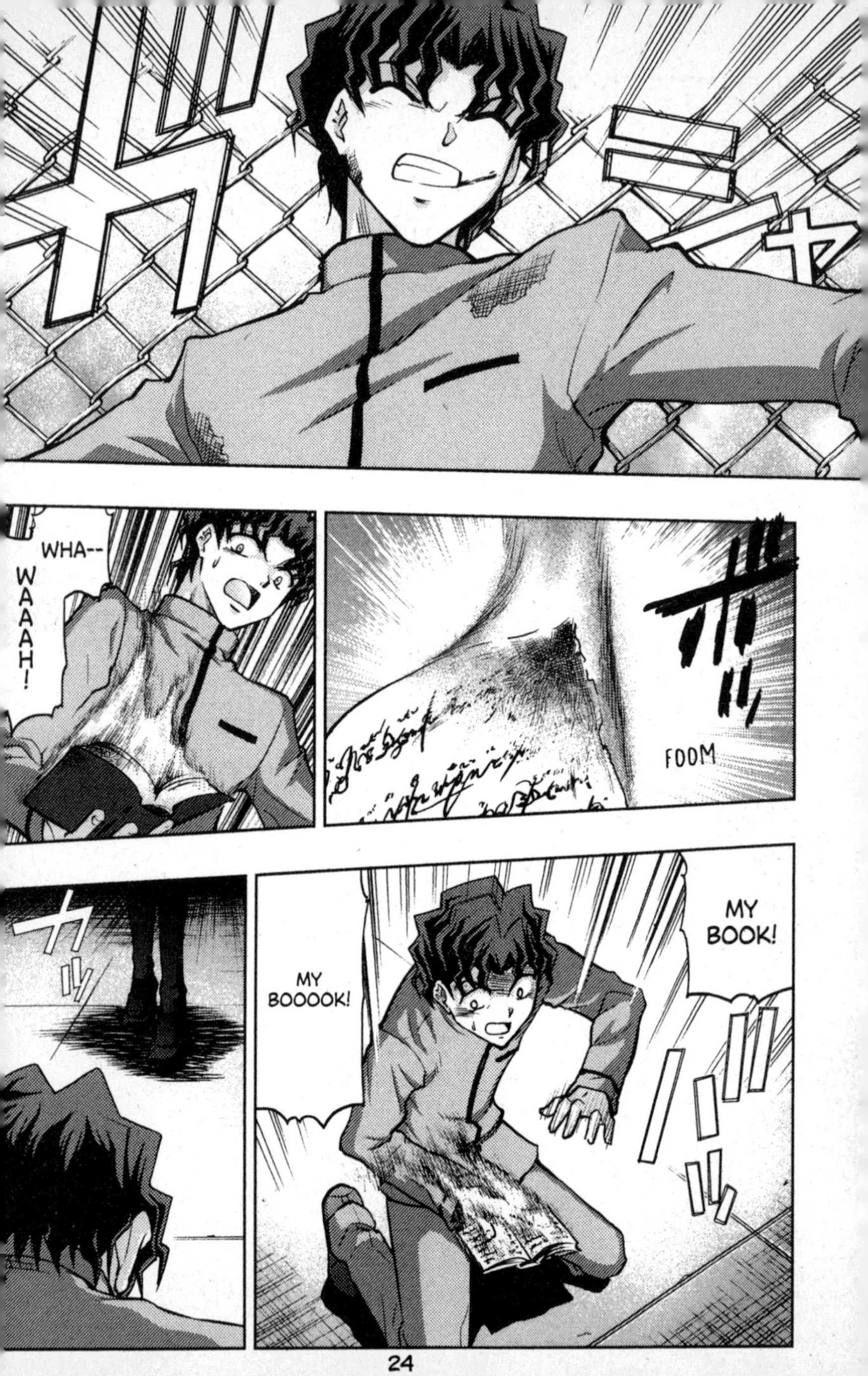
FOOM
WHA--
WAAAAH!
MY BOOK!
MY BOOOOK!

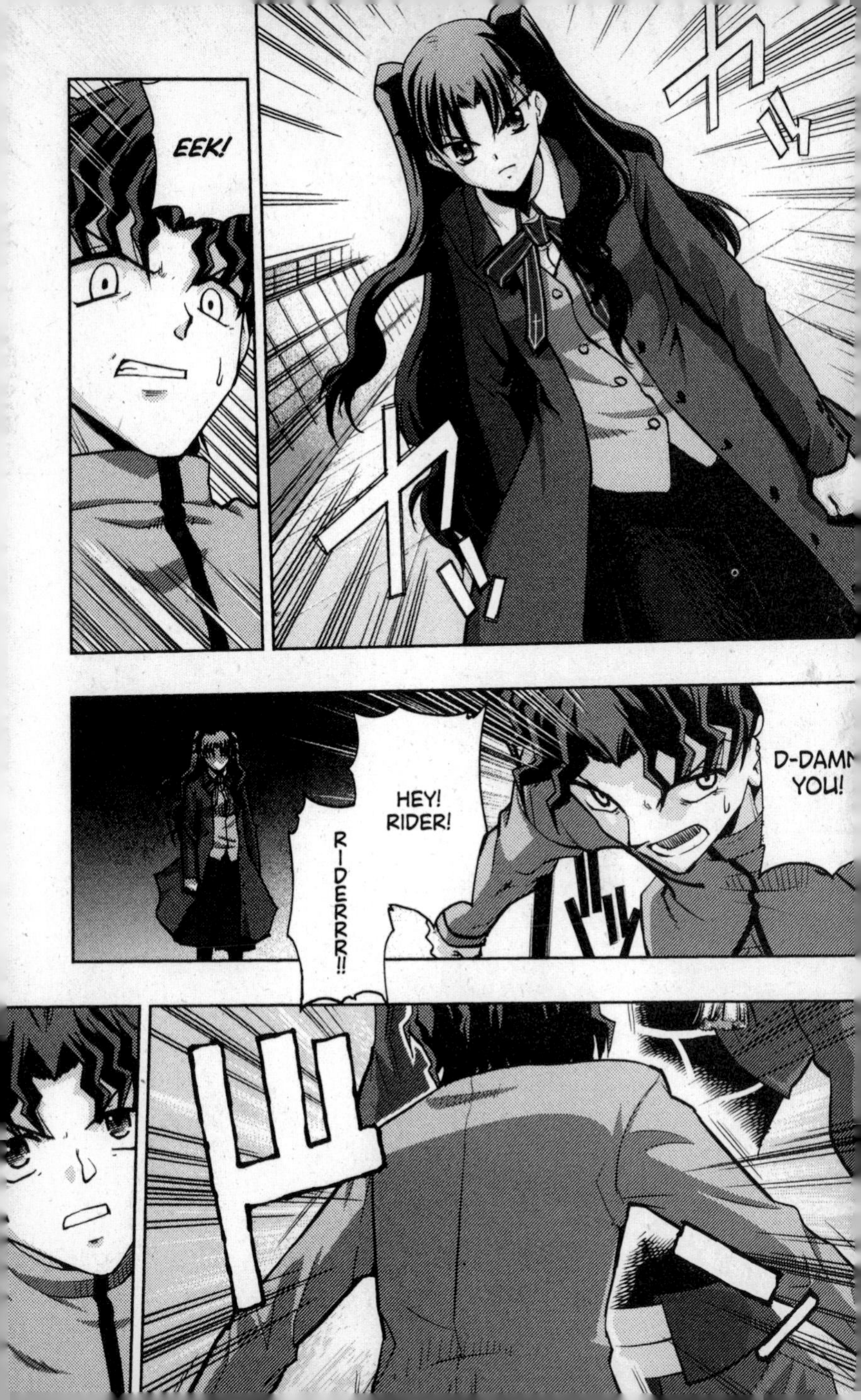
EEK!
D-DAMN YOU!
HEY! RIDER!
RIDERRR!!

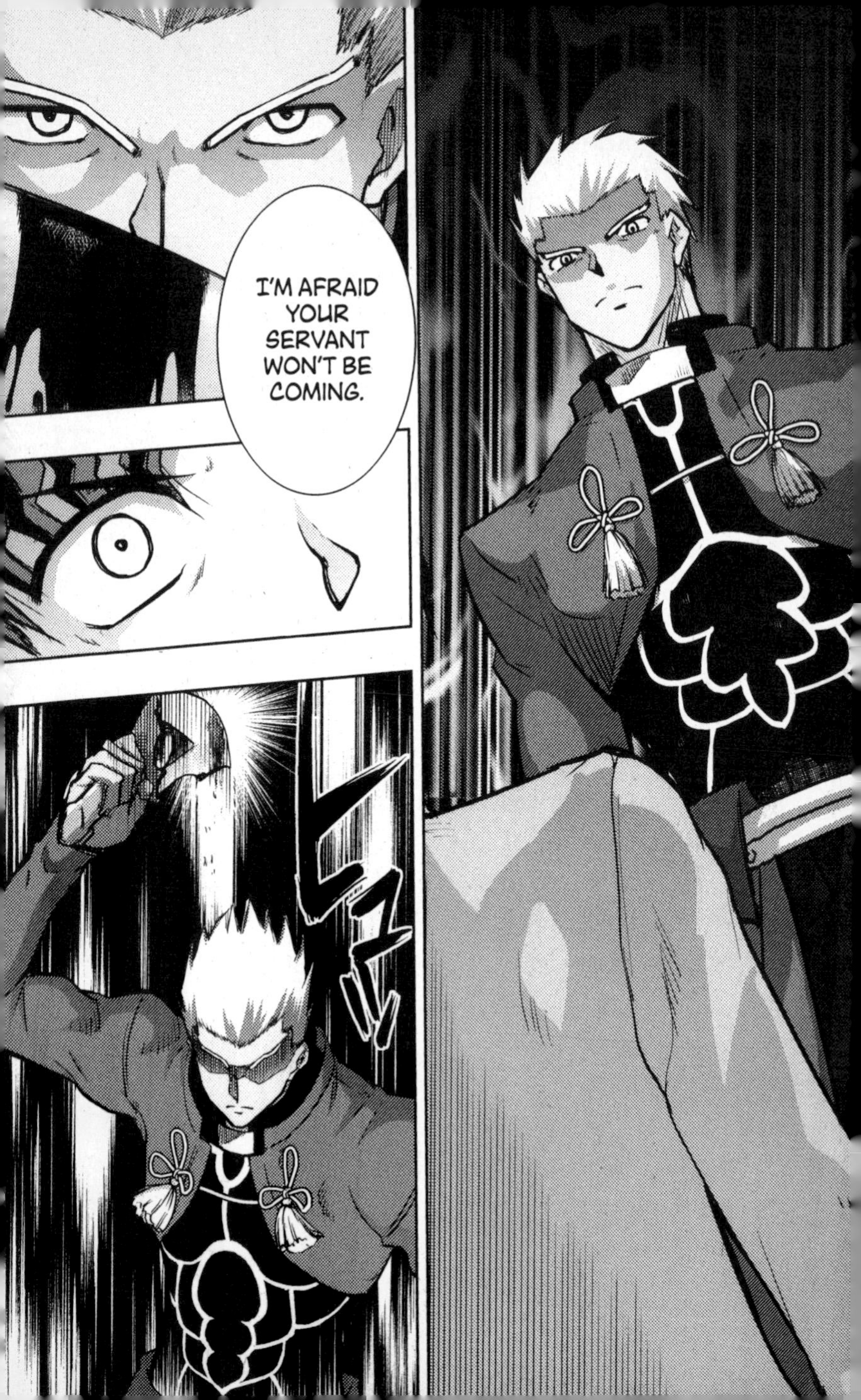
I'M AFRAID YOUR SERVANT WON'T BE COMING.

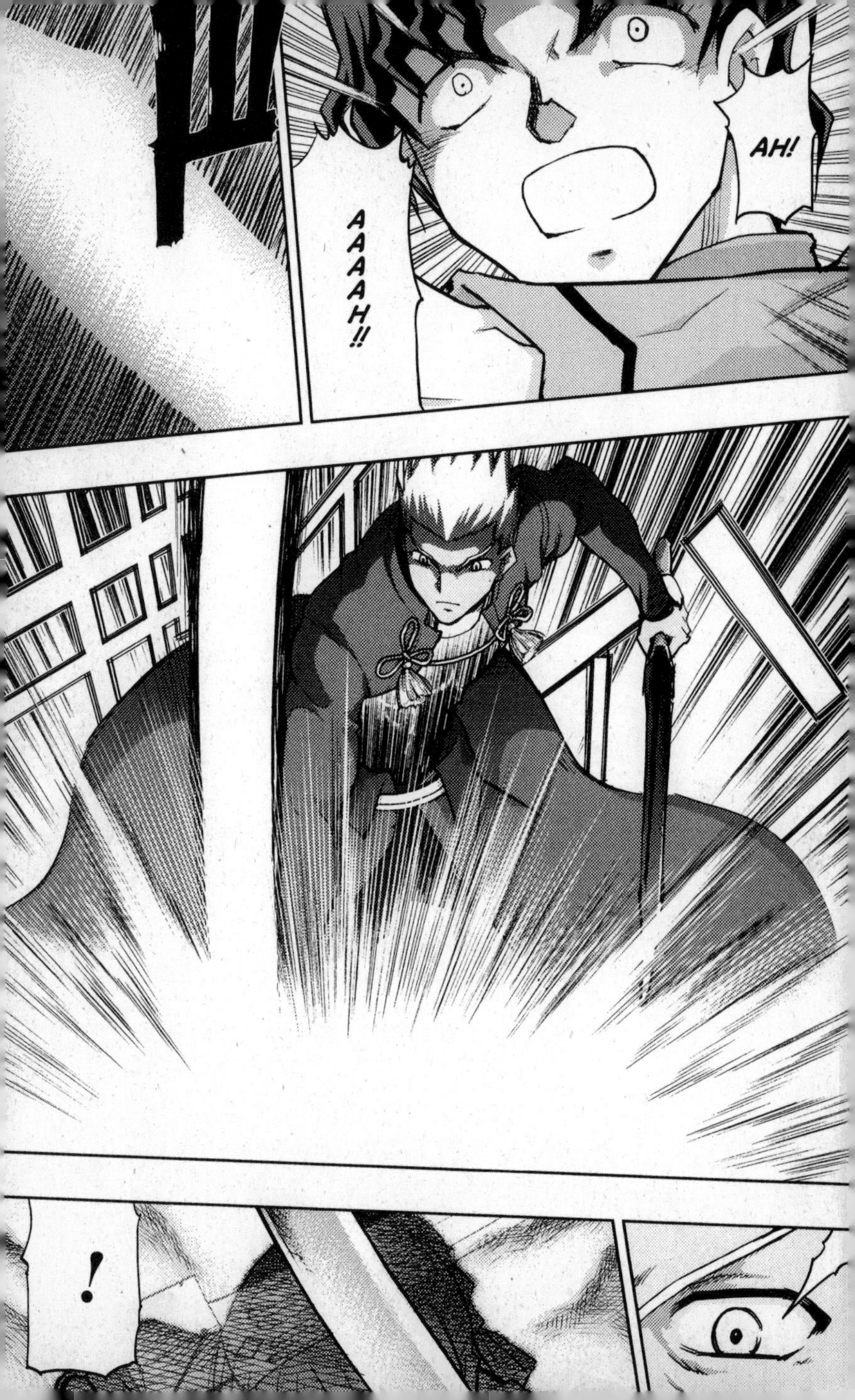
AH!
AAAAAH!!
!

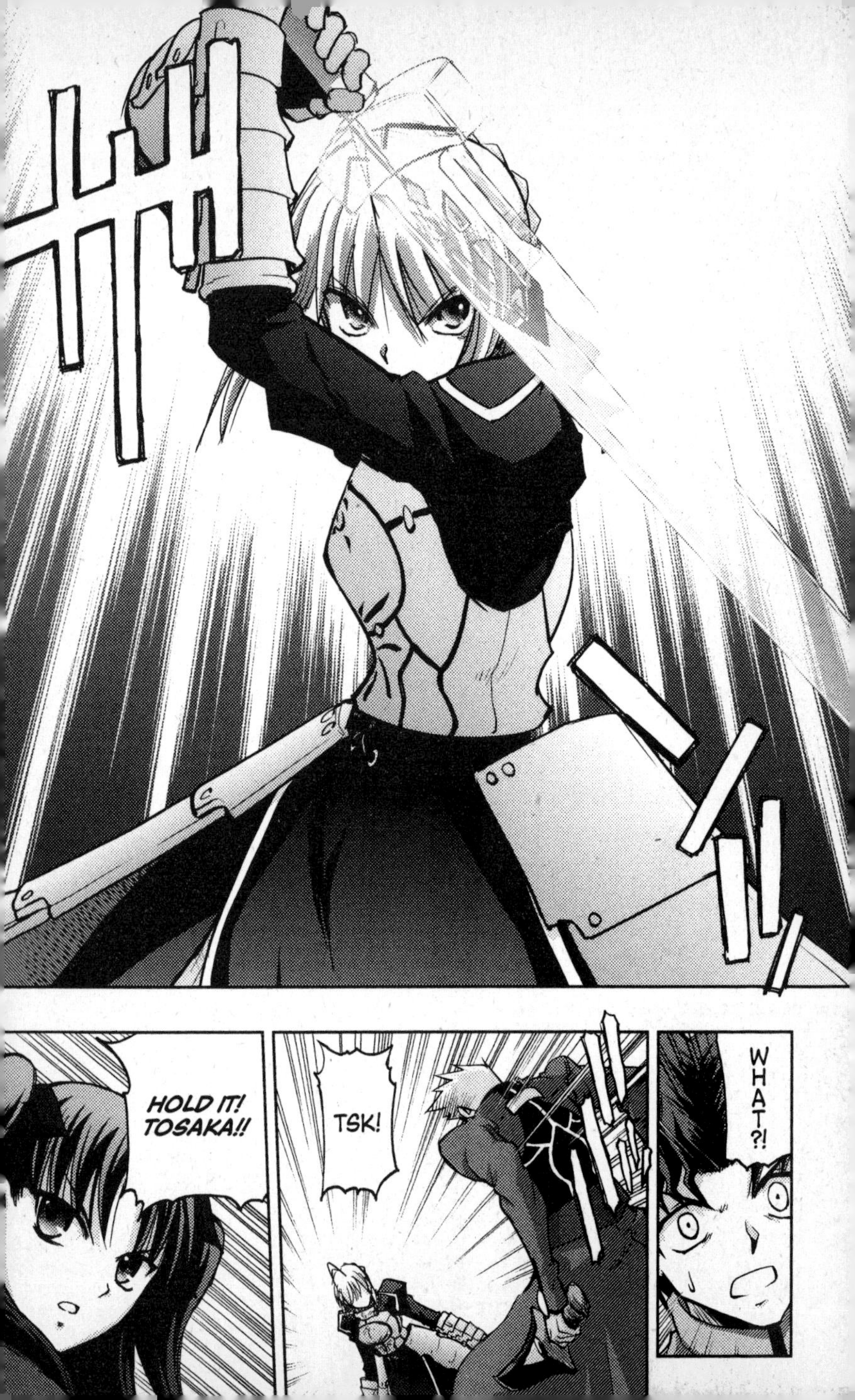
WHAT?!
TSK!
HOLD IT! TOSAKA!!

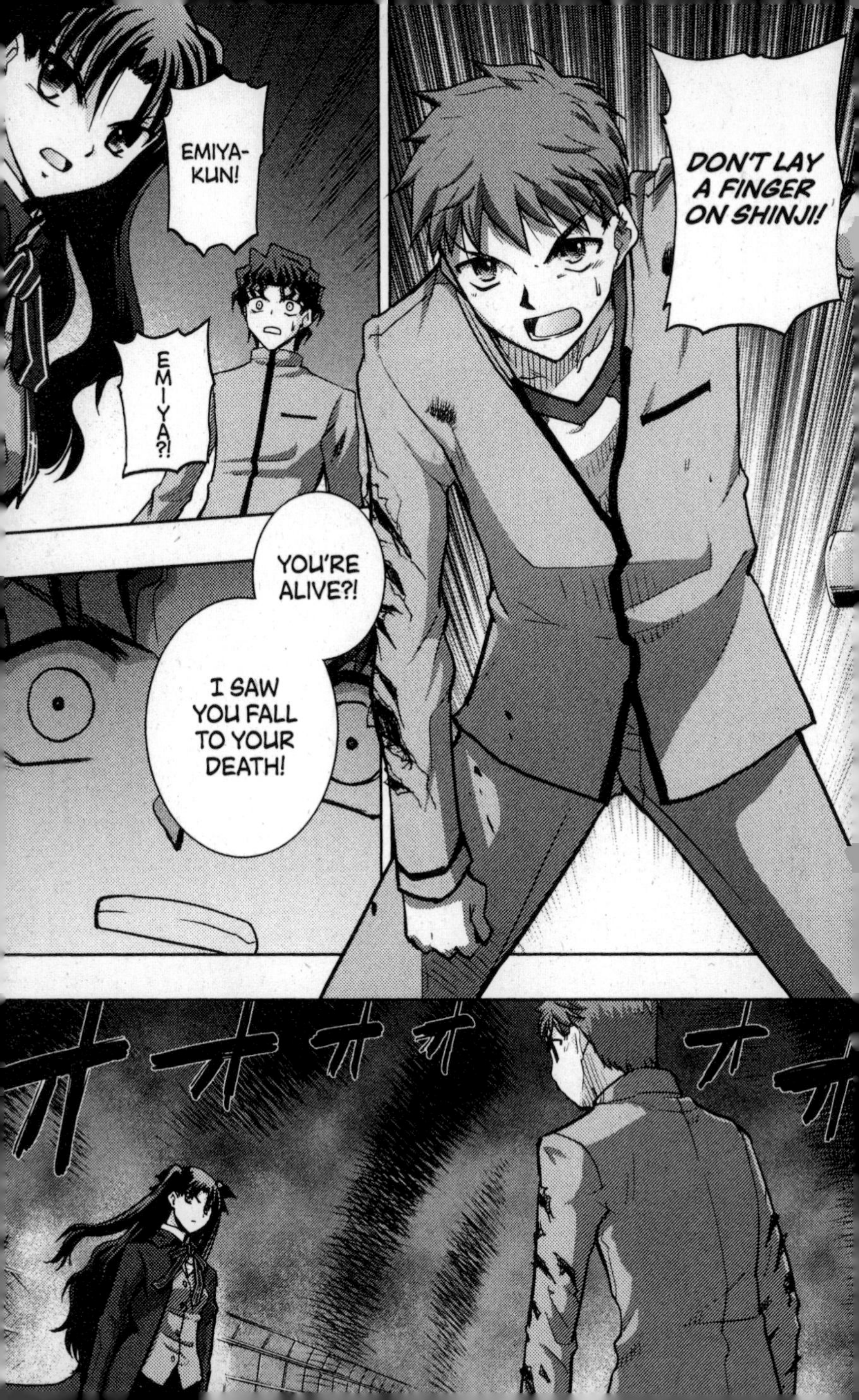
DON'T LAY A FINGER ON SHINJI!
EMIYA-KUN!
EMIYA?!
YOU'RE ALIVE?!
I SAW YOU FALL TO YOUR DEATH!

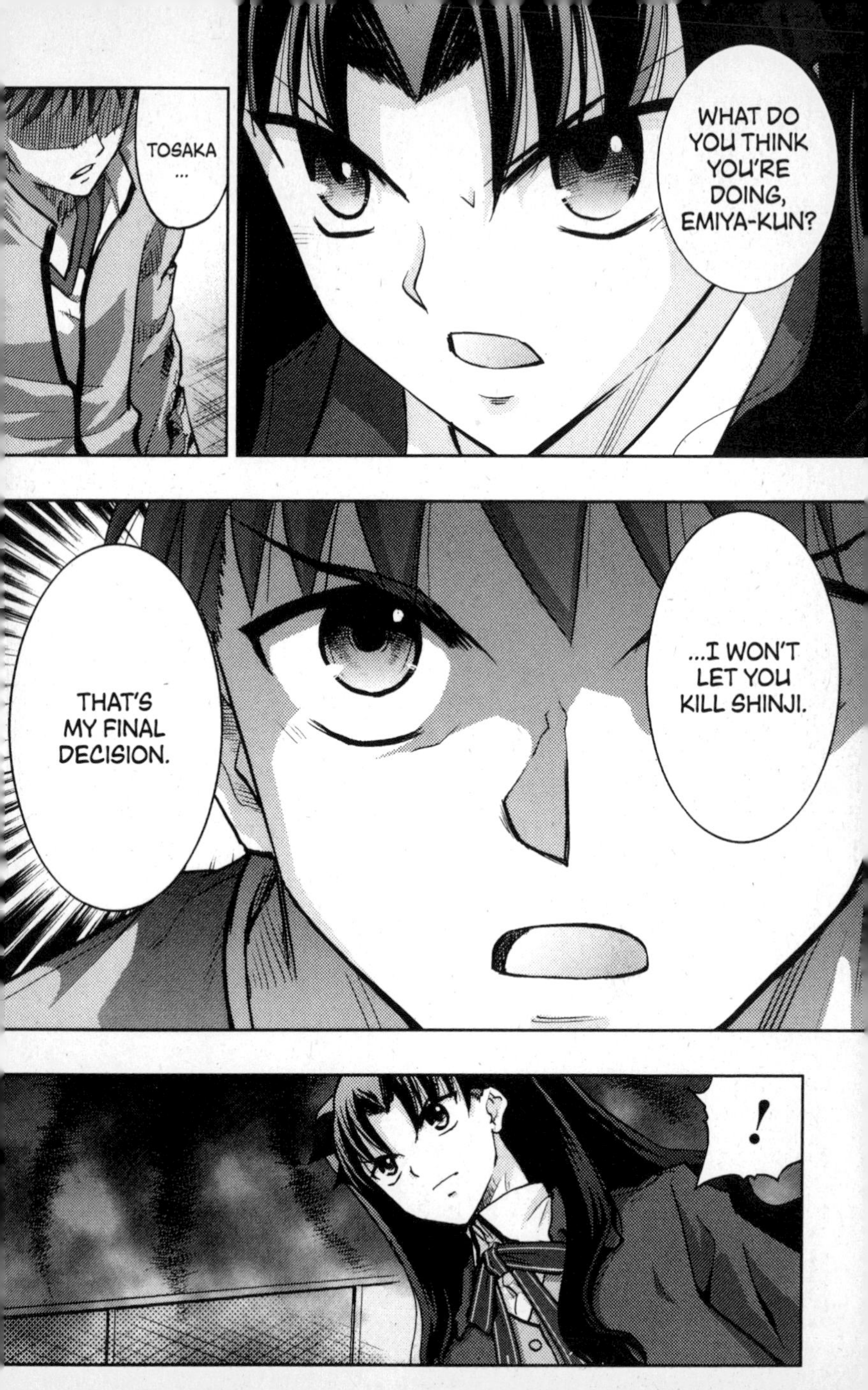
WHAT DO YOU THINK YOU'RE DOING, EMIYA-KUN?
TOSAKA ...
...I WON'T LET YOU KILL SHINJI.
THAT'S MY FINAL DECISION.
!

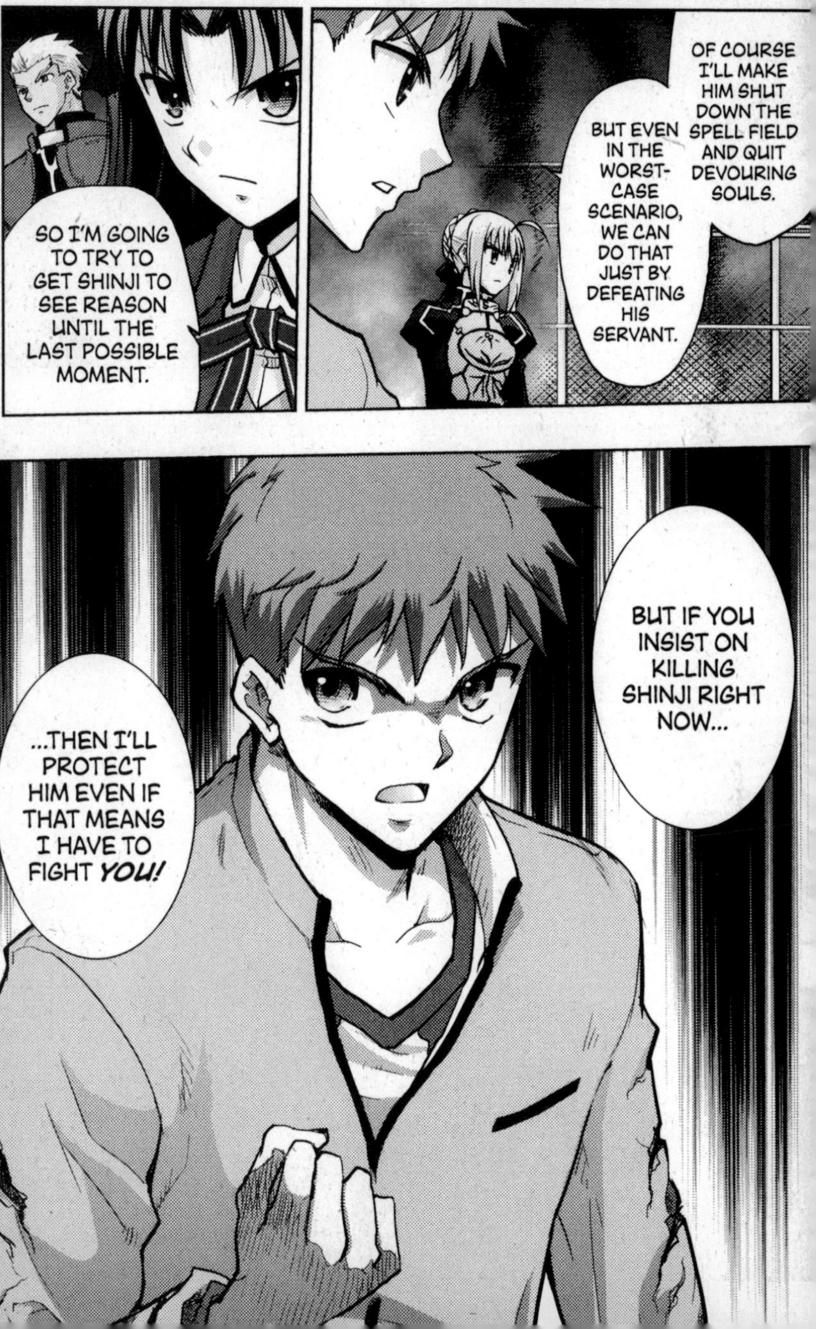
OF COURSE I'LL MAKE HIM SHUT DOWN THE SPELL FIELD AND QUIT DEVOURING SOULS.
BUT EVEN IN THE WORST-CASE SCENARIO, WE CAN DO THAT JUST BY DEFEATING HIS SERVANT.
SO I'M GOING TO TRY TO GET SHINJI TO SEE REASON UNTIL THE LAST POSSIBLE MOMENT.
BUT IF YOU INSIST ON KILLING SHINJI RIGHT NOW...
...THEN I'LL PROTECT HIM EVEN IF THAT MEANS I HAVE TO FIGHT *YOU!*

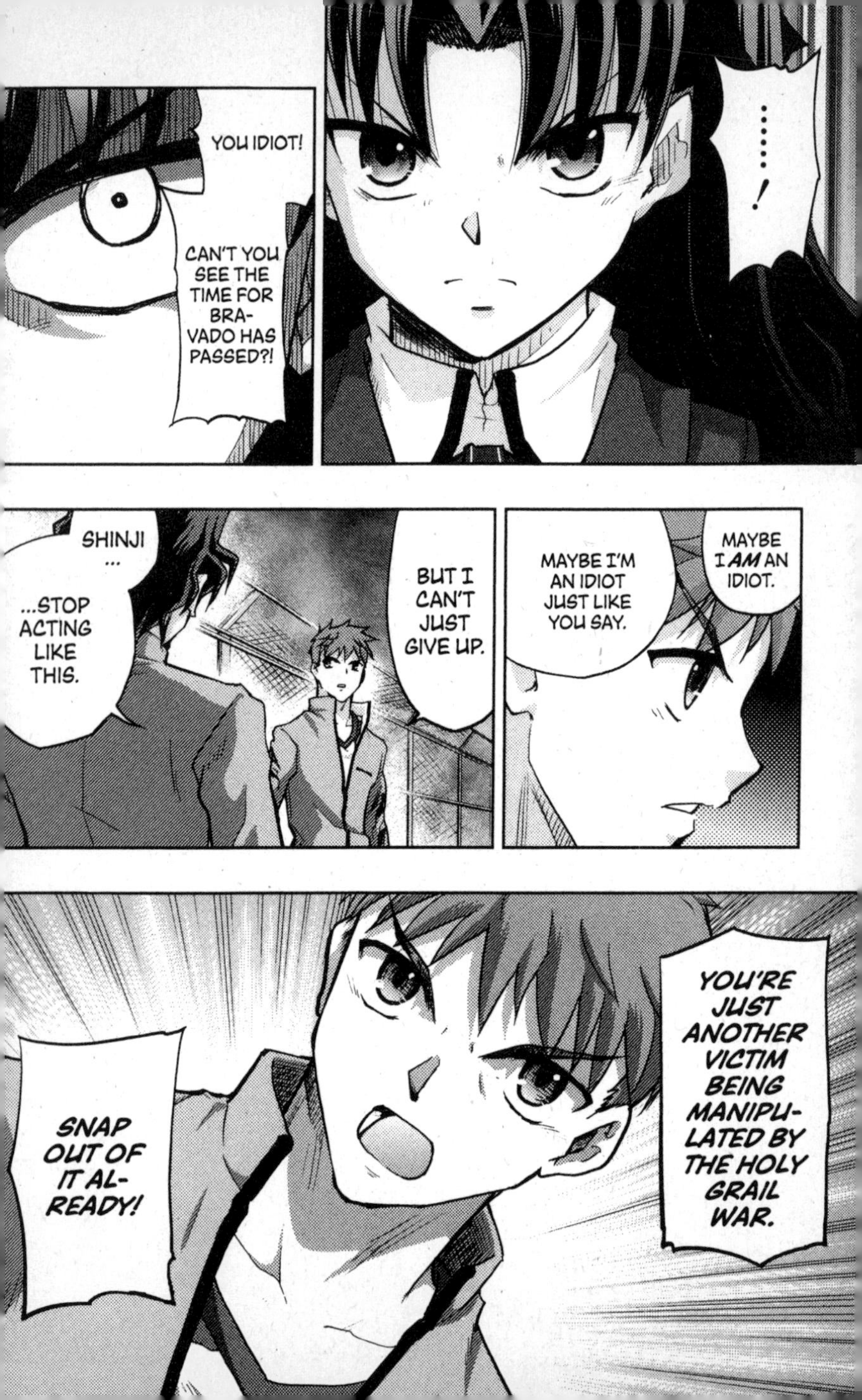
……!
YOU IDIOT!
CAN'T YOU SEE THE TIME FOR BRAVADO HAS PASSED?!
MAYBE I *AM* AN IDIOT.
MAYBE I'M AN IDIOT JUST LIKE YOU SAY.
BUT I CAN'T JUST GIVE UP.
SHINJI ...
...STOP ACTING LIKE THIS.
YOU'RE JUST ANOTHER VICTIM BEING MANIPULATED BY THE HOLY GRAIL WAR.
SNAP OUT OF IT ALREADY!

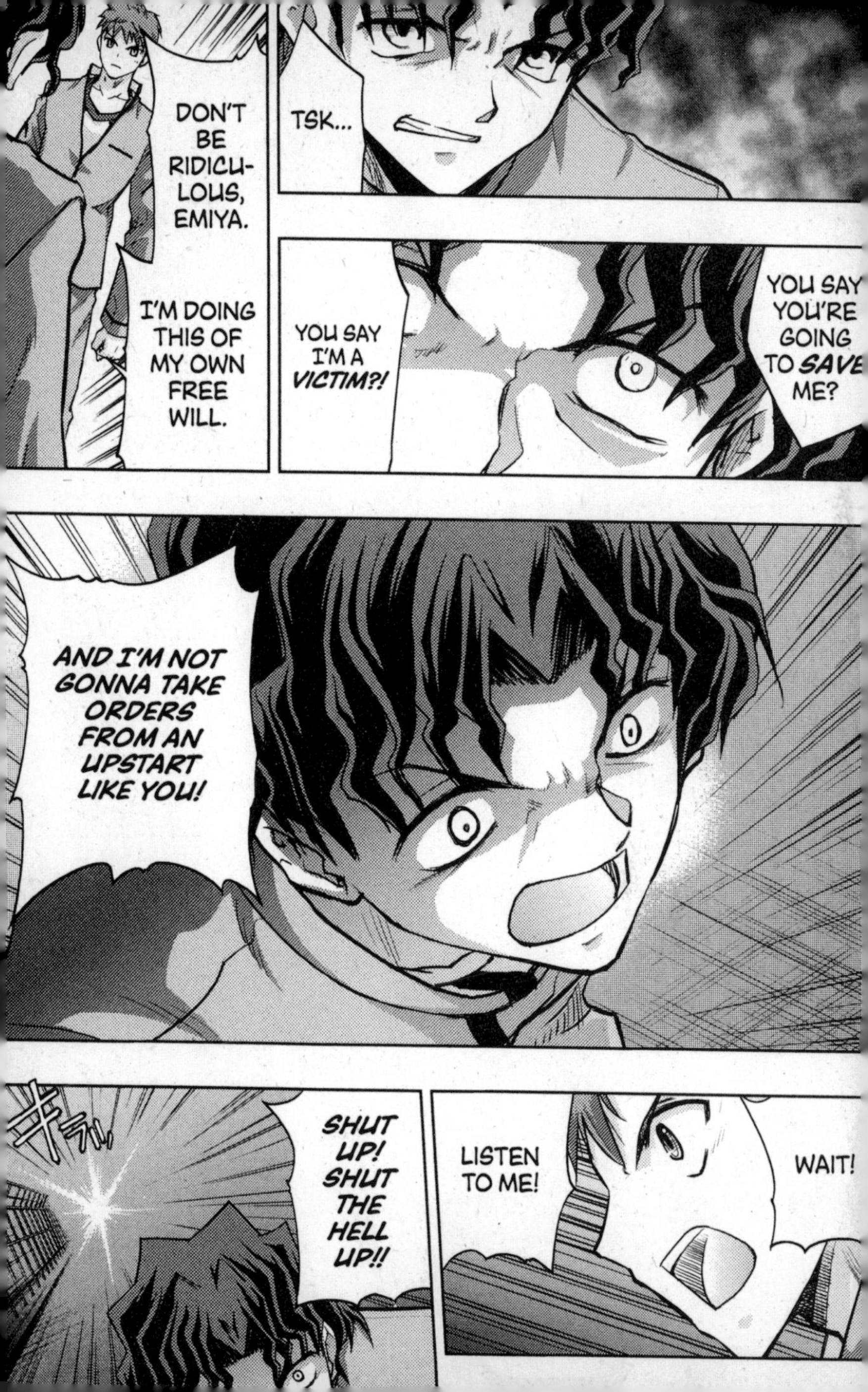
TSK...
YOU SAY YOU'RE GOING TO *SAVE* ME?
YOU SAY I'M A *VICTIM?!*
DON'T BE RIDICULOUS, EMIYA.
I'M DOING THIS OF MY OWN FREE WILL.
AND I'M NOT GONNA TAKE ORDERS FROM AN UPSTART LIKE YOU!
WAIT!
LISTEN TO ME!
SHUT UP! SHUT THE HELL UP!!

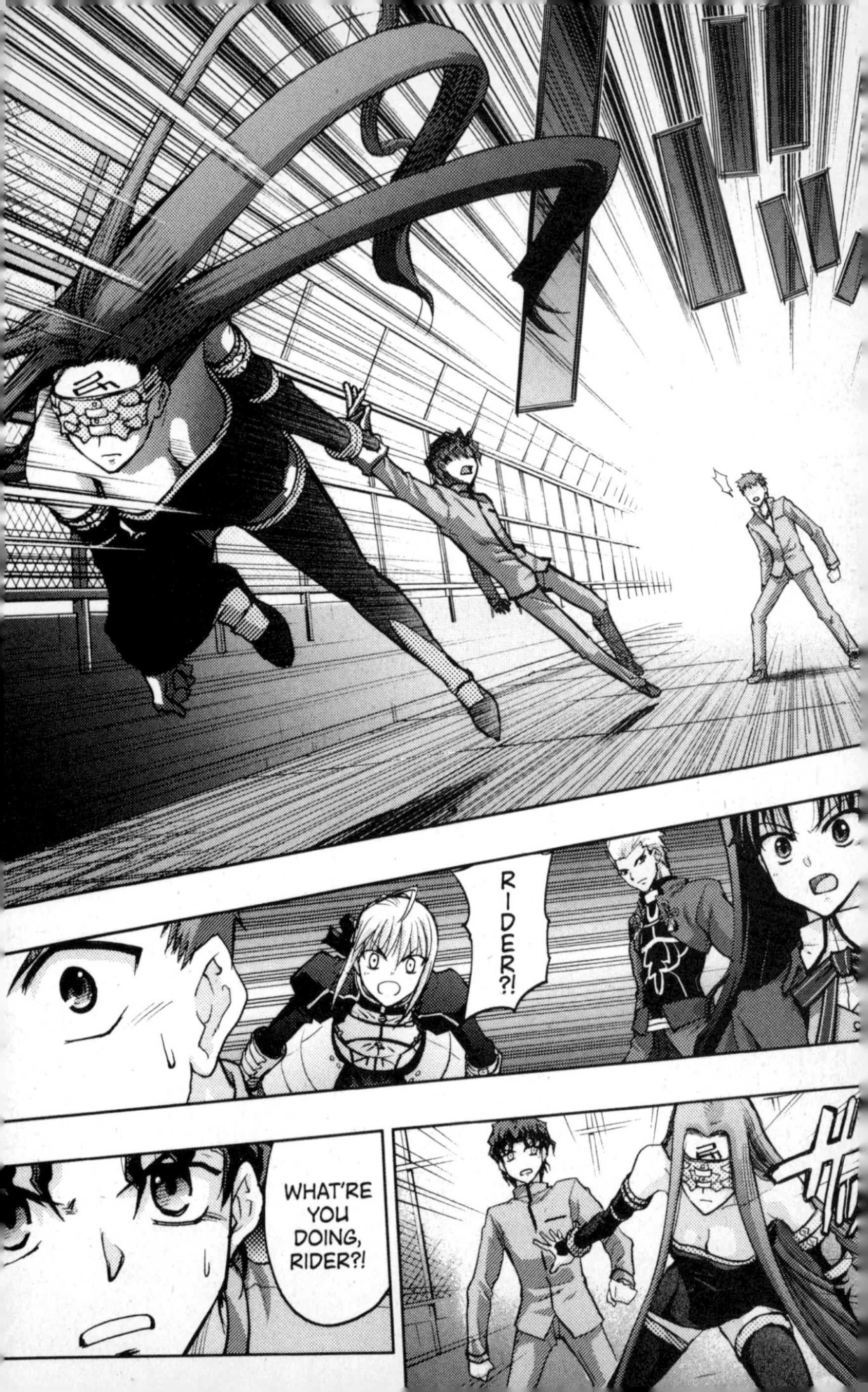
RIDER?!
WHAT'RE YOU DOING, RIDER?!

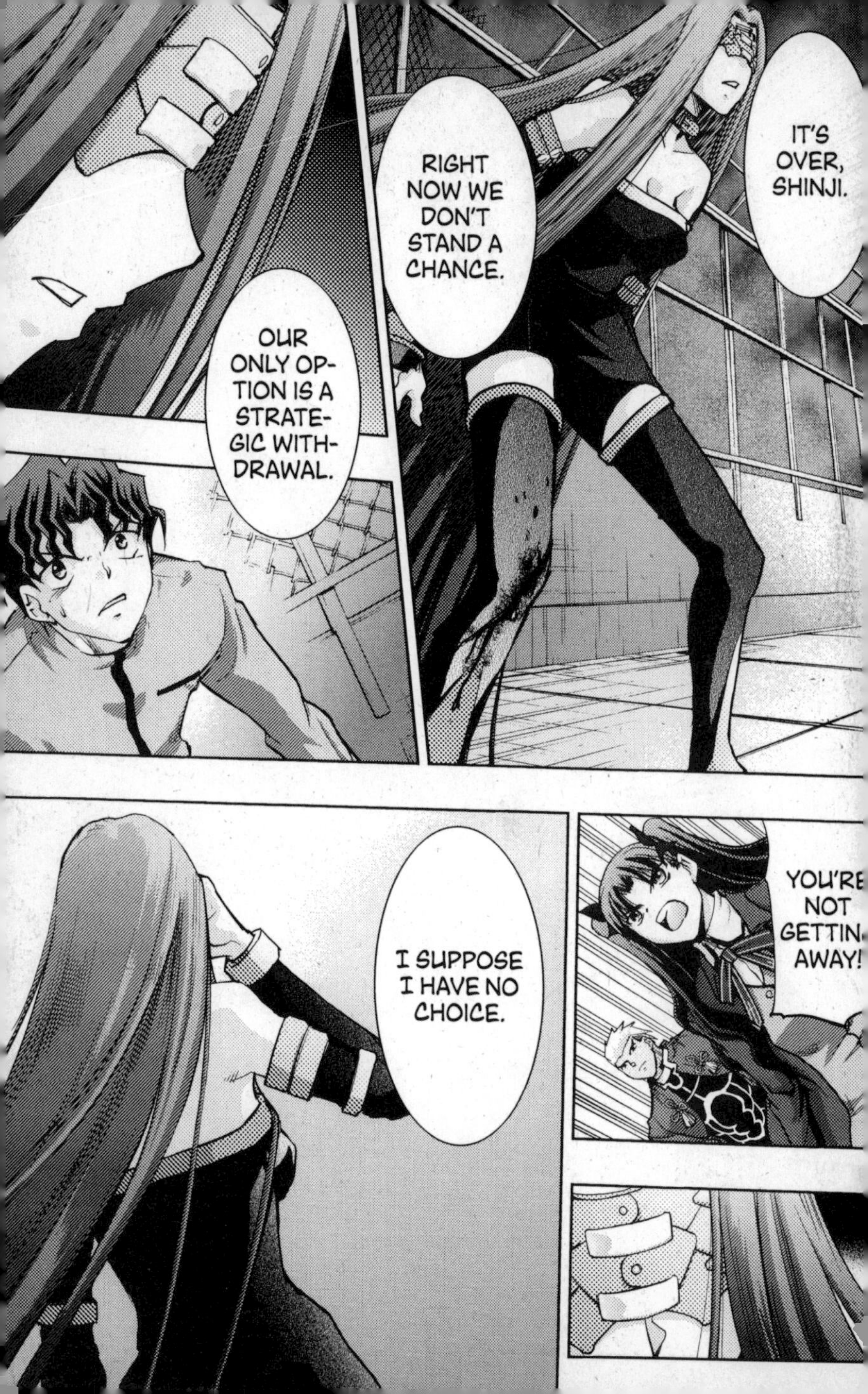
IT'S OVER, SHINJI.
RIGHT NOW WE DON'T STAND A CHANCE.
OUR ONLY OP-TION IS A STRATE-GIC WITH-DRAWAL.
YOU'RE NOT GETTIN AWAY!
I SUPPOSE I HAVE NO CHOICE.

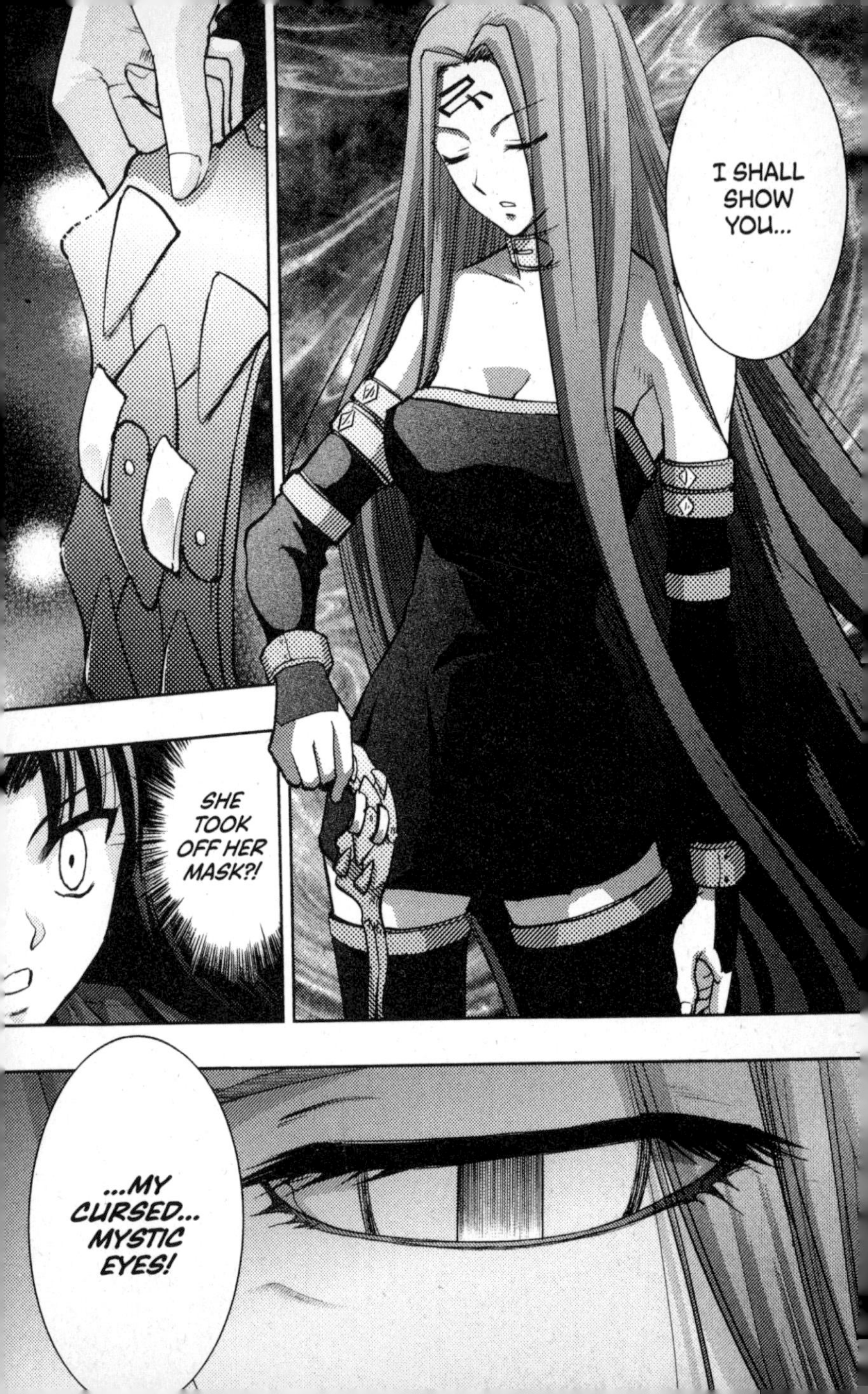
I SHALL SHOW YOU...
SHE TOOK OFF HER MASK?!
...MY CURSED... MYSTIC EYES!

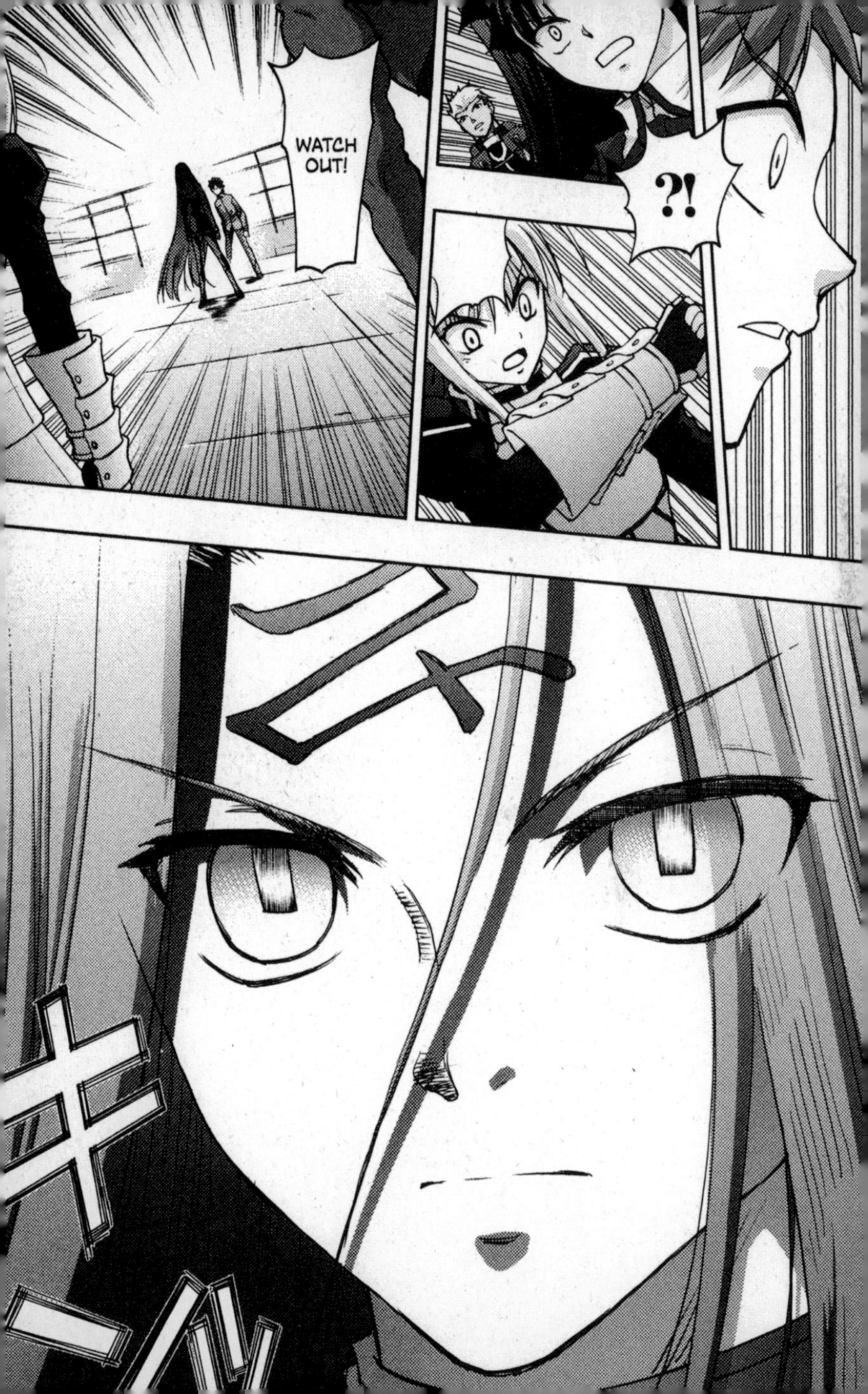
?!
WATCH OUT!

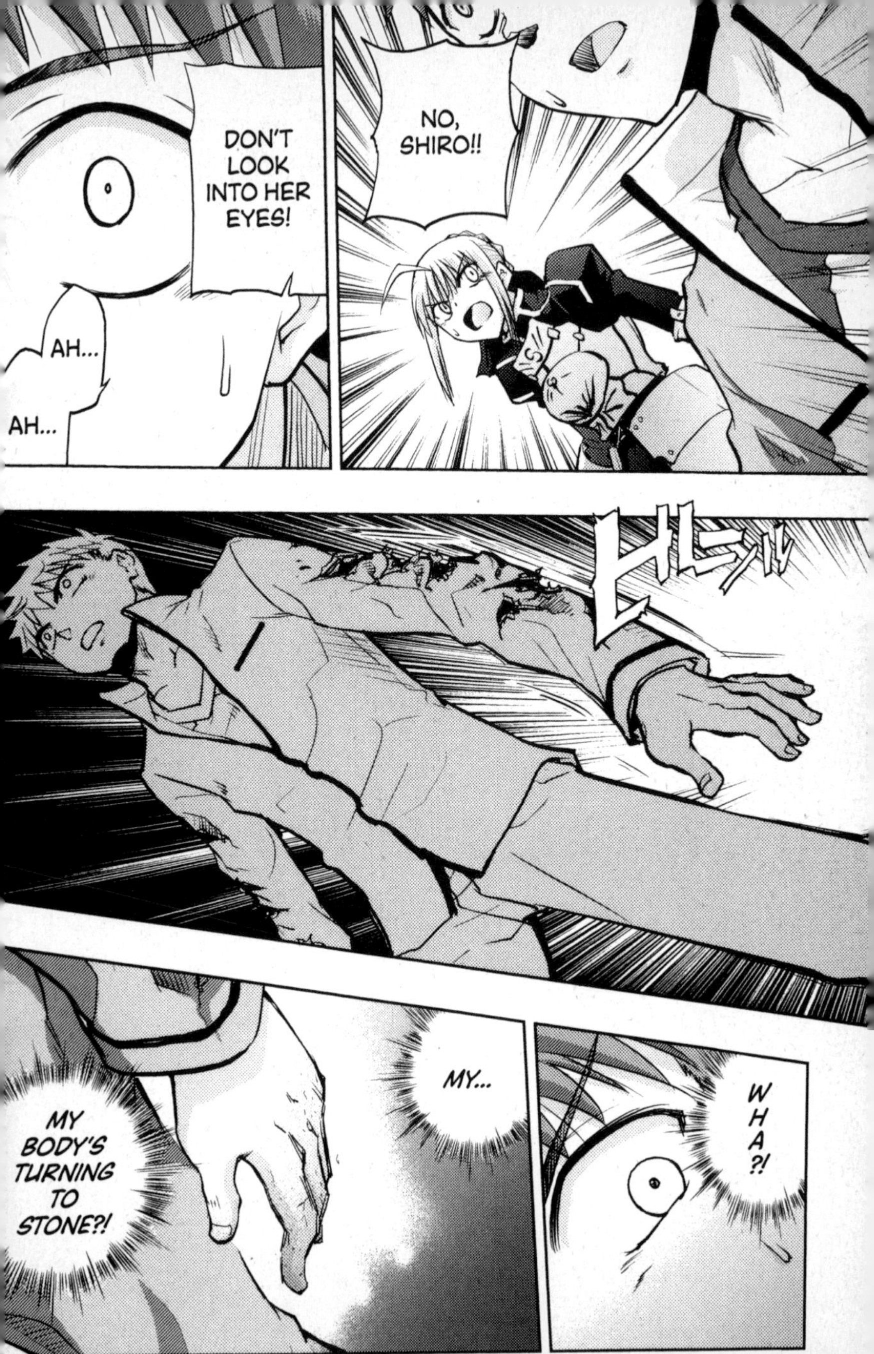
NO, SHIRO!!
DON'T LOOK INTO HER EYES!
AH...
AH...
WHA?!
MY...
MY BODY'S TURNING TO STONE?!

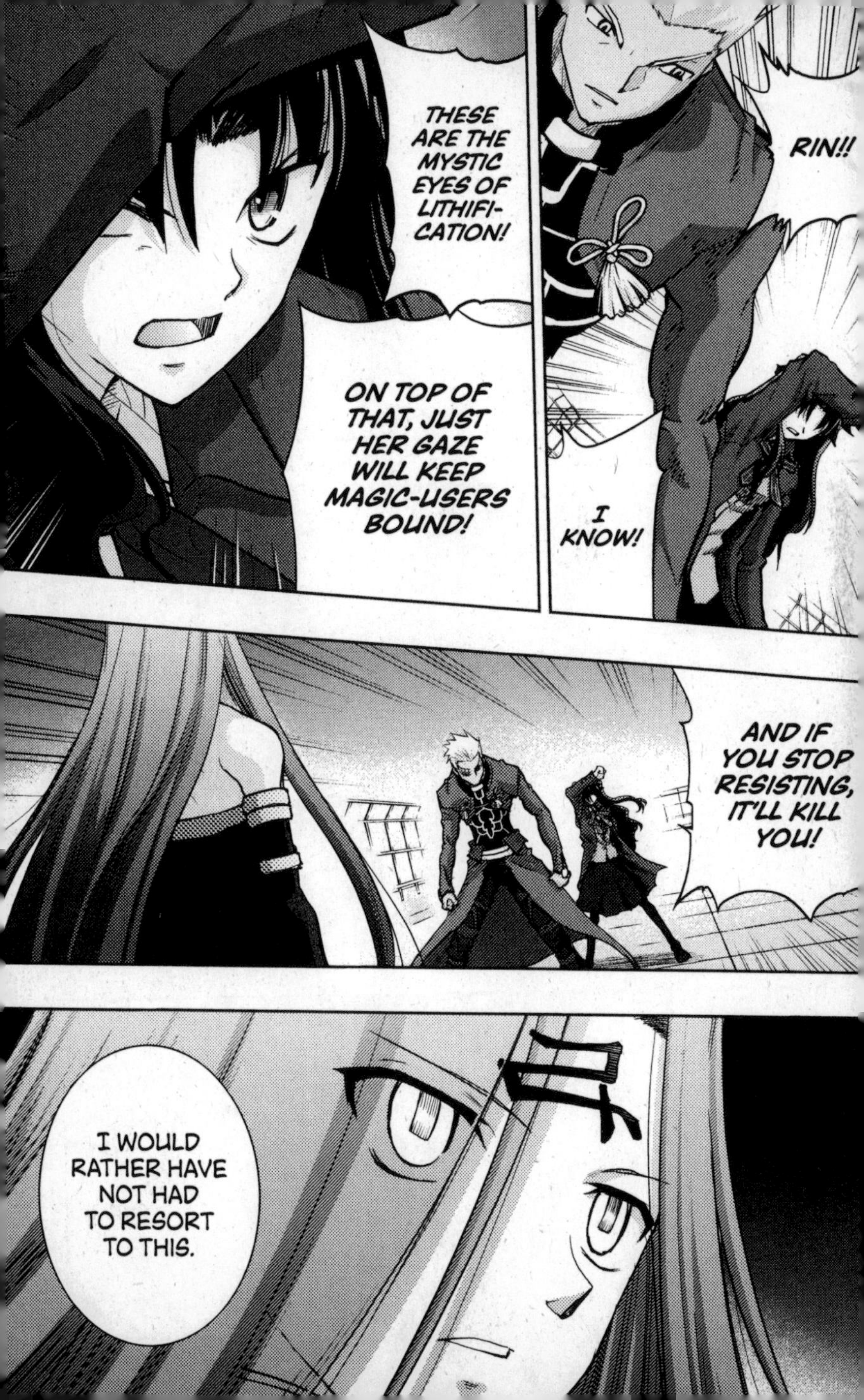
RIN!!
I KNOW!
THESE ARE THE MYSTIC EYES OF LITHIFI-CATION!
ON TOP OF THAT, JUST HER GAZE WILL KEEP MAGIC-USERS BOUND!
AND IF YOU STOP RESISTING, IT'LL KILL YOU!
I WOULD RATHER HAVE NOT HAD TO RESORT TO THIS.

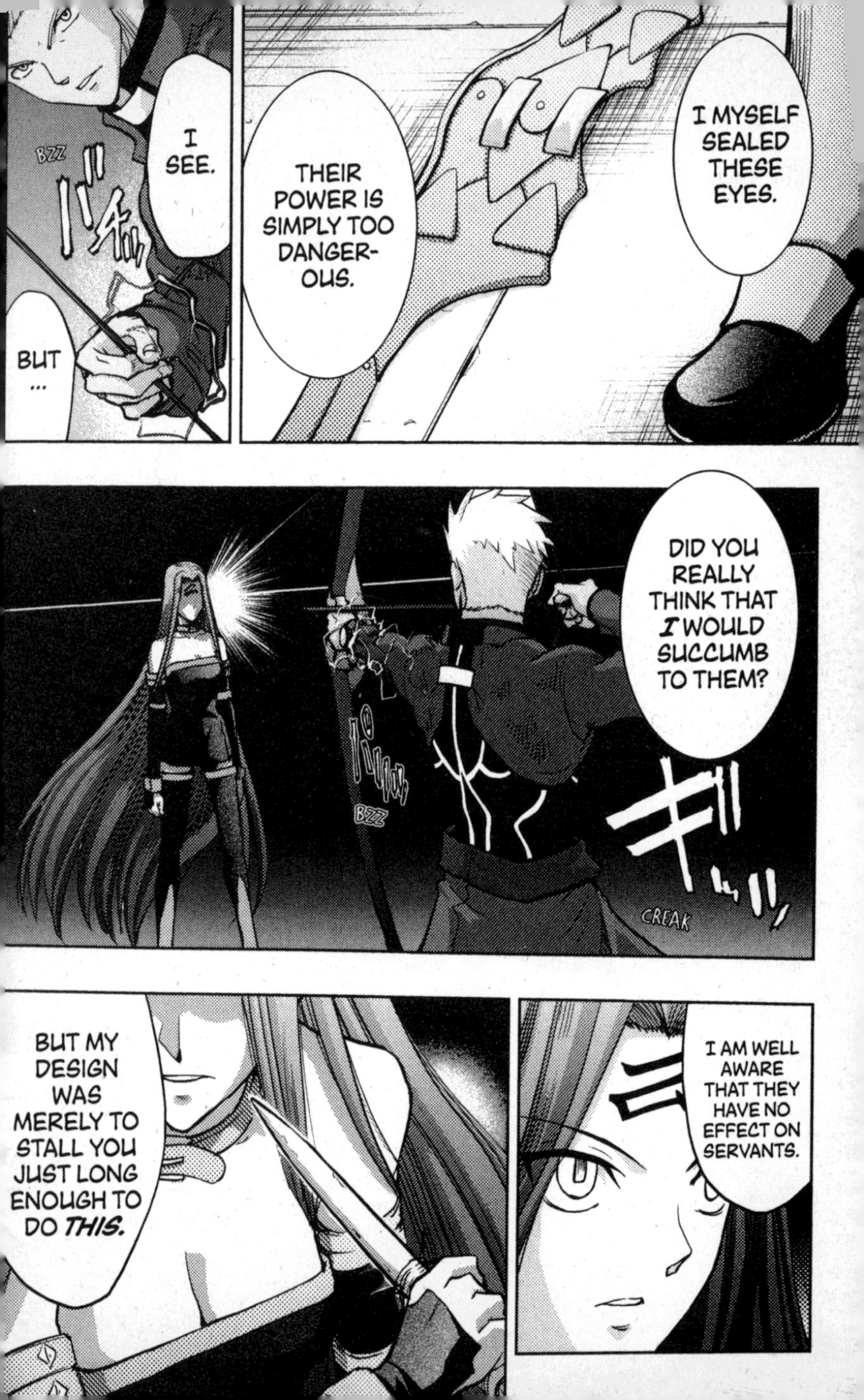
I MYSELF SEALED THESE EYES.
THEIR POWER IS SIMPLY TOO DANGER-OUS.
I SEE.
BZZ
BUT ...
DID YOU REALLY THINK THAT *I* WOULD SUCCUMB TO THEM?
BZZ
CREAK
I AM WELL AWARE THAT THEY HAVE NO EFFECT ON SERVANTS.
BUT MY DESIGN WAS MERELY TO STALL YOU JUST LONG ENOUGH TO DO ***THIS.***

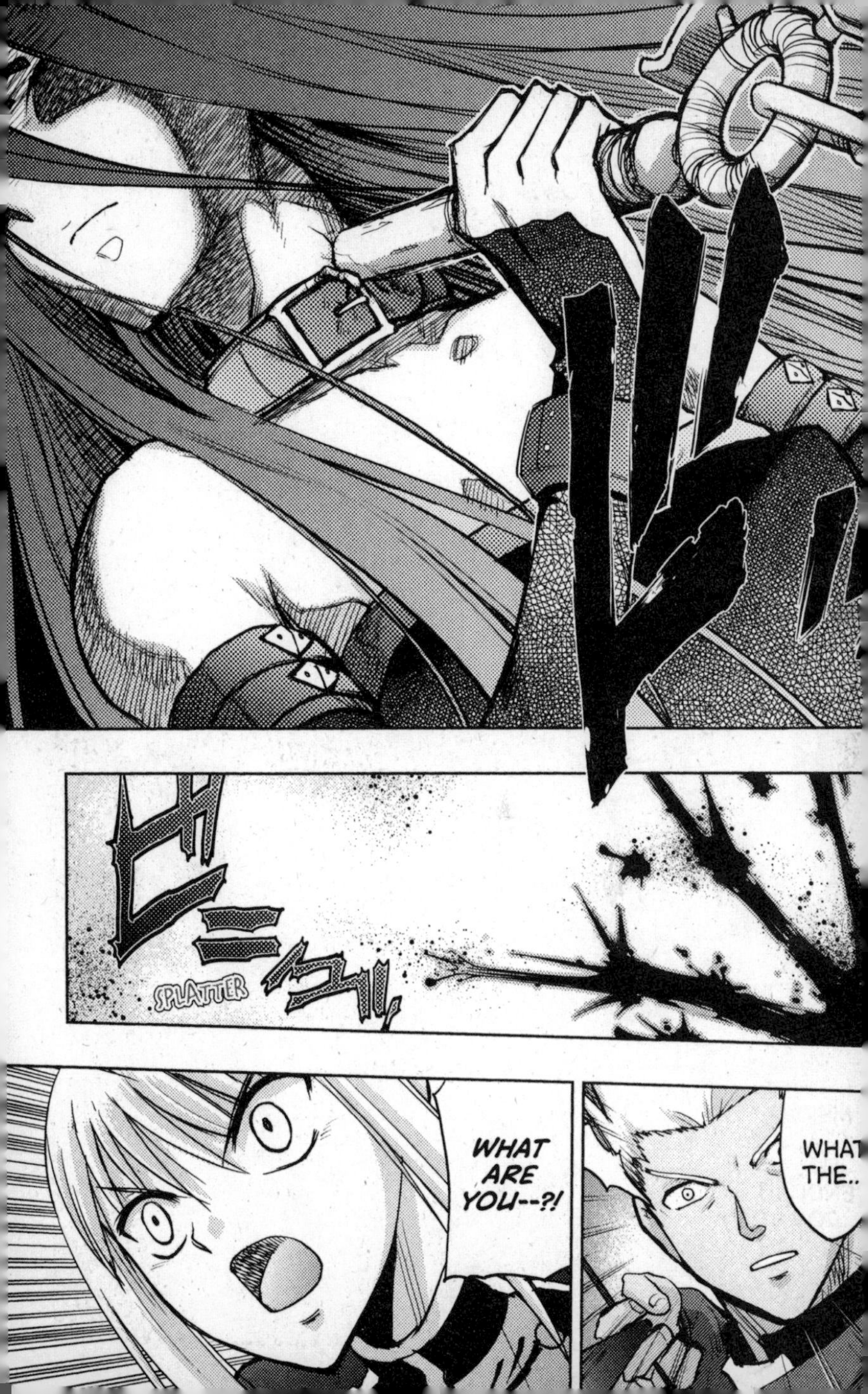
SPLATTER
WHAT THE...
WHAT ARE YOU--?!

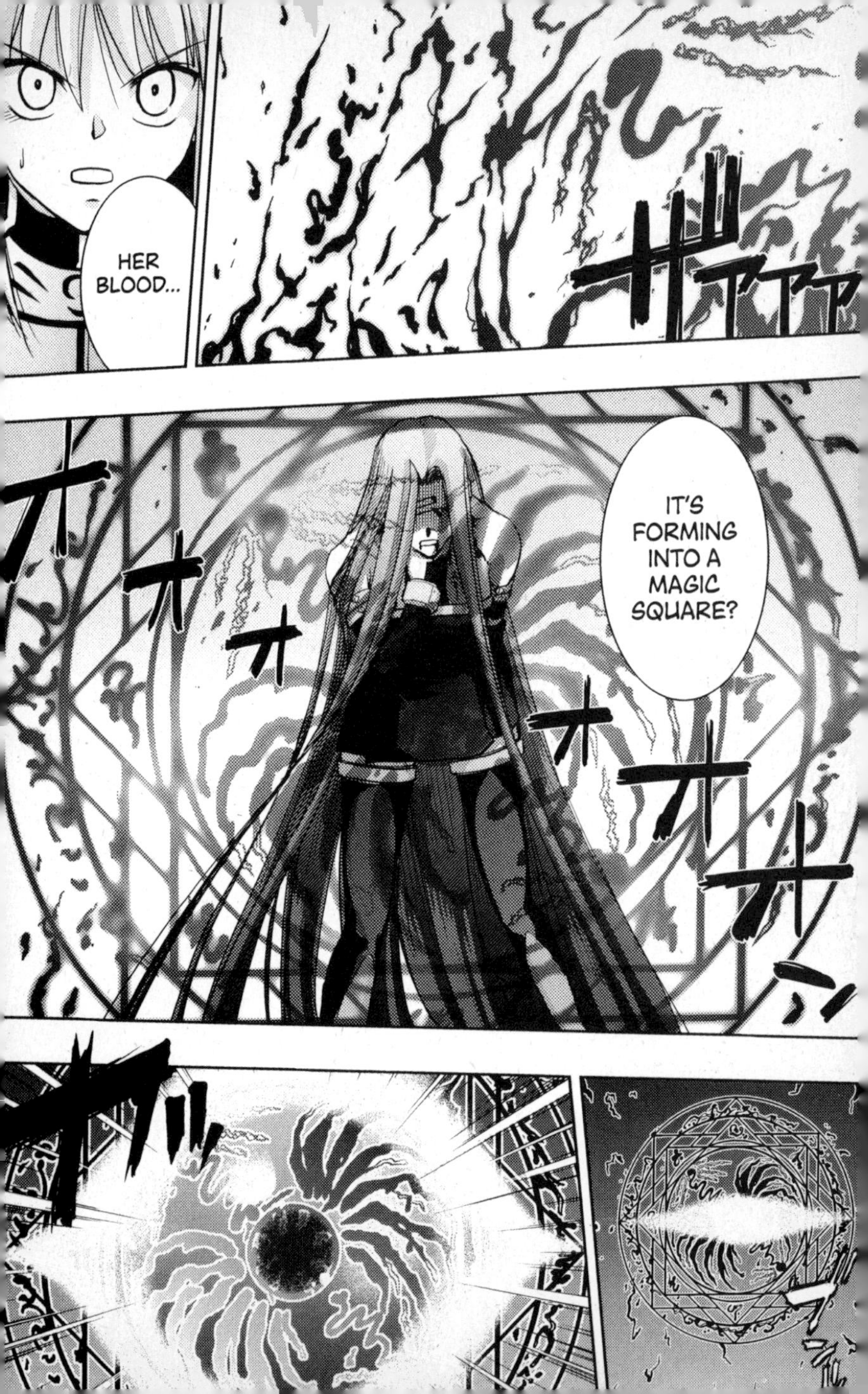
HER BLOOD...
IT'S FORMING INTO A MAGIC SQUARE?

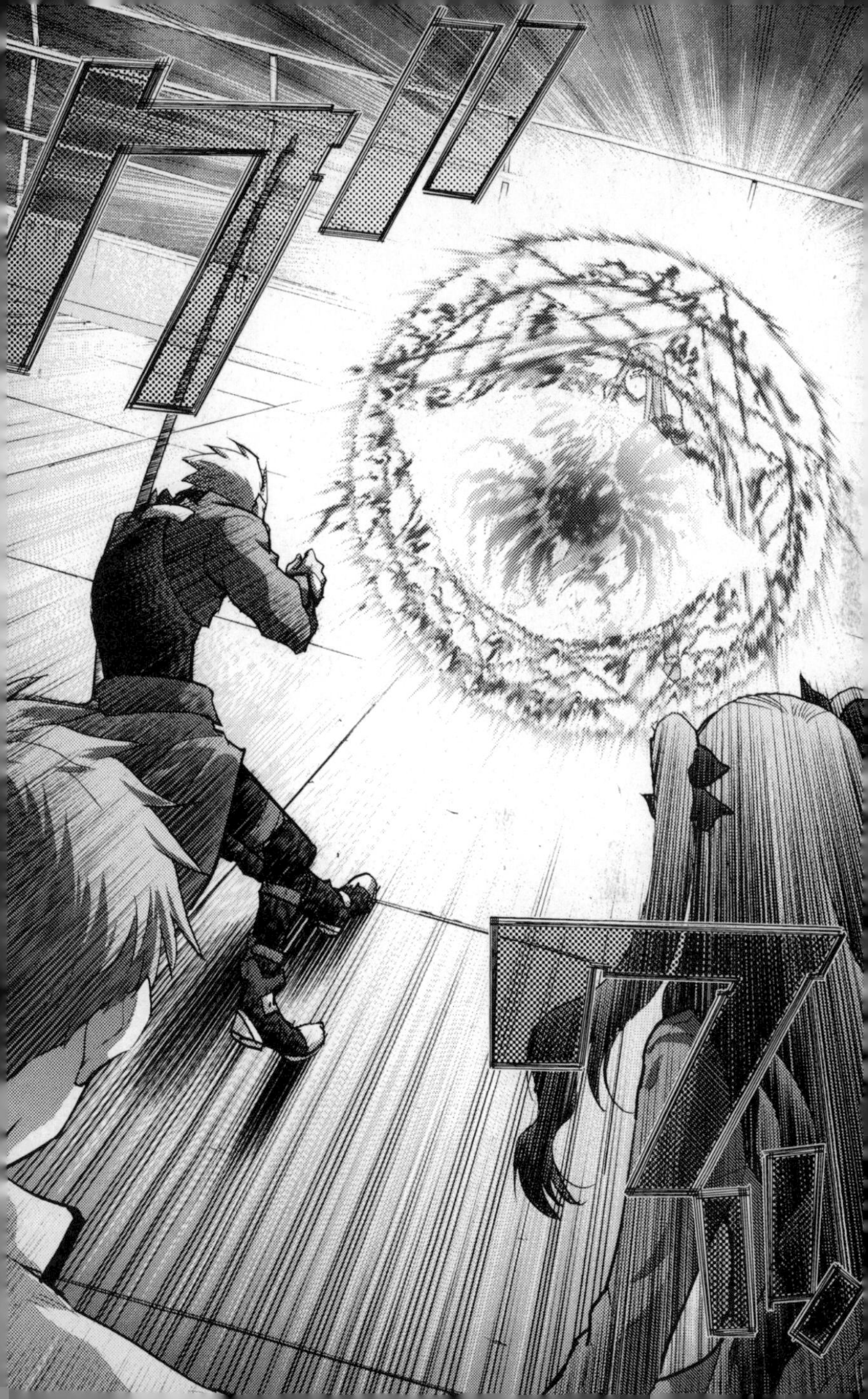

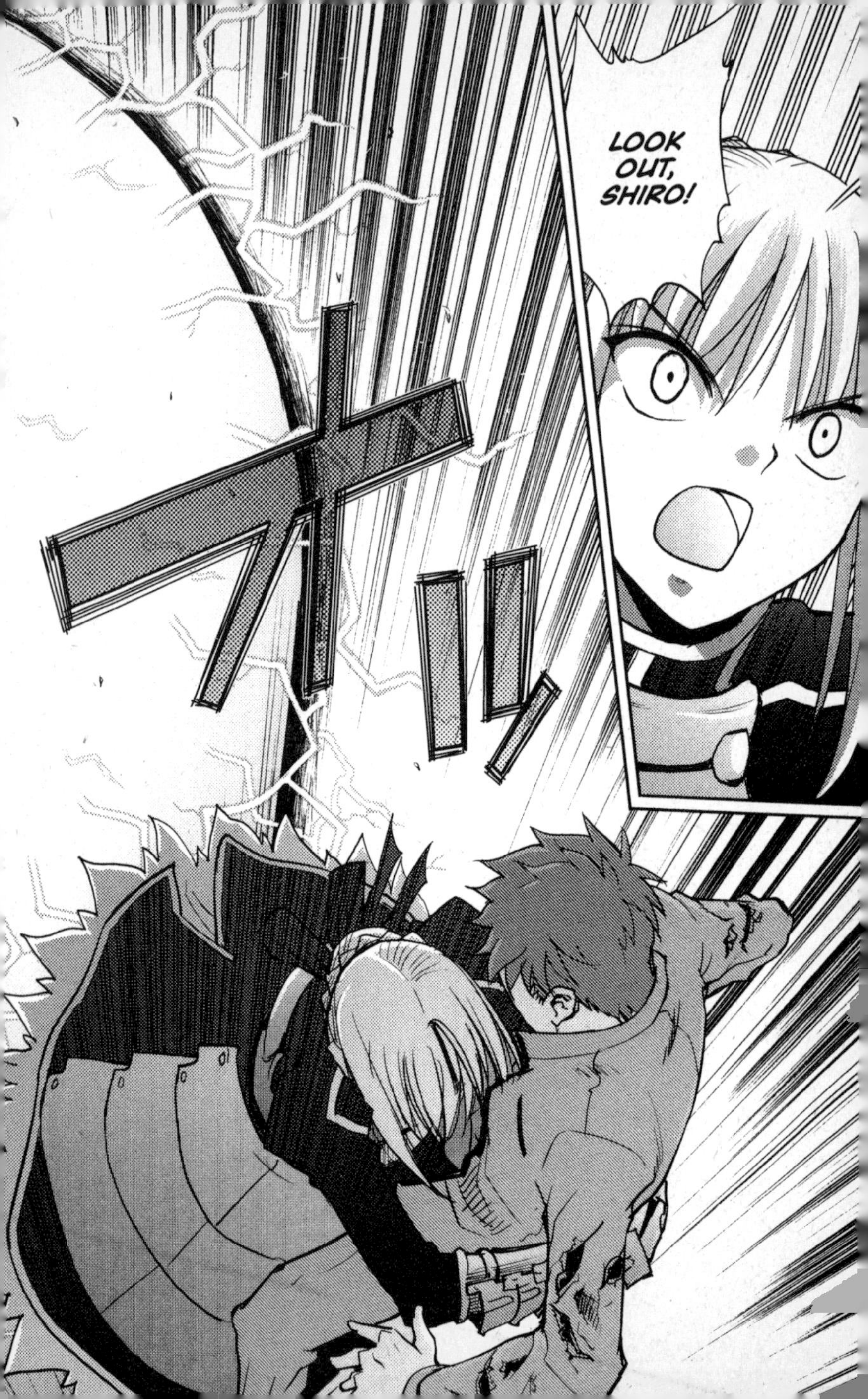
LOOK OUT, SHIRO!

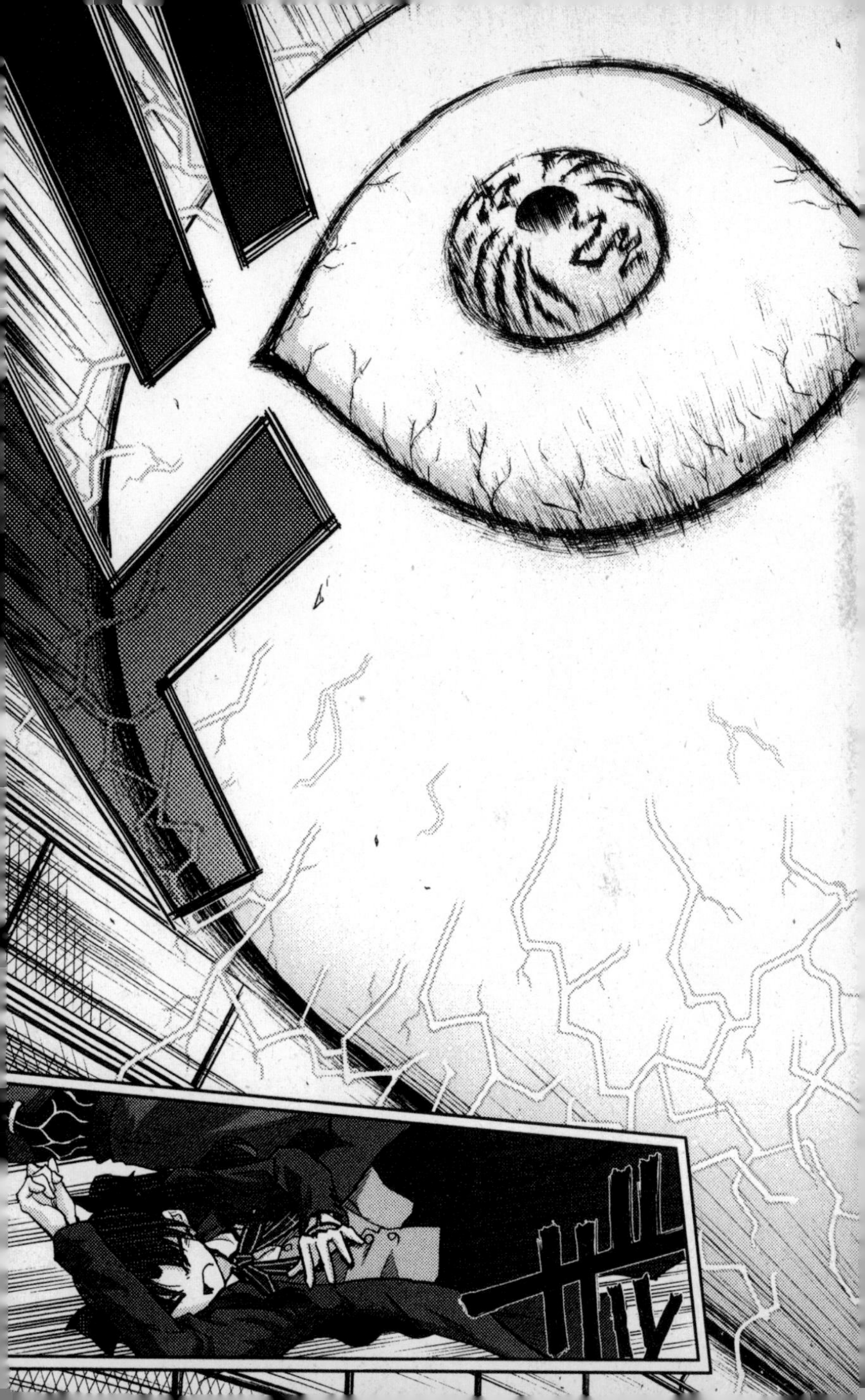

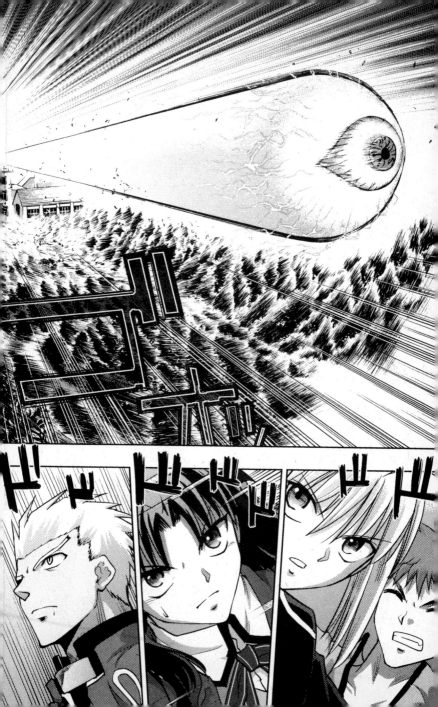

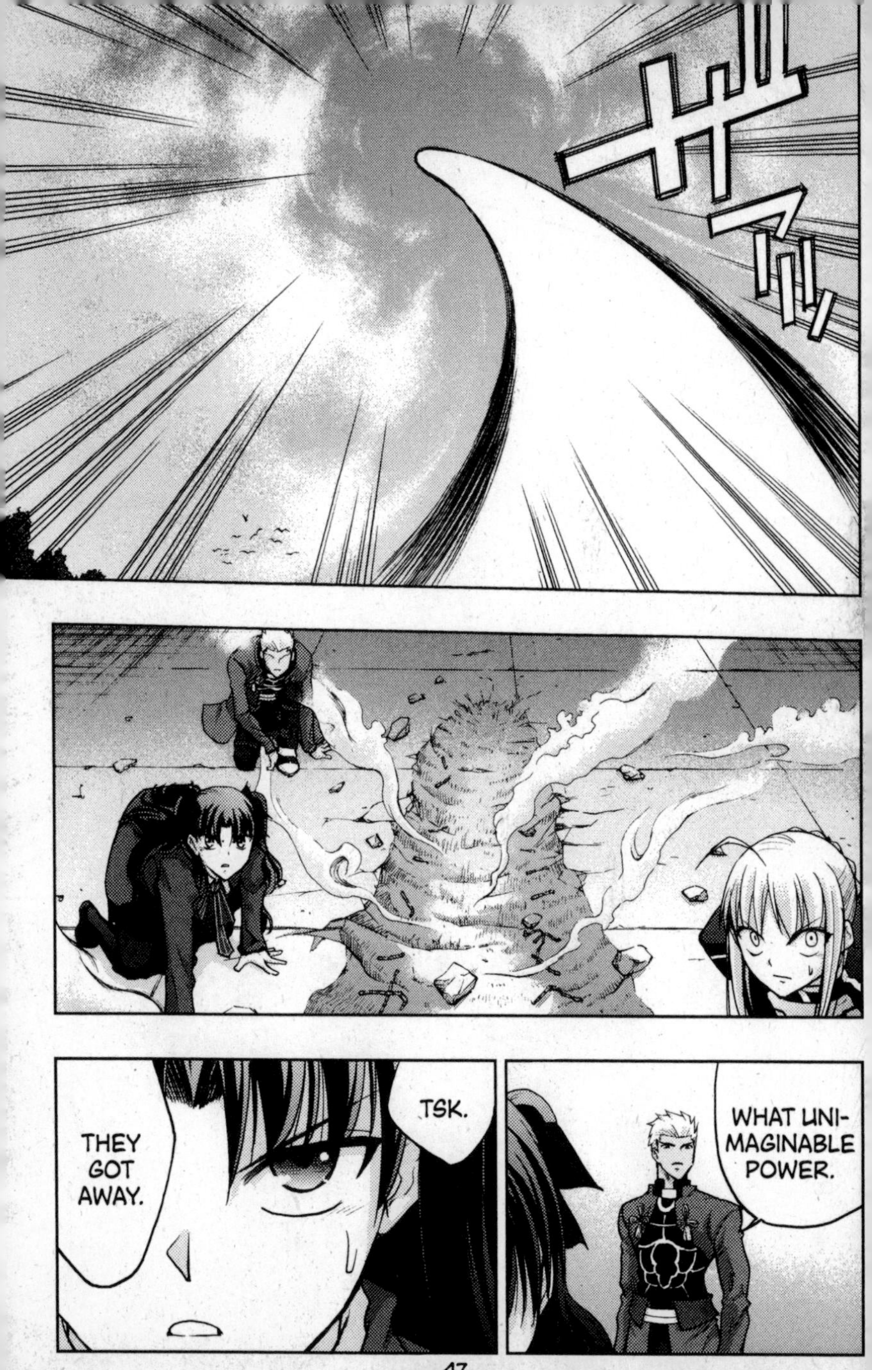
WHAT UNI-MAGINABLE POWER.
TSK.
THEY GOT AWAY.

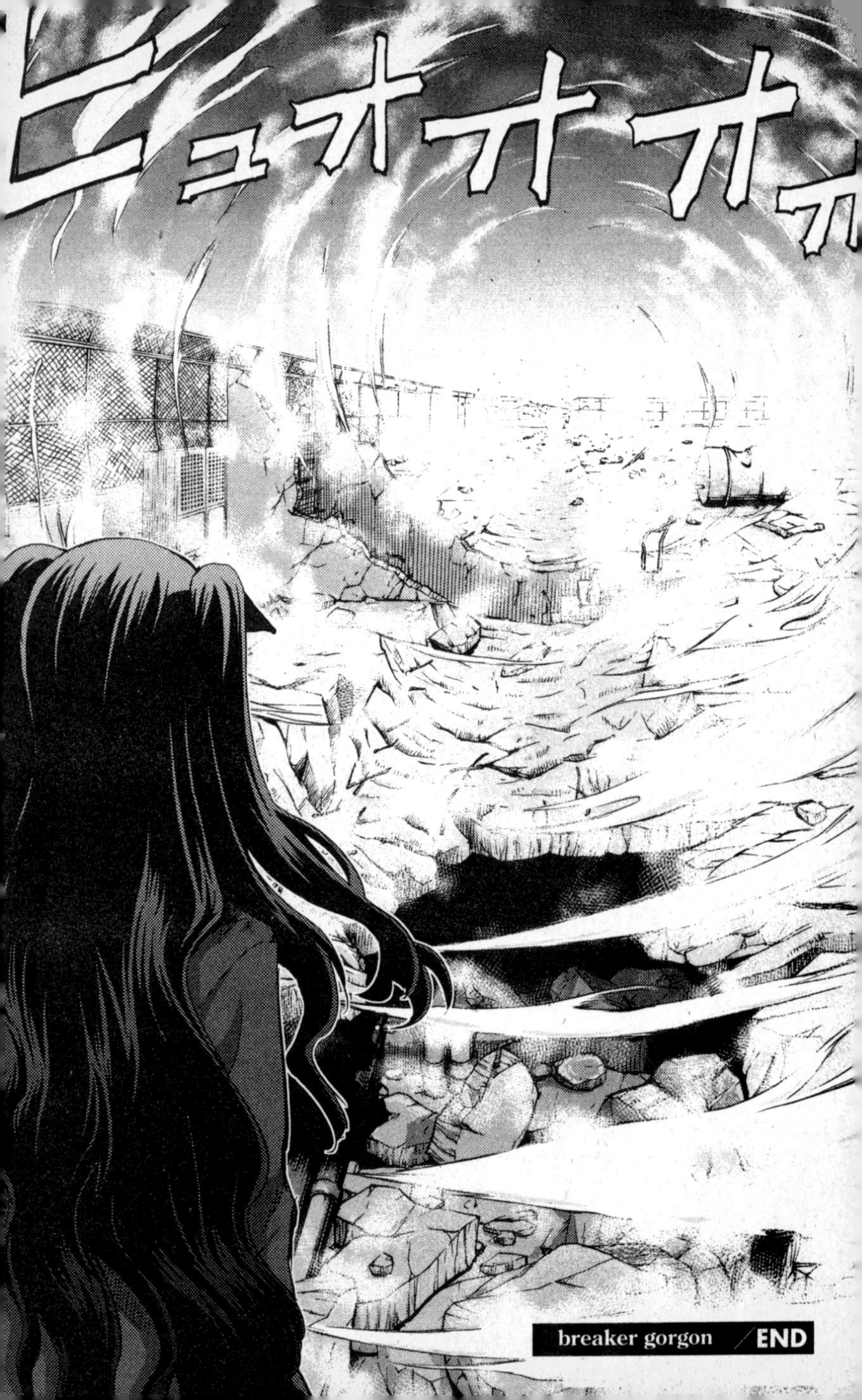
ヒュオオオォ
breaker gorgon ／END

Fate
stay night
フェイト/ステイナイト

skyscraper (I)

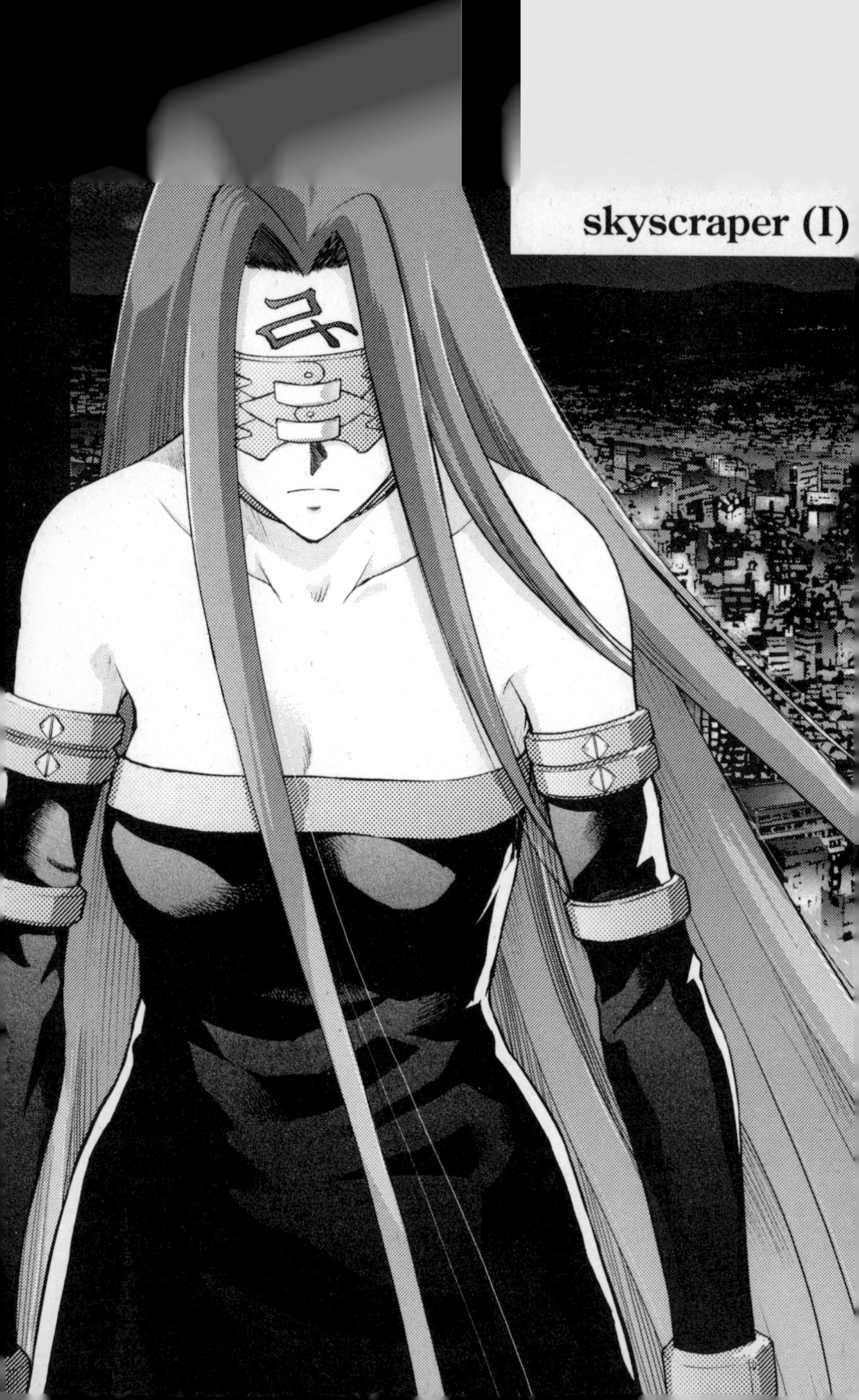

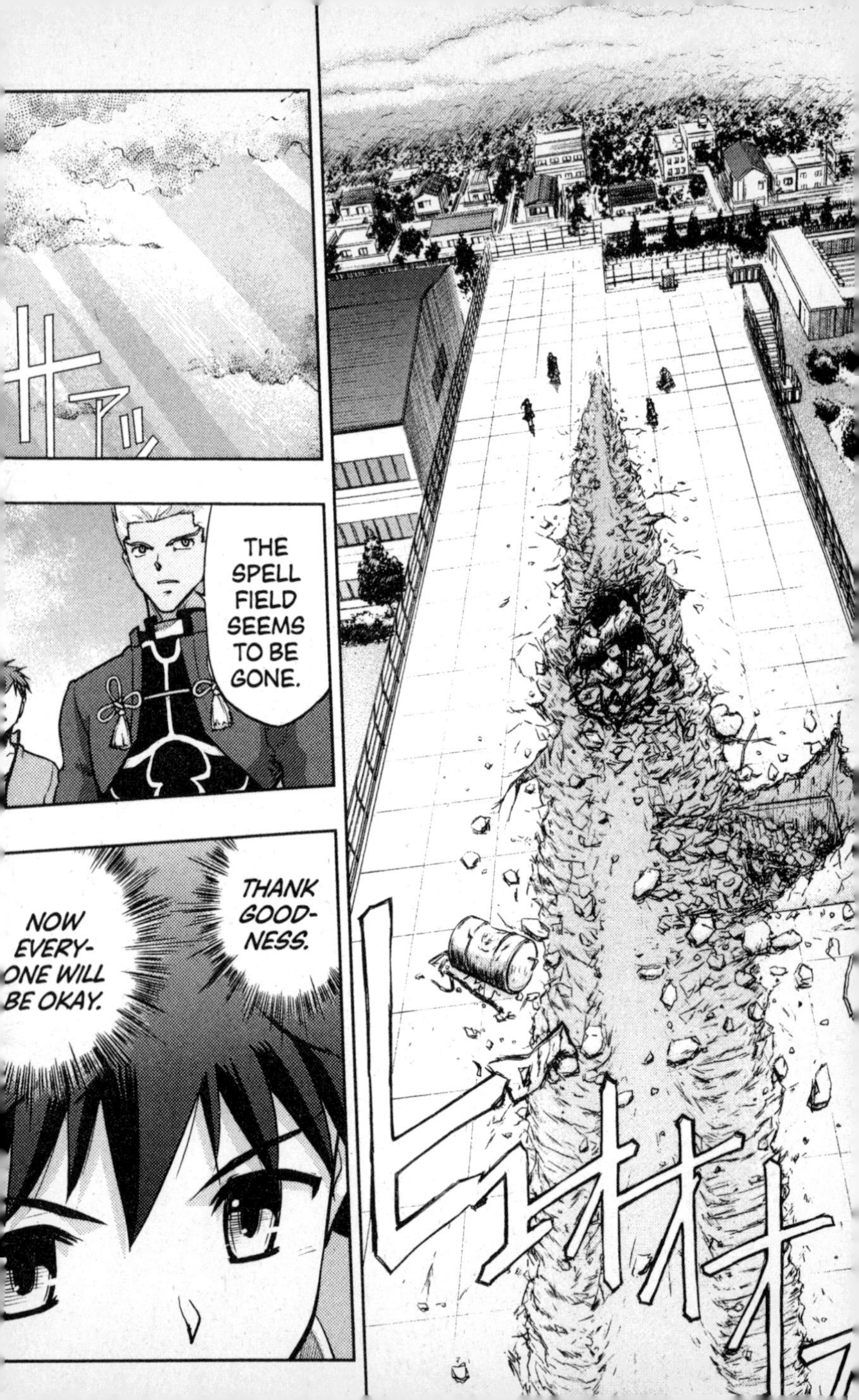

ヒュオオオ
サァッ
THE SPELL FIELD SEEMS TO BE GONE.
THANK GOODNESS.
NOW EVERYONE WILL BE OKAY.

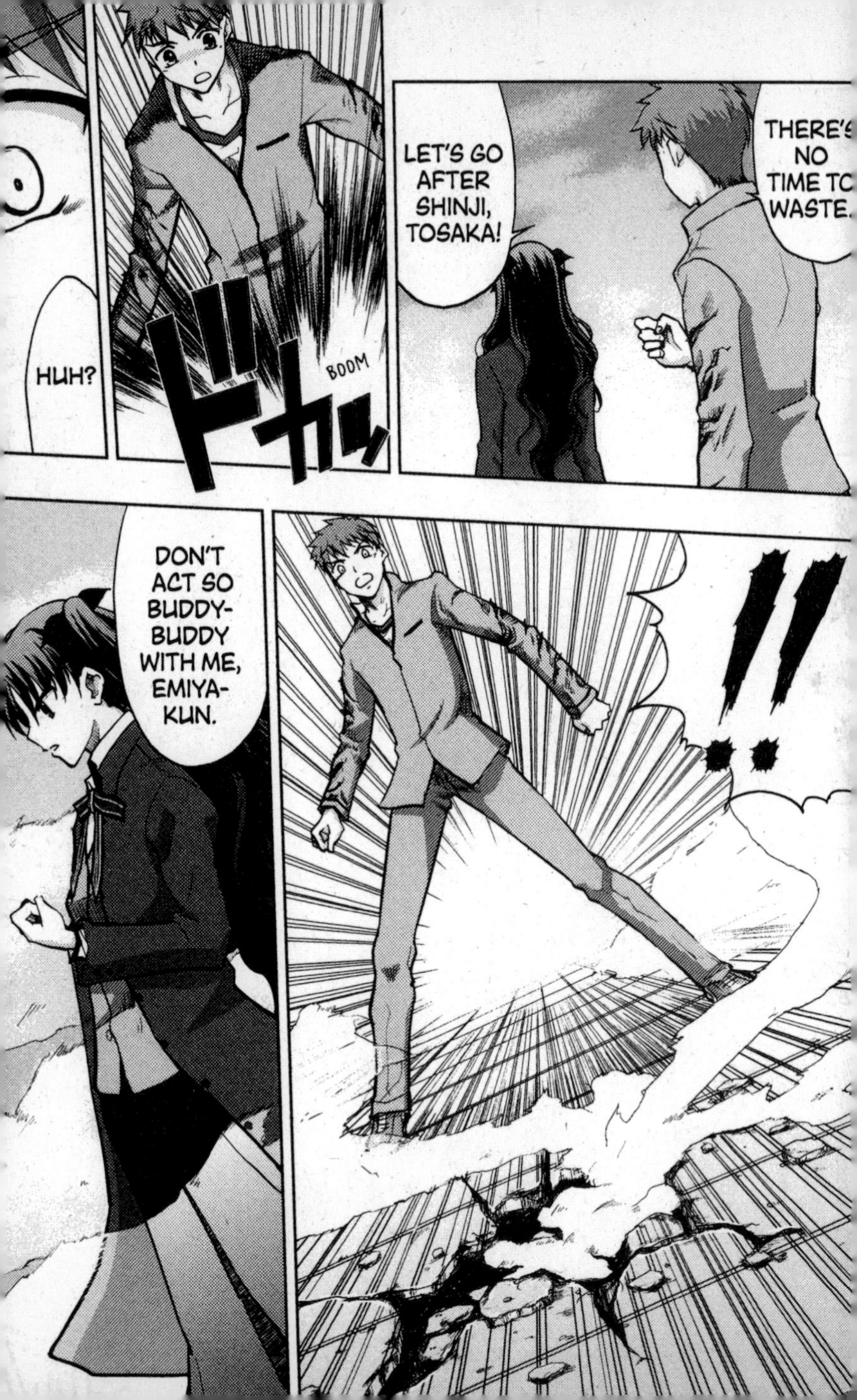
THERE'S NO TIME TO WASTE.
LET'S GO AFTER SHINJI, TOSAKA!
ドカッ
BOOM
HUH?
!!
DON'T ACT SO BUDDY-BUDDY WITH ME, EMIYA-KUN.

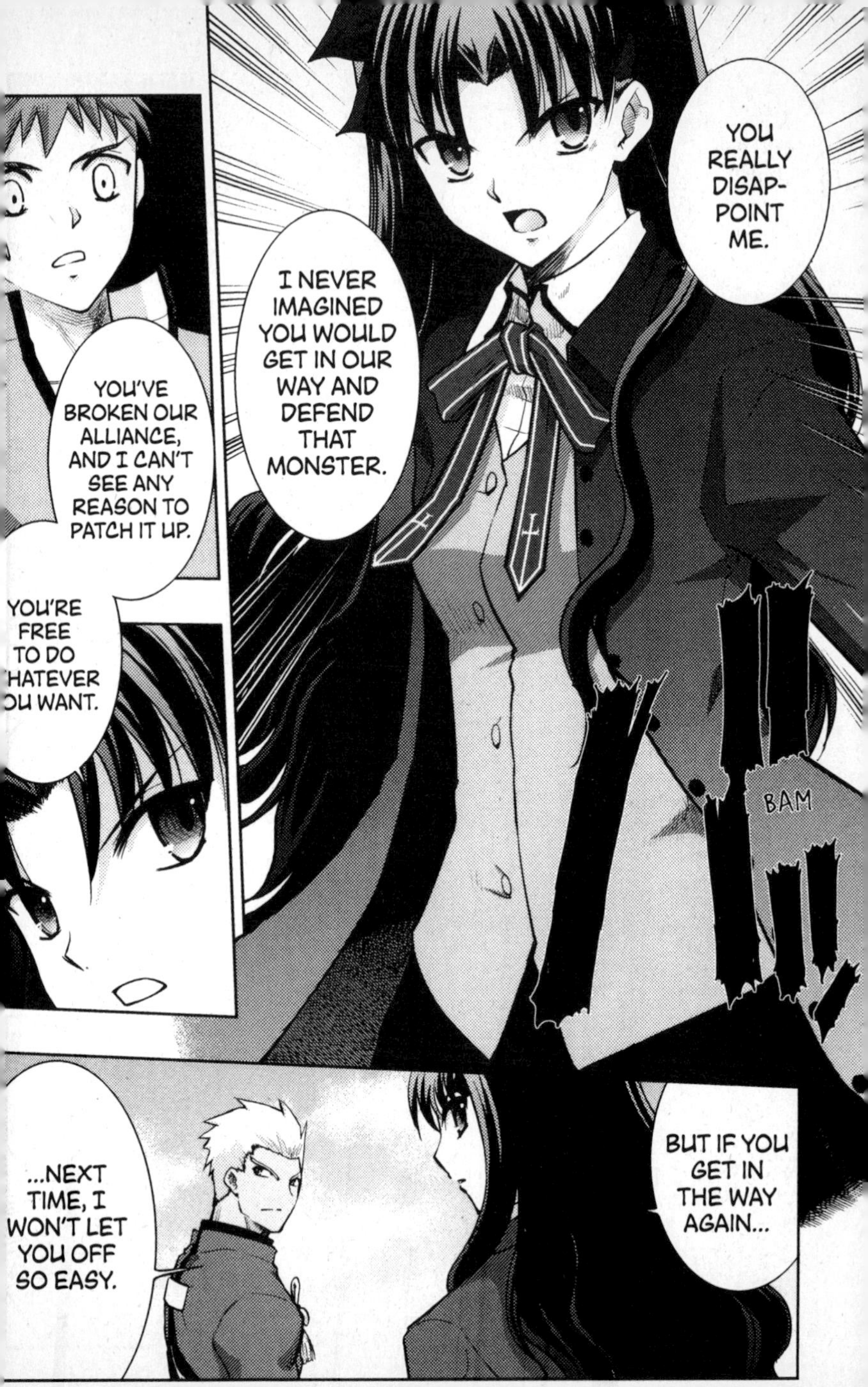
YOU REALLY DISAP- POINT ME.
I NEVER IMAGINED YOU WOULD GET IN OUR WAY AND DEFEND THAT MONSTER.
BAM
YOU'VE BROKEN OUR ALLIANCE, AND I CAN'T SEE ANY REASON TO PATCH IT UP.
YOU'RE FREE TO DO HATEVER OU WANT.
BUT IF YOU GET IN THE WAY AGAIN...
...NEXT TIME, I WON'T LET YOU OFF SO EASY.

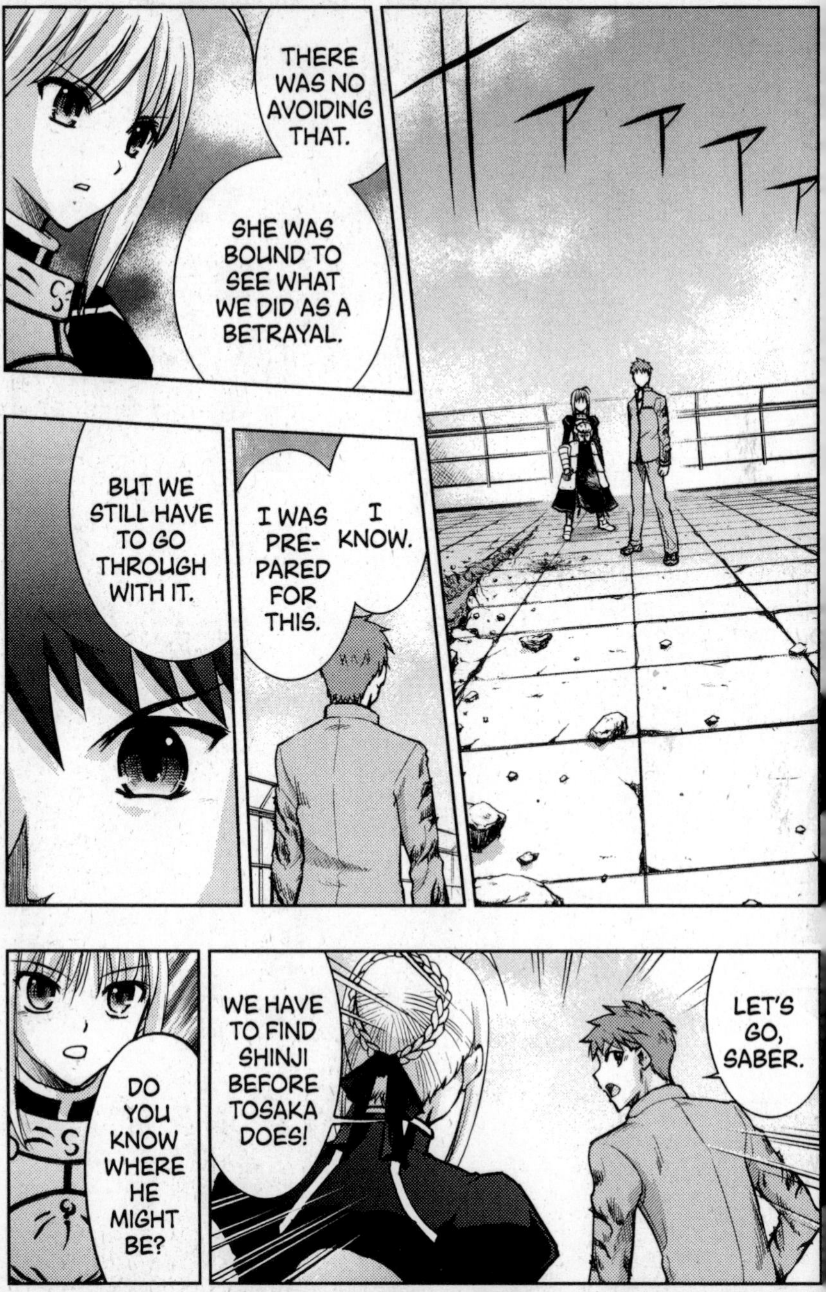
THERE WAS NO AVOIDING THAT.
SHE WAS BOUND TO SEE WHAT WE DID AS A BETRAYAL.
I KNOW.
I WAS PRE-PARED FOR THIS.
BUT WE STILL HAVE TO GO THROUGH WITH IT.
LET'S GO, SABER.
WE HAVE TO FIND SHINJI BEFORE TOSAKA DOES!
DO YOU KNOW WHERE HE MIGHT BE?

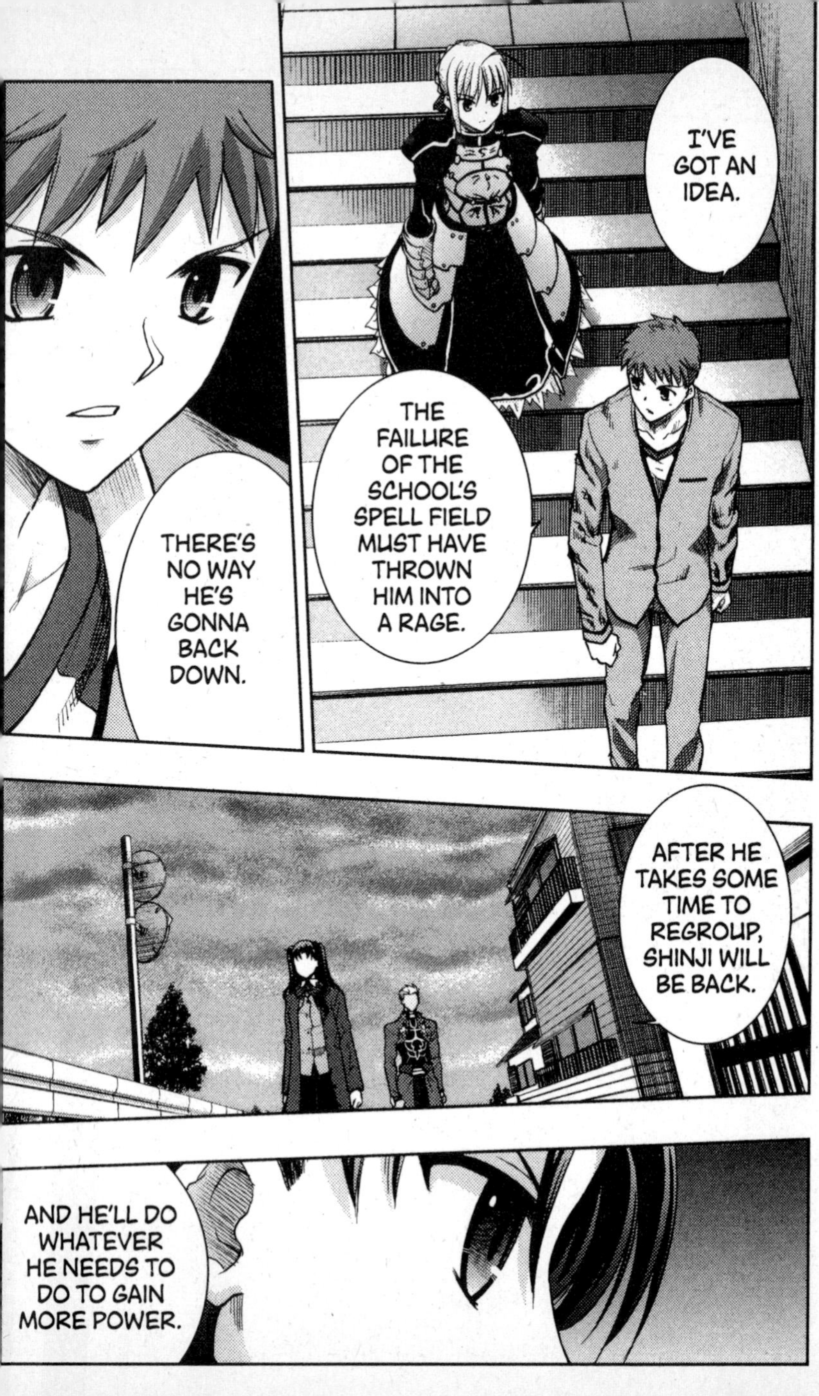
I'VE GOT AN IDEA.
THE FAILURE OF THE SCHOOL'S SPELL FIELD MUST HAVE THROWN HIM INTO A RAGE.
THERE'S NO WAY HE'S GONNA BACK DOWN.
AFTER HE TAKES SOME TIME TO REGROUP, SHINJI WILL BE BACK.
AND HE'LL DO WHATEVER HE NEEDS TO DO TO GAIN MORE POWER.

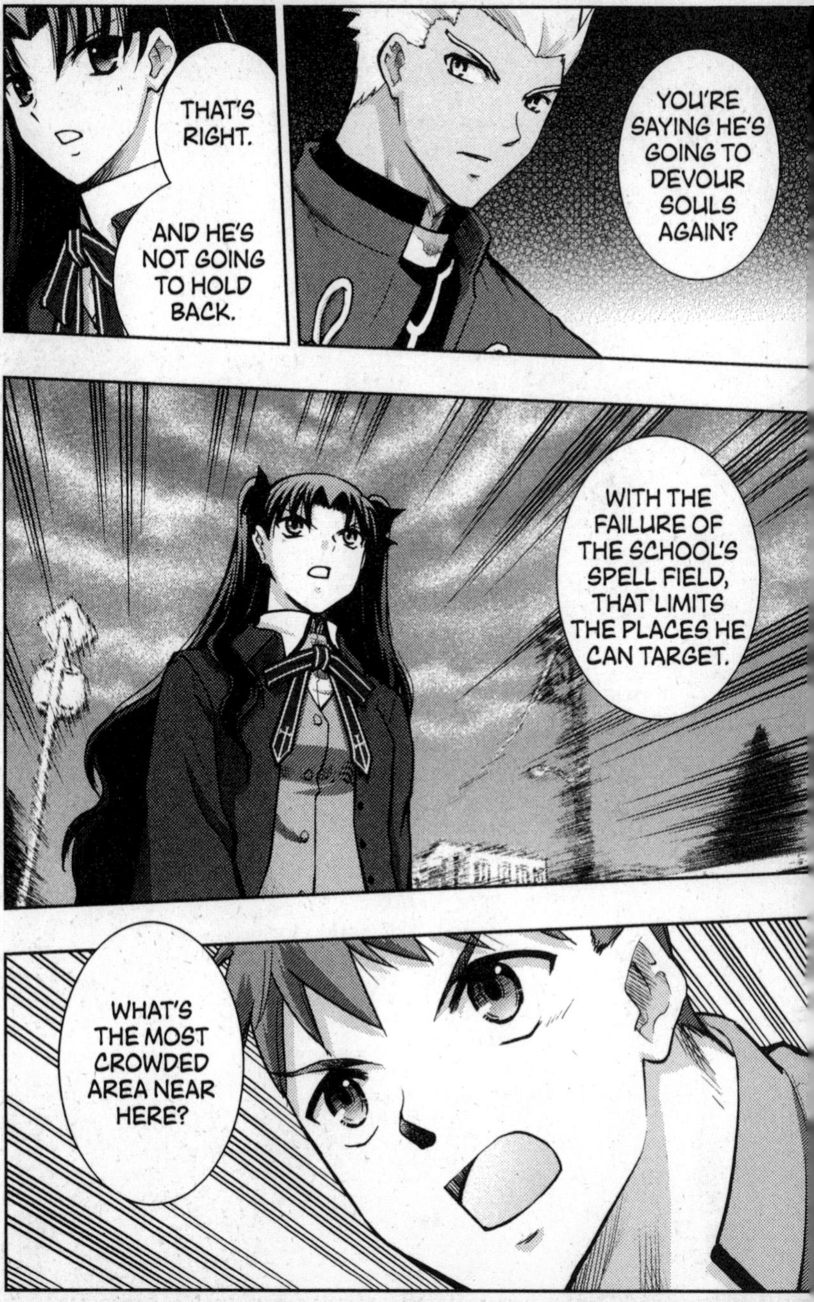
YOU'RE SAYING HE'S GOING TO DEVOUR SOULS AGAIN?
THAT'S RIGHT.
AND HE'S NOT GOING TO HOLD BACK.
WITH THE FAILURE OF THE SCHOOL'S SPELL FIELD, THAT LIMITS THE PLACES HE CAN TARGET.
WHAT'S THE MOST CROWDED AREA NEAR HERE?

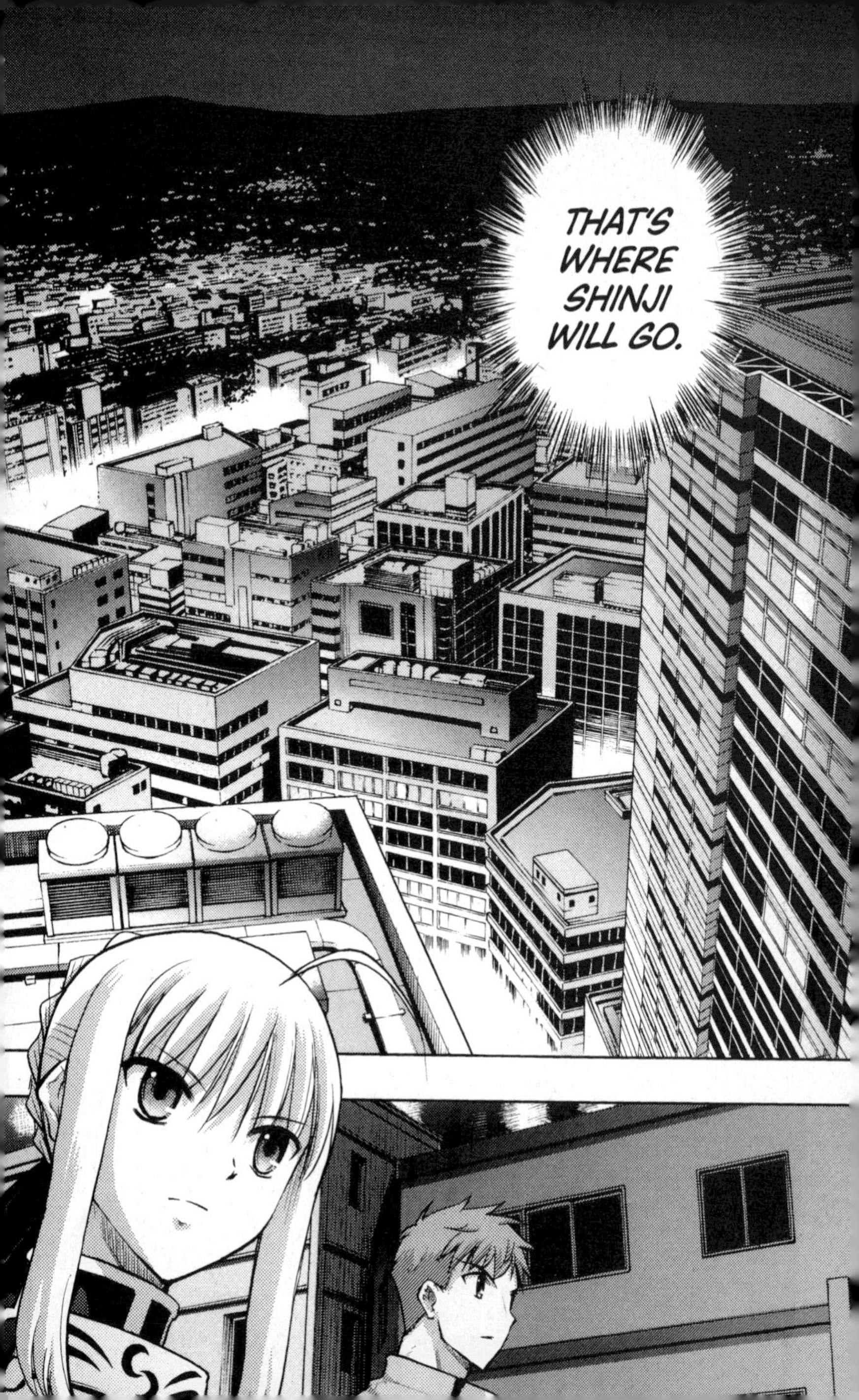
THAT'S WHERE SHINJI WILL GO.

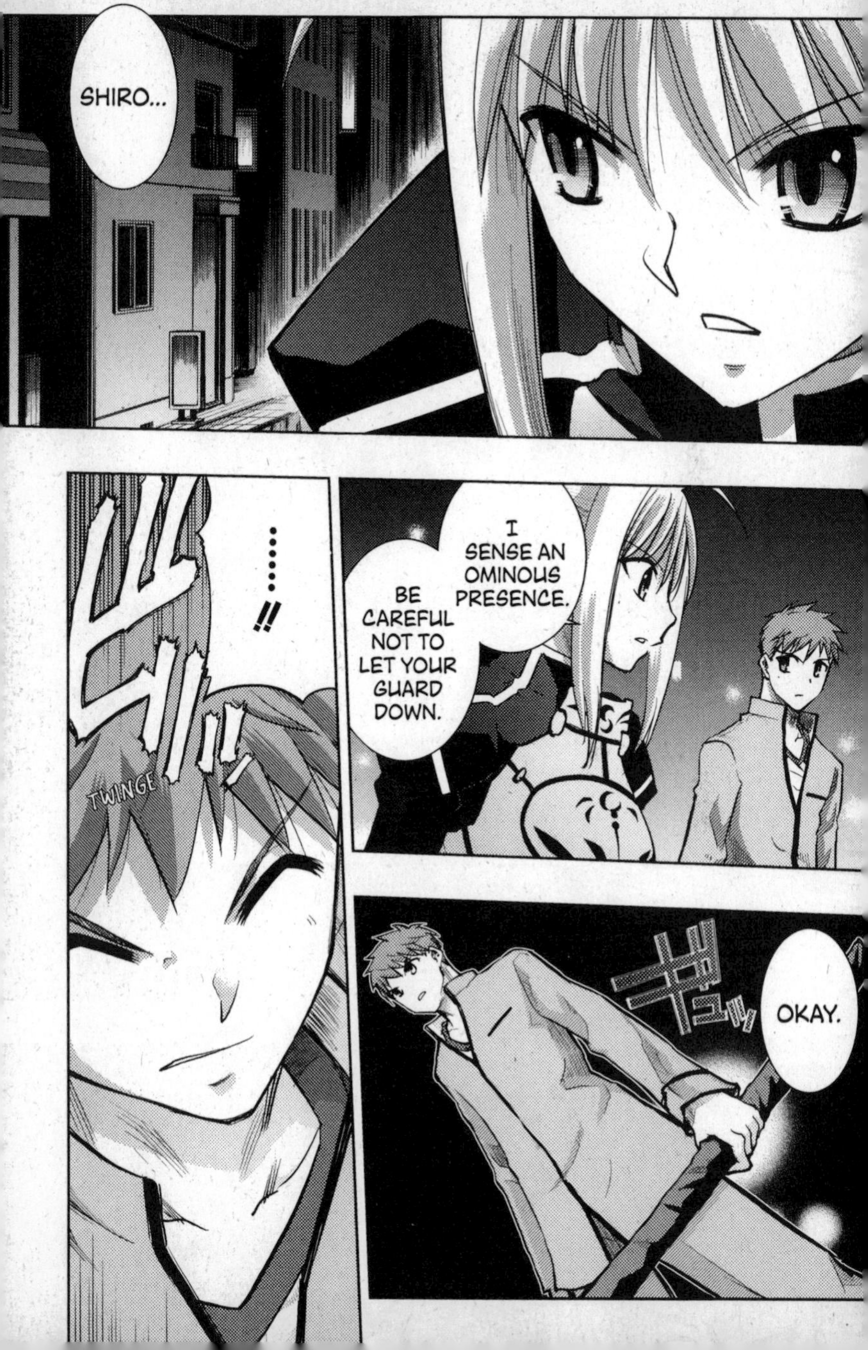
SHIRO...
I SENSE AN OMINOUS PRESENCE.
BE CAREFUL NOT TO LET YOUR GUARD DOWN.
OKAY.
......!!
TWINGE

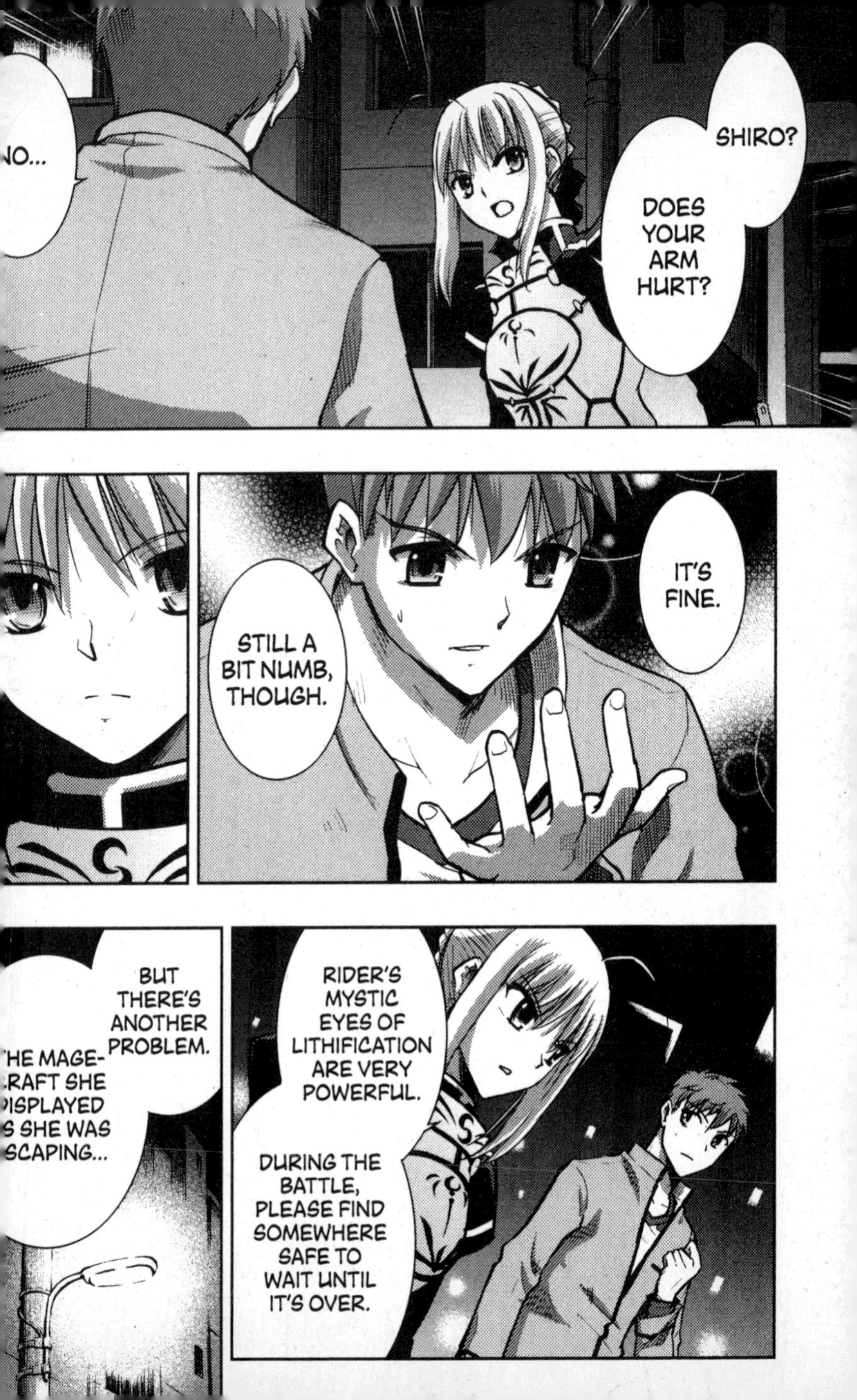
SHIRO?
DOES YOUR ARM HURT?
NO...
IT'S FINE.
STILL A BIT NUMB, THOUGH.
RIDER'S MYSTIC EYES OF LITHIFICATION ARE VERY POWERFUL.
DURING THE BATTLE, PLEASE FIND SOMEWHERE SAFE TO WAIT UNTIL IT'S OVER.
BUT THERE'S ANOTHER PROBLEM.
HE MAGE- RAFT SHE ISPLAYED S SHE WAS SCAPING...

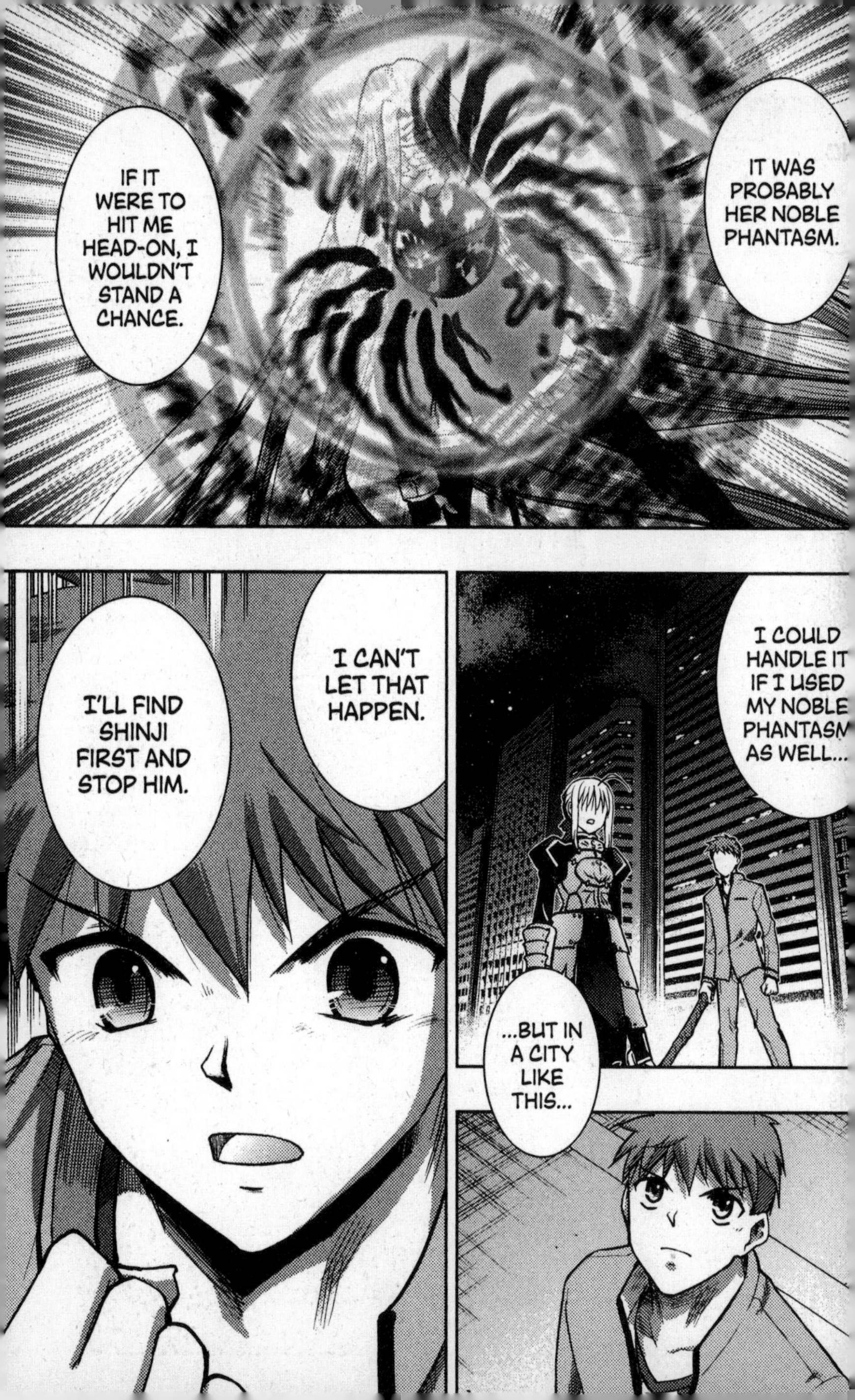
IT WAS PROBABLY HER NOBLE PHANTASM.
IF IT WERE TO HIT ME HEAD-ON, I WOULDN'T STAND A CHANCE.
I COULD HANDLE IT IF I USED MY NOBLE PHANTASM AS WELL...
...BUT IN A CITY LIKE THIS...
I CAN'T LET THAT HAPPEN.
I'LL FIND SHINJI FIRST AND STOP HIM.

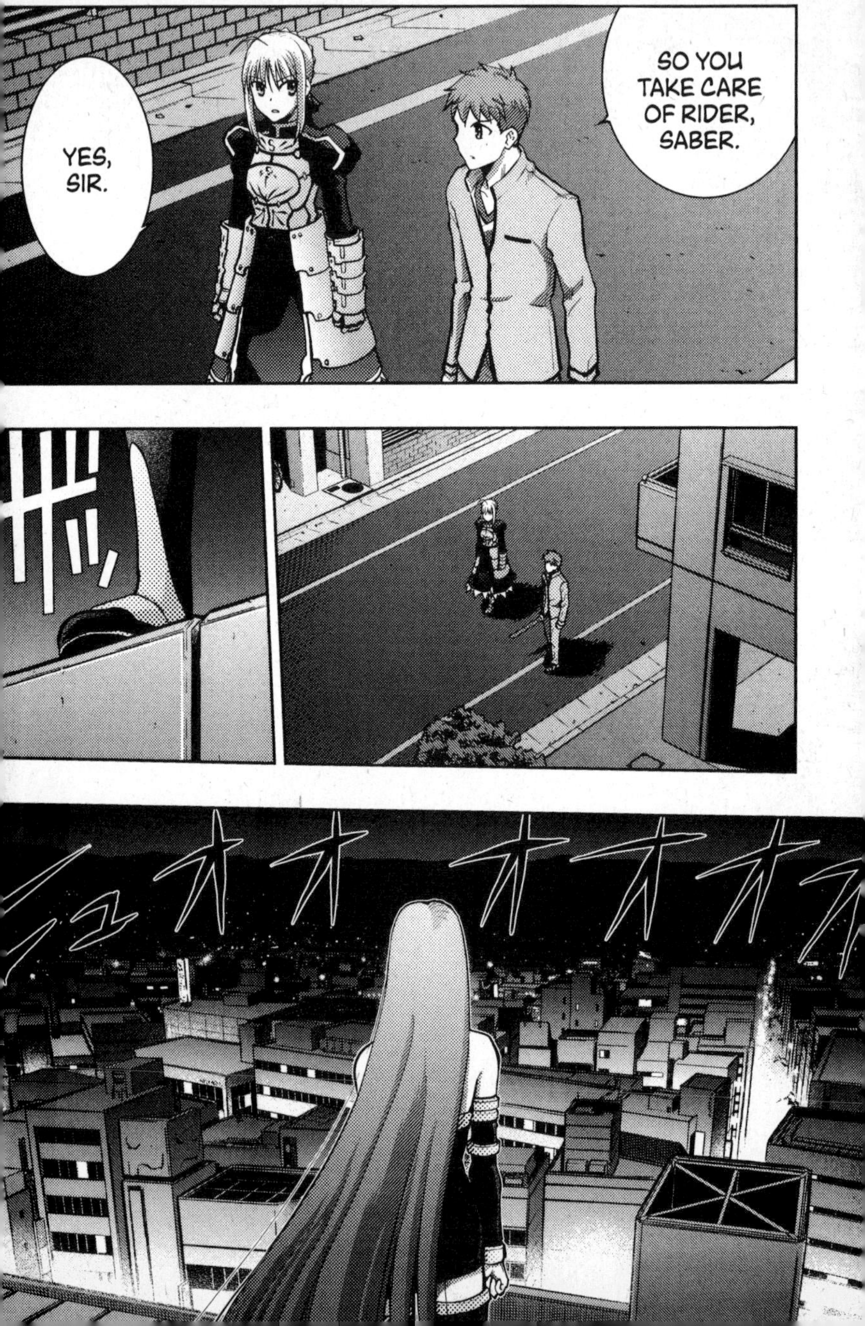
SO YOU TAKE CARE OF RIDER, SABER.
YES, SIR.

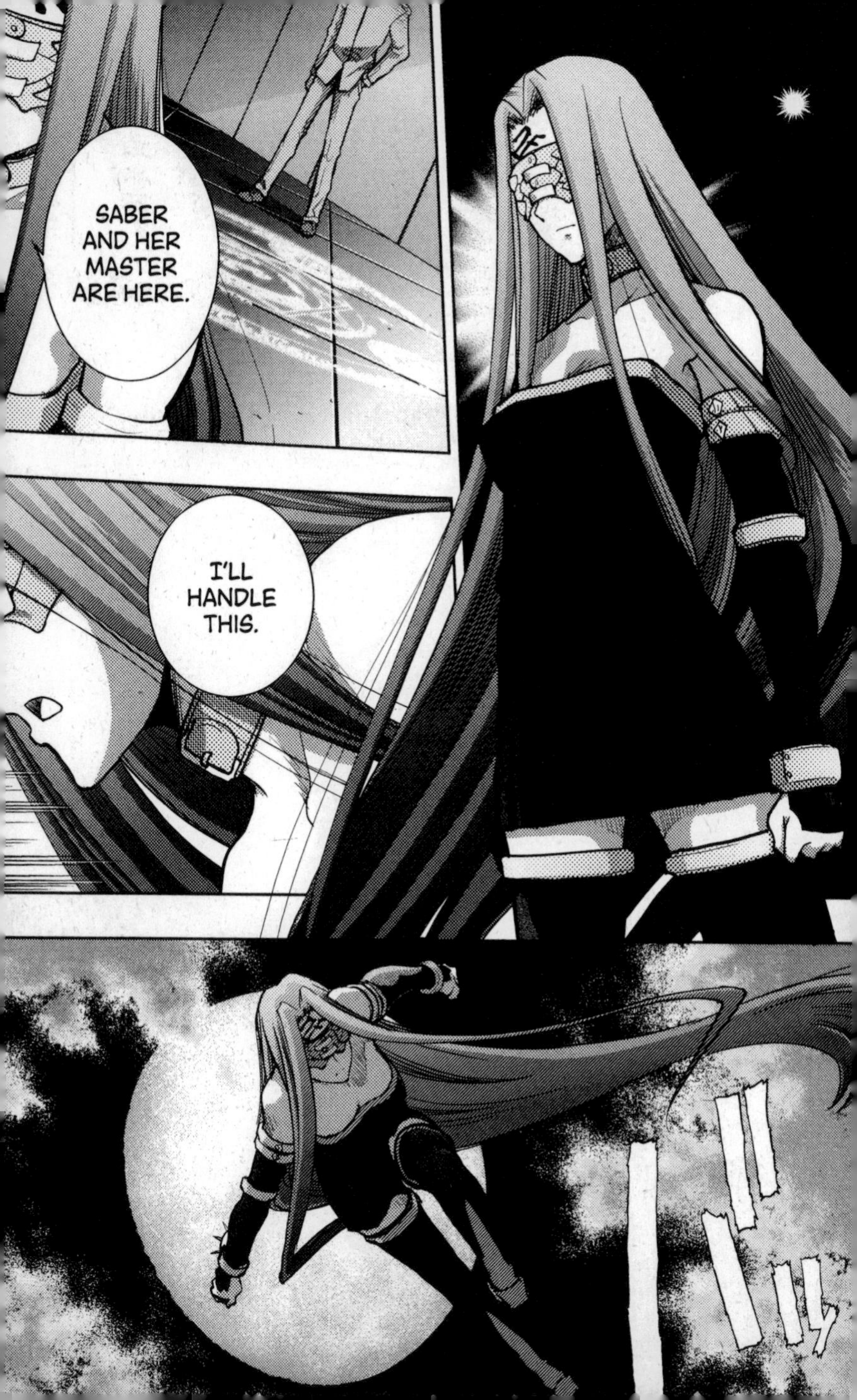
SABER AND HER MASTER ARE HERE.
I'LL HANDLE THIS.

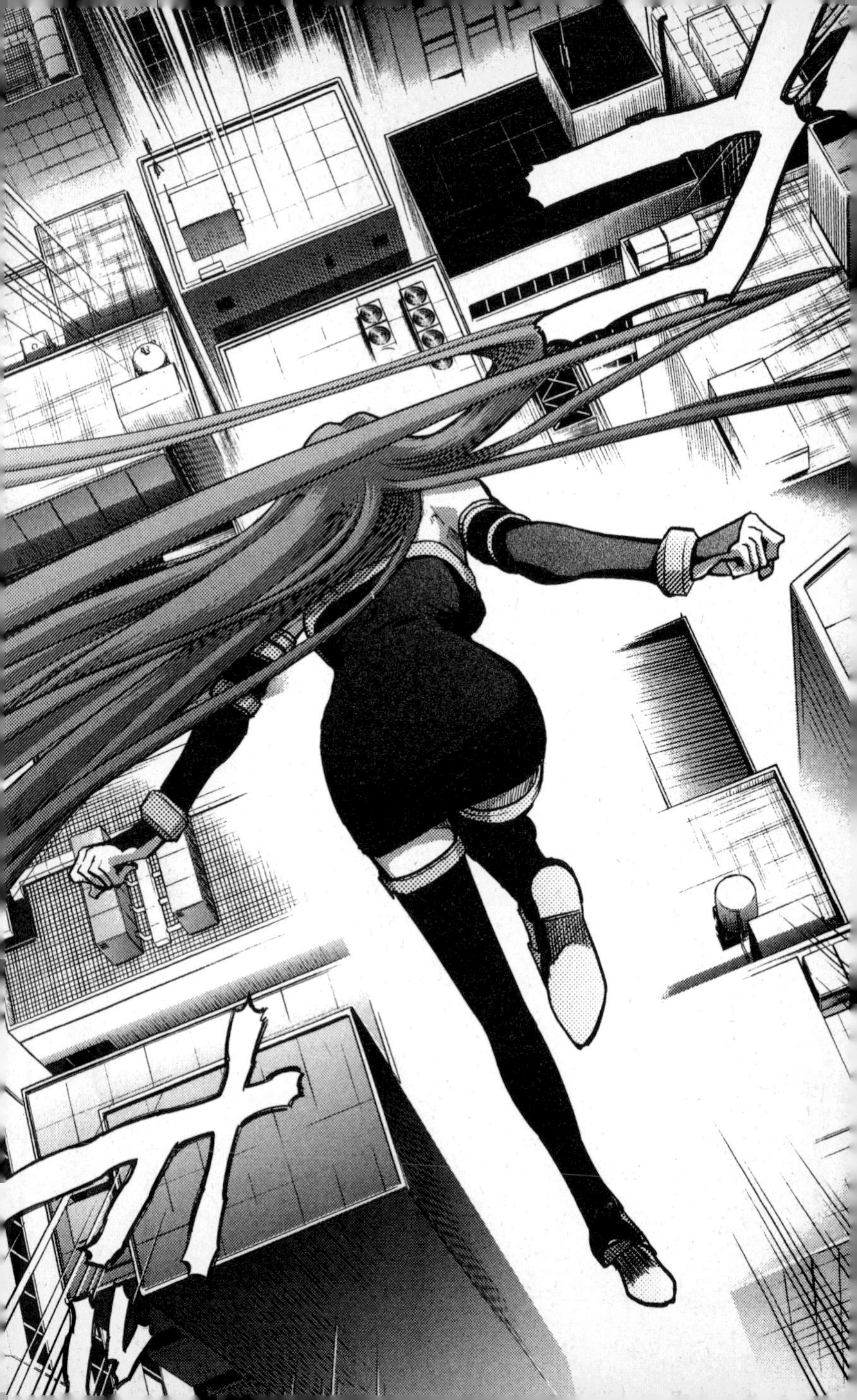

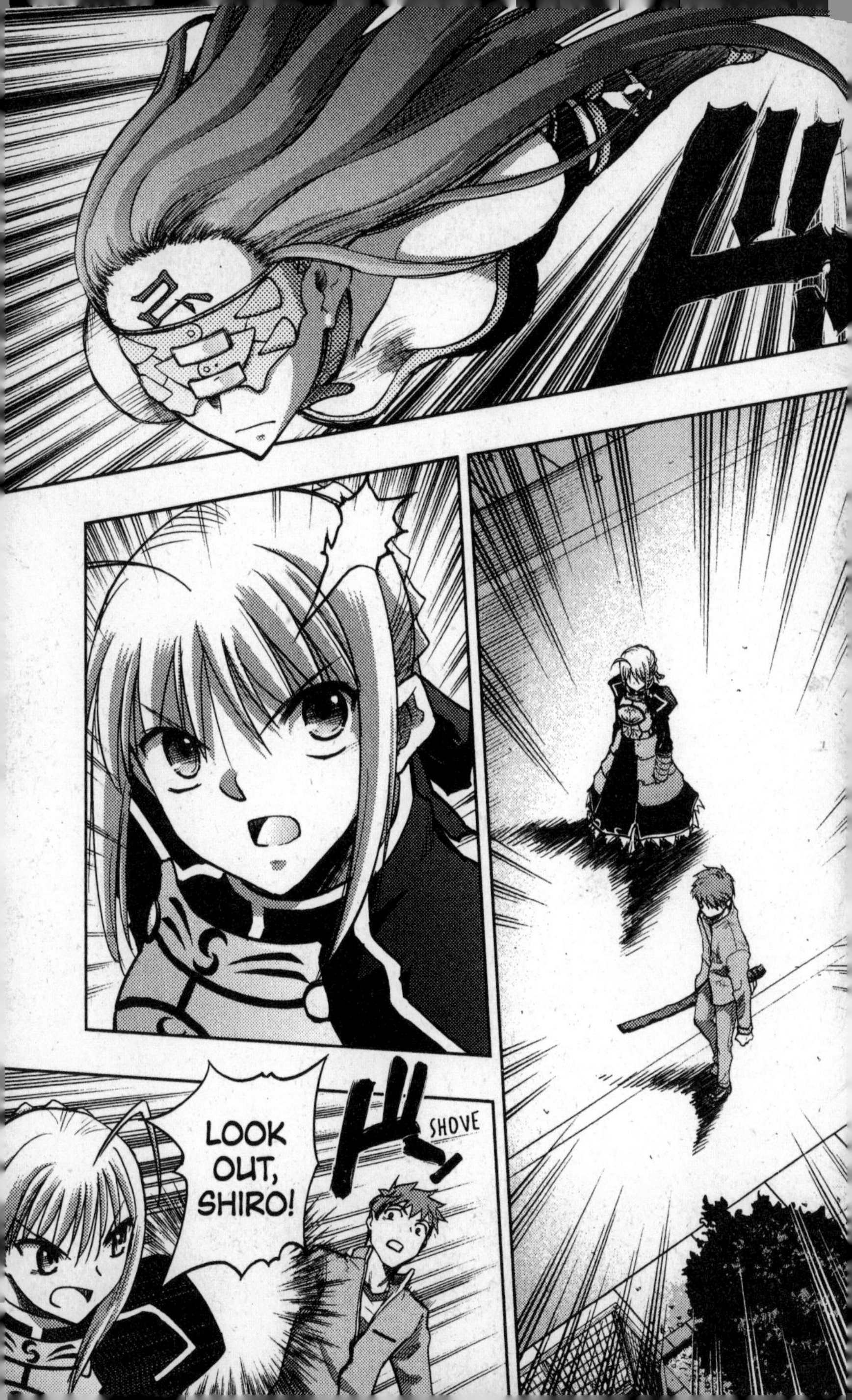
LOOK OUT, SHIRO!
SHOVE

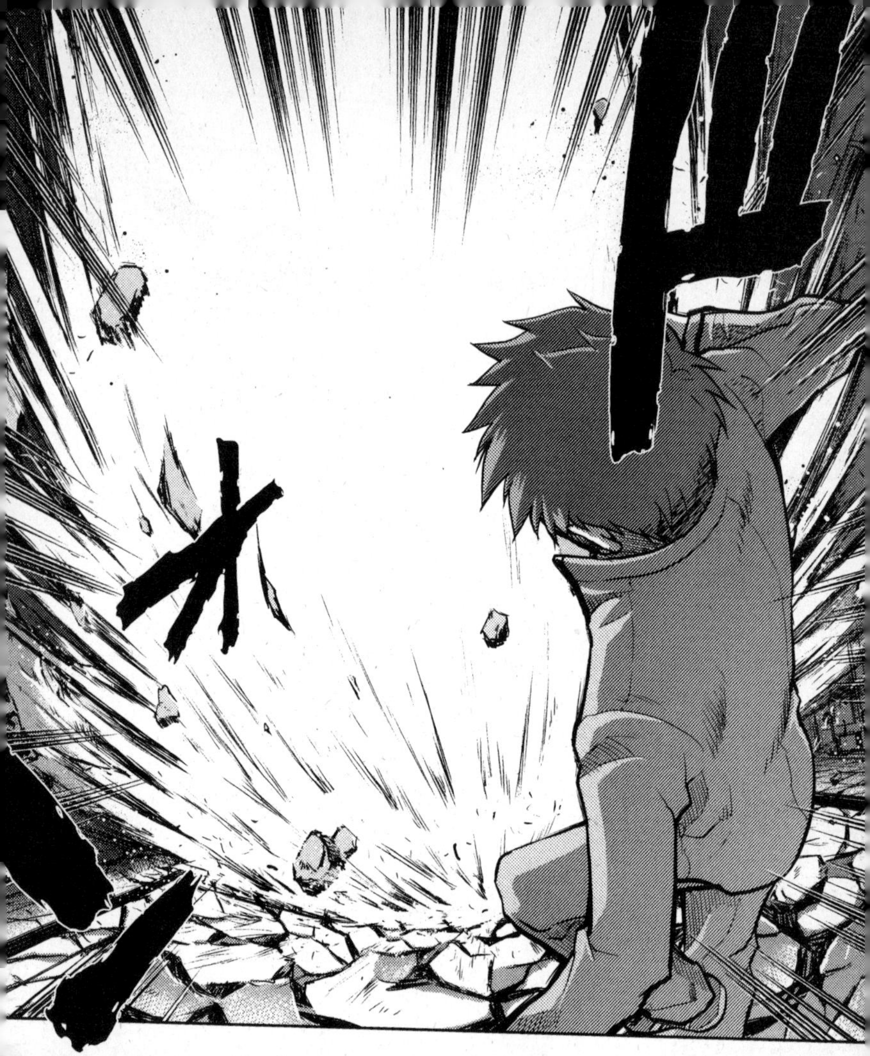

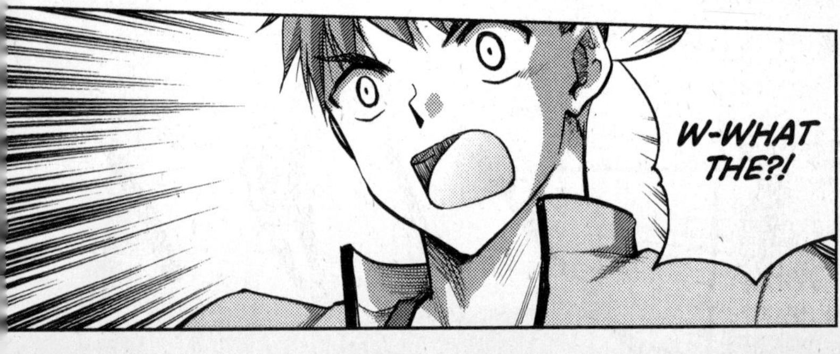
W-WHAT THE?!

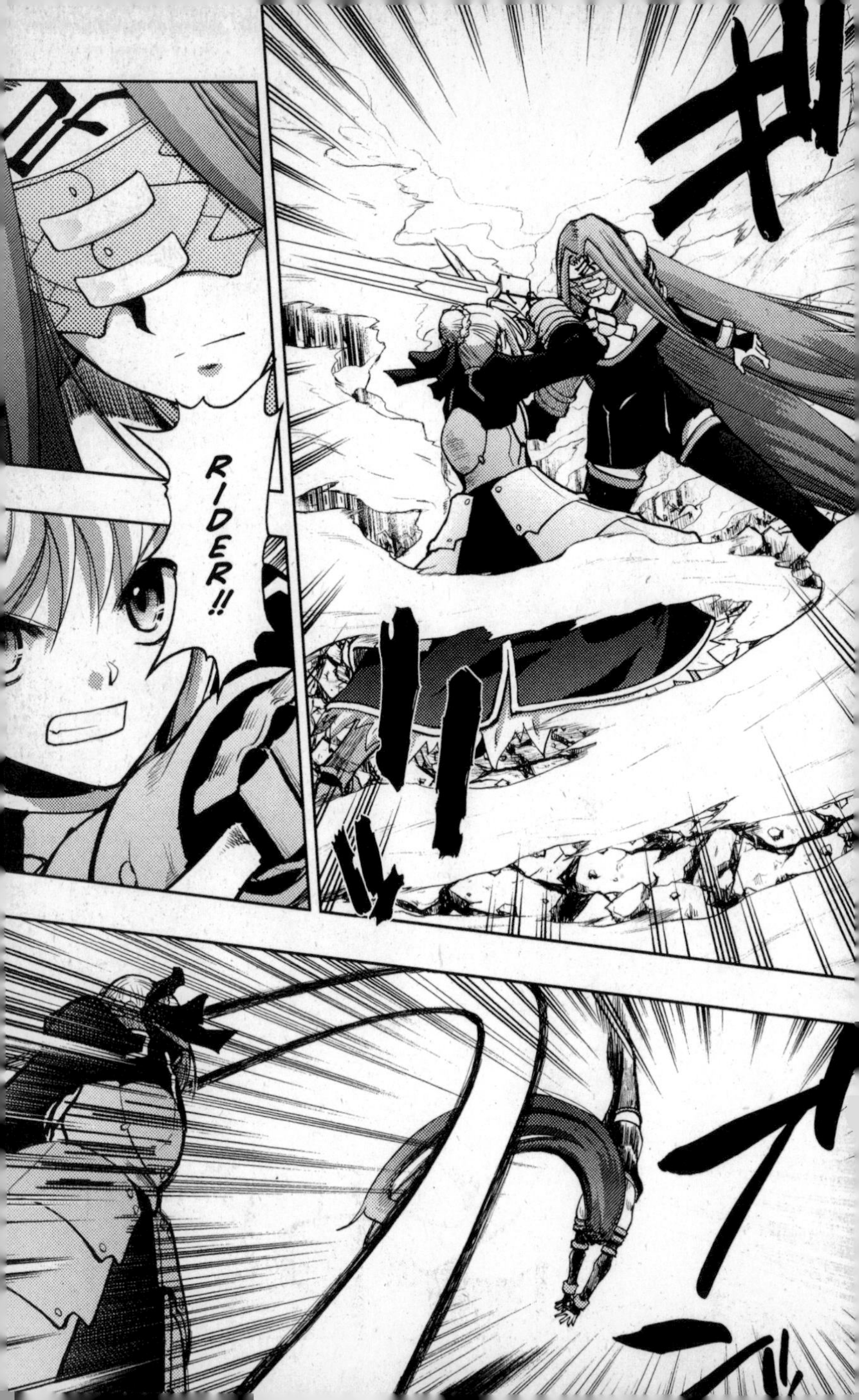
RIDER!!

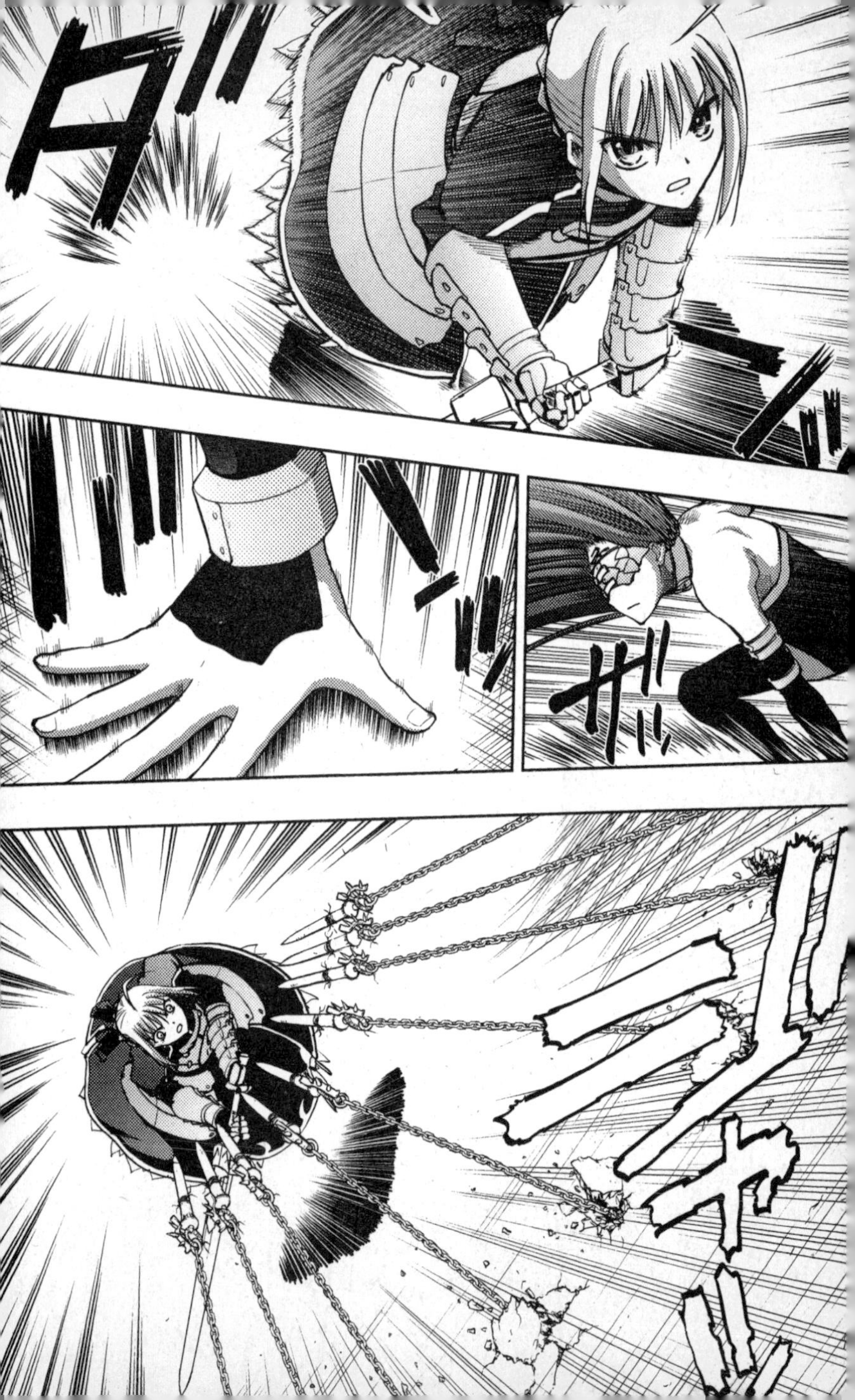
ダッ
ザッ

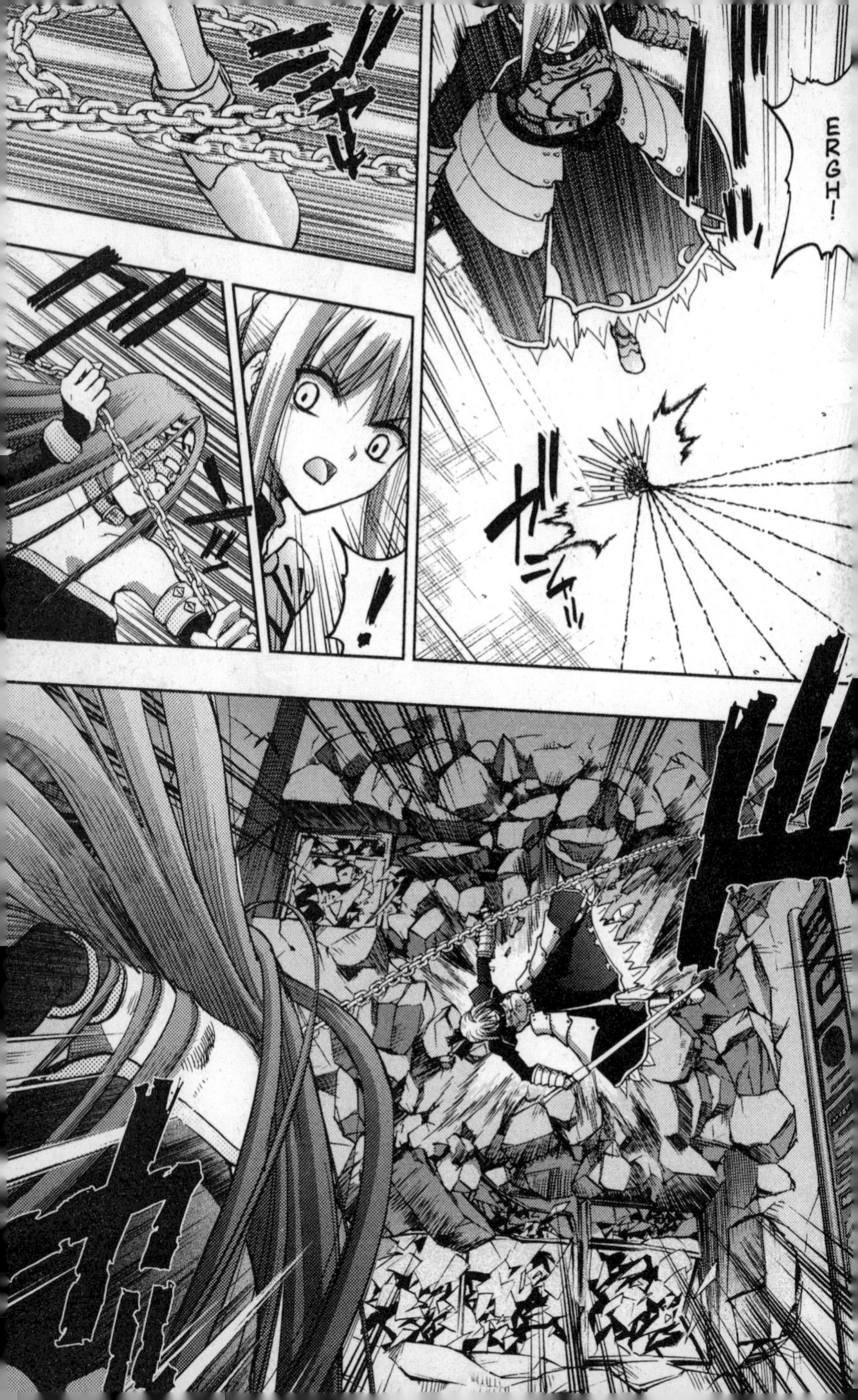
ERGH!

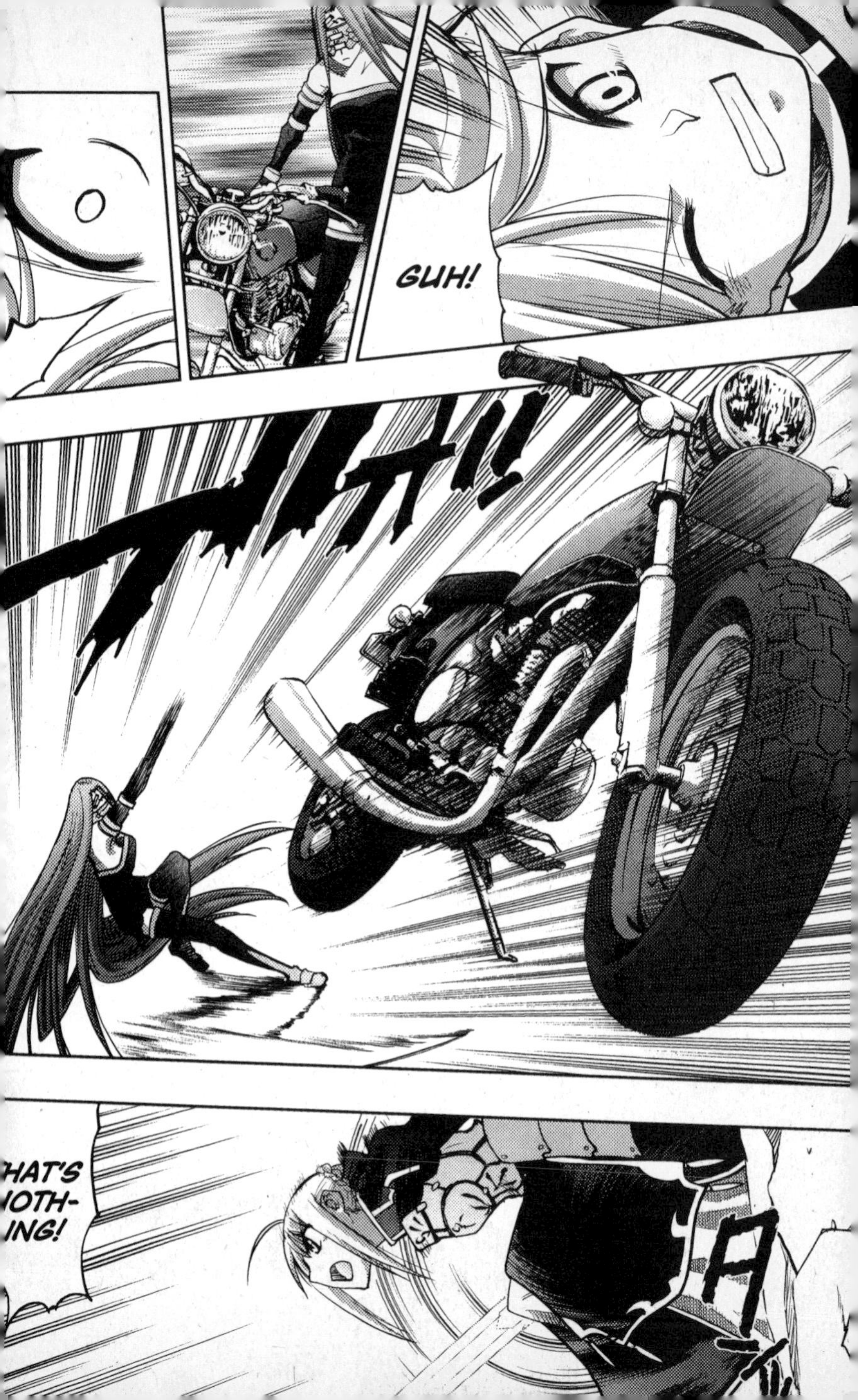
GUH!
HAT'S
IOTH-
ING!

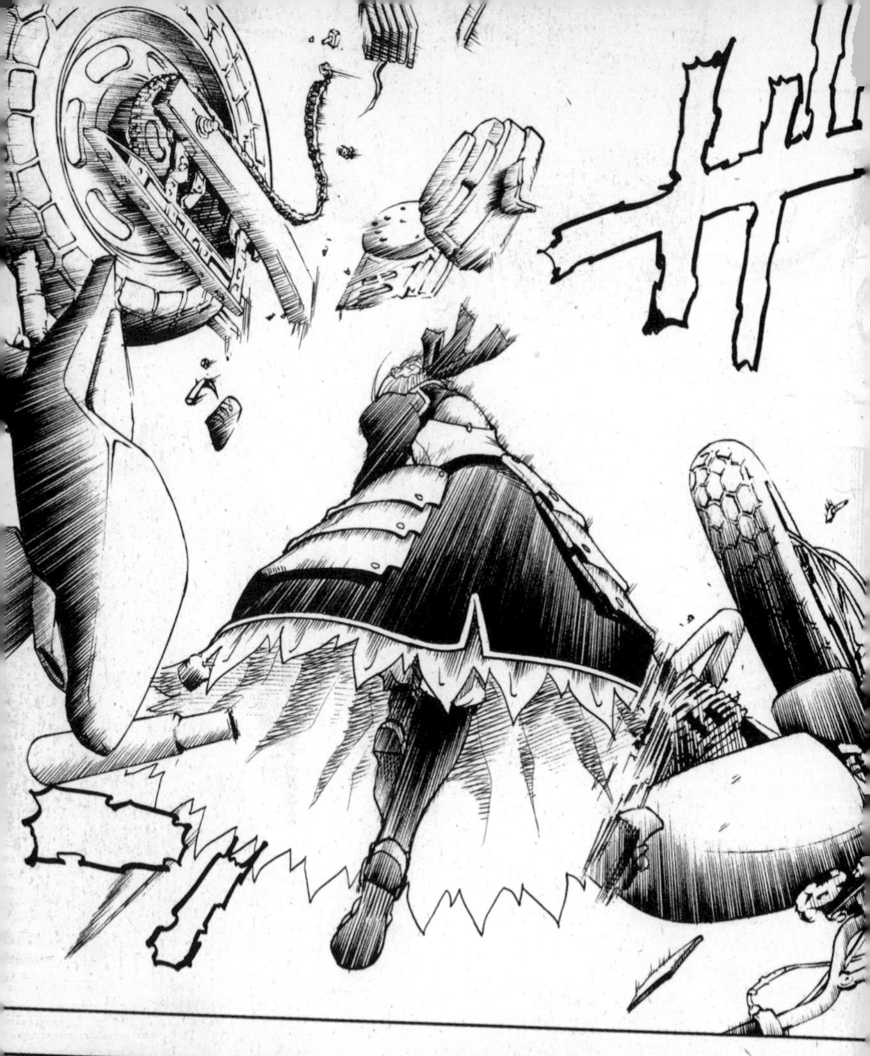
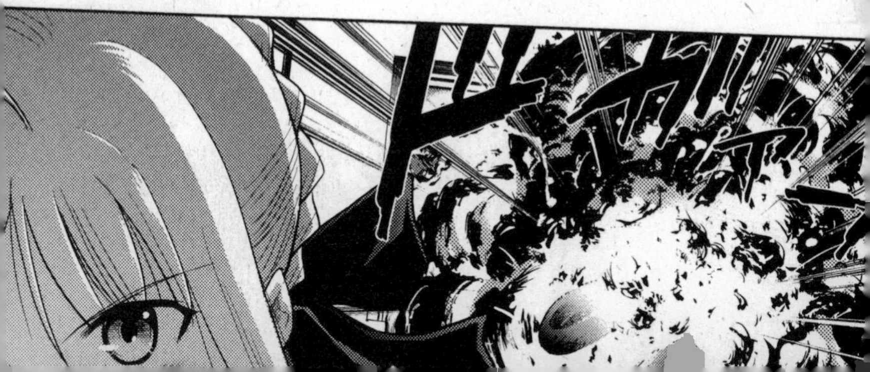

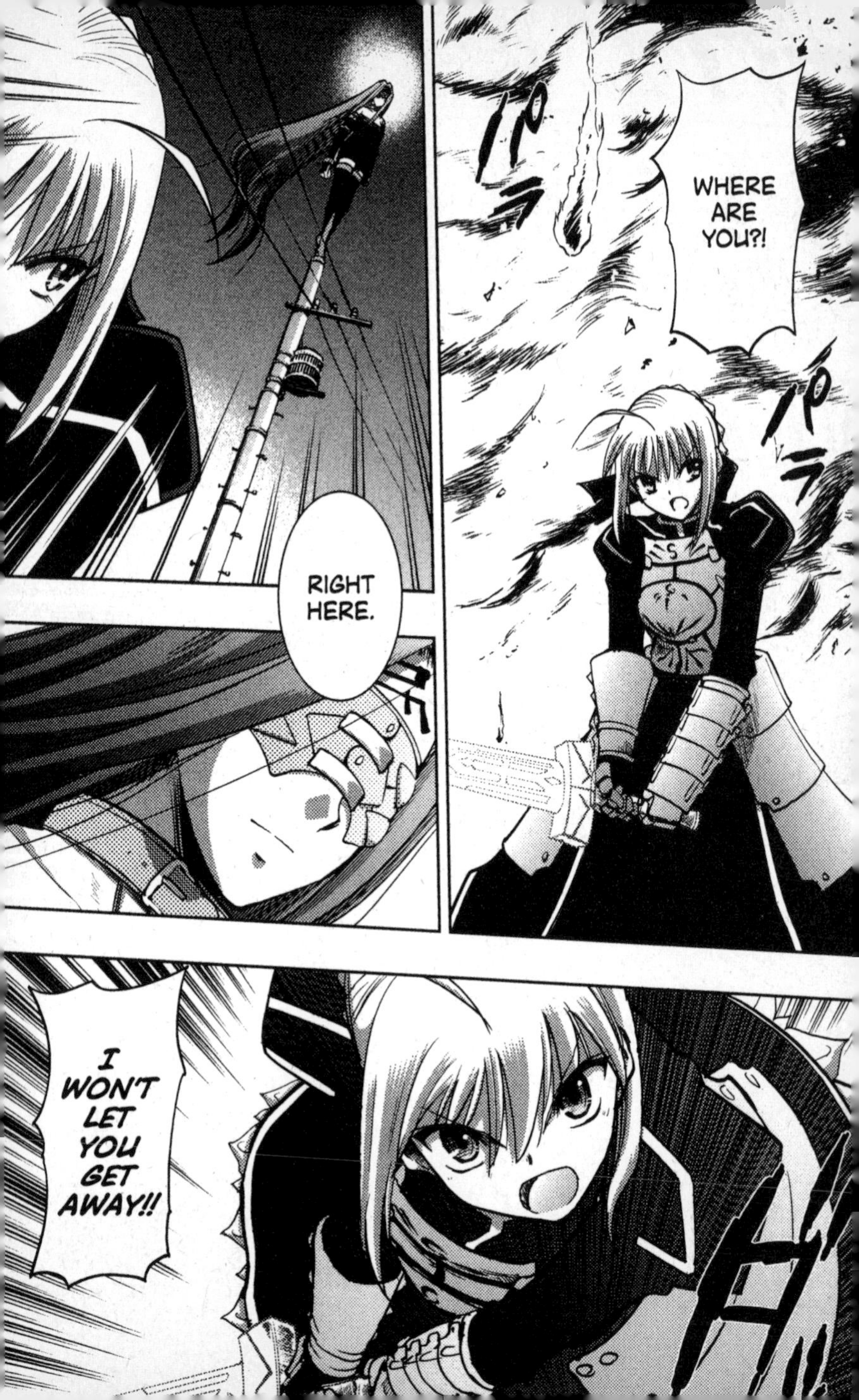
パラ
WHERE ARE YOU?!
パラ
RIGHT HERE.
I WON'T LET YOU GET AWAY!!

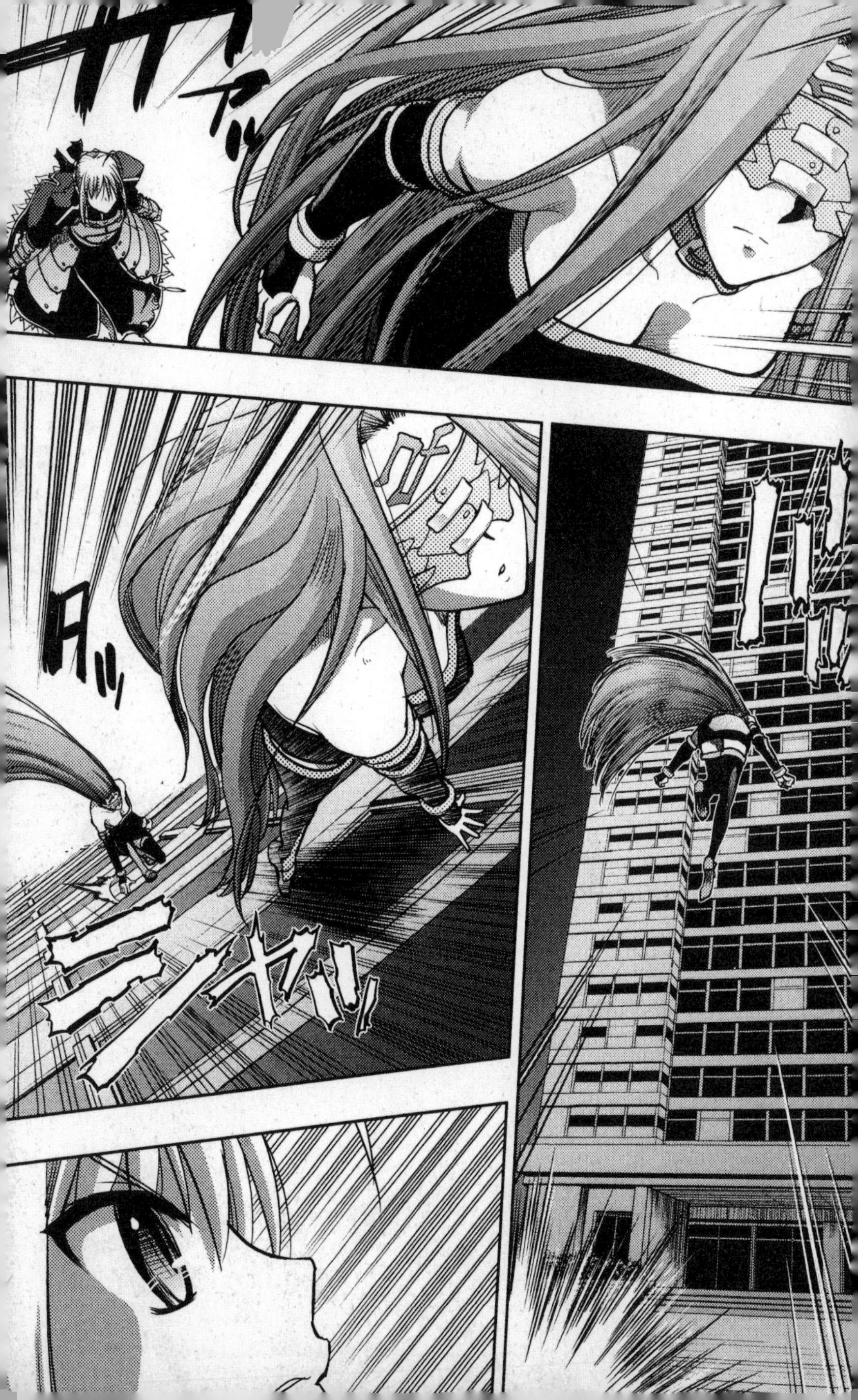

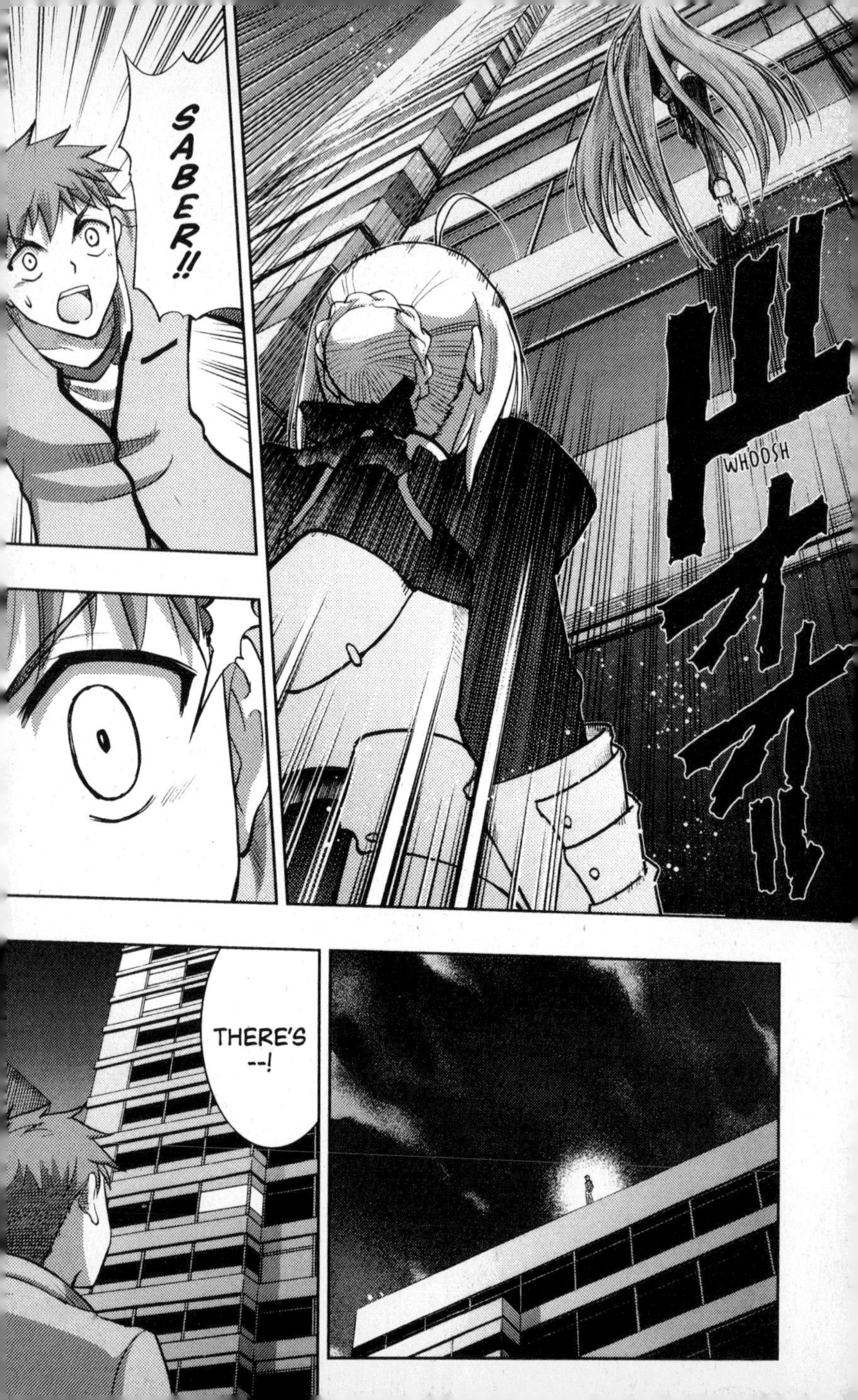
SABER!!
WHOOSH
THERE'S --!

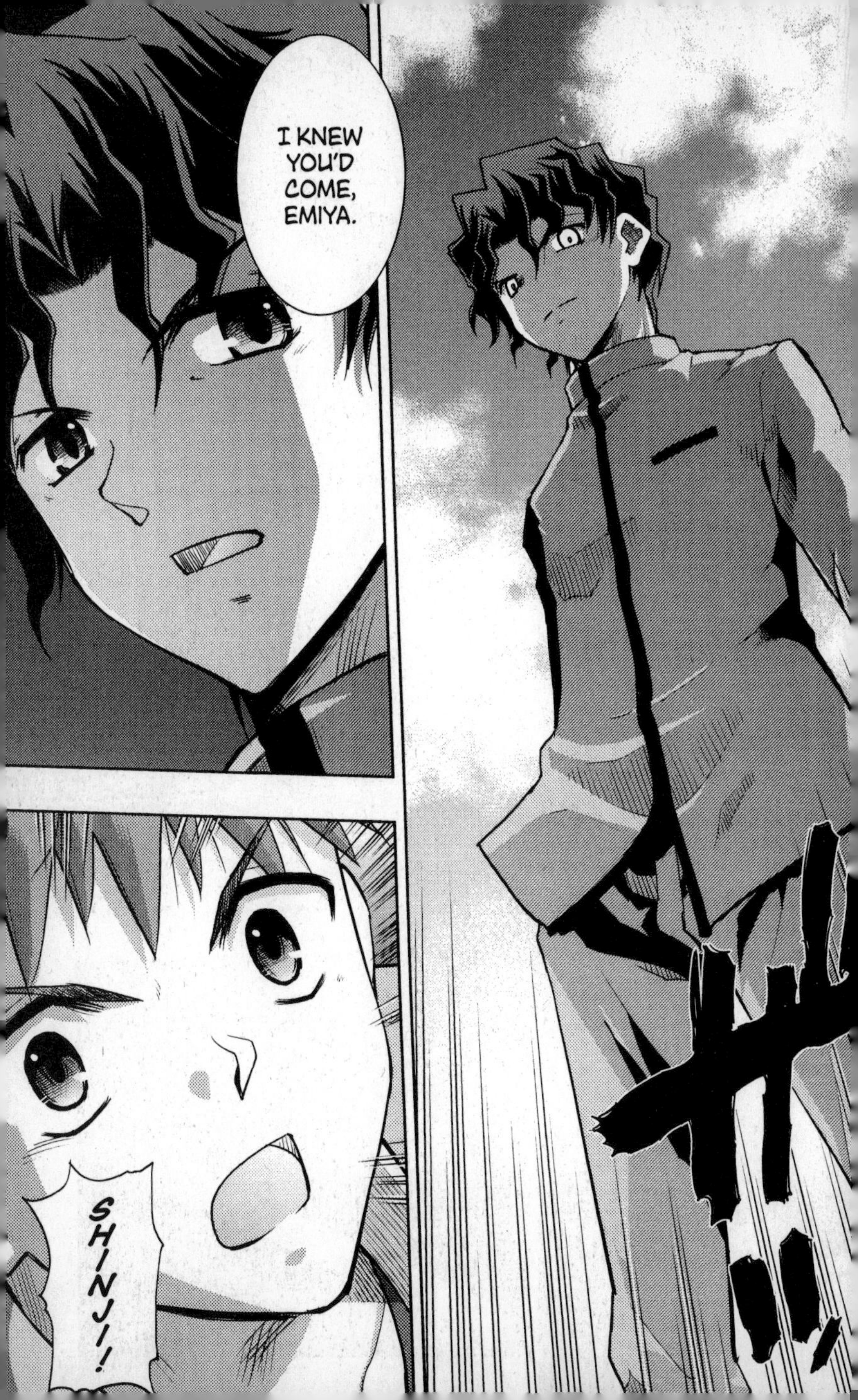
I KNEW YOU'D COME, EMIYA.
SHINJI!

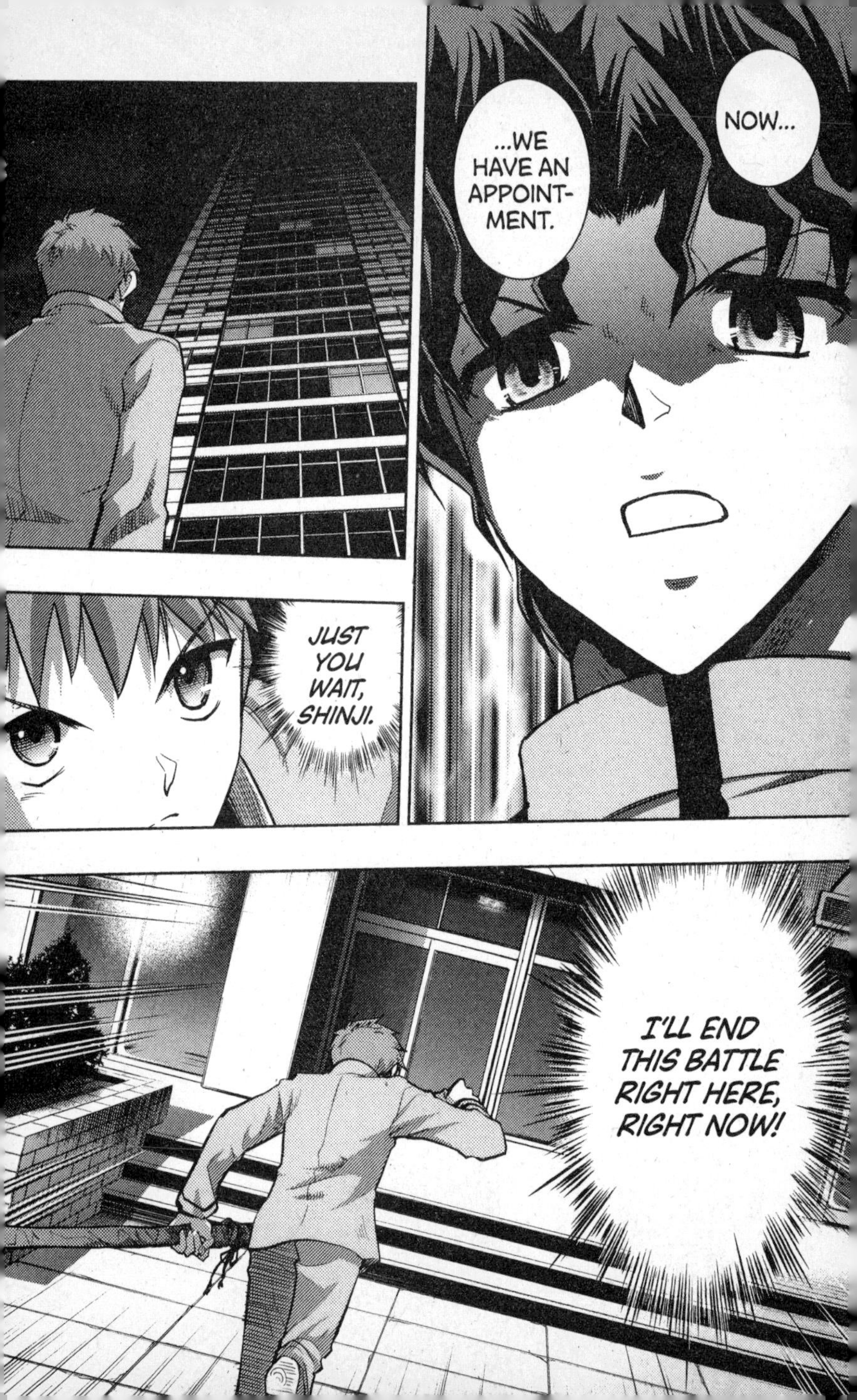
NOW...
...WE HAVE AN APPOINT-MENT.
JUST YOU WAIT, SHINJI.
I'LL END THIS BATTLE RIGHT HERE, RIGHT NOW!

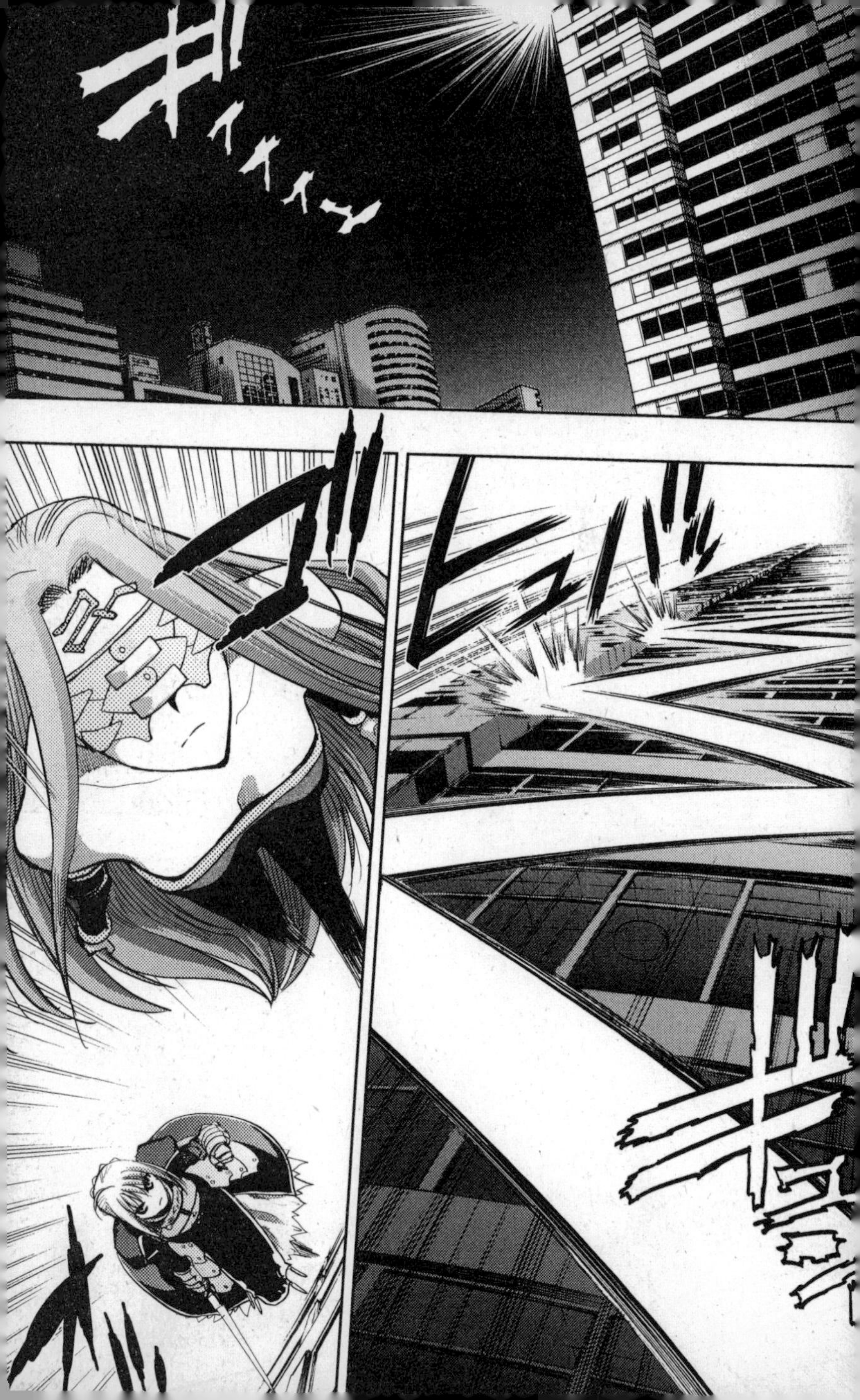
ギイイイン
ヒュバ

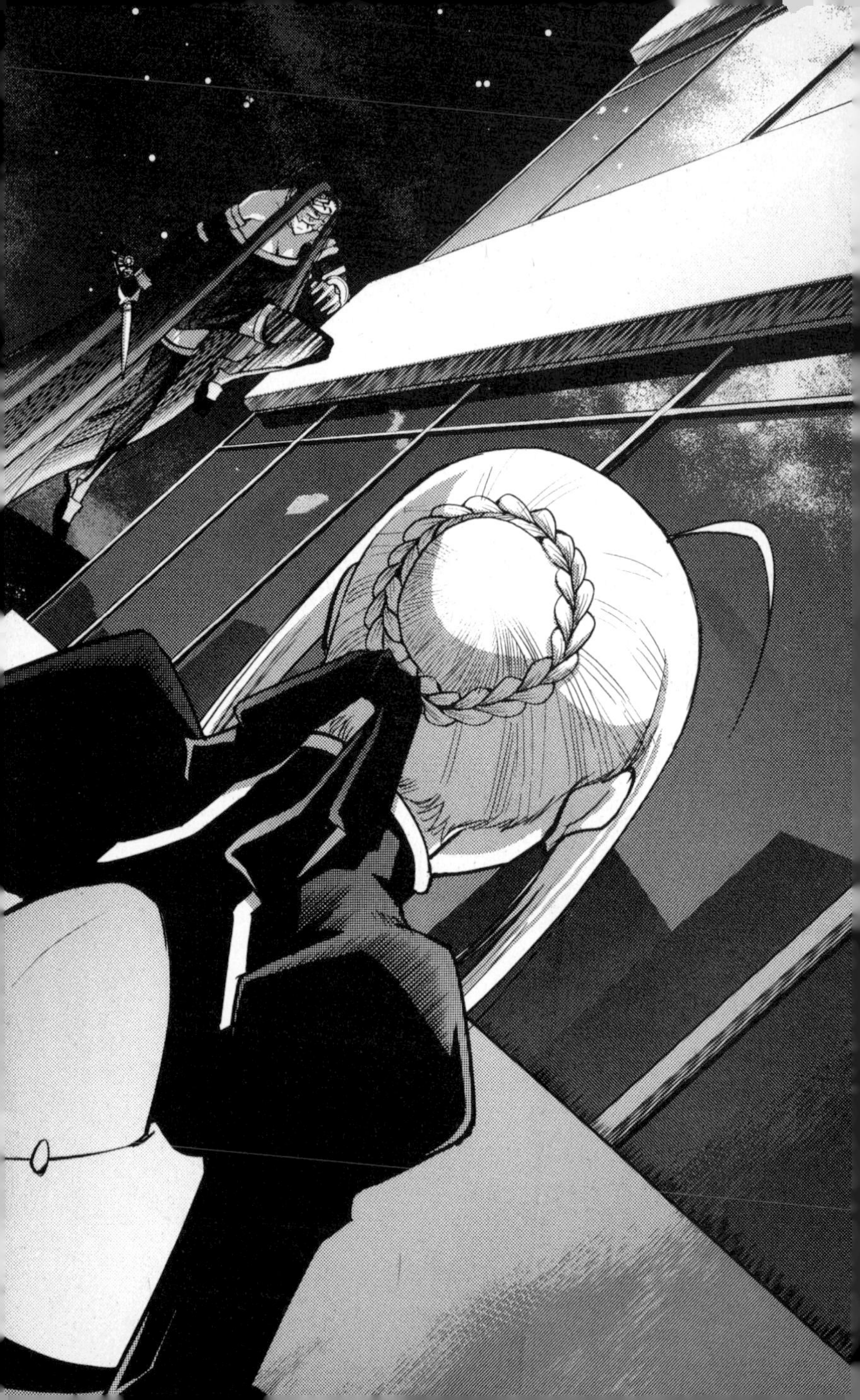

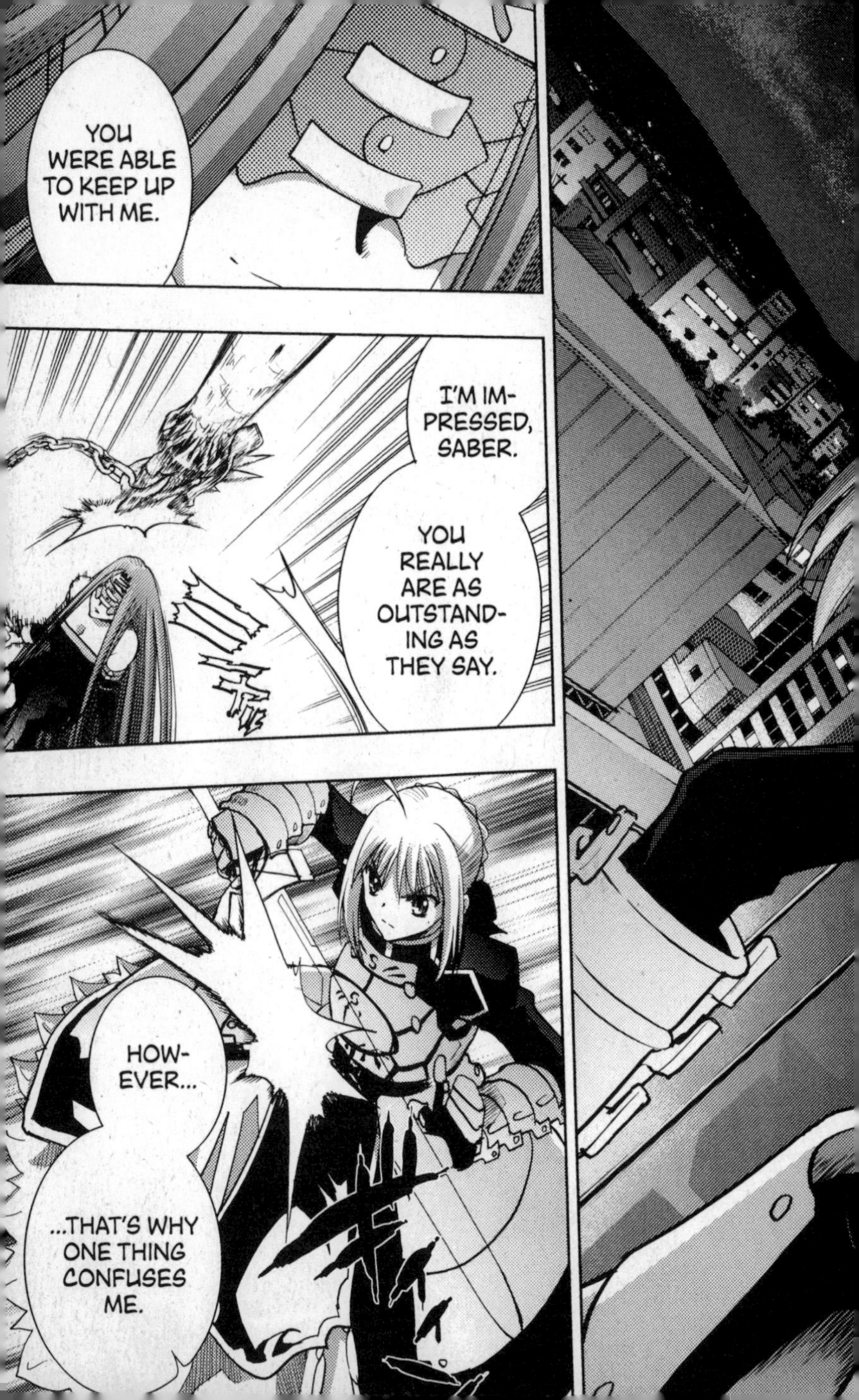
YOU WERE ABLE TO KEEP UP WITH ME.
I'M IM-PRESSED, SABER.
YOU REALLY ARE AS OUTSTAND-ING AS THEY SAY.
HOW-EVER...
...THAT'S WHY ONE THING CONFUSES ME.

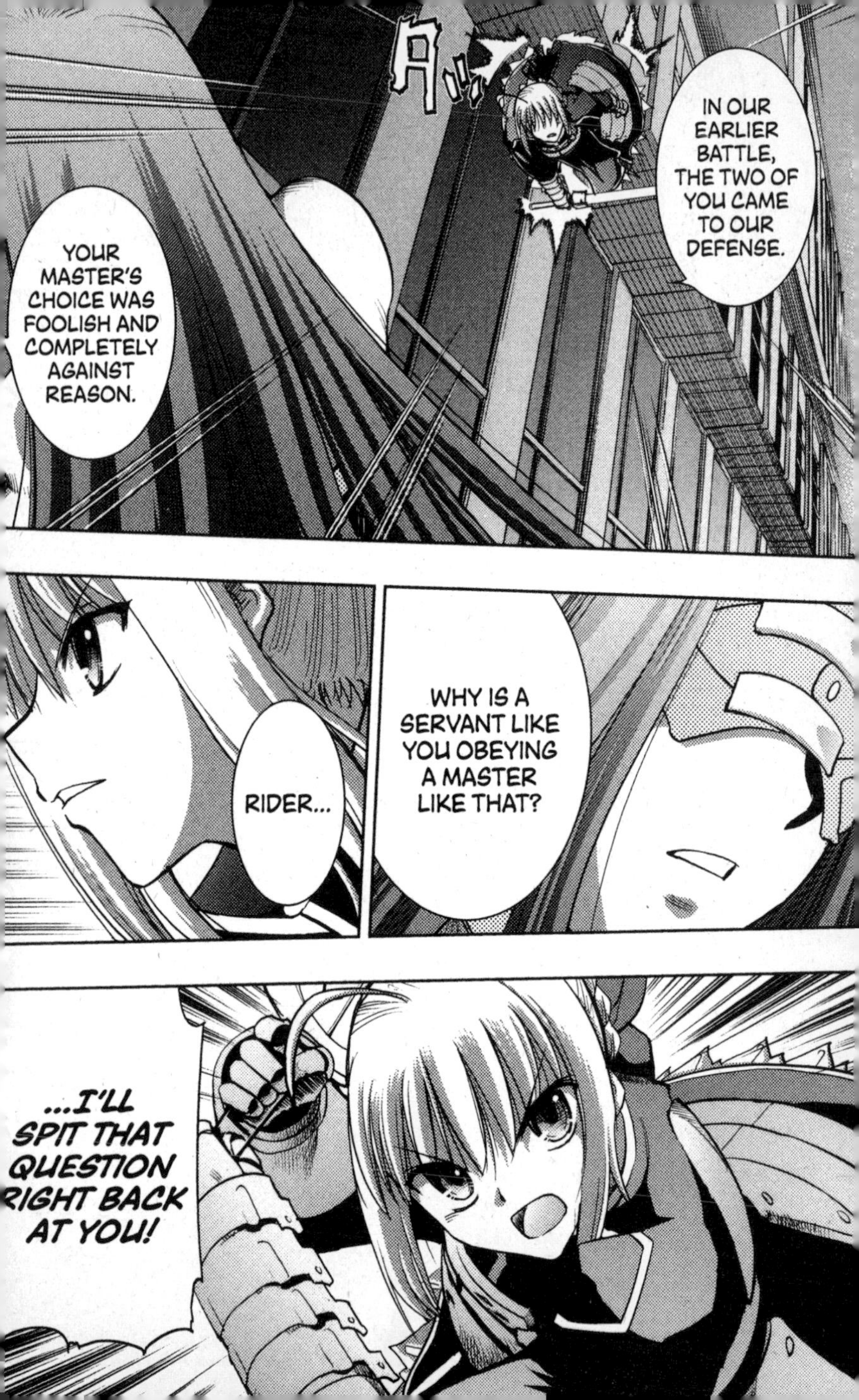
IN OUR EARLIER BATTLE, THE TWO OF YOU CAME TO OUR DEFENSE.
YOUR MASTER'S CHOICE WAS FOOLISH AND COMPLETELY AGAINST REASON.
WHY IS A SERVANT LIKE YOU OBEYING A MASTER LIKE THAT?
RIDER...
...I'LL SPIT THAT QUESTION RIGHT BACK AT YOU!

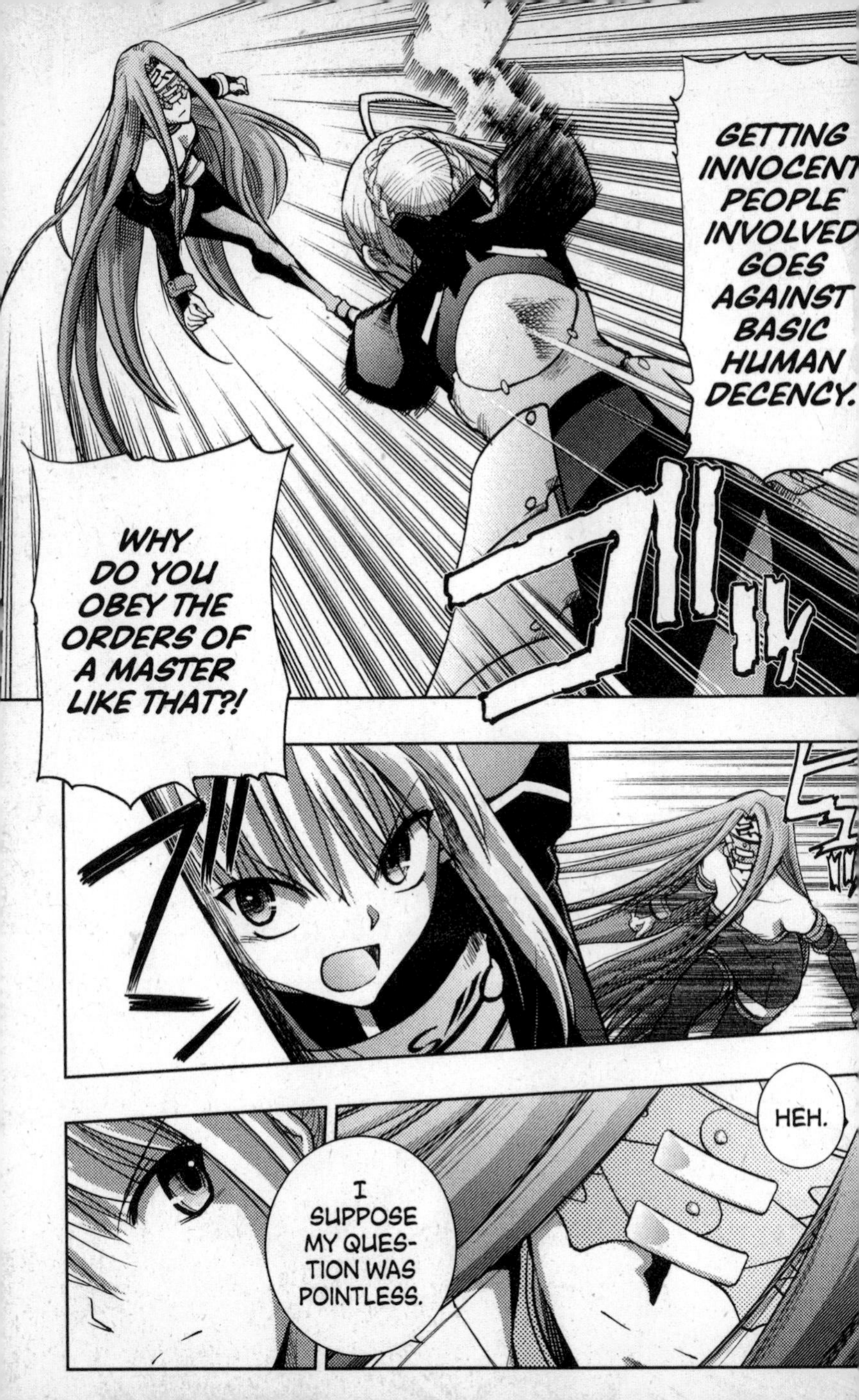
GETTING INNOCENT PEOPLE INVOLVED GOES AGAINST BASIC HUMAN DECENCY.
WHY DO YOU OBEY THE ORDERS OF A MASTER LIKE THAT?!
HEH.
I SUPPOSE MY QUES-TION WAS POINTLESS.

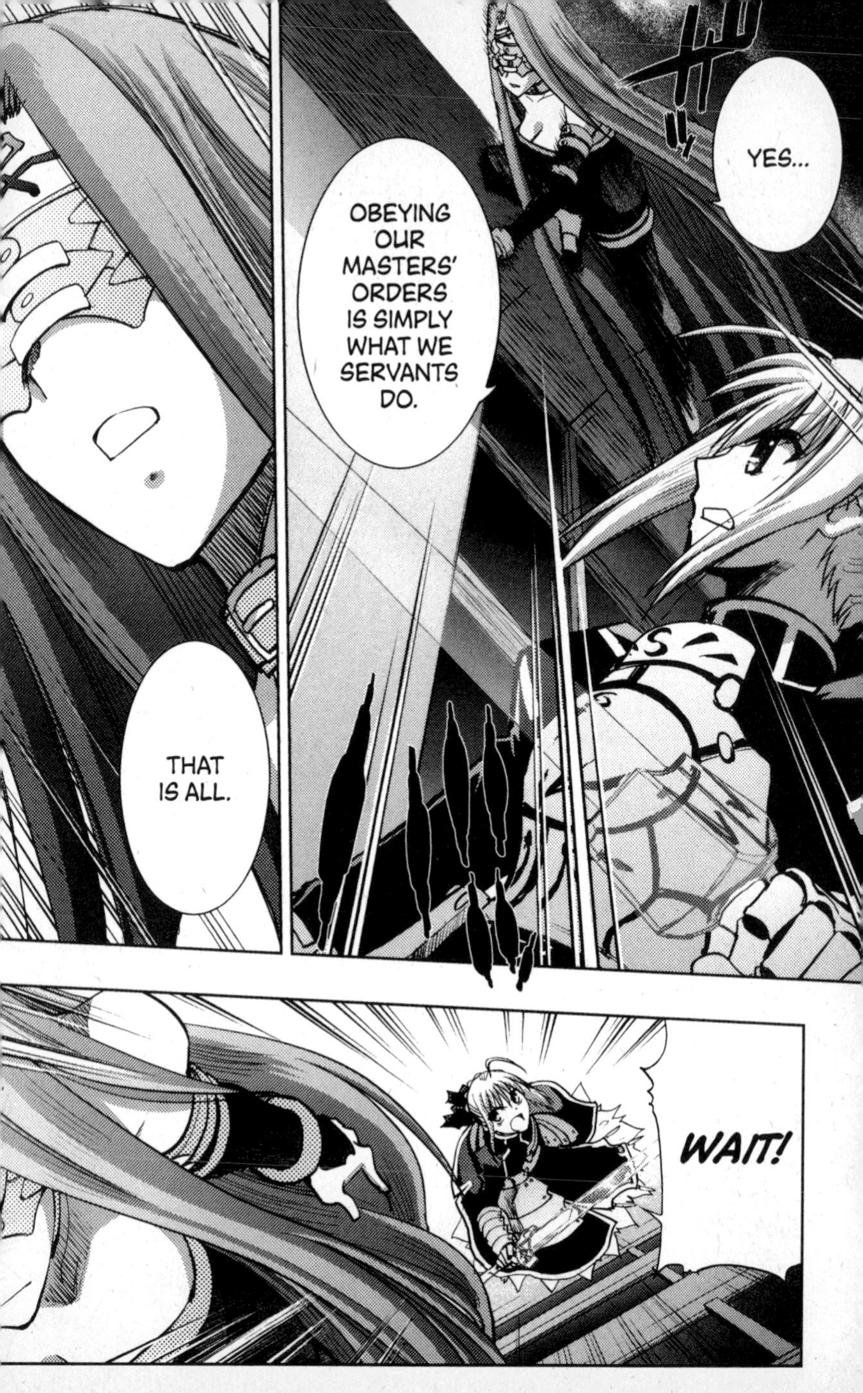
YES...
OBEYING OUR MASTERS' ORDERS IS SIMPLY WHAT WE SERVANTS DO.
THAT IS ALL.
WAIT!

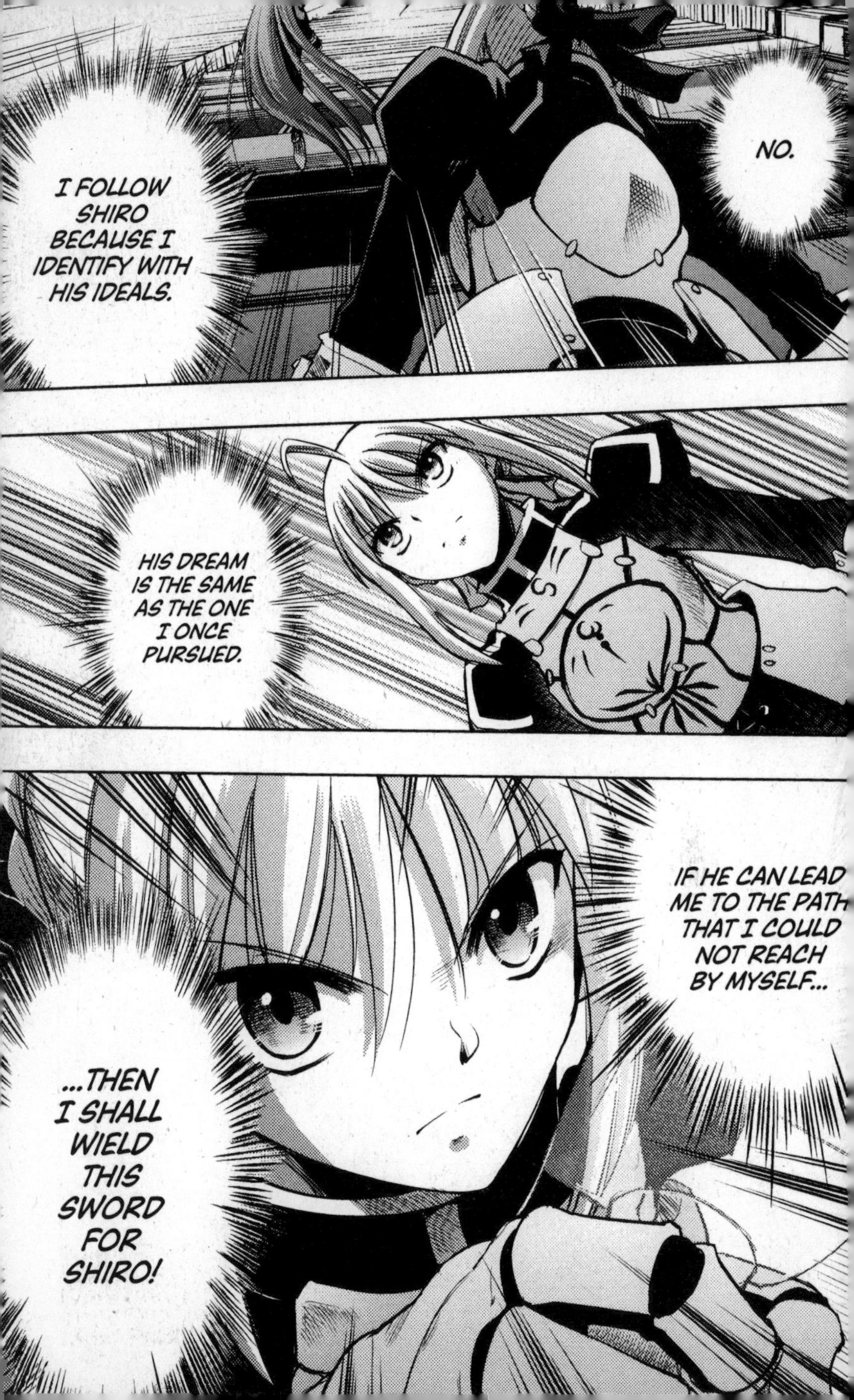
NO.
I FOLLOW SHIRO BECAUSE I IDENTIFY WITH HIS IDEALS.
HIS DREAM IS THE SAME AS THE ONE I ONCE PURSUED.
IF HE CAN LEAD ME TO THE PATH THAT I COULD NOT REACH BY MYSELF...
...THEN I SHALL WIELD THIS SWORD FOR SHIRO!

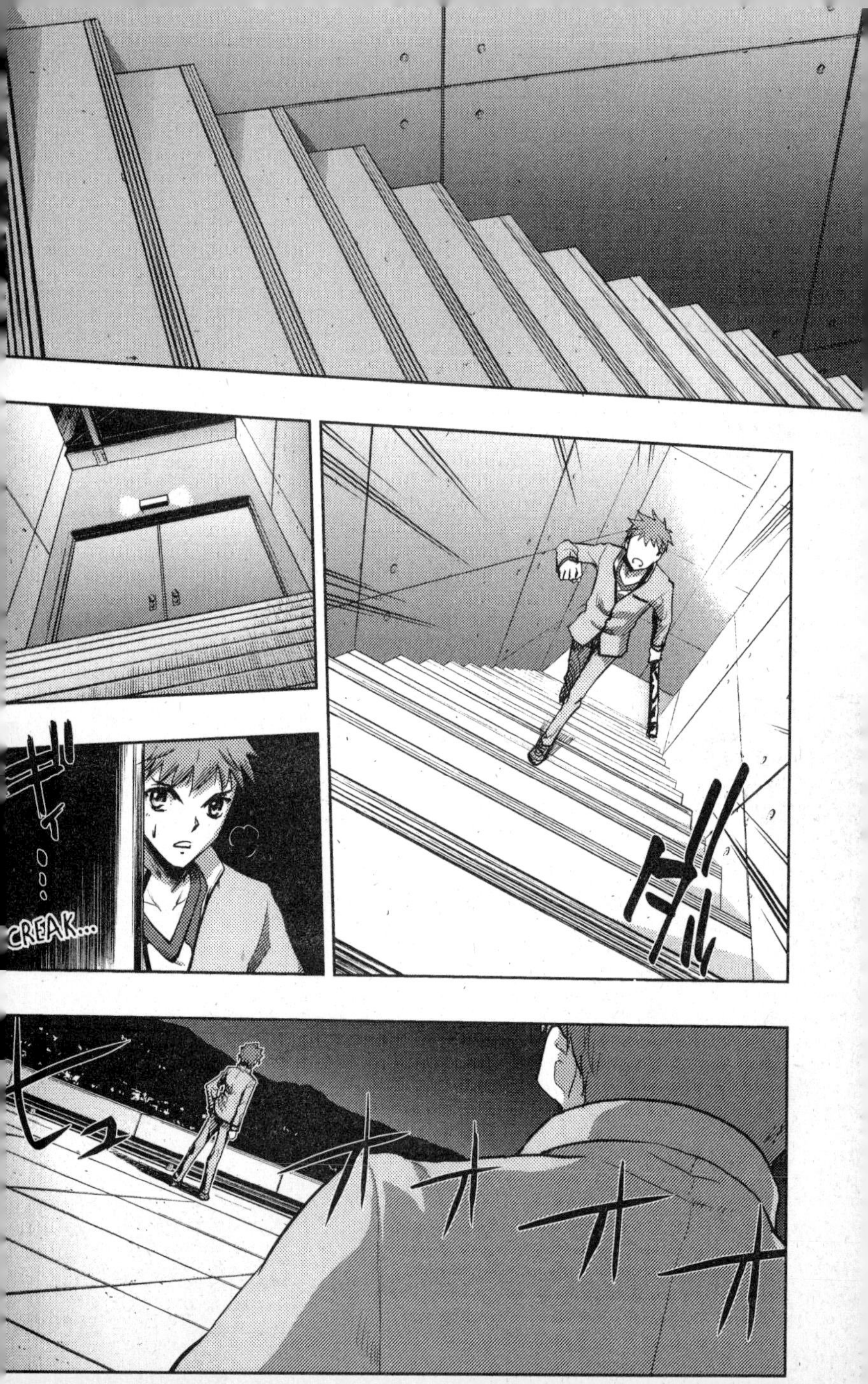
CREAK...

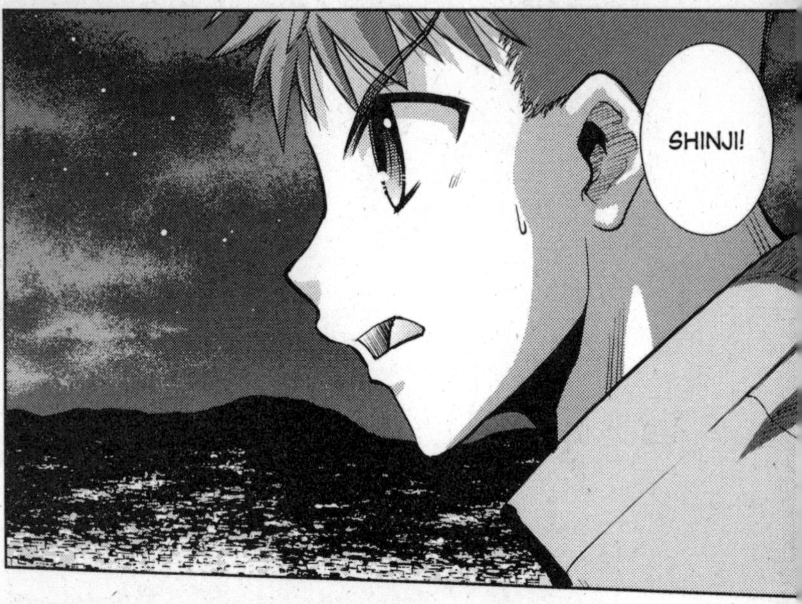
SHINJI!
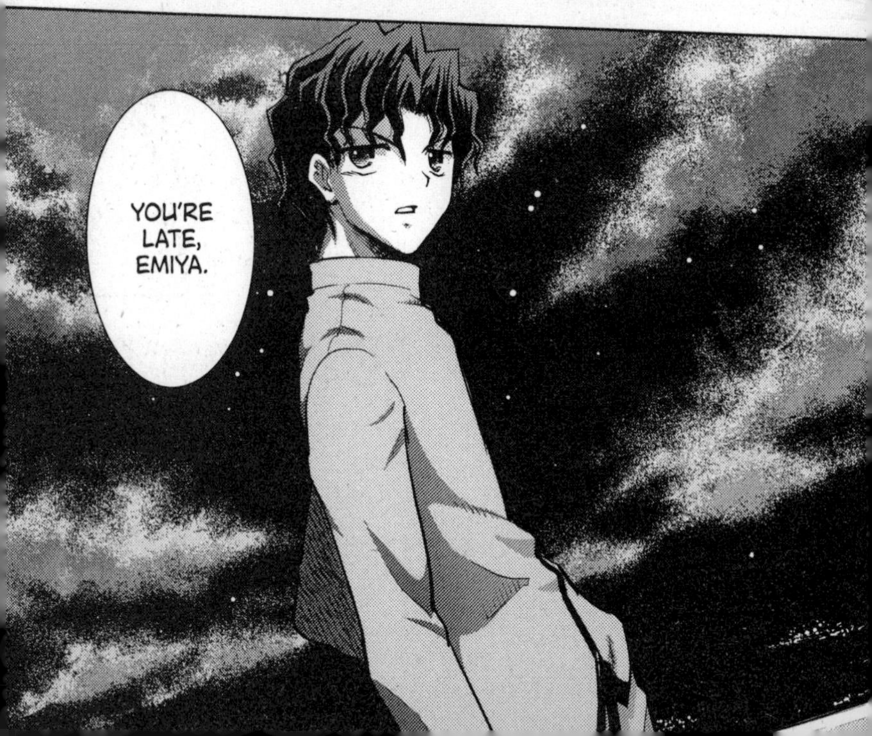
YOU'RE LATE, EMIYA.

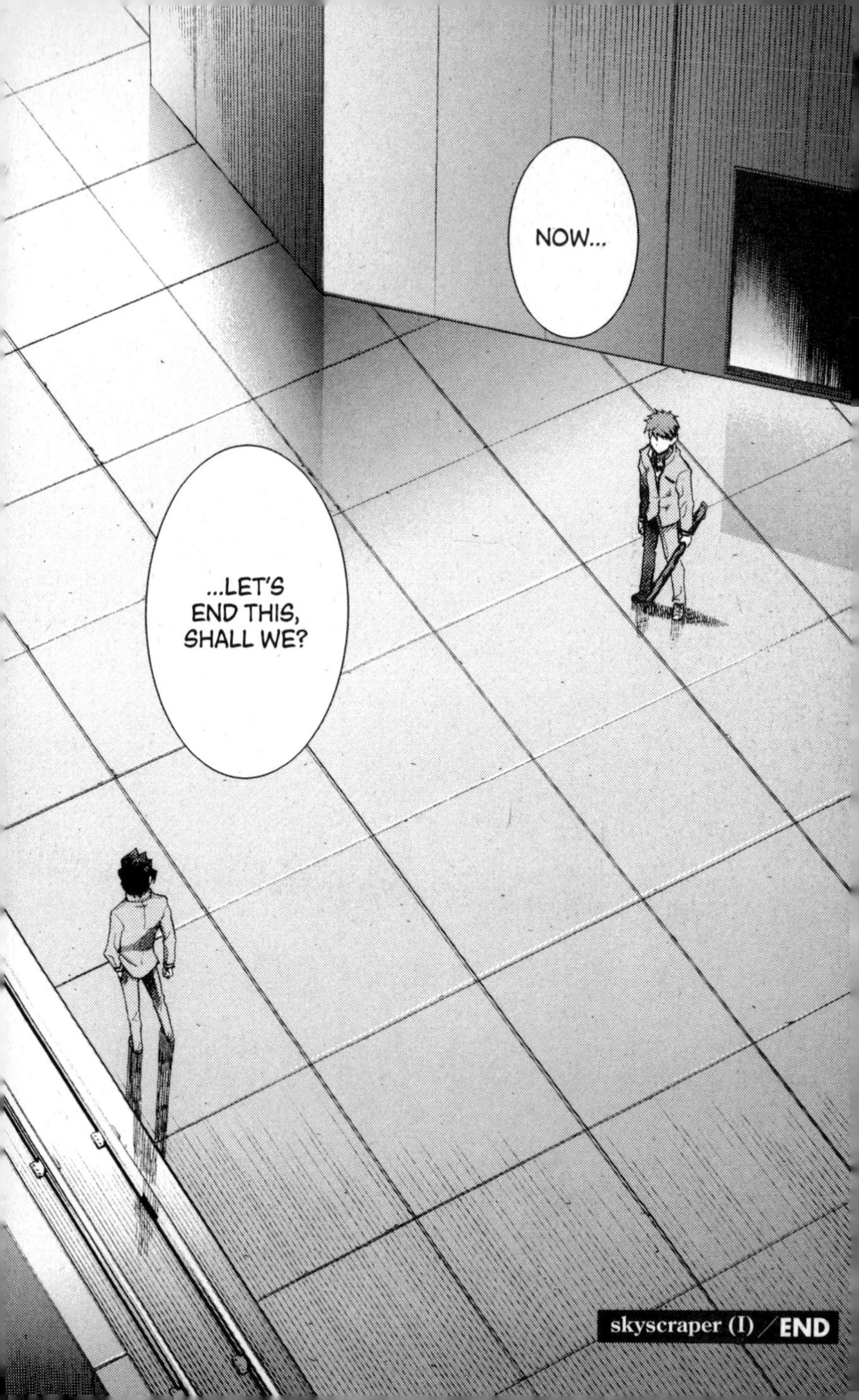
NOW...
...LET'S END THIS, SHALL WE?
skyscraper (I) / END

Fate

stay night

フェイト/ステイナイト

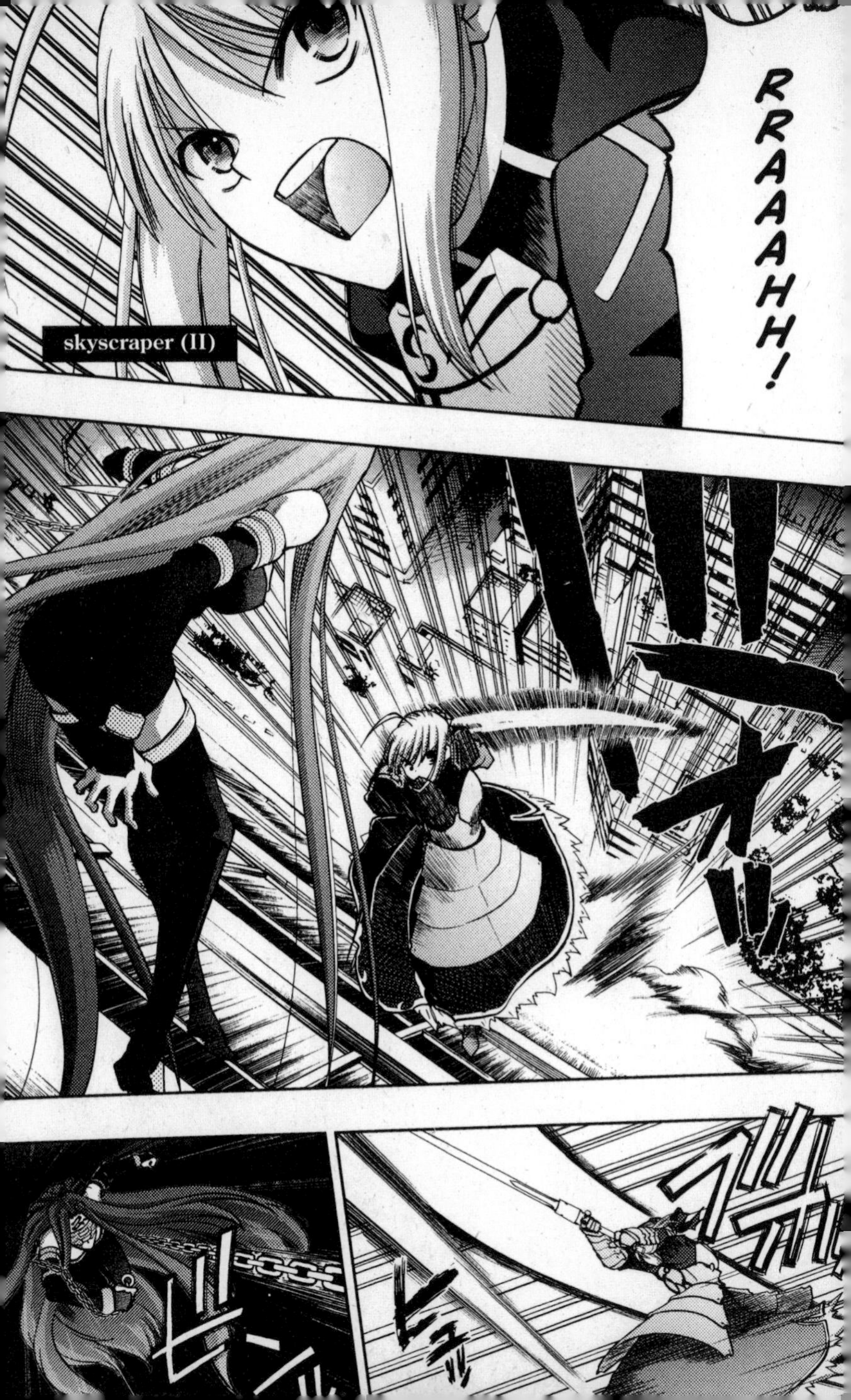
RRAAAHH!
skyscraper (II)

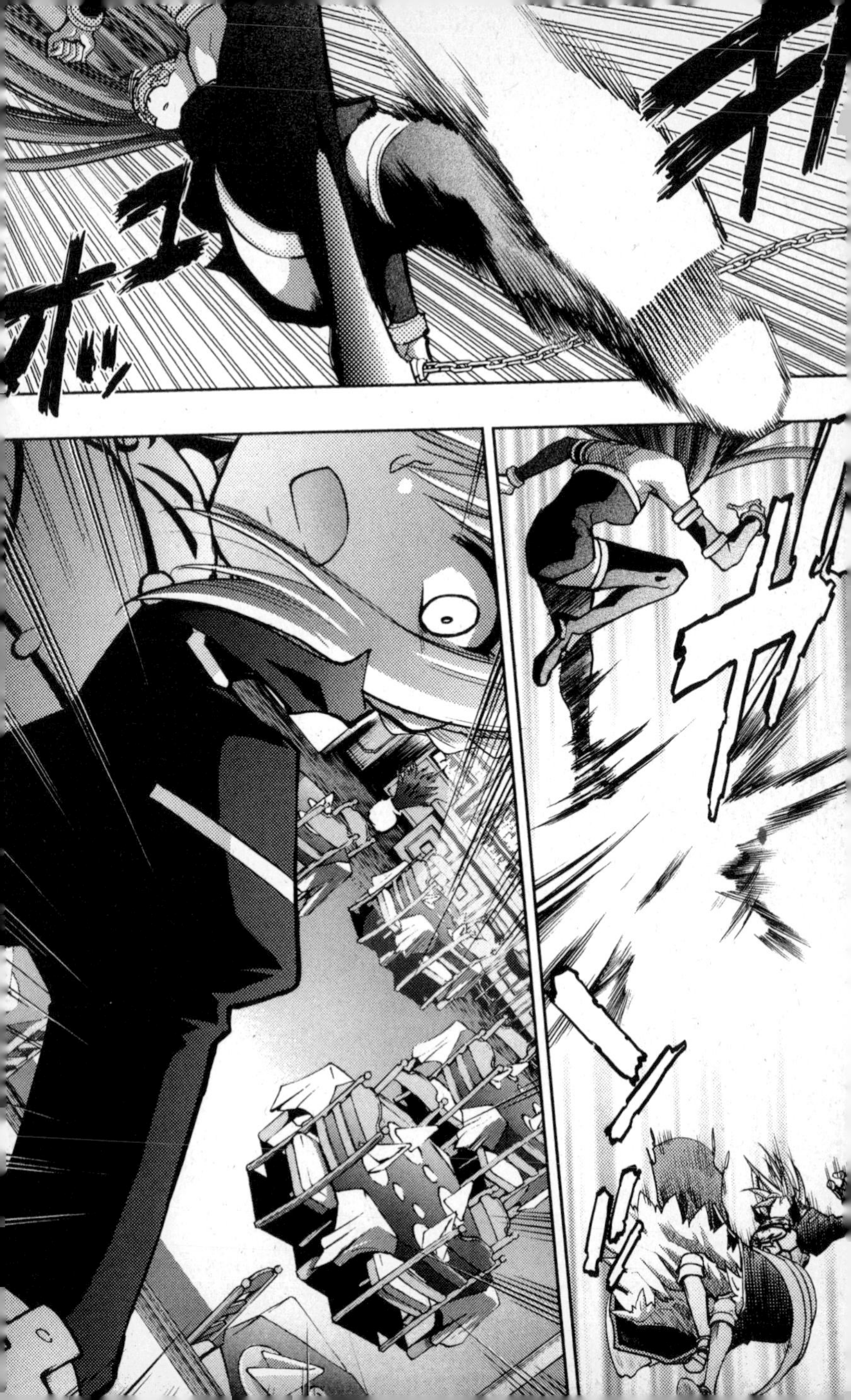

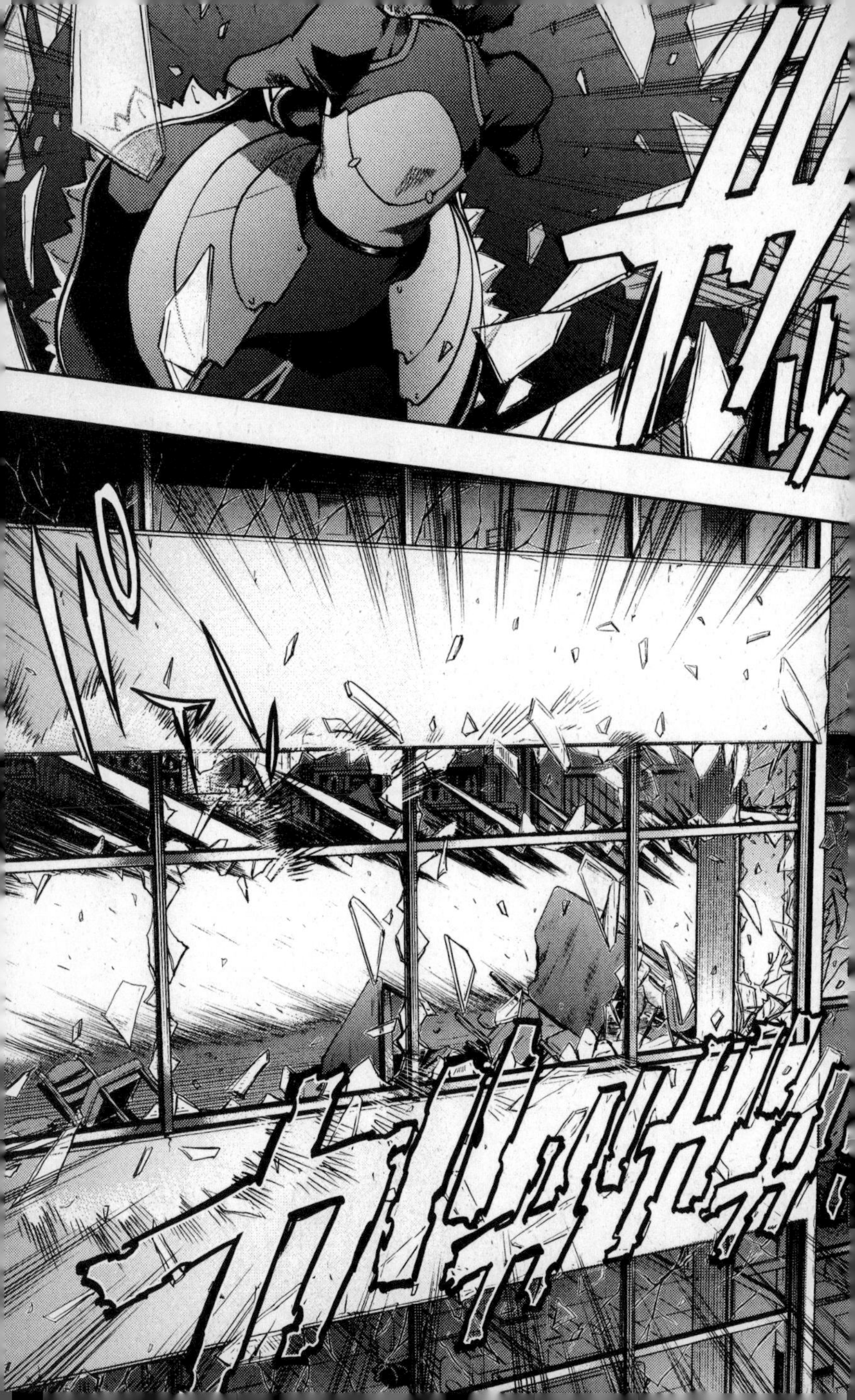

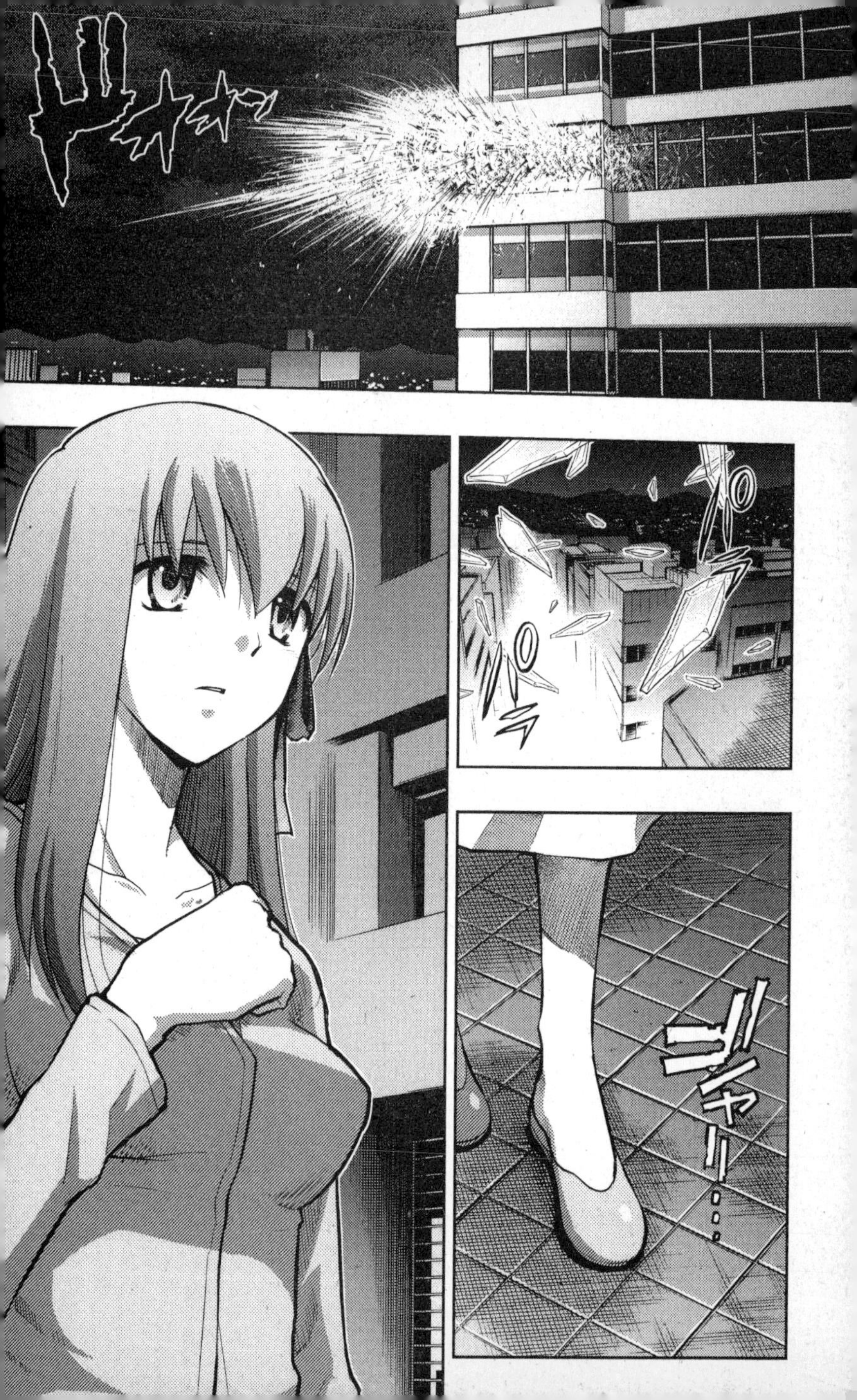

skyscraper (II)

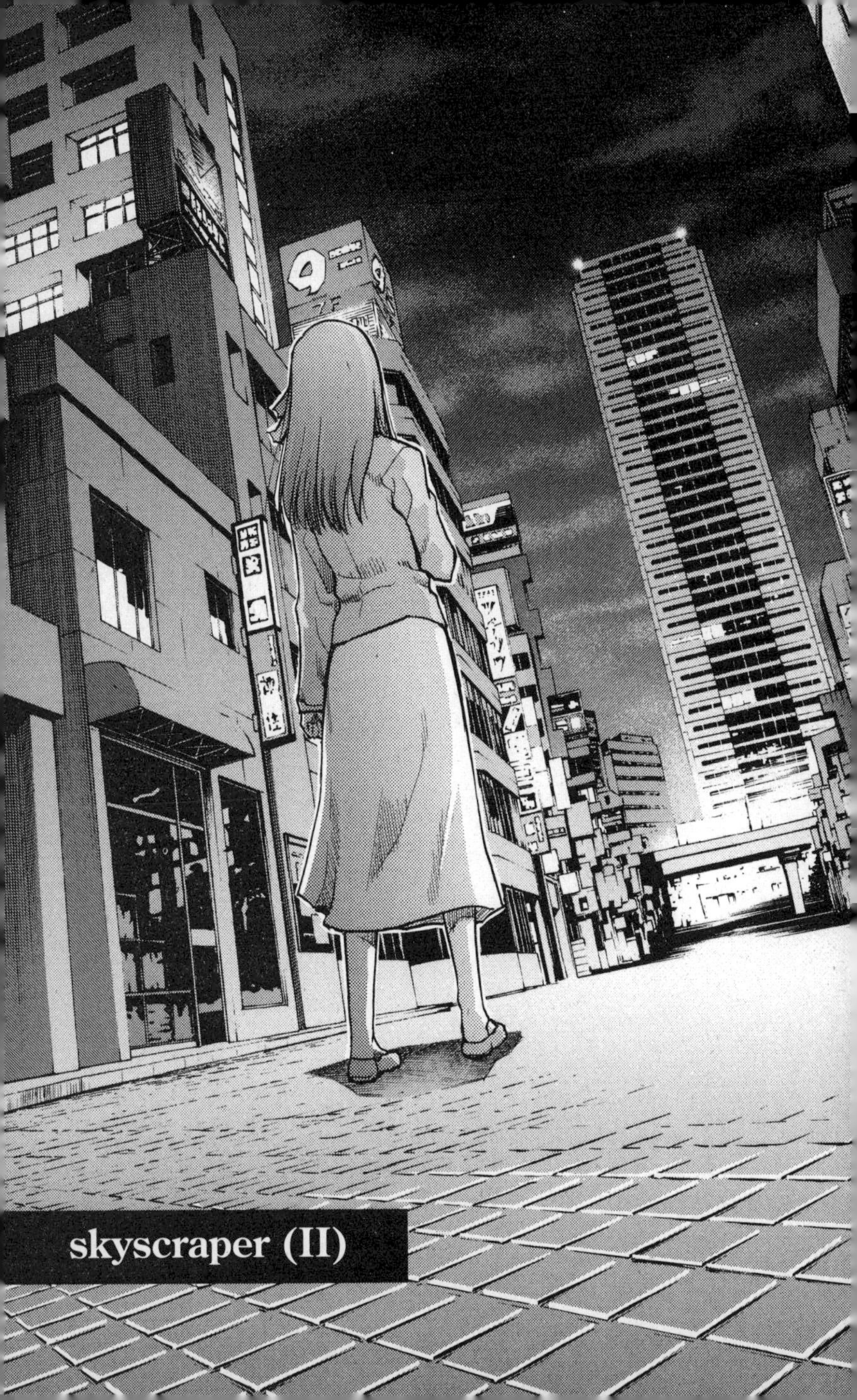

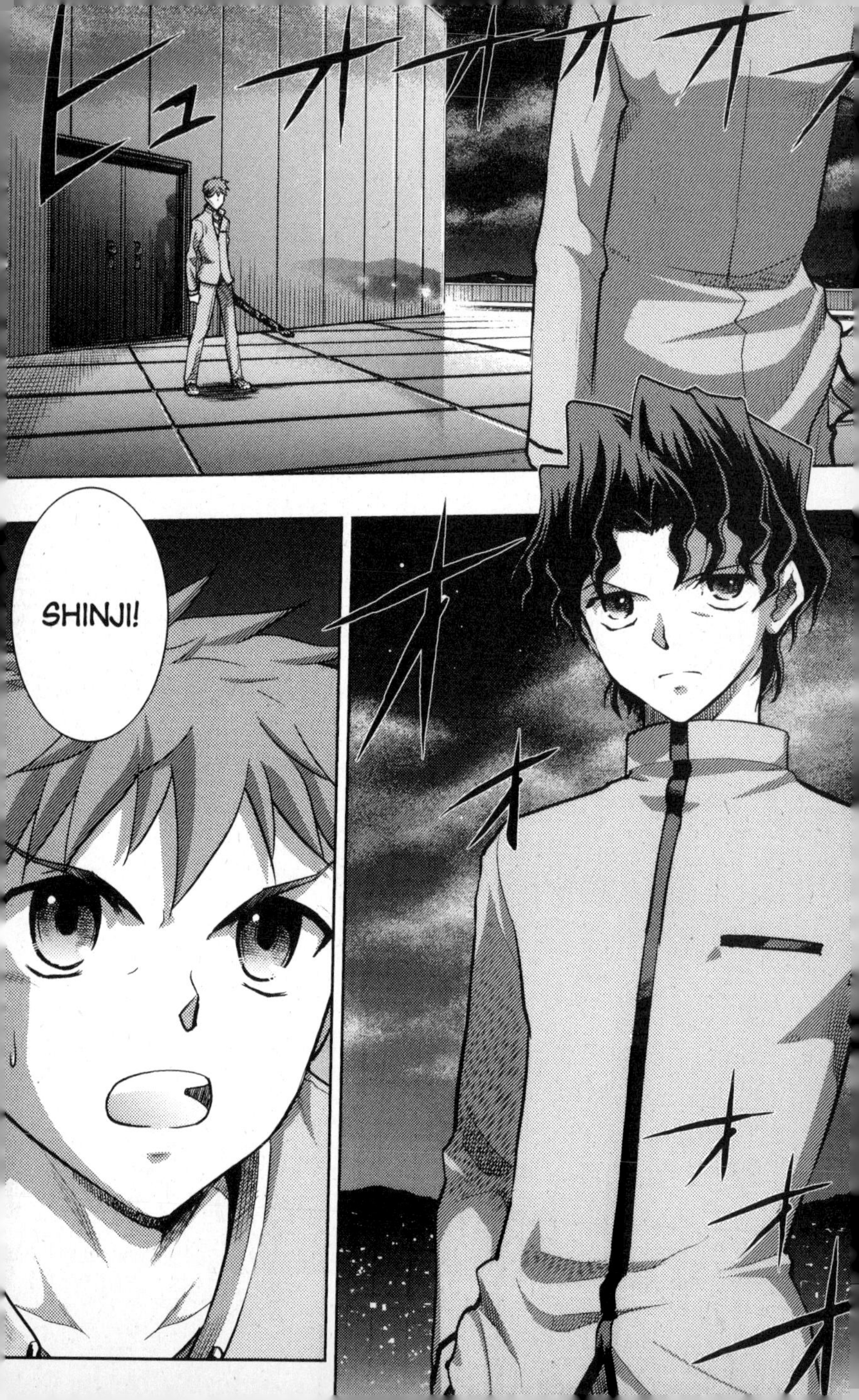
ヒュオオオオ
オオオオオ
SHINJI!

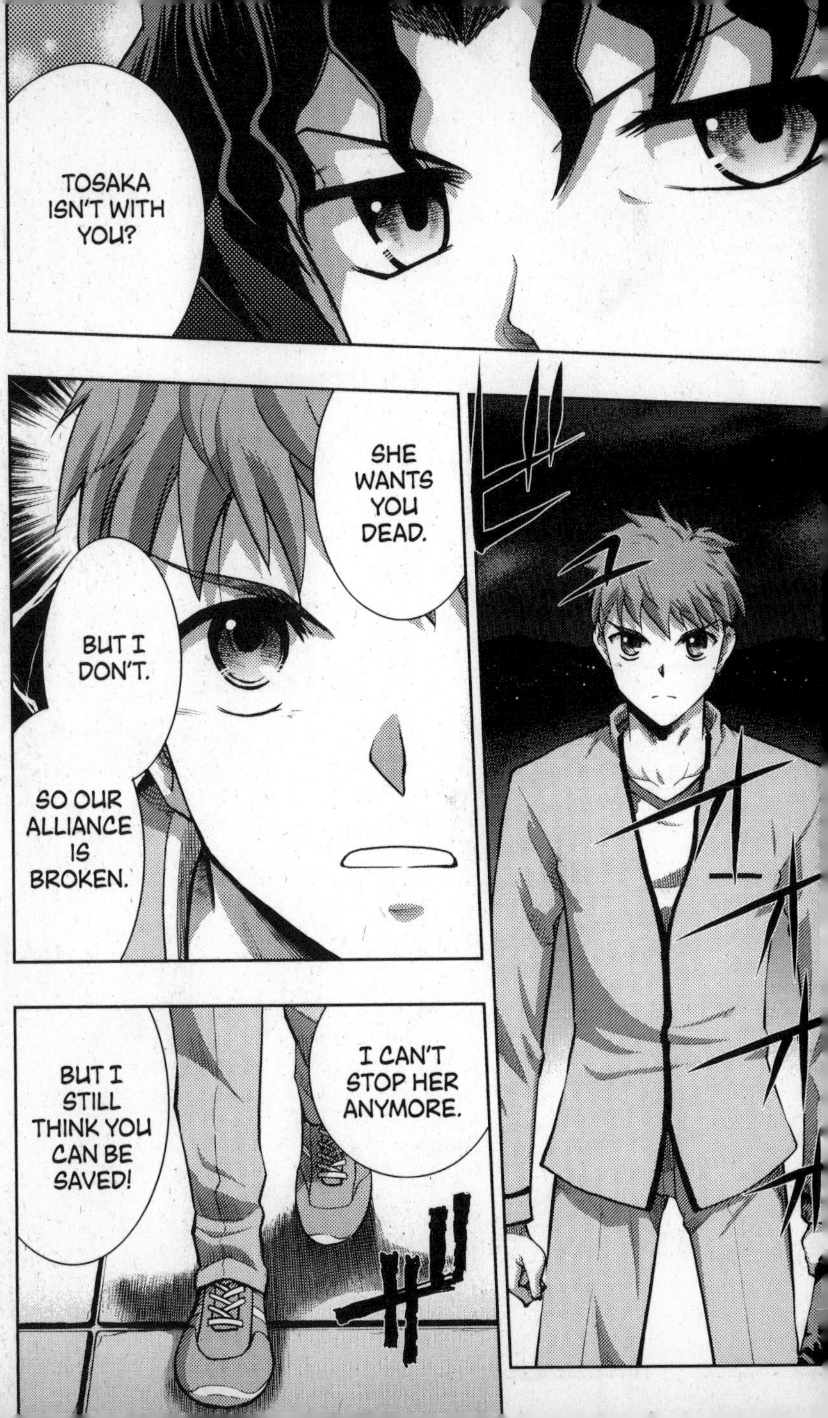
TOSAKA ISN'T WITH YOU?
SHE WANTS YOU DEAD.
BUT I DON'T.
SO OUR ALLIANCE IS BROKEN.
I CAN'T STOP HER ANYMORE.
BUT I STILL THINK YOU CAN BE SAVED!

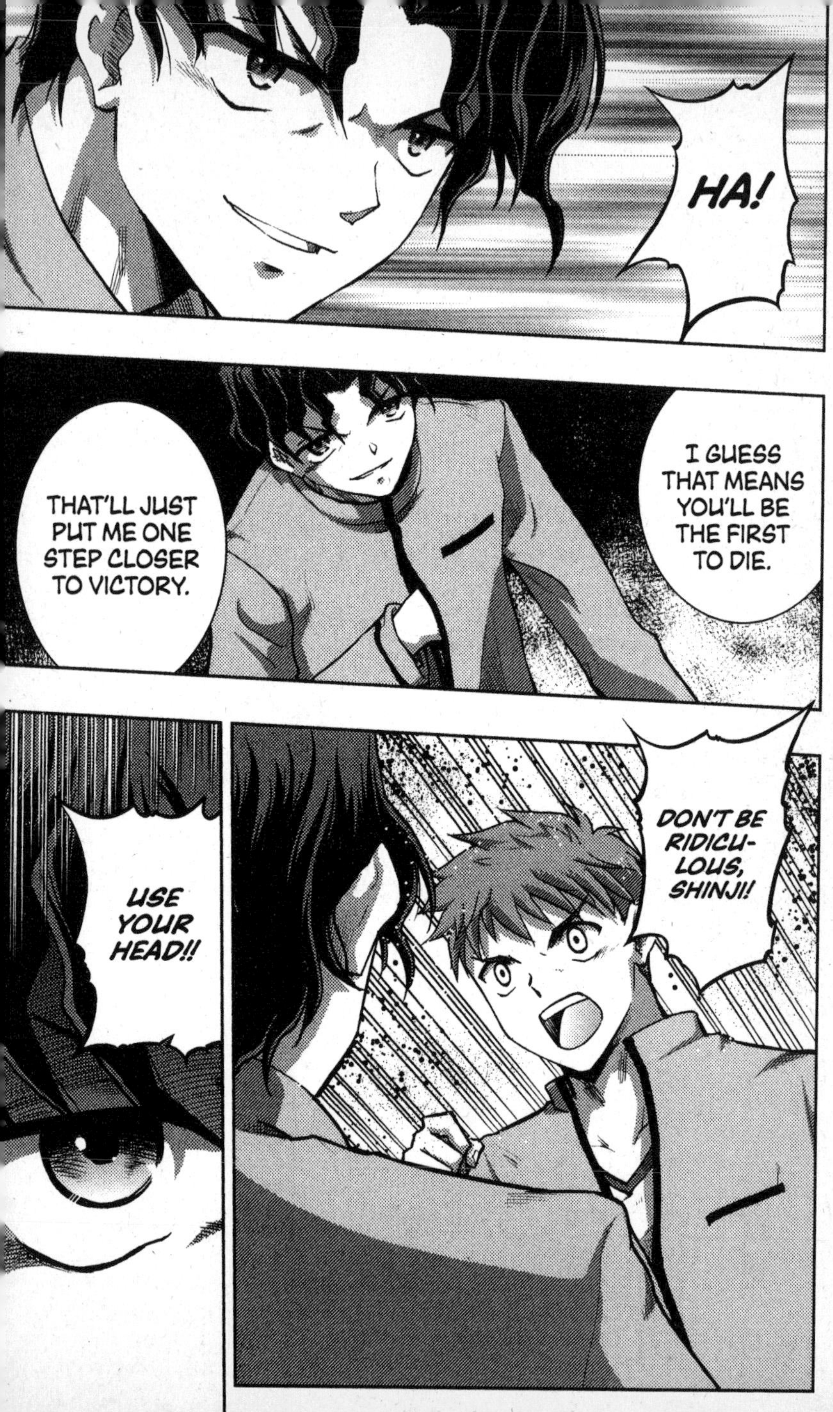
HA!
I GUESS THAT MEANS YOU'LL BE THE FIRST TO DIE.
THAT'LL JUST PUT ME ONE STEP CLOSER TO VICTORY.
DON'T BE RIDICU-LOUS, SHINJI!
USE YOUR HEAD!!

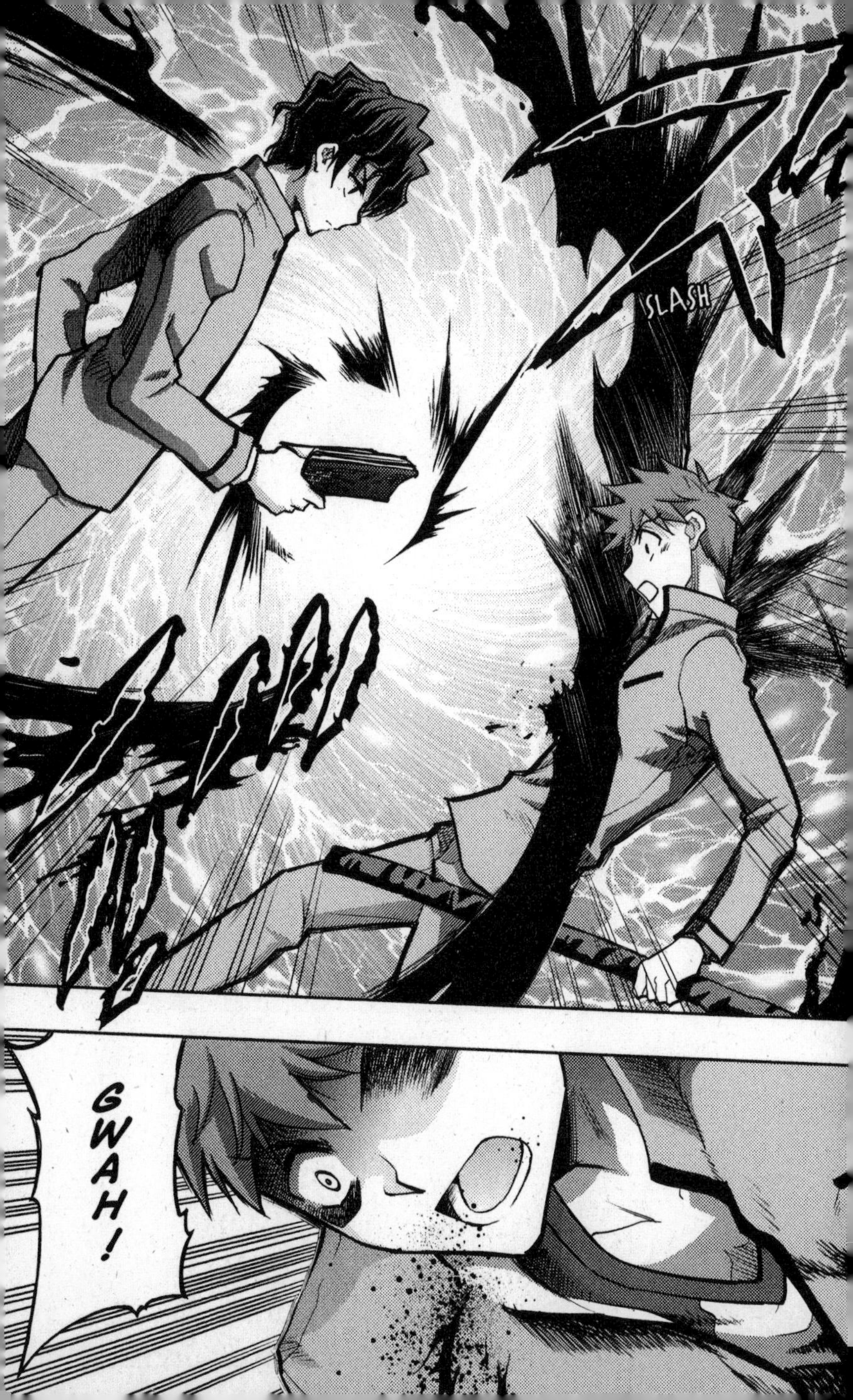
SLASH
GWAH!

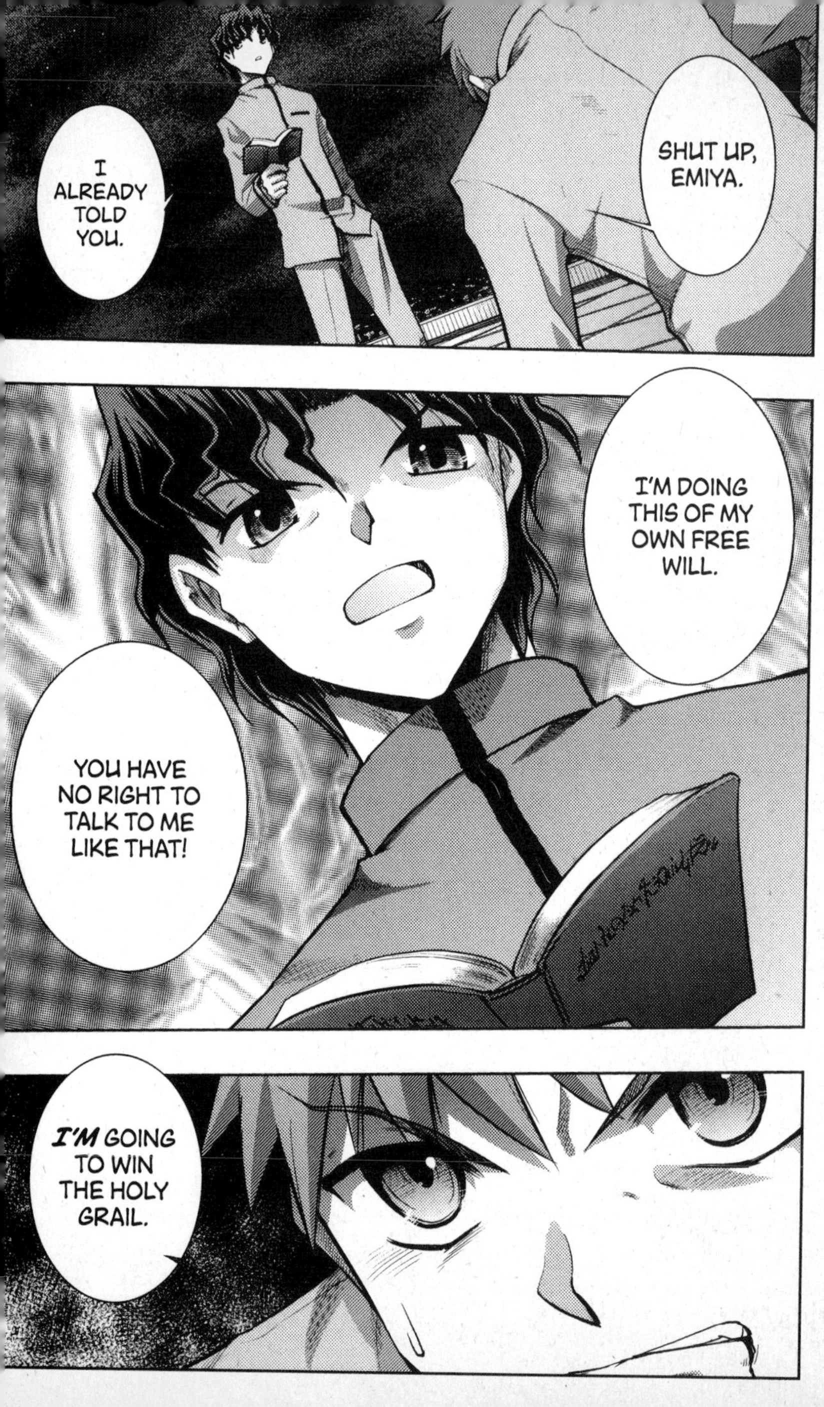
SHUT UP, EMIYA.
I ALREADY TOLD YOU.
I'M DOING THIS OF MY OWN FREE WILL.
YOU HAVE NO RIGHT TO TALK TO ME LIKE THAT!
I'M GOING TO WIN THE HOLY GRAIL.

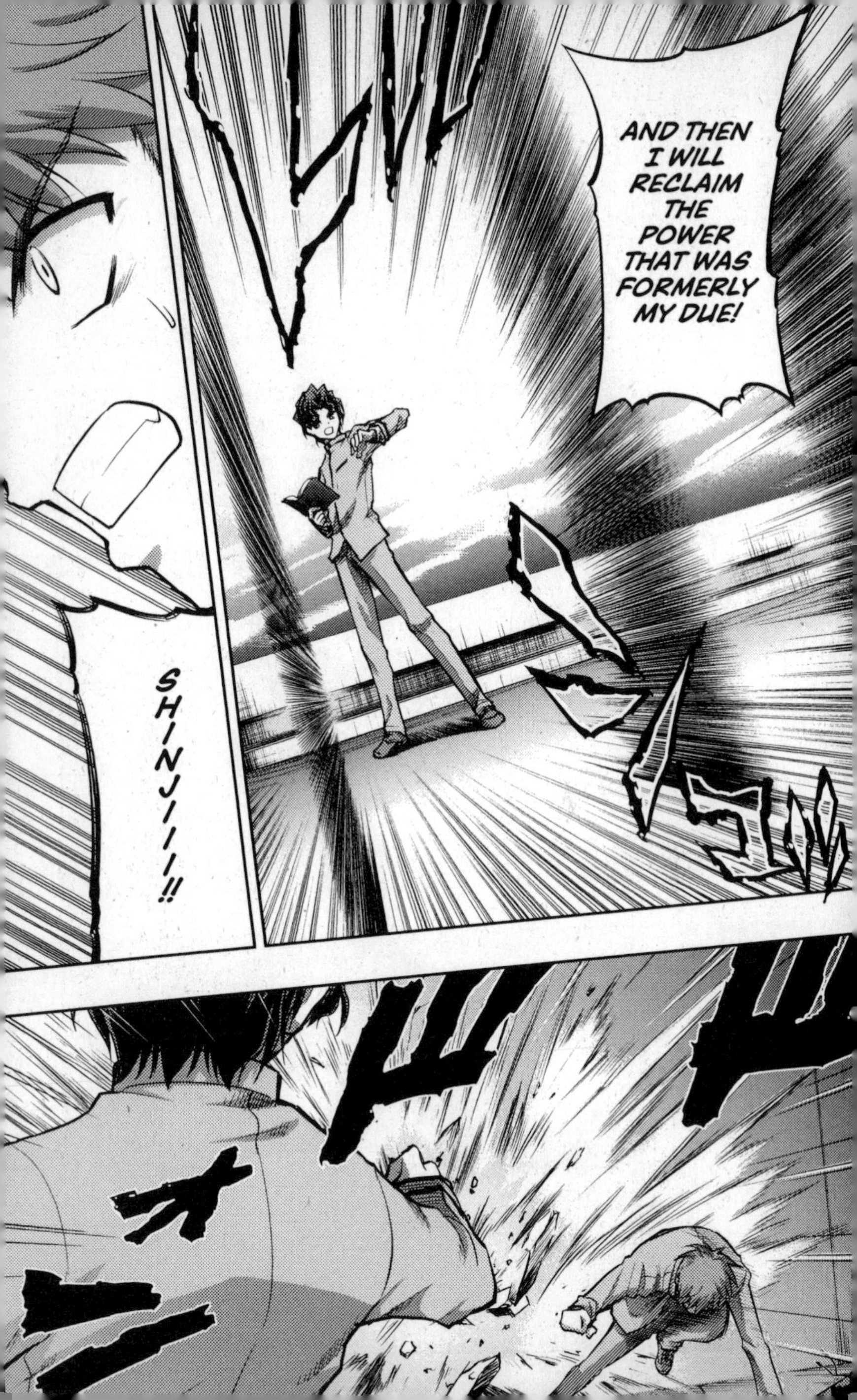
AND THEN I WILL RECLAIM THE POWER THAT WAS FORMERLY MY DUE!
SHINJIIIII!!

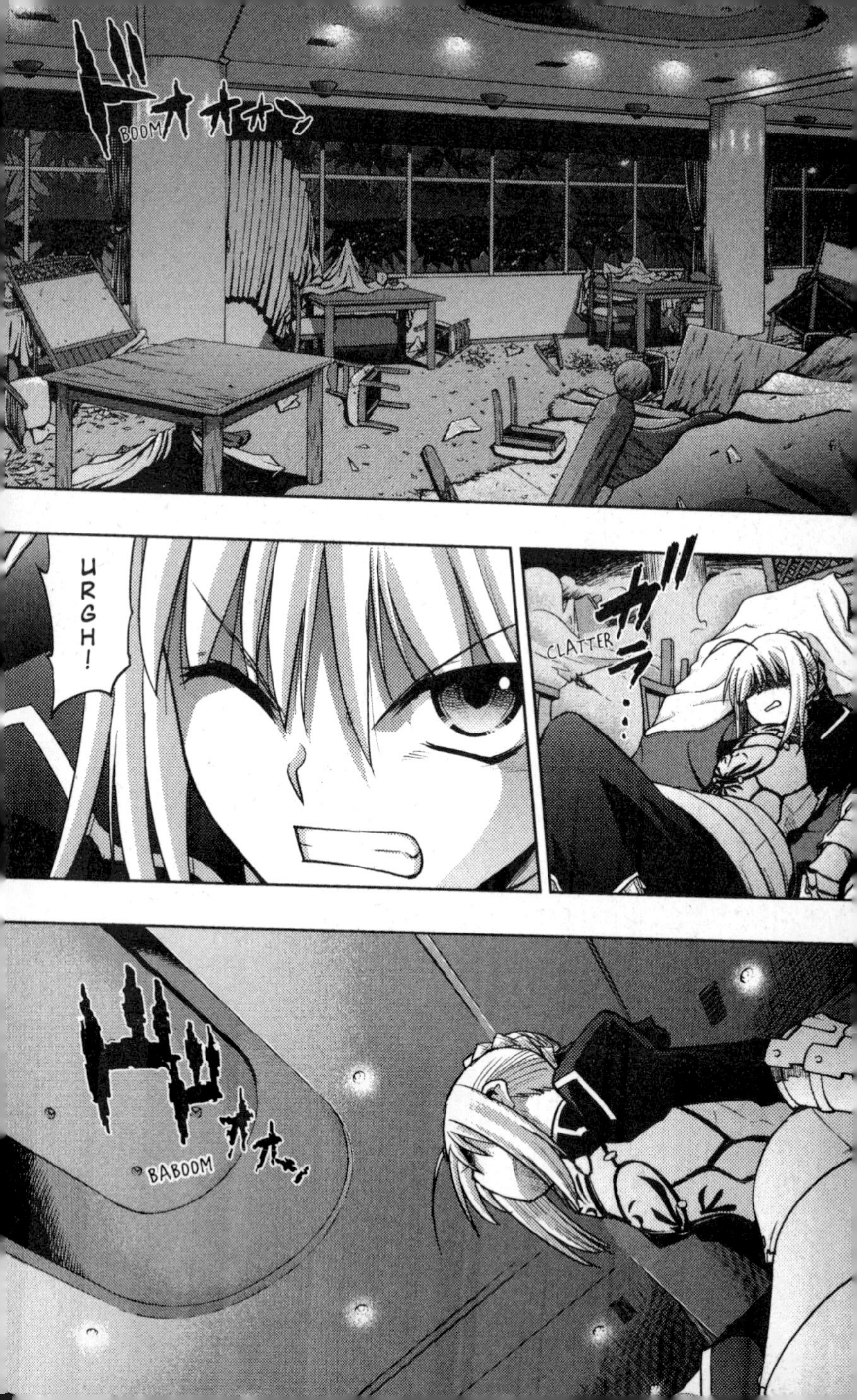
BOOM
CLATTER
URGH!
BABOOM

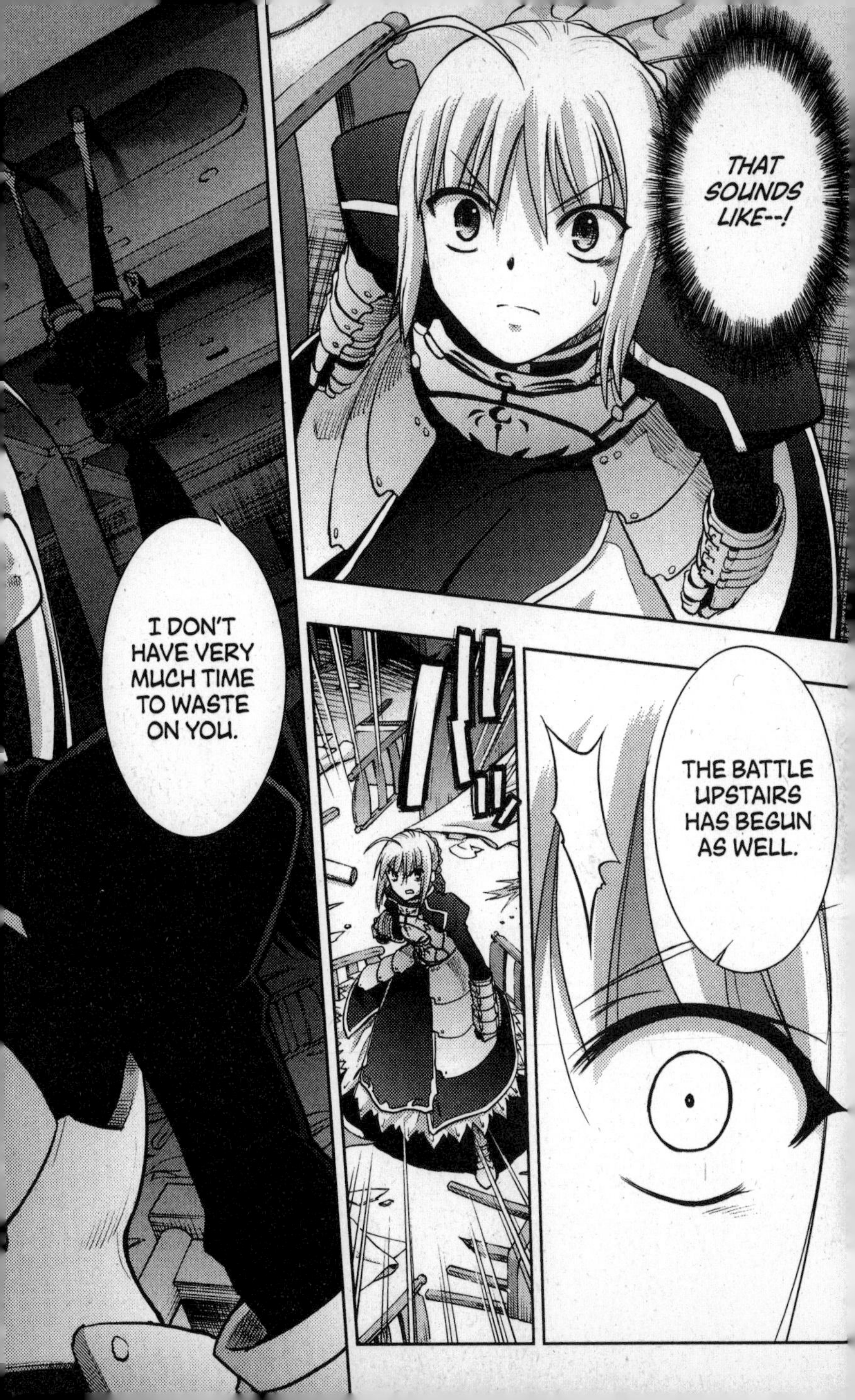
THAT SOUNDS LIKE--!
THE BATTLE UPSTAIRS HAS BEGUN AS WELL.
I DON'T HAVE VERY MUCH TIME TO WASTE ON YOU.

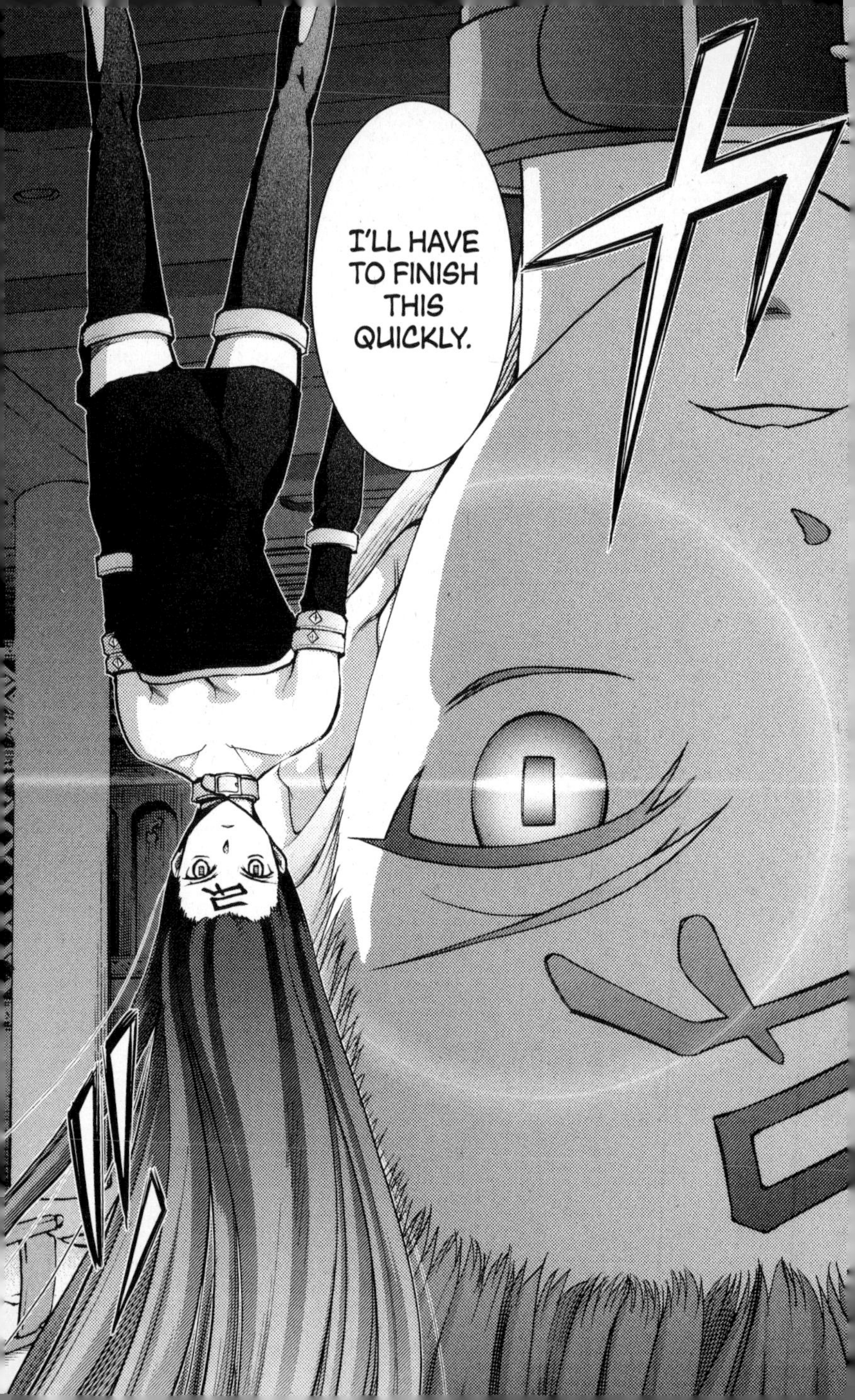
I'LL HAVE TO FINISH THIS QUICKLY.

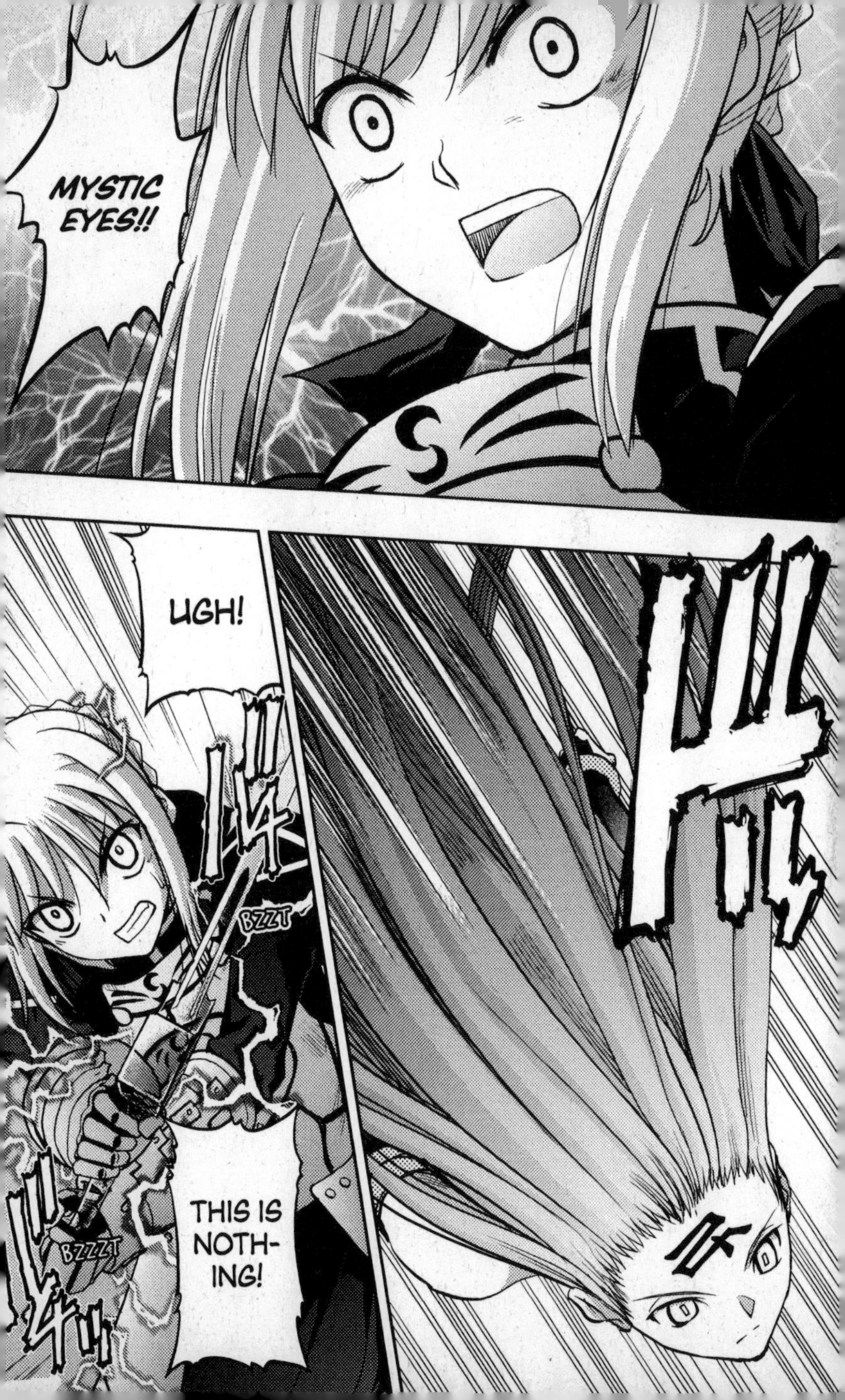
MYSTIC EYES!!
UGH!
BZZT
THIS IS NOTHING!
BZZZZT

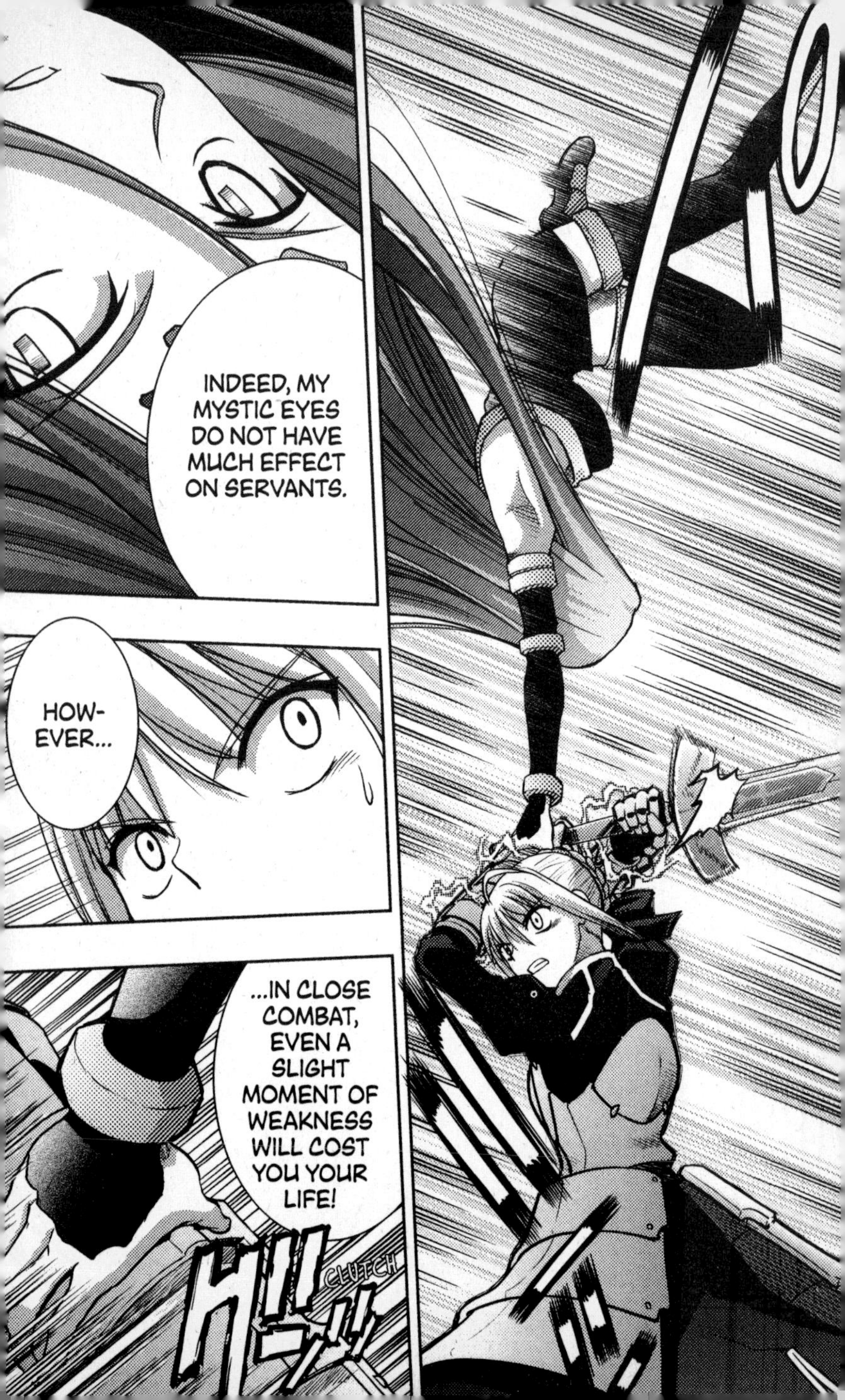
INDEED, MY MYSTIC EYES DO NOT HAVE MUCH EFFECT ON SERVANTS.
HOW-EVER...
...IN CLOSE COMBAT, EVEN A SLIGHT MOMENT OF WEAKNESS WILL COST YOU YOUR LIFE!
CLUTCH

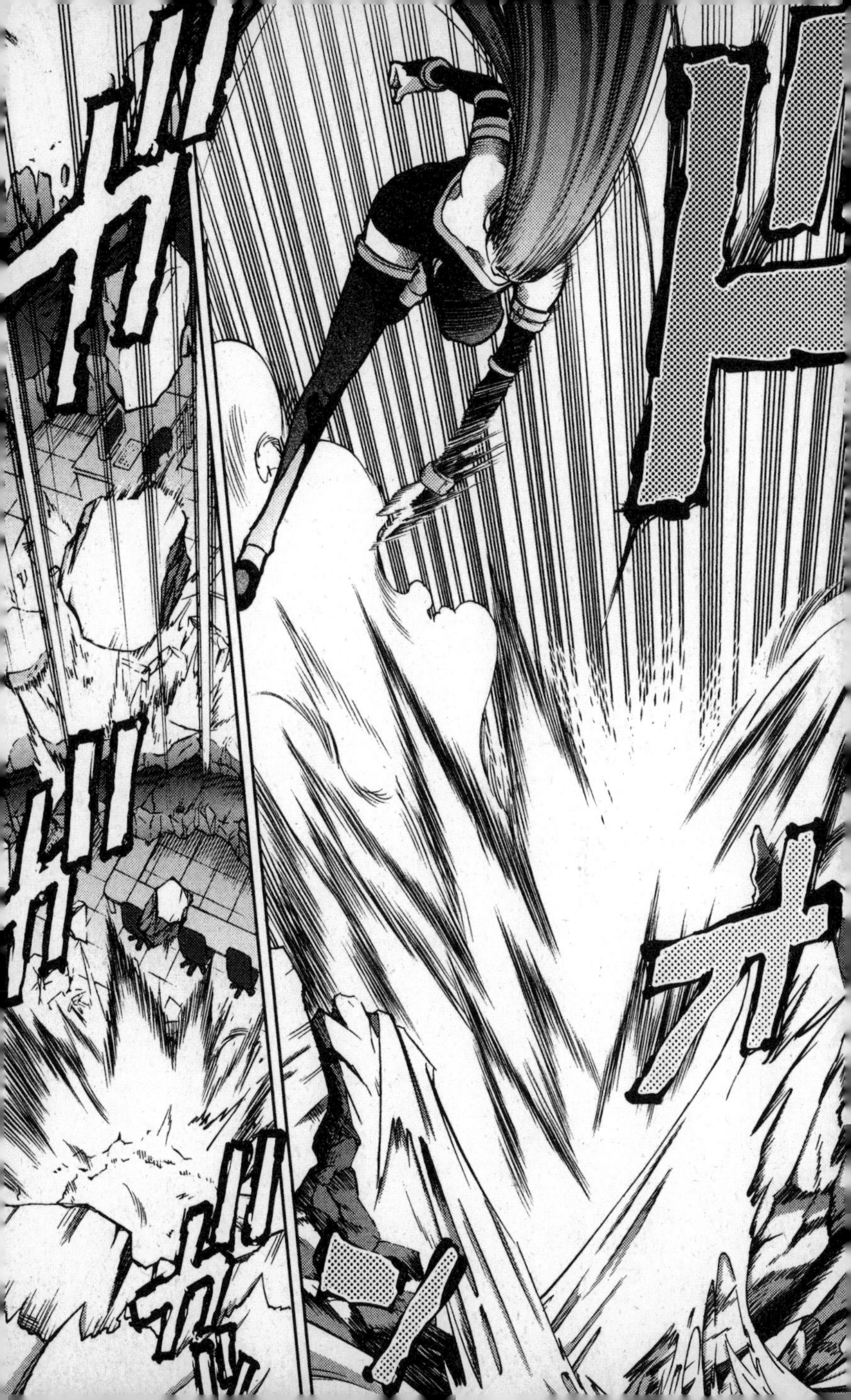

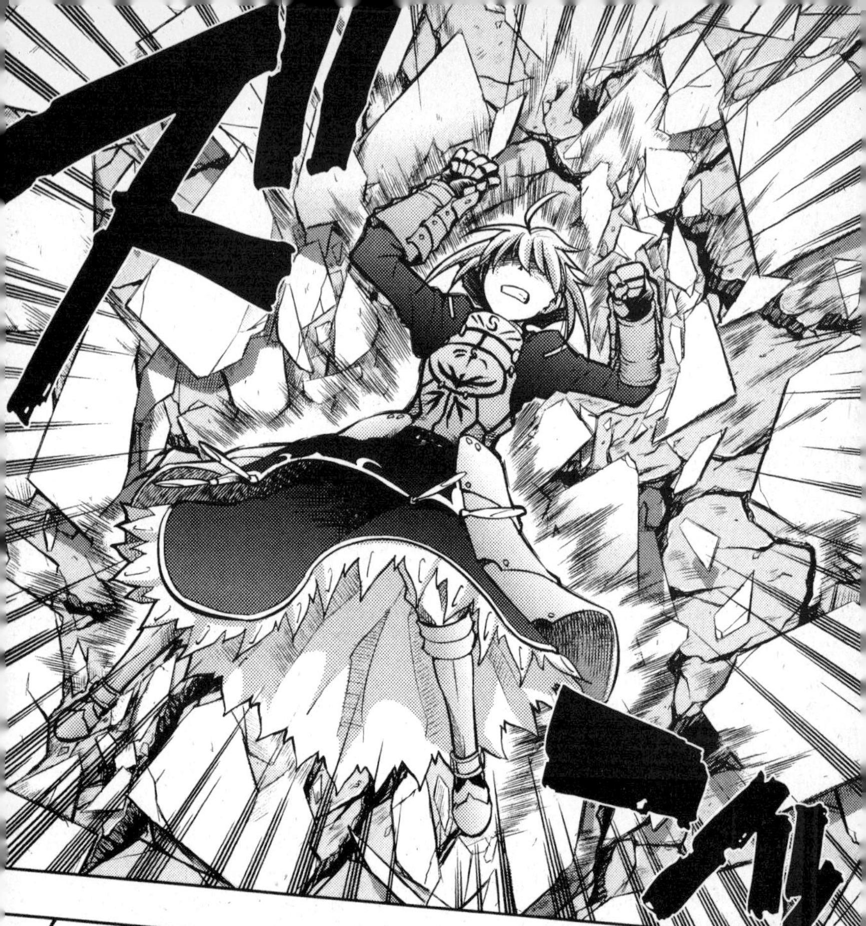

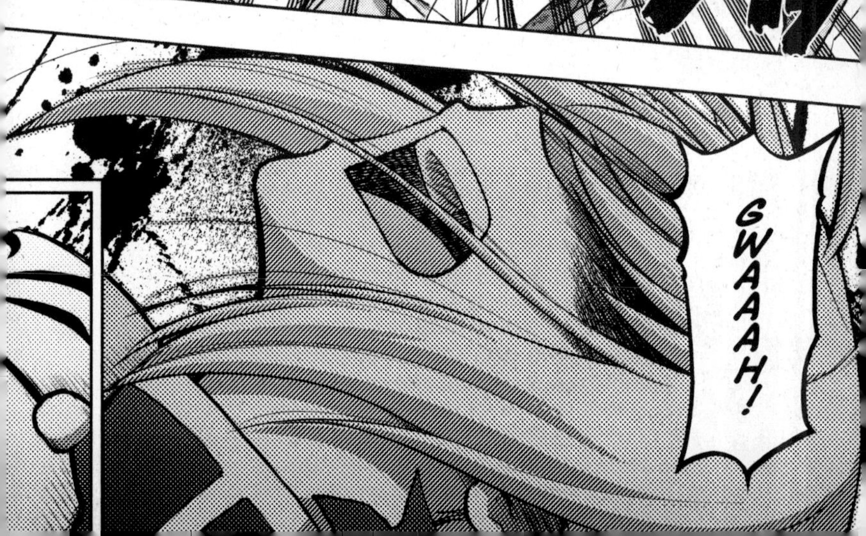
GWAAAAH!

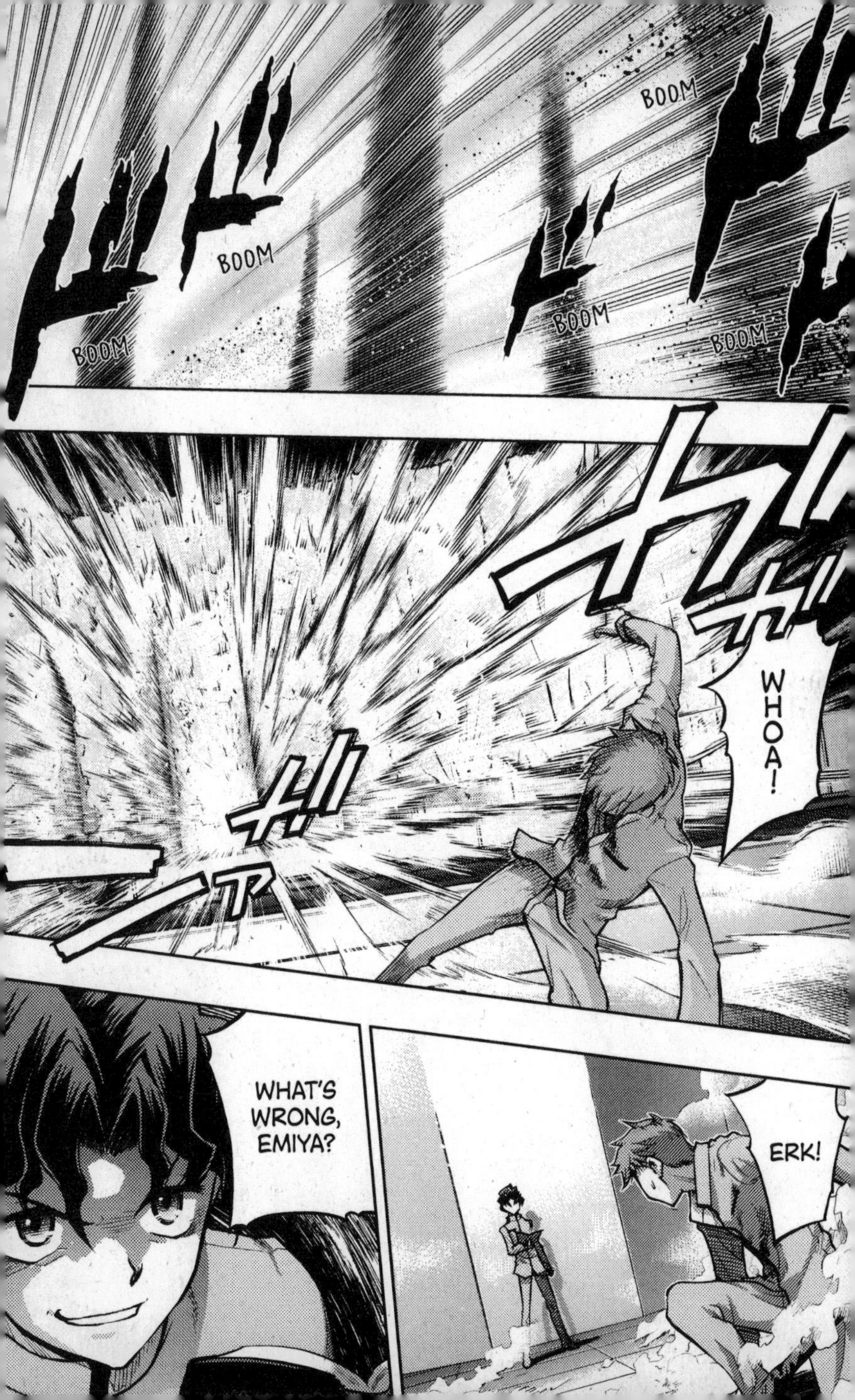
BOOM
BOOM
BOOM
BOOM
BOOM
WHOA!
ERK!
WHAT'S WRONG, EMIYA?

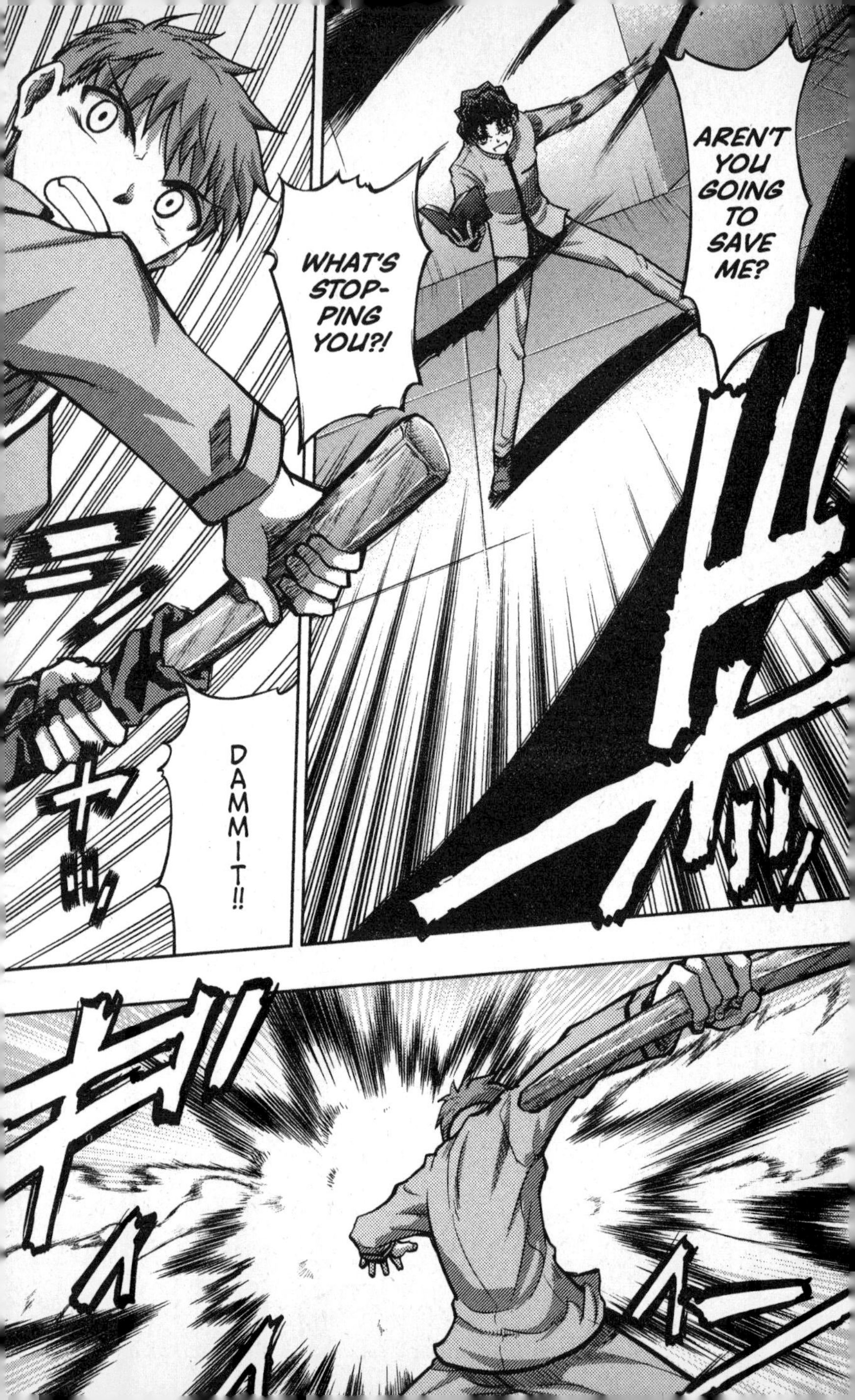

AREN'T YOU GOING TO SAVE ME?
WHAT'S STOP-PING YOU?!
DAMMIT!!

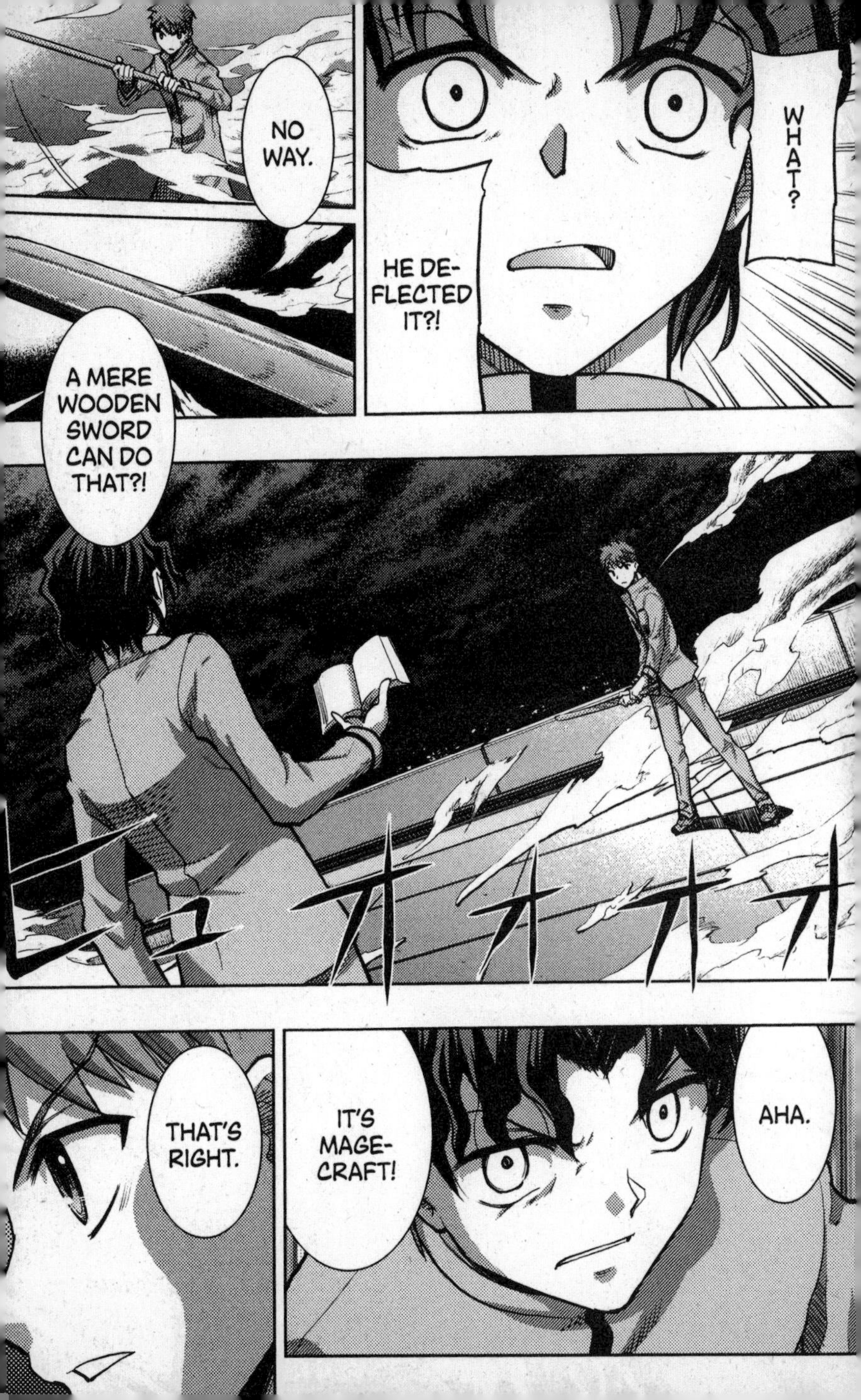
WHAT?
HE DE-FLECTED IT?!
NO WAY.
A MERE WOODEN SWORD CAN DO THAT?!
AHA.
IT'S MAGE-CRAFT!
THAT'S RIGHT.

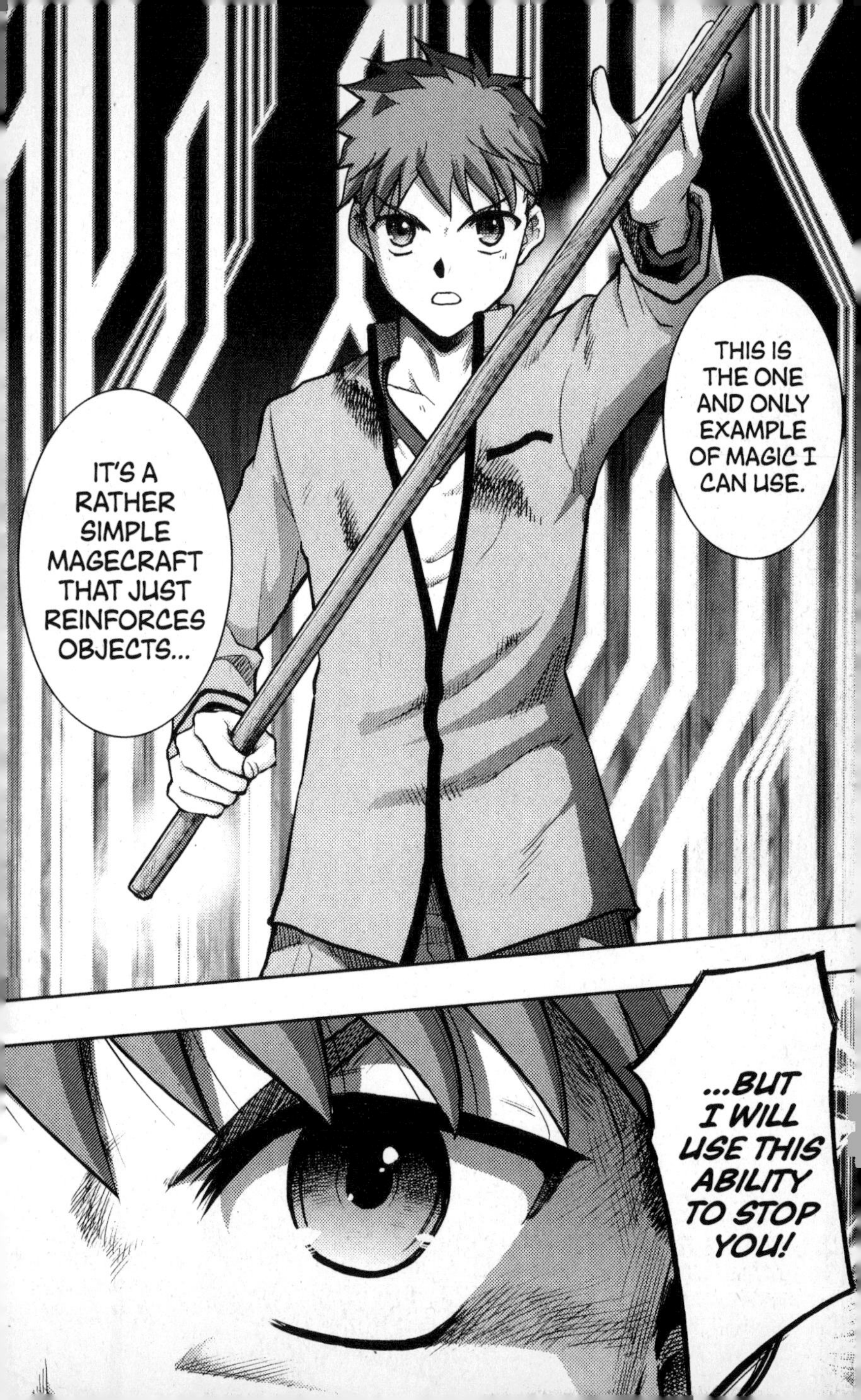
THIS IS THE ONE AND ONLY EXAMPLE OF MAGIC I CAN USE.
IT'S A RATHER SIMPLE MAGECRAFT THAT JUST REINFORCES OBJECTS...
...BUT I WILL USE THIS ABILITY TO STOP YOU!

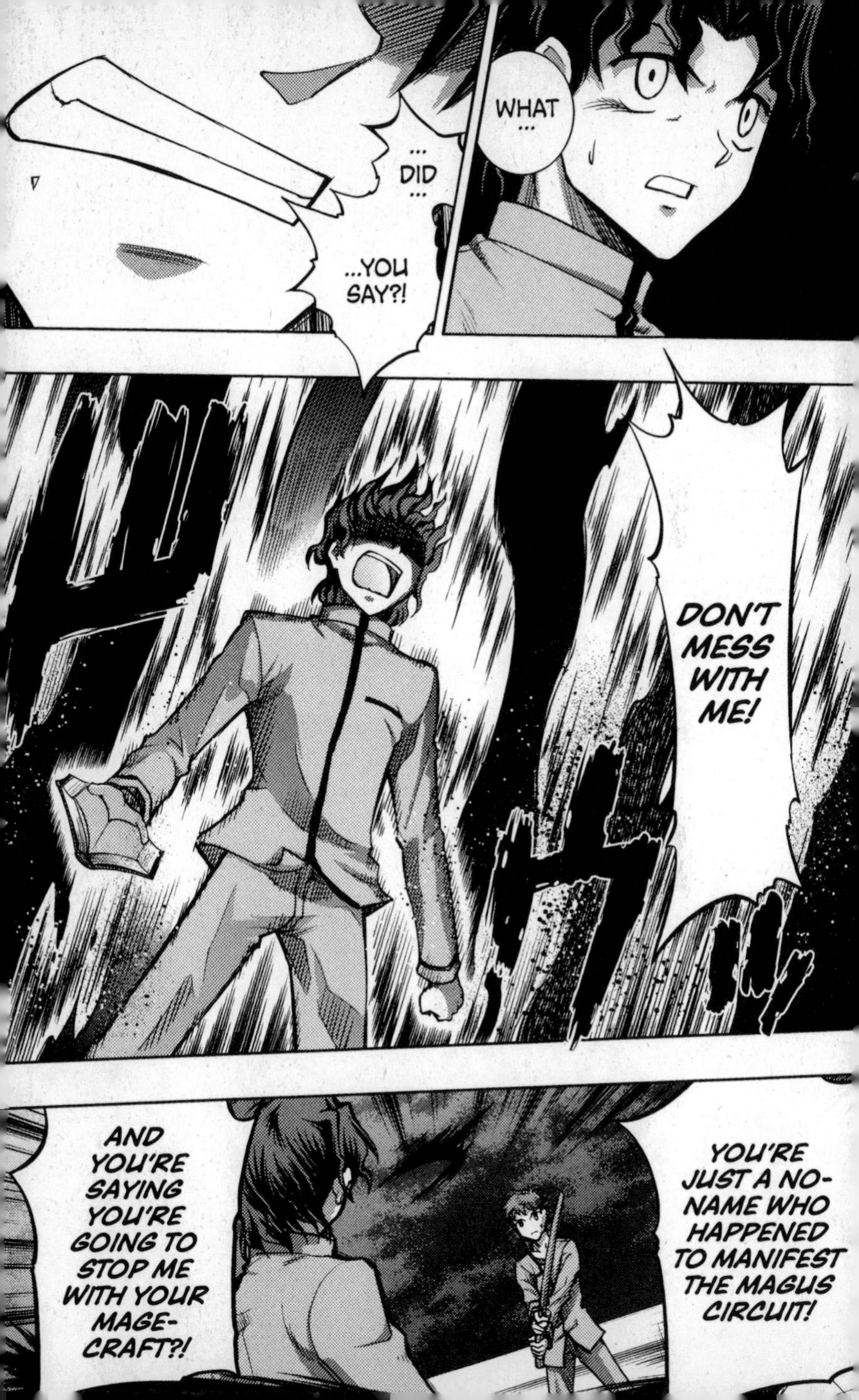
WHAT ...
... DID ...
...YOU SAY?!
DON'T MESS WITH ME!
YOU'RE JUST A NO-NAME WHO HAPPENED TO MANIFEST THE MAGUS CIRCUIT!
AND YOU'RE SAYING YOU'RE GOING TO STOP ME WITH YOUR MAGE-CRAFT?!

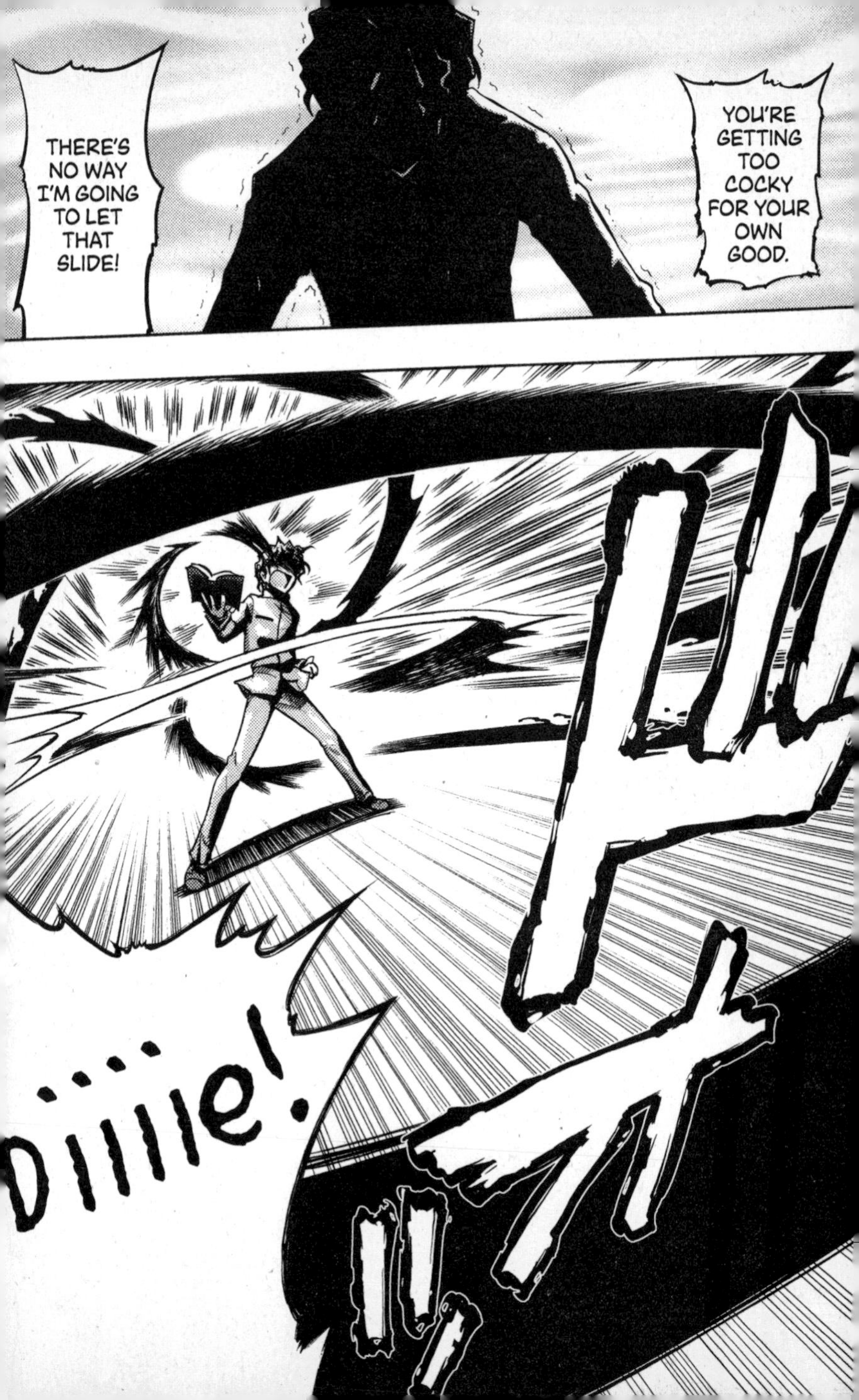
YOU'RE GETTING TOO COCKY FOR YOUR OWN GOOD.
THERE'S NO WAY I'M GOING TO LET THAT SLIDE!
Diiiie!

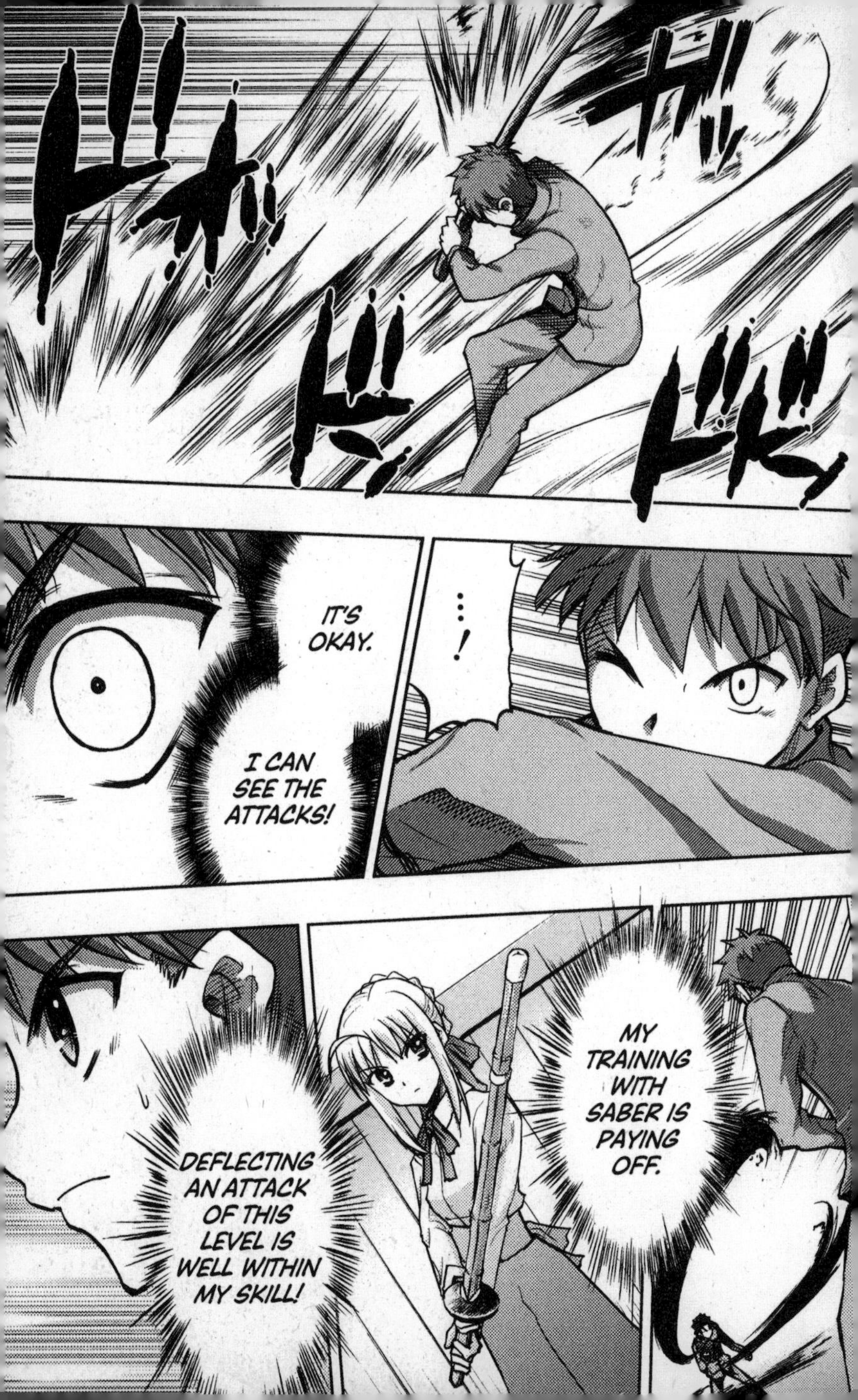
...!
IT'S OKAY.
I CAN SEE THE ATTACKS!
MY TRAINING WITH SABER IS PAYING OFF.
DEFLECTING AN ATTACK OF THIS LEVEL IS WELL WITHIN MY SKILL!

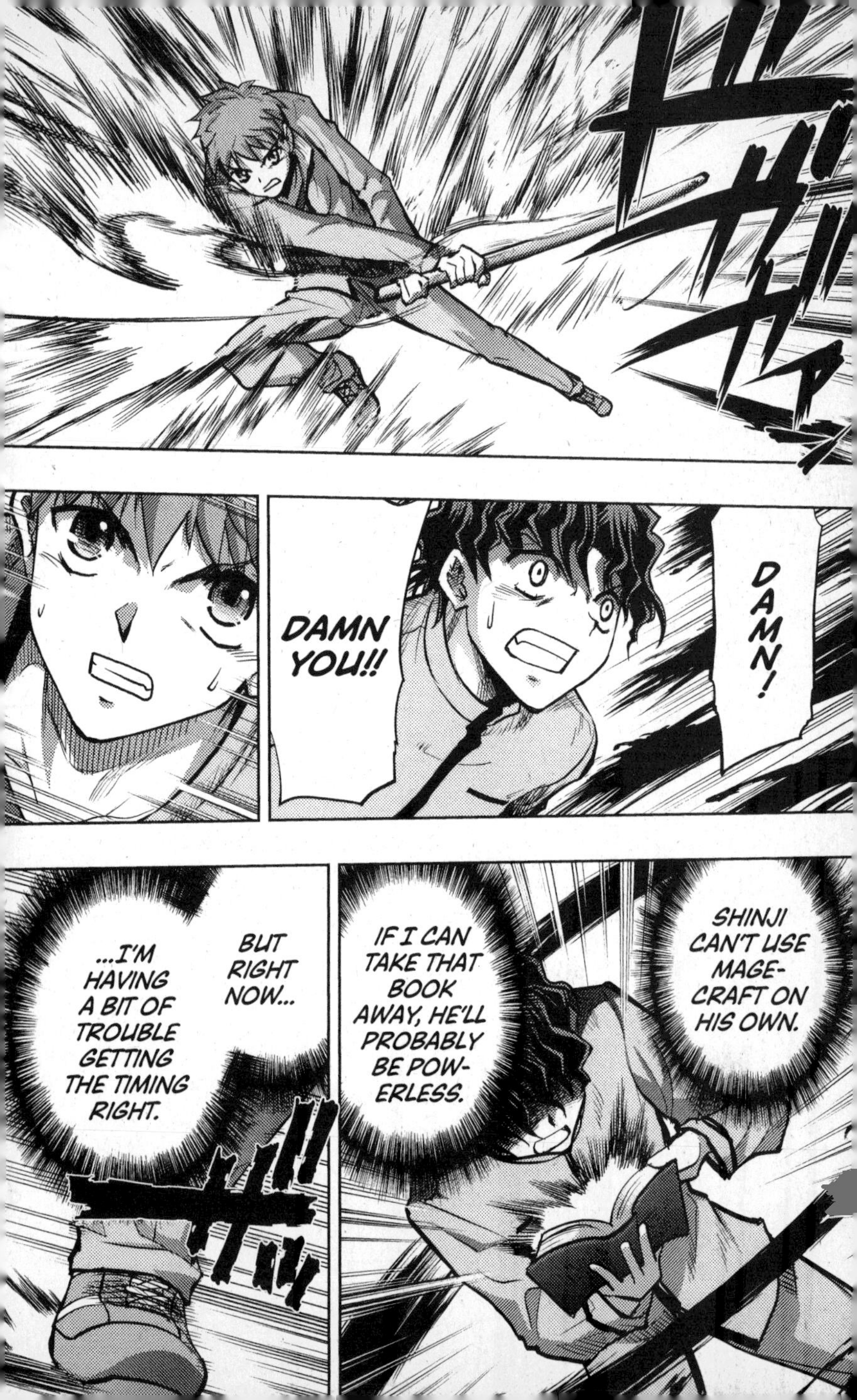
DAMN!
DAMN YOU!!
SHINJI CAN'T USE MAGE-CRAFT ON HIS OWN.
IF I CAN TAKE THAT BOOK AWAY, HE'LL PROBABLY BE POW-ERLESS.
BUT RIGHT NOW...
...I'M HAVING A BIT OF TROUBLE GETTING THE TIMING RIGHT.

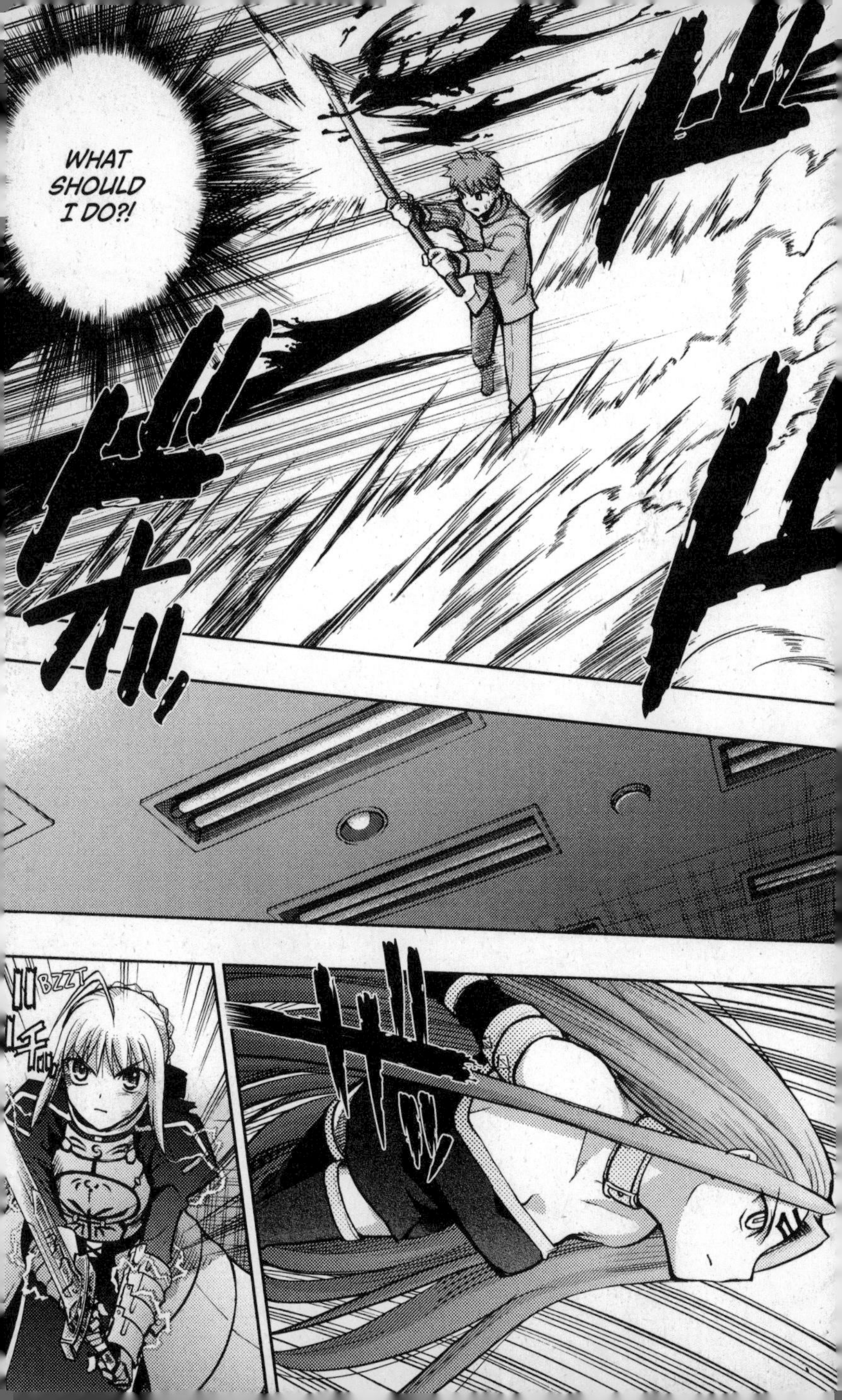
WHAT SHOULD I DO?!
BZZT

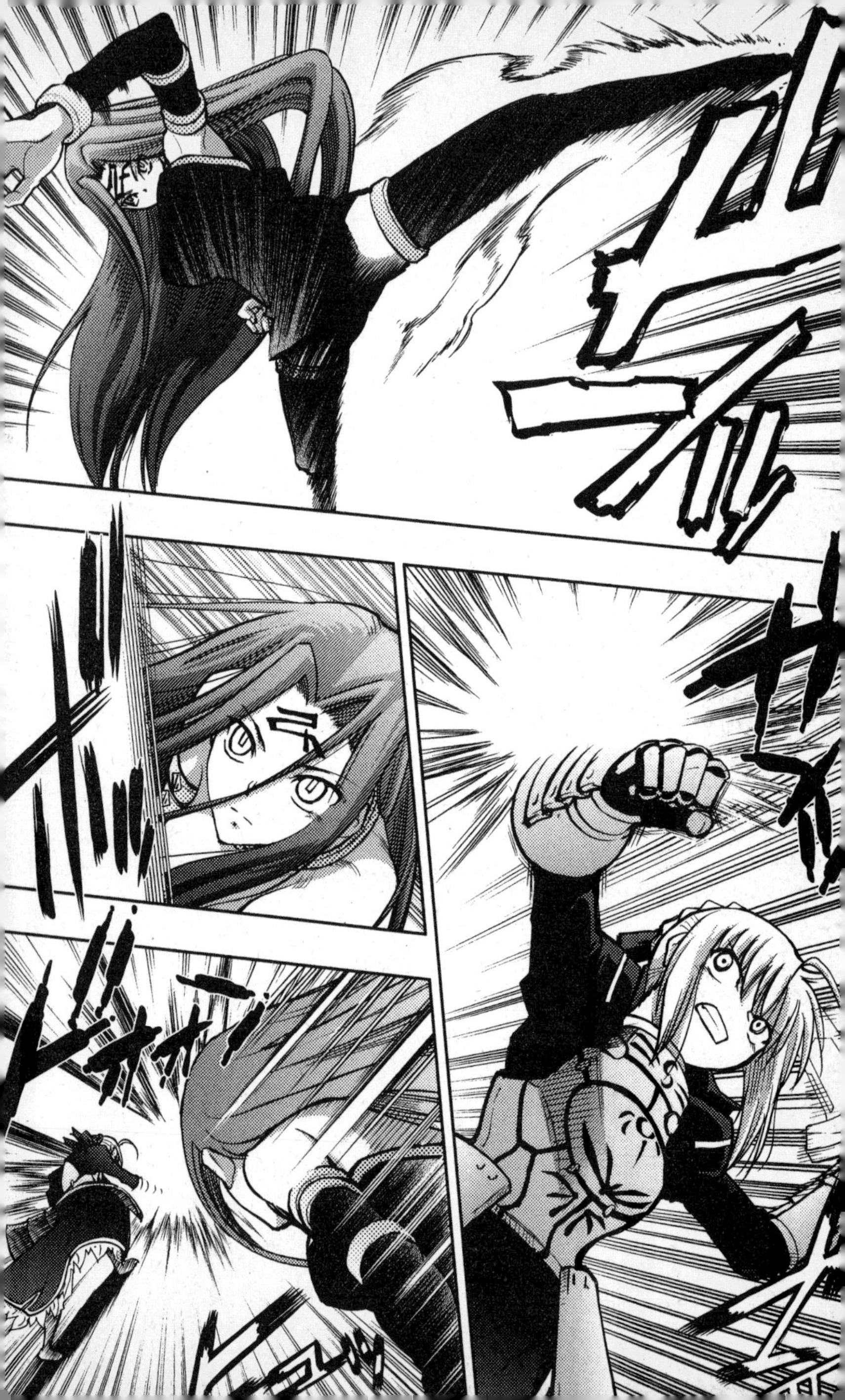

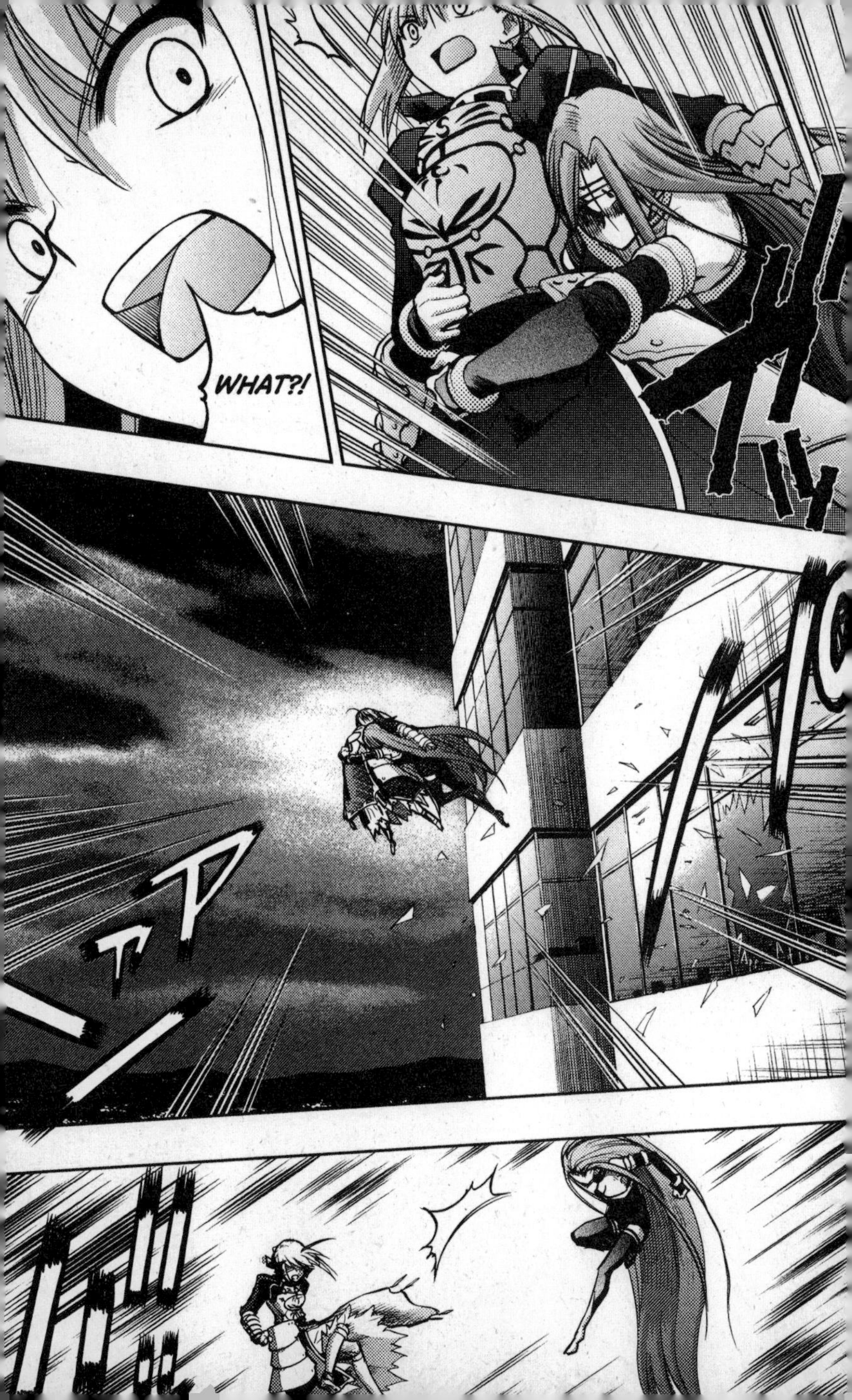
WHAT?!

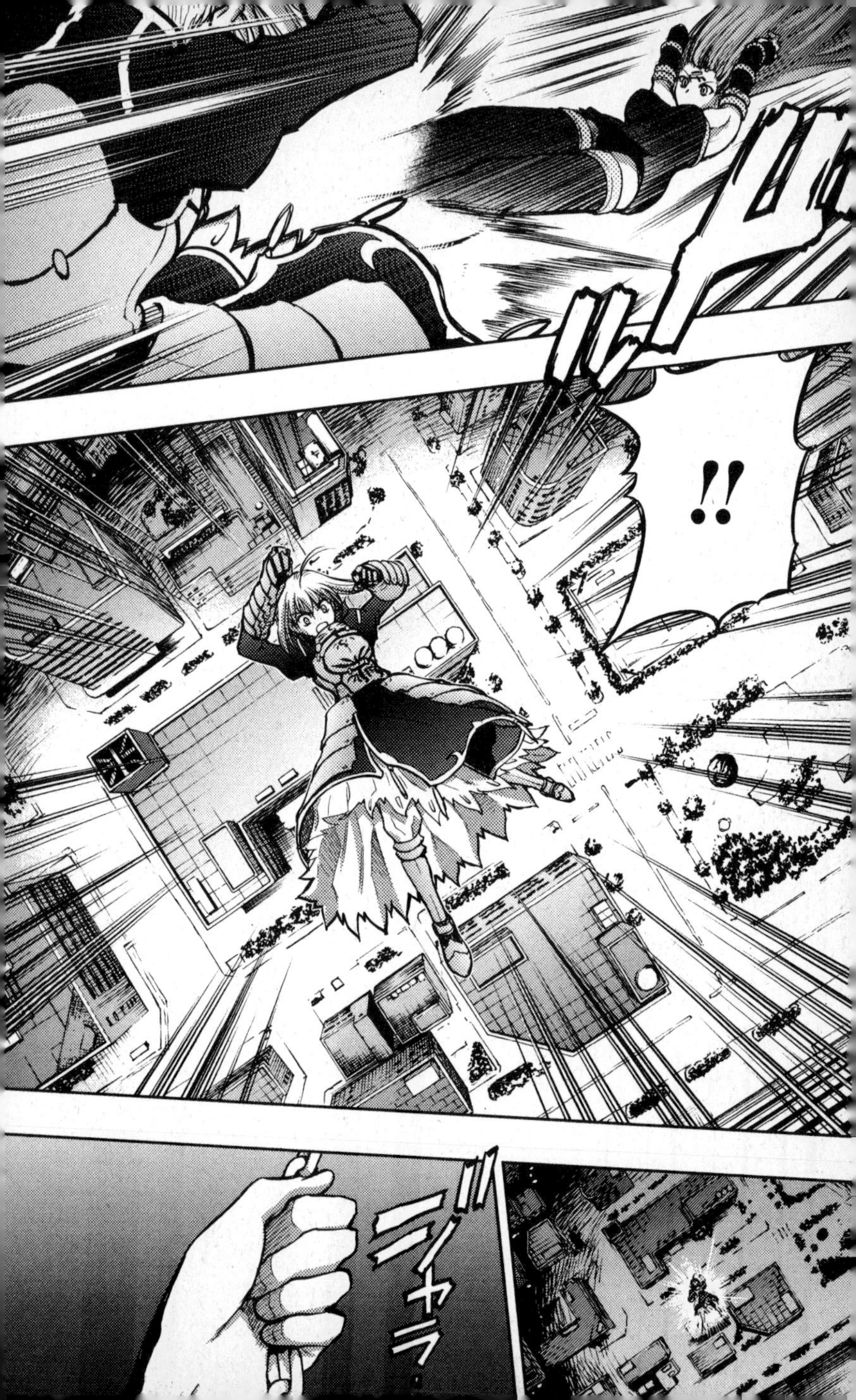
!!
ジャラ

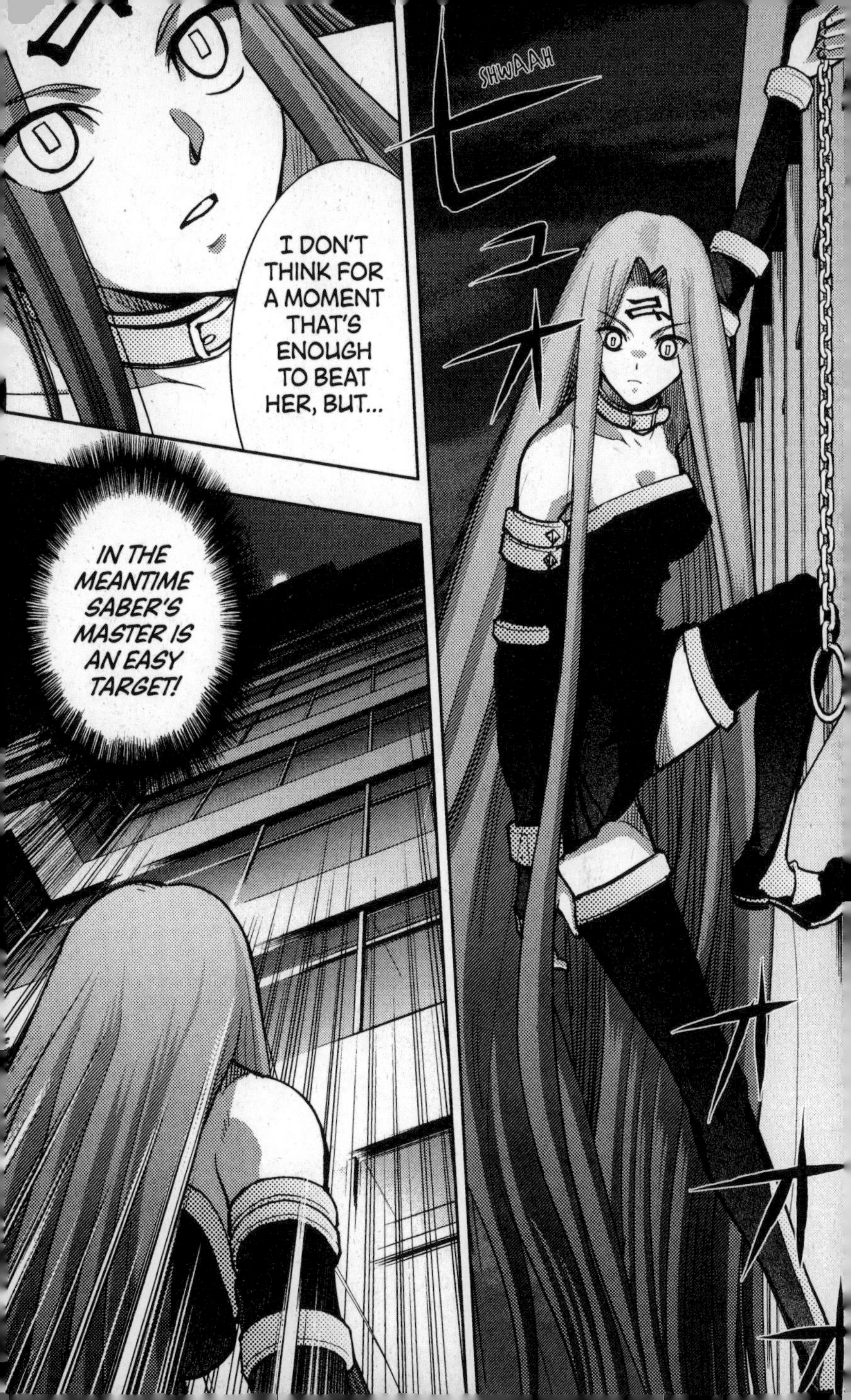
SHWAAH
I DON'T THINK FOR A MOMENT THAT'S ENOUGH TO BEAT HER, BUT...
IN THE MEANTIME SABER'S MASTER IS AN EASY TARGET!

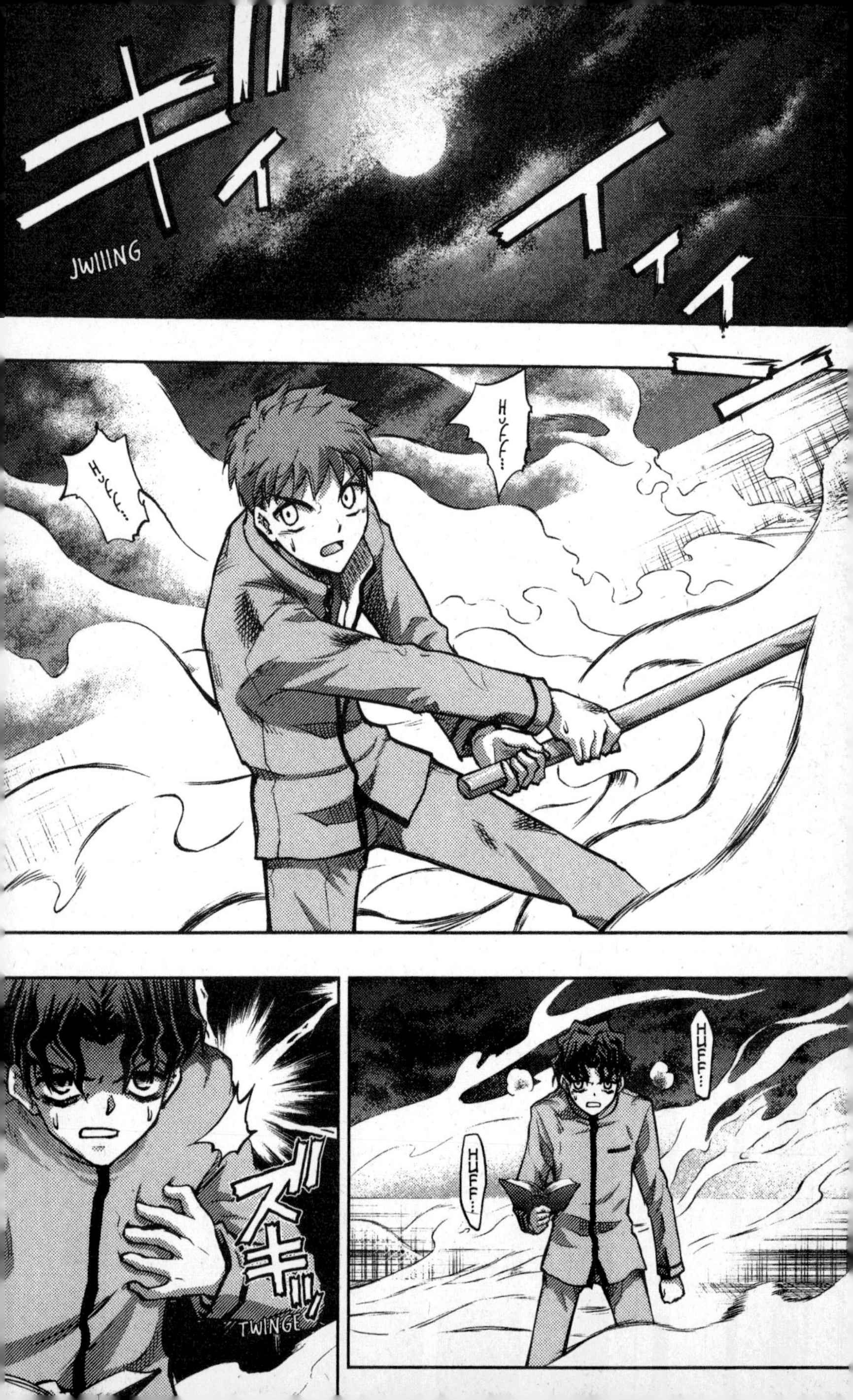
JWIIING
HUFF...
HUFF...
TWINGE
HUFF...
HUFF...

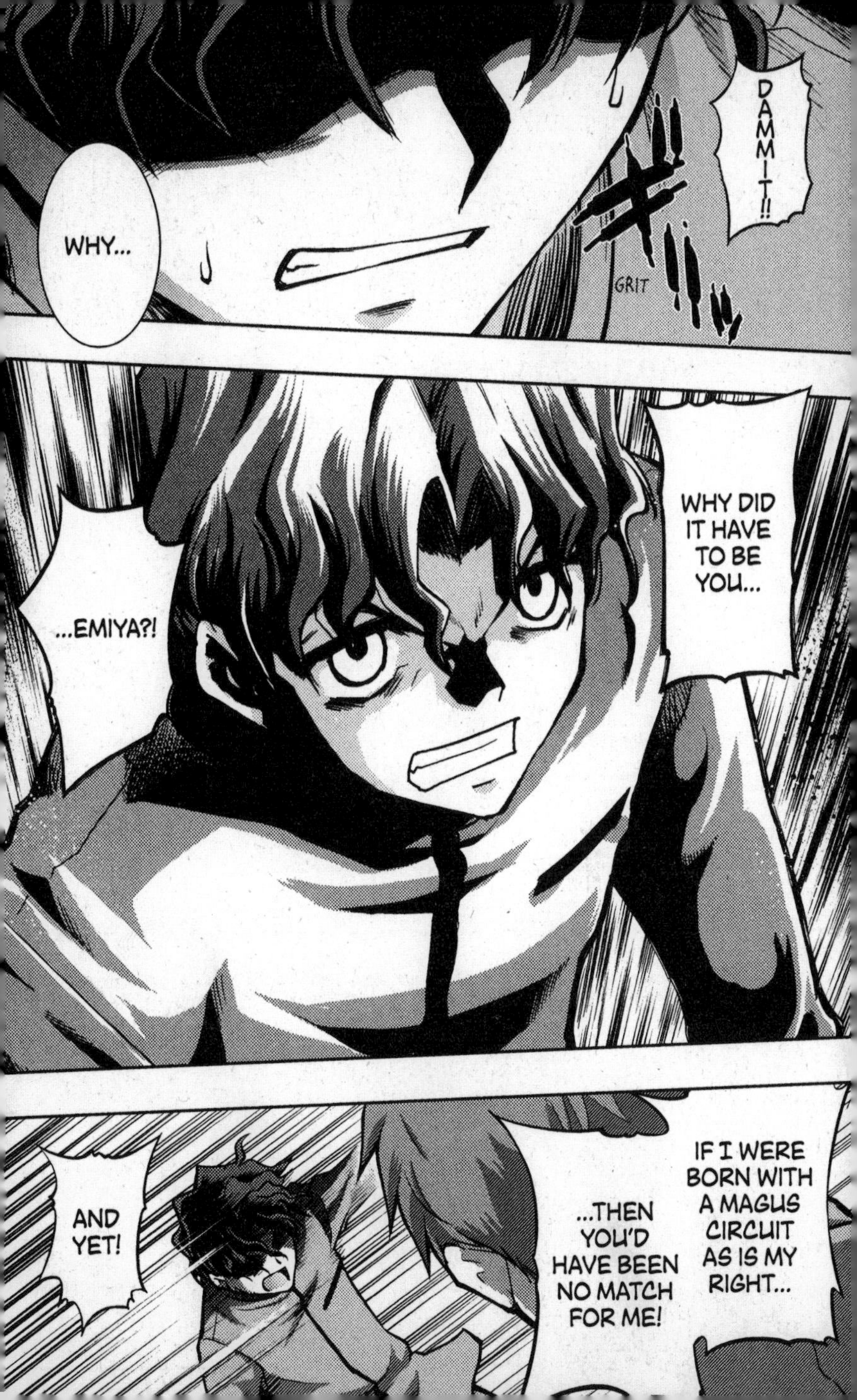
DAMMIT!!
GRIT
WHY...
WHY DID IT HAVE TO BE YOU...
...EMIYA?!
IF I WERE BORN WITH A MAGUS CIRCUIT AS IS MY RIGHT...
...THEN YOU'D HAVE BEEN NO MATCH FOR ME!
AND YET!

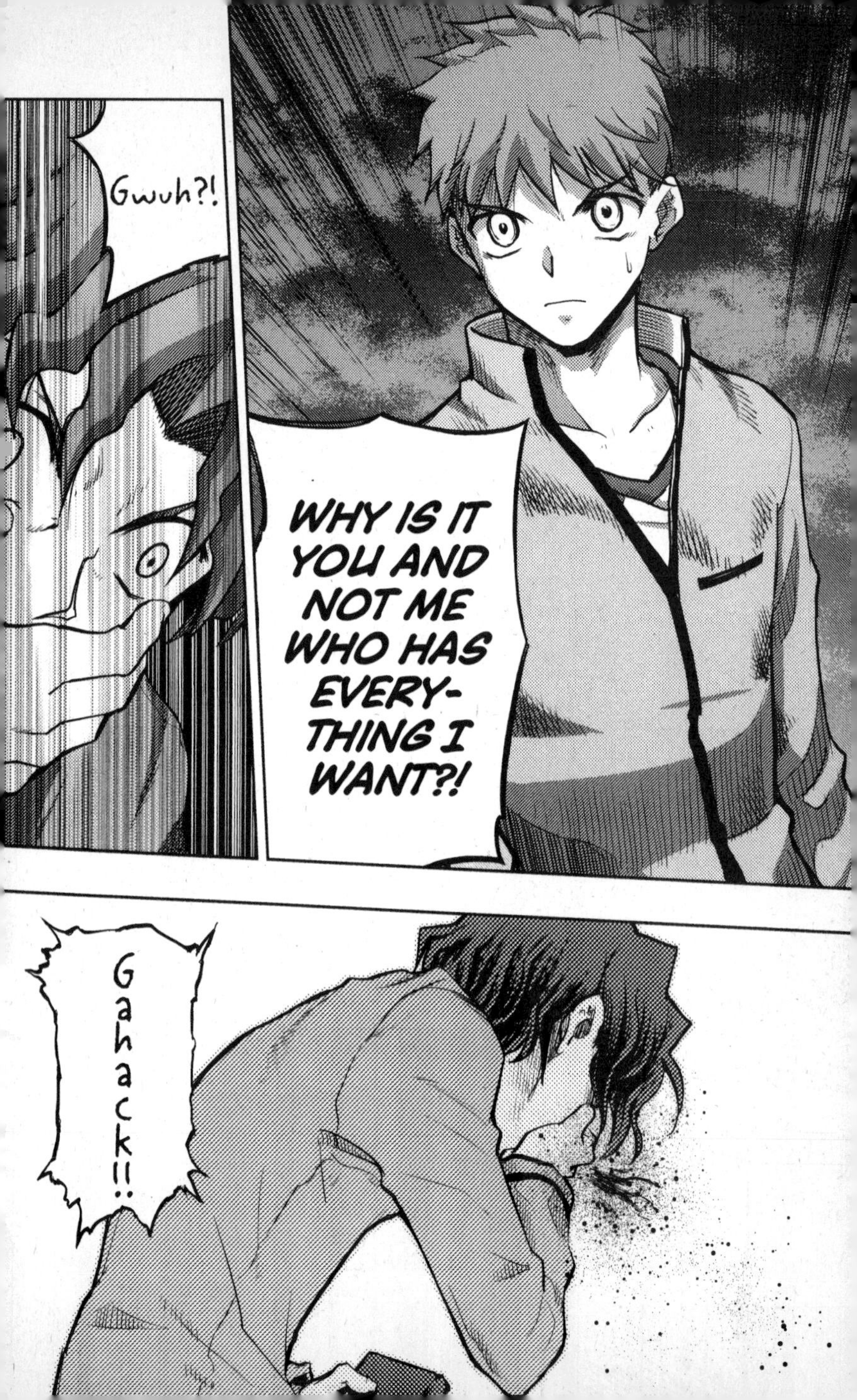
WHY IS IT YOU AND NOT ME WHO HAS EVERY-THING I WANT?!
Gwuh?!
Gahack!!

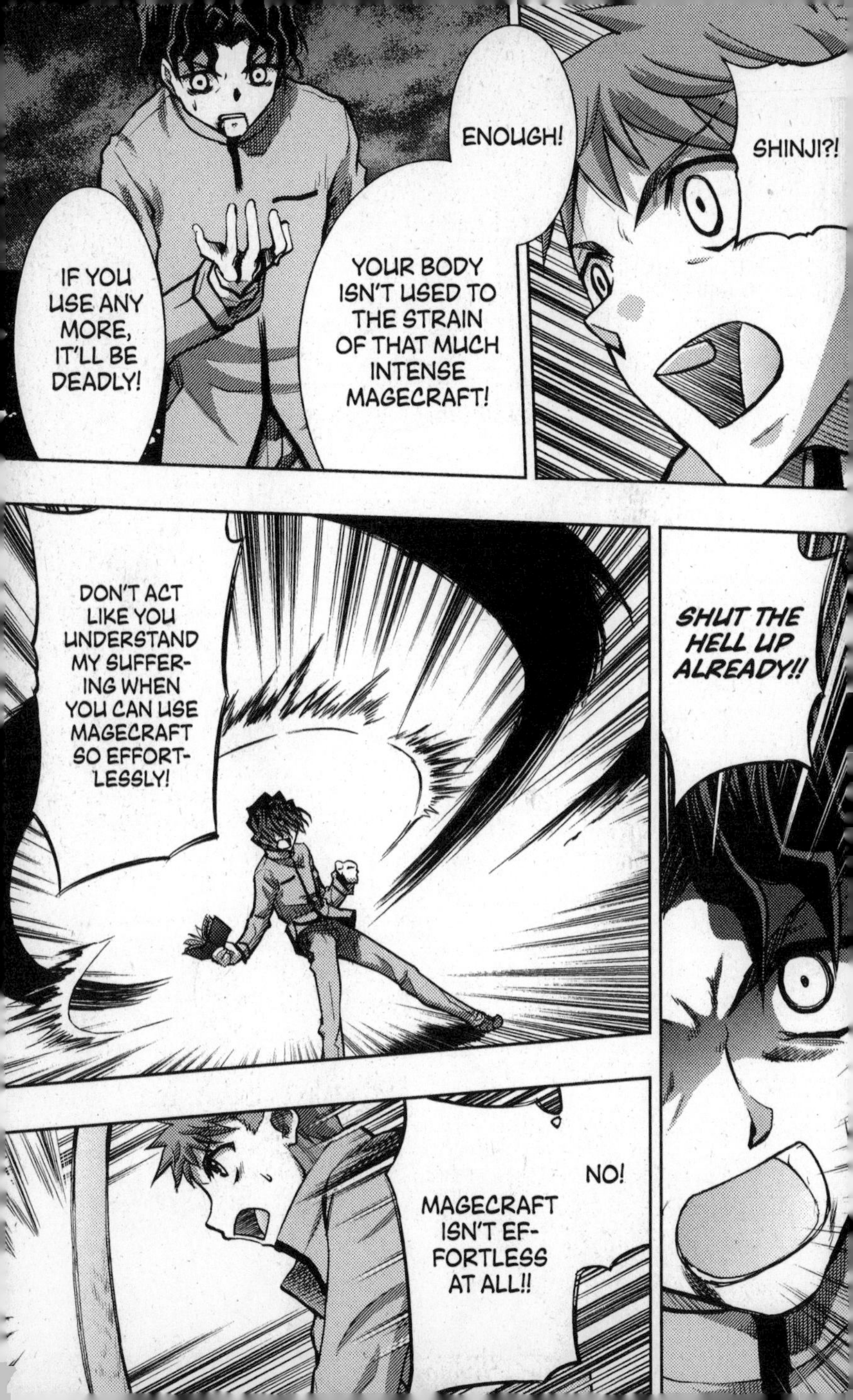
SHINJI?!
ENOUGH!
YOUR BODY ISN'T USED TO THE STRAIN OF THAT MUCH INTENSE MAGECRAFT!
IF YOU USE ANY MORE, IT'LL BE DEADLY!
SHUT THE HELL UP ALREADY!!
DON'T ACT LIKE YOU UNDERSTAND MY SUFFER-ING WHEN YOU CAN USE MAGECRAFT SO EFFORT-LESSLY!
NO!
MAGECRAFT ISN'T EF-FORTLESS AT ALL!!

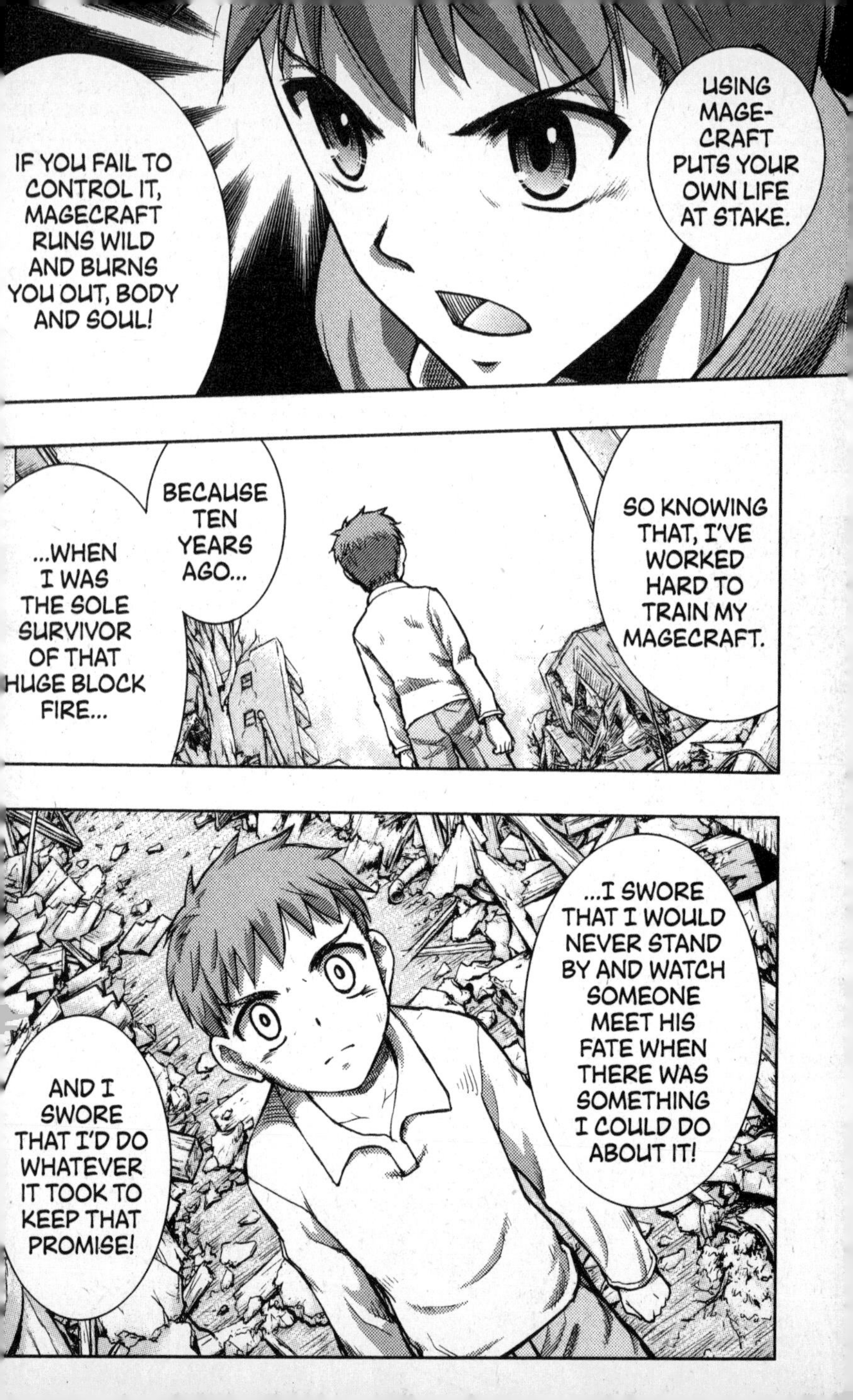
USING MAGE-CRAFT PUTS YOUR OWN LIFE AT STAKE.
IF YOU FAIL TO CONTROL IT, MAGECRAFT RUNS WILD AND BURNS YOU OUT, BODY AND SOUL!
SO KNOWING THAT, I'VE WORKED HARD TO TRAIN MY MAGECRAFT.
BECAUSE TEN YEARS AGO...
...WHEN I WAS THE SOLE SURVIVOR OF THAT HUGE BLOCK FIRE...
...I SWORE THAT I WOULD NEVER STAND BY AND WATCH SOMEONE MEET HIS FATE WHEN THERE WAS SOMETHING I COULD DO ABOUT IT!
AND I SWORE THAT I'D DO WHATEVER IT TOOK TO KEEP THAT PROMISE!

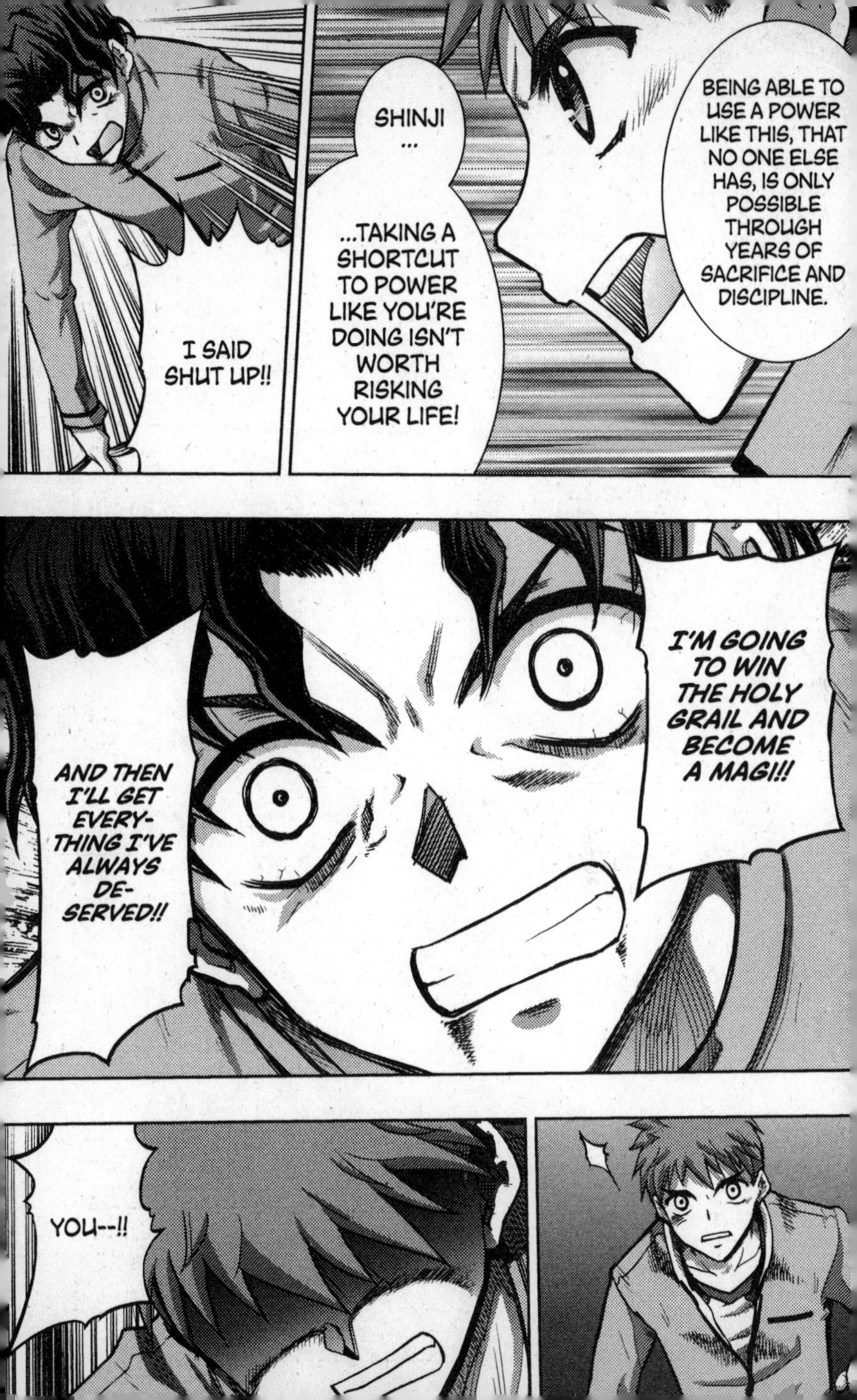
BEING ABLE TO USE A POWER LIKE THIS, THAT NO ONE ELSE HAS, IS ONLY POSSIBLE THROUGH YEARS OF SACRIFICE AND DISCIPLINE.
SHINJI ...
...TAKING A SHORTCUT TO POWER LIKE YOU'RE DOING ISN'T WORTH RISKING YOUR LIFE!
I SAID SHUT UP!!
I'M GOING TO WIN THE HOLY GRAIL AND BECOME A MAGI!!
AND THEN I'LL GET EVERY-THING I'VE ALWAYS DE-SERVED!!
YOU--!!

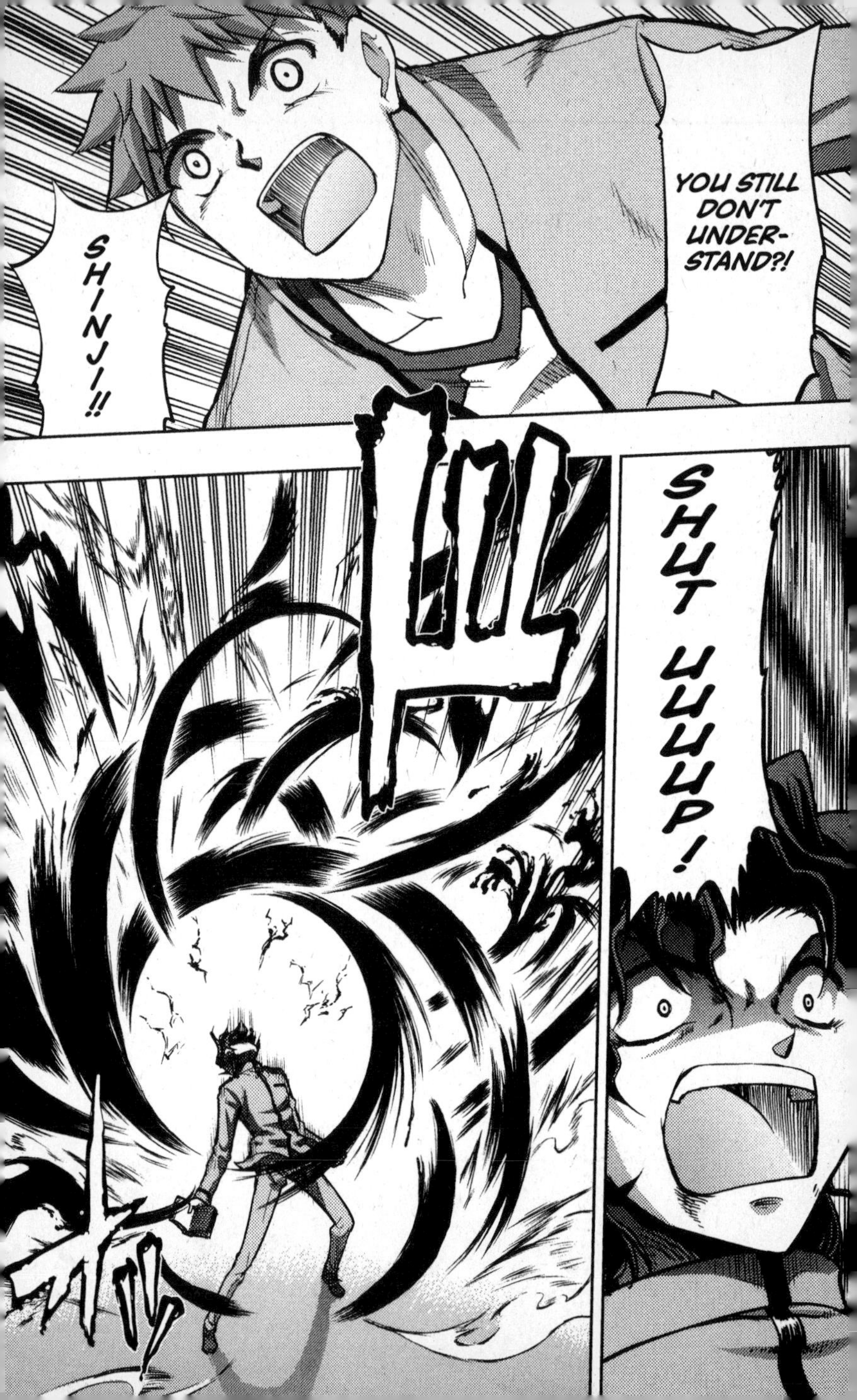
YOU STILL DON'T UNDER-STAND?!
SHINJI!!
SHUT UUUUUP!

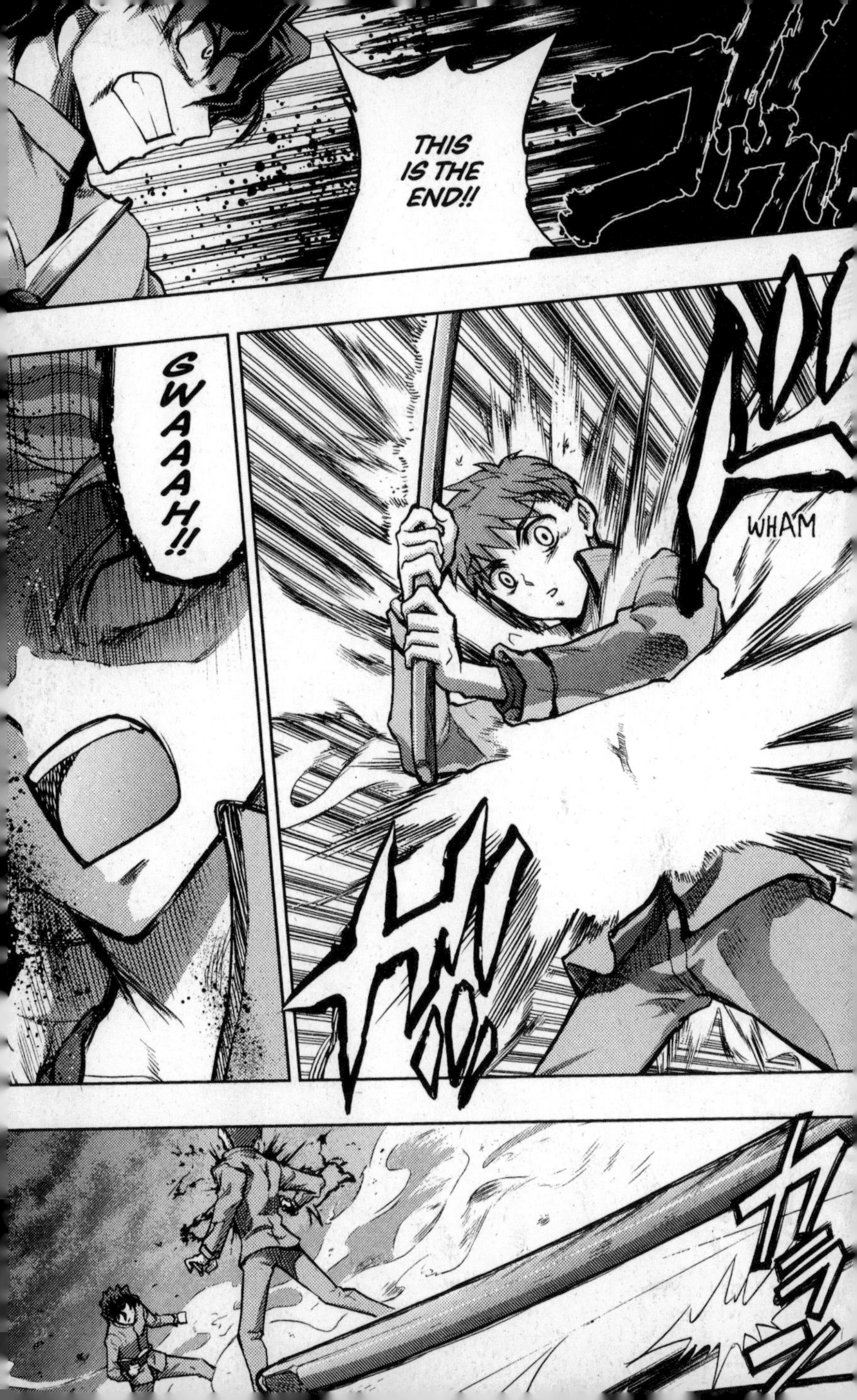
THIS IS THE END!!
WHAM
GWAAAAH!!

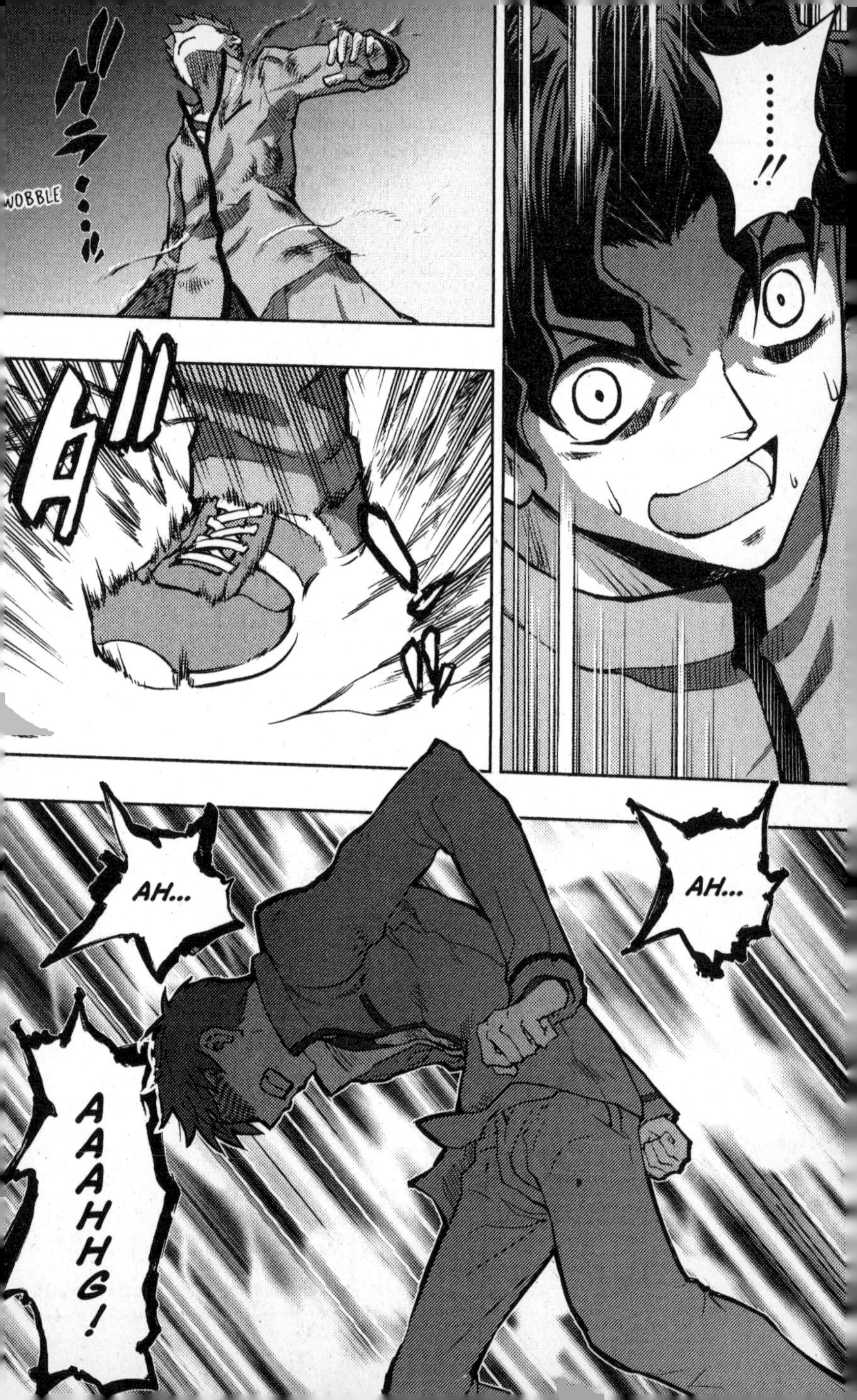
......!!
WOBBLE
AH...
AH...
AAAAHHG!

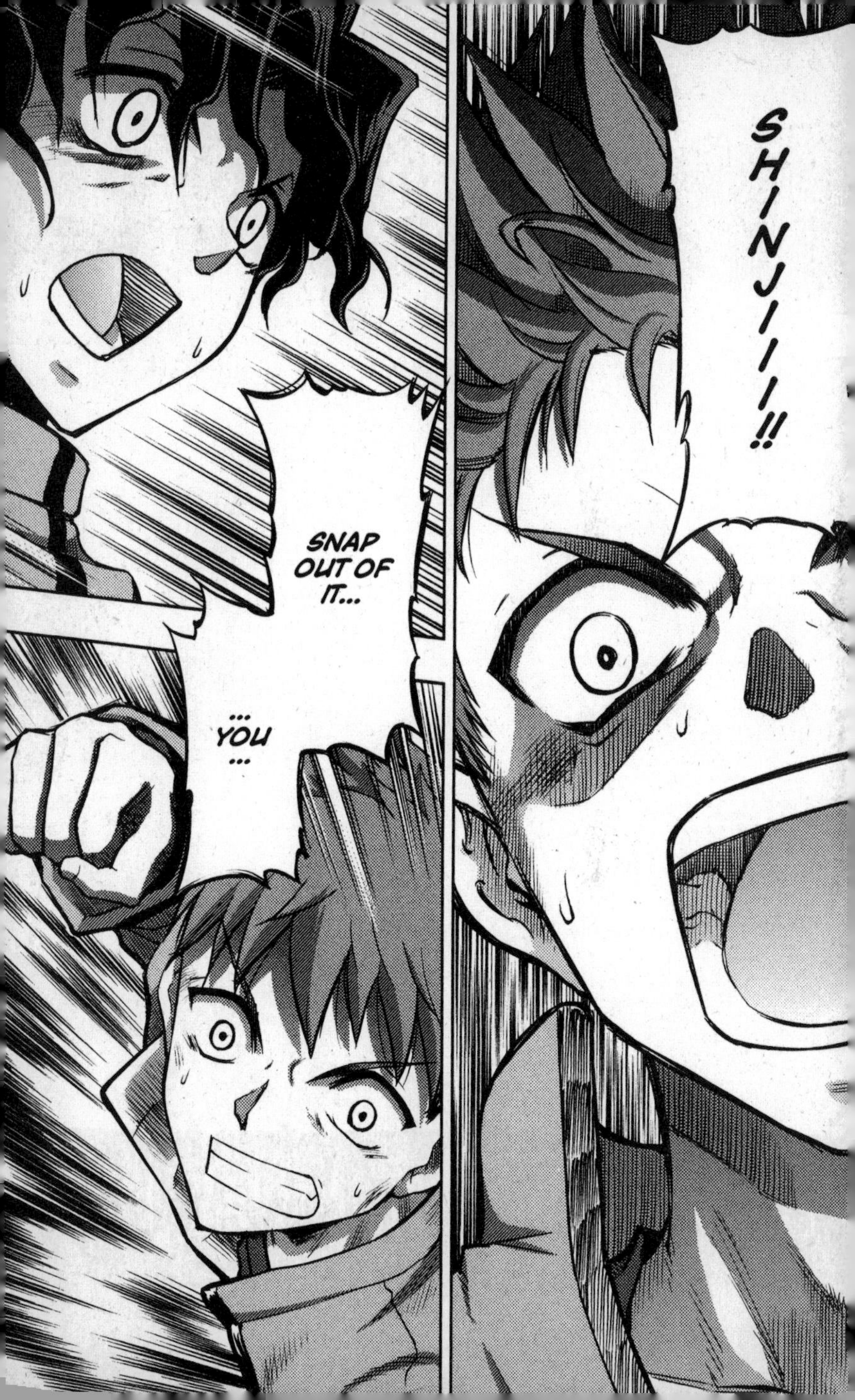
SHINJIII!!
SNAP OUT OF IT...
...YOU ...

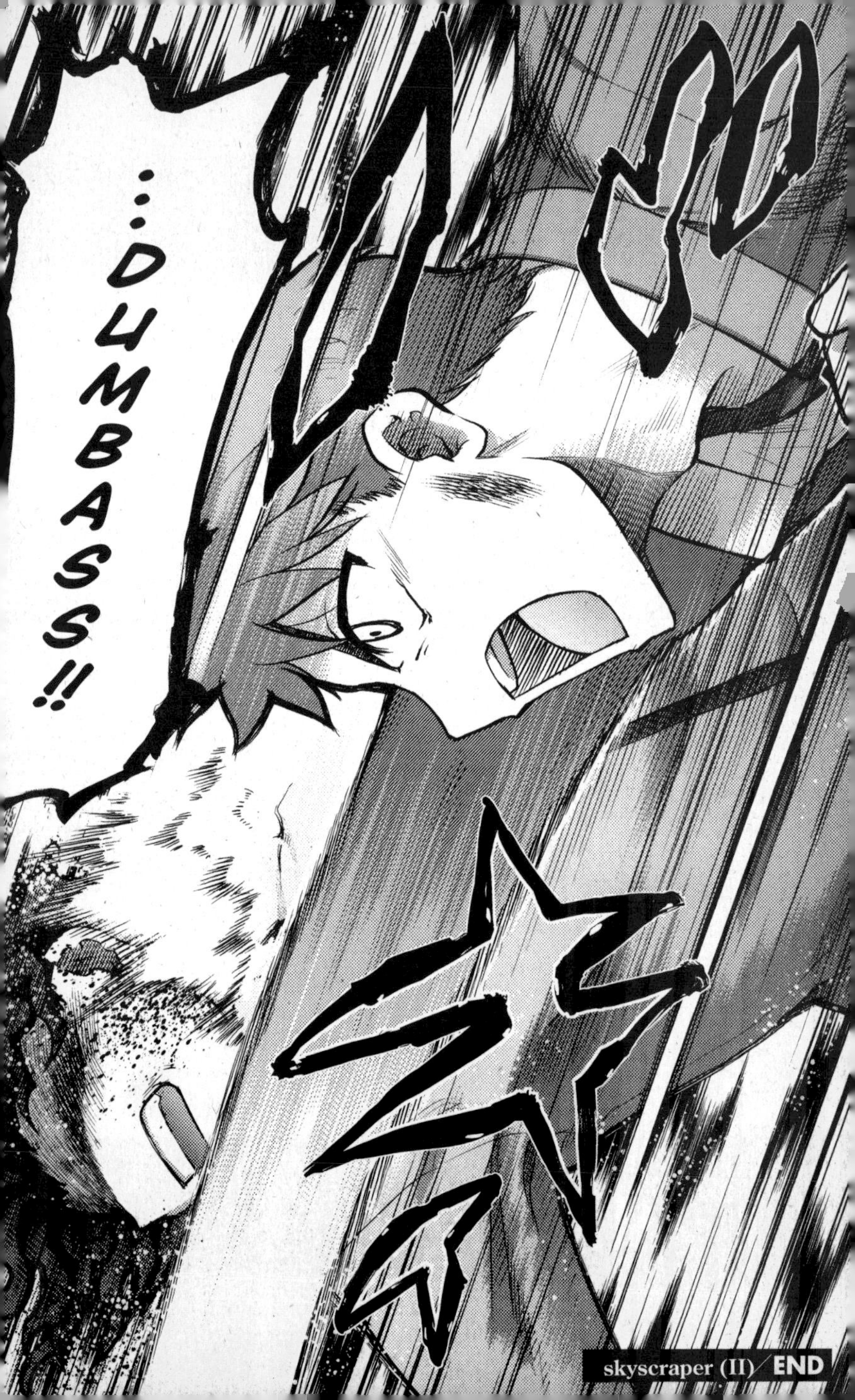
...DUMBASS!!

skyscraper (II) / END

Fate
stay night
フェイト/ステイナイト

WHOOOSH

noble phantasm

GAH...

URK...

Gahack
hgck!!

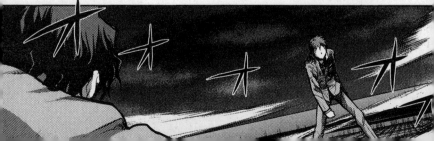

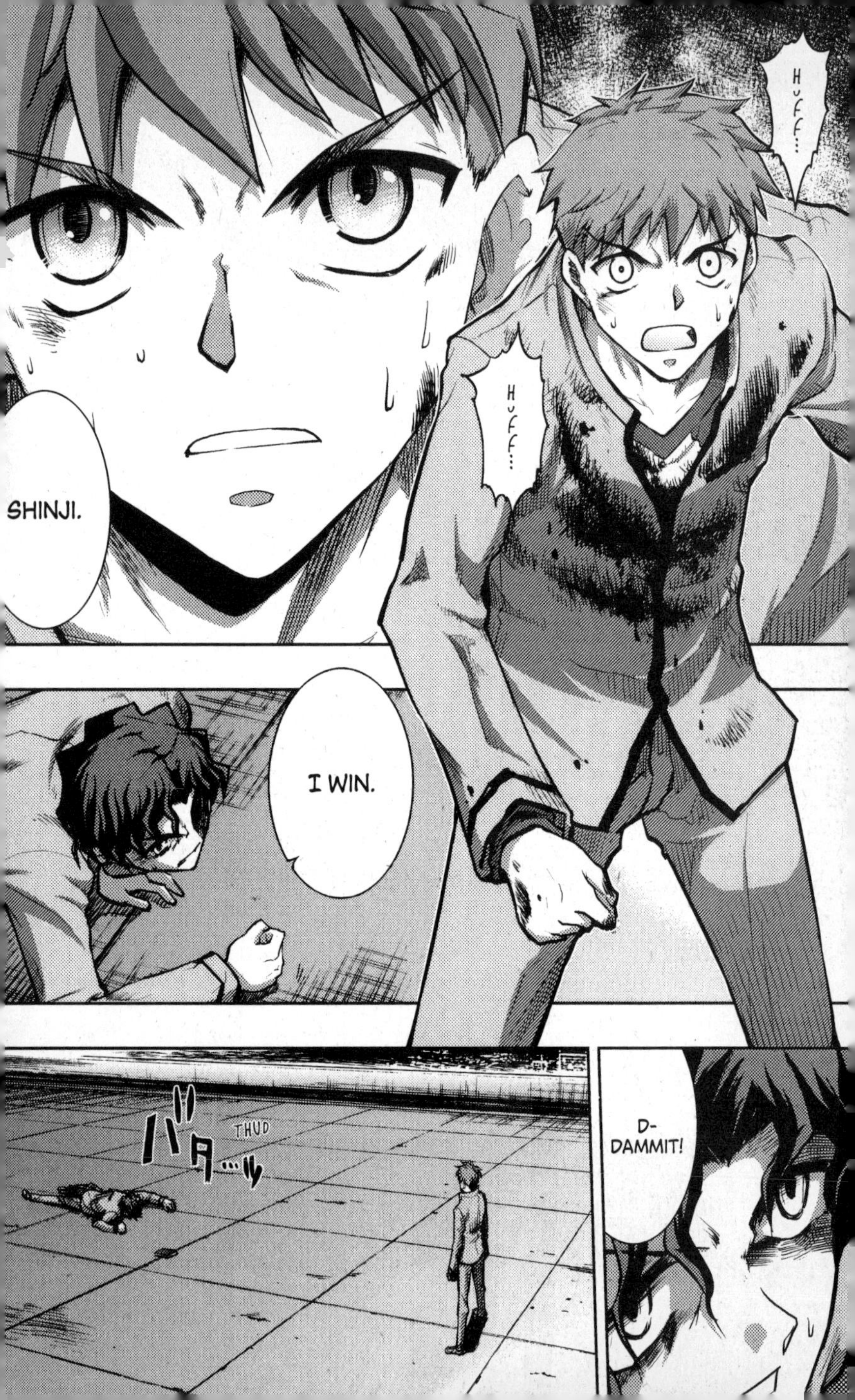
HUFF...
HUFF...
SHINJI.
I WIN.
D-DAMMIT!
バタ…ッ
THUD

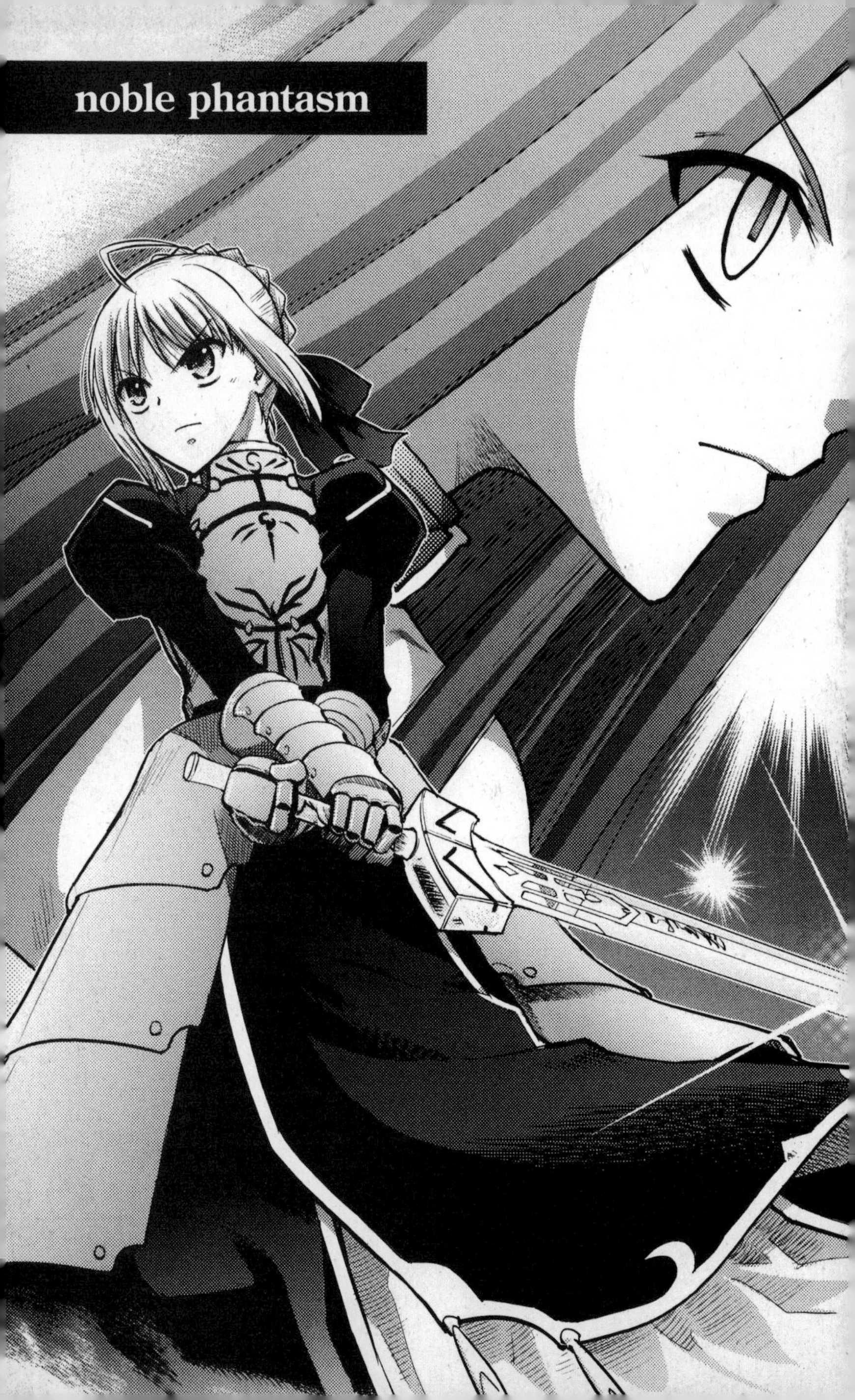
noble phantasm

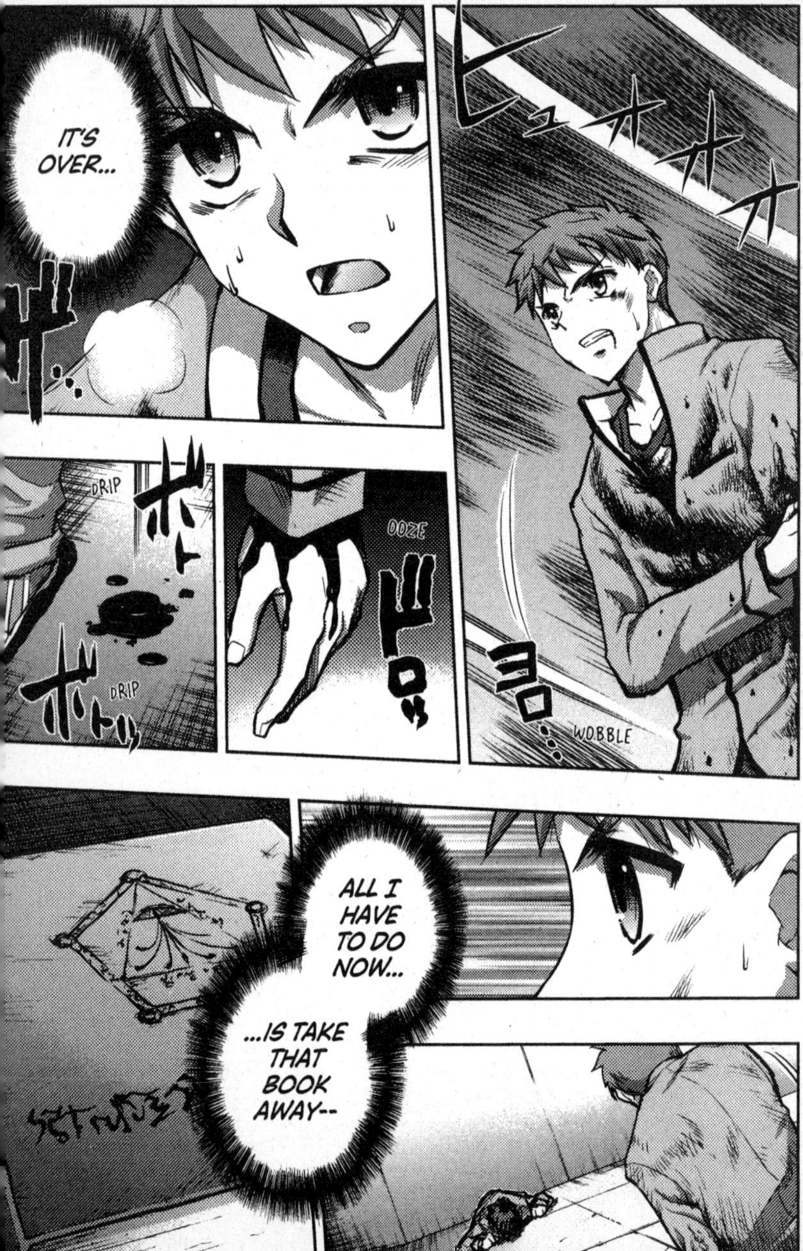
ヒュォォォォ
ヨロ...
WOBBLE
IT'S OVER...
OOZE
DRIP
DRIP
ALL I HAVE TO DO NOW...
...IS TAKE THAT BOOK AWAY--

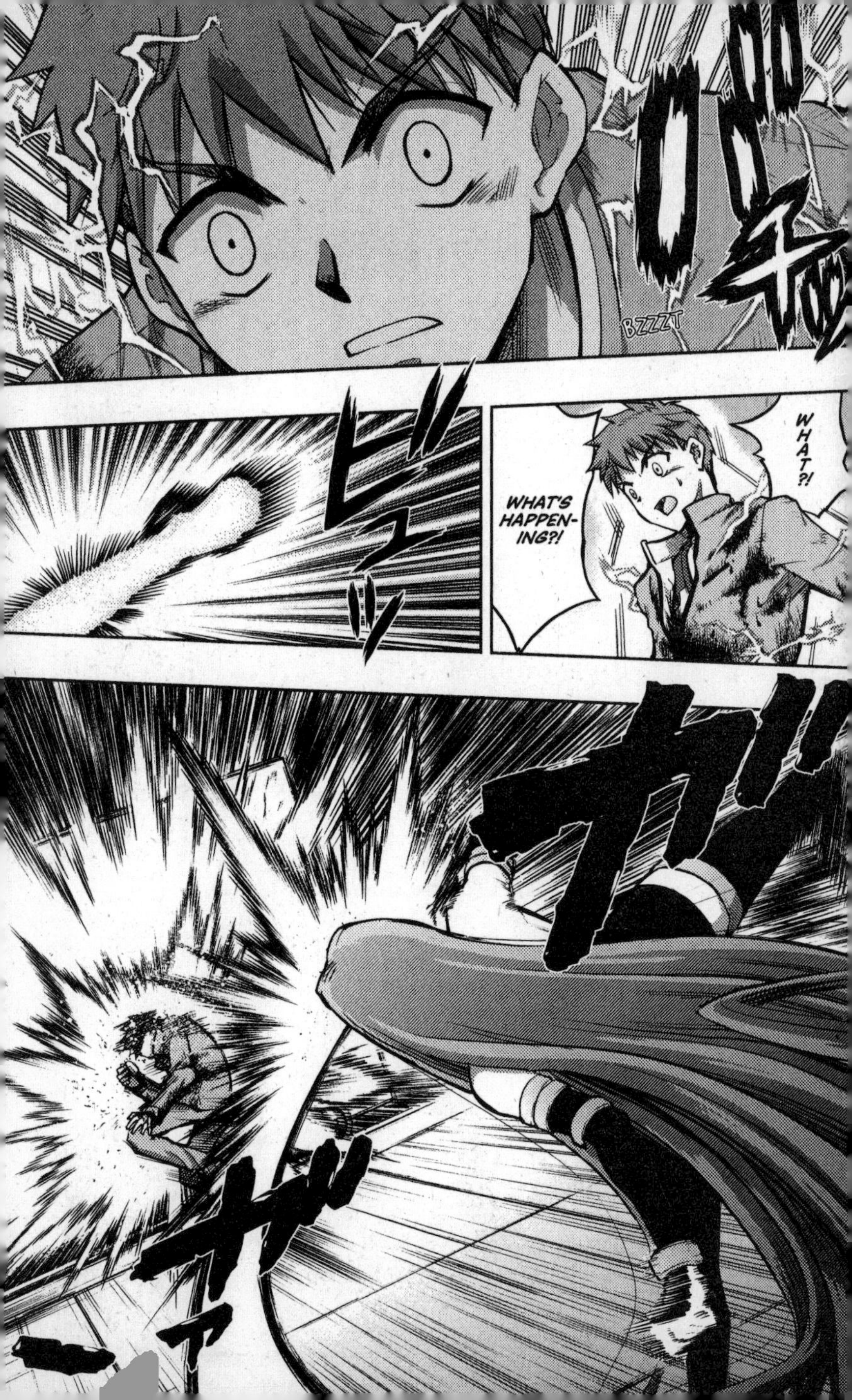
BZZZT
WHAT?!
WHAT'S HAPPENING?!

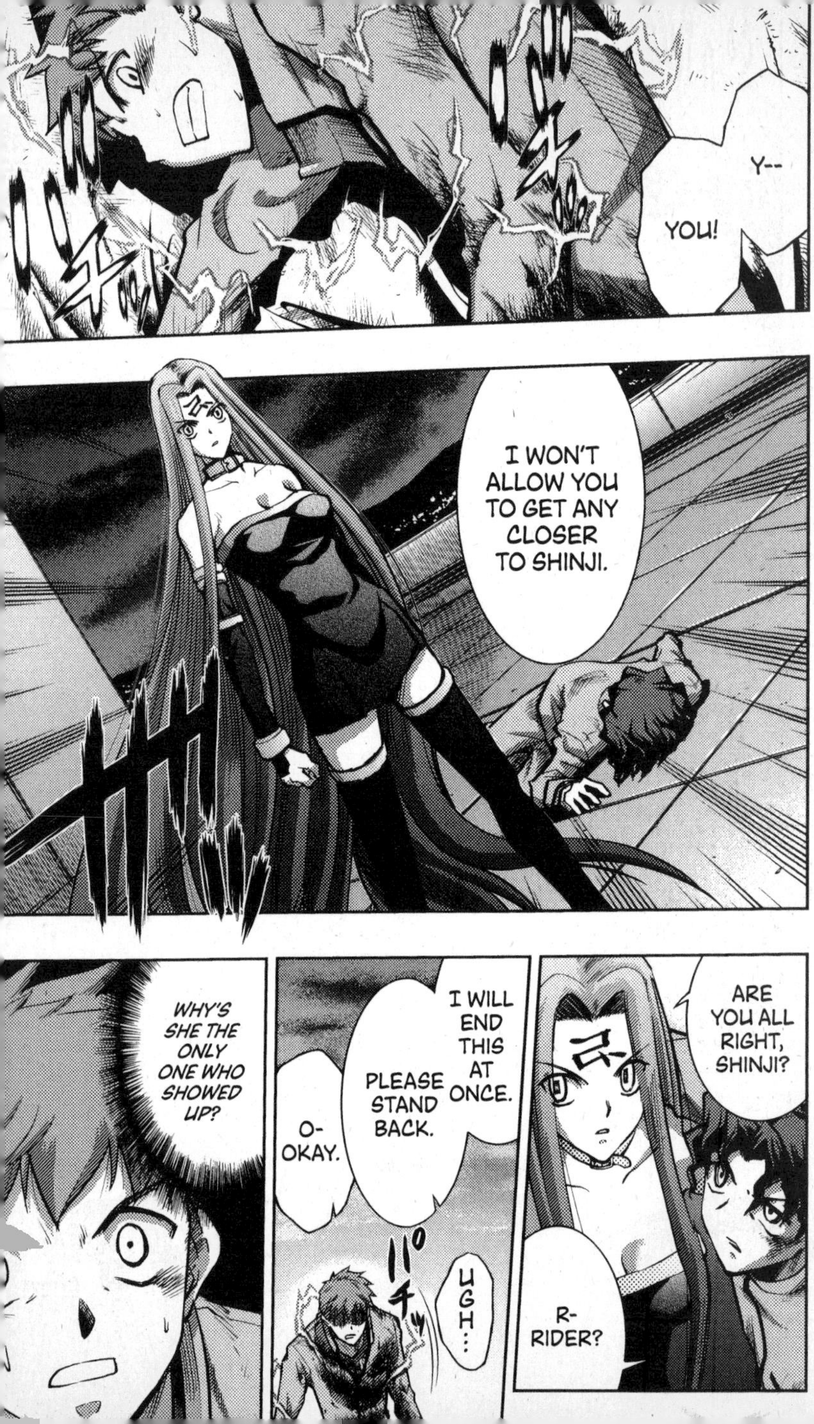
Y--
YOU!
I WON'T ALLOW YOU TO GET ANY CLOSER TO SHINJI.
ARE YOU ALL RIGHT, SHINJI?
R-RIDER?
I WILL END THIS AT ONCE.
PLEASE STAND BACK.
O-OKAY.
UGH...
WHY'S SHE THE ONLY ONE WHO SHOWED UP?

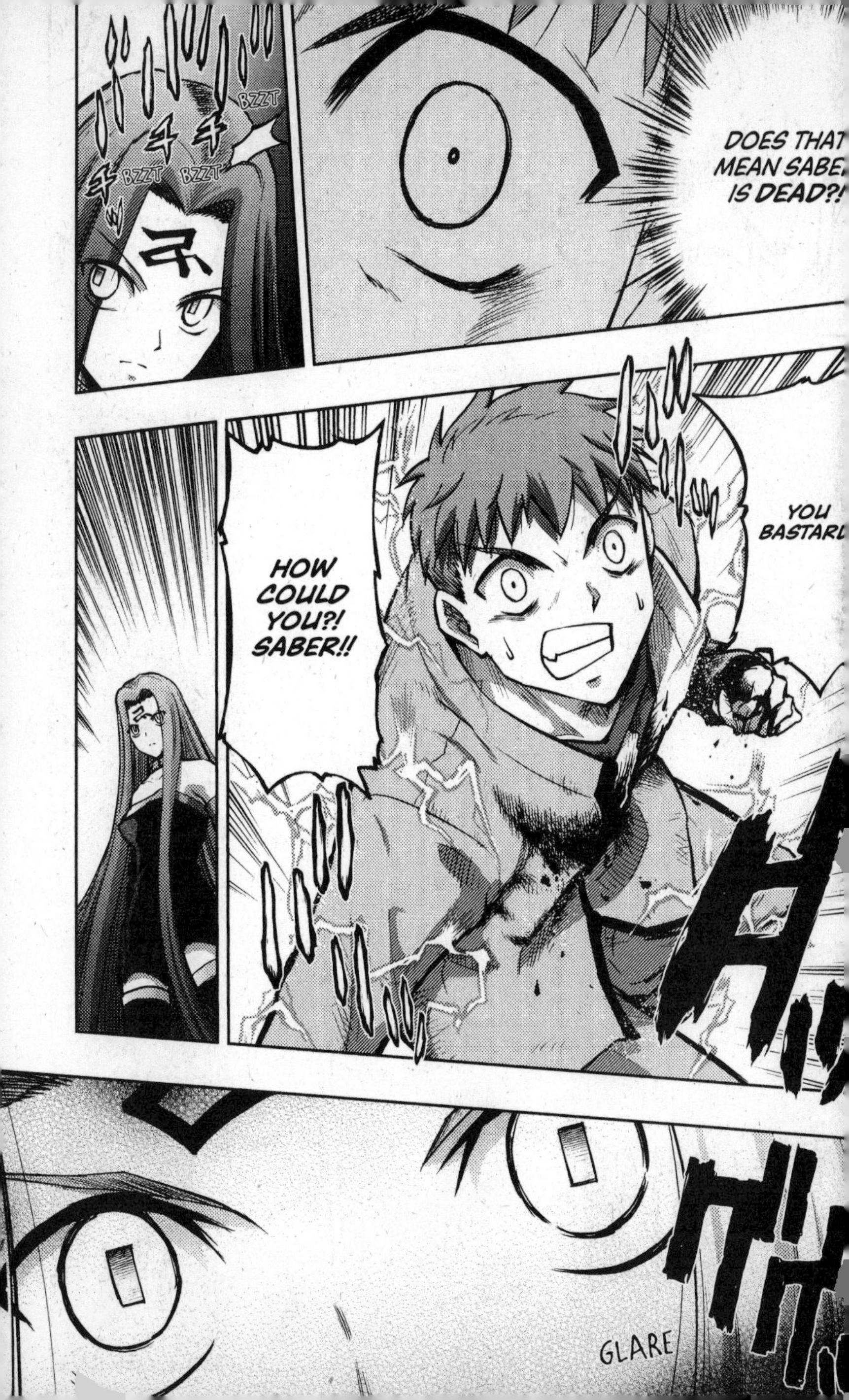
DOES THAT
MEAN SABE
IS DEAD?!
BZZT
BZZT
BZZT
YOU
BASTAR
HOW
COULD
YOU?!
SABER!!
GLARE

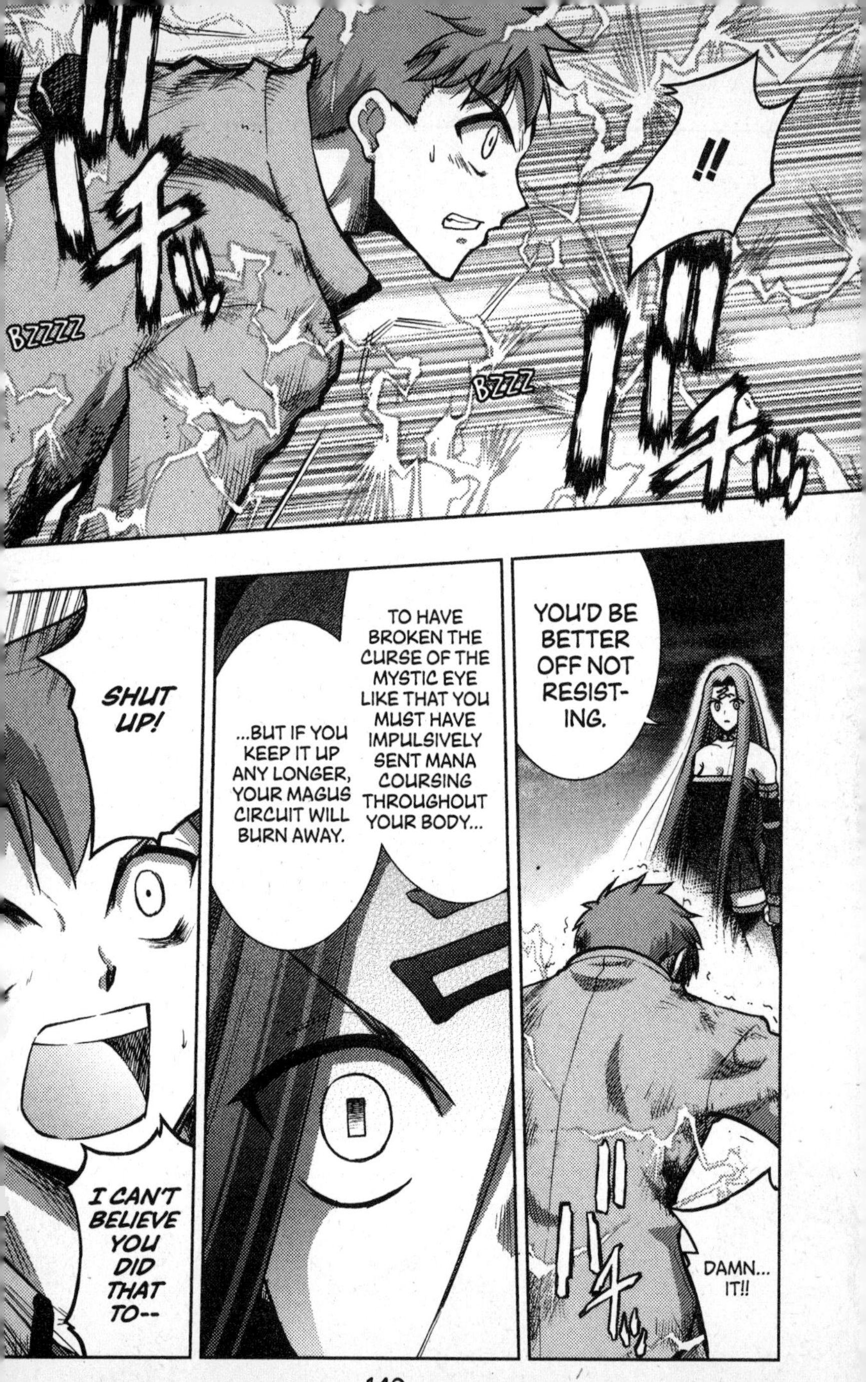
!!
BZZZ
BZZZZZ
YOU'D BE BETTER OFF NOT RESIST-ING.
DAMN... IT!!
TO HAVE BROKEN THE CURSE OF THE MYSTIC EYE LIKE THAT YOU MUST HAVE IMPULSIVELY SENT MANA COURSING THROUGHOUT YOUR BODY...
...BUT IF YOU KEEP IT UP ANY LONGER, YOUR MAGUS CIRCUIT WILL BURN AWAY.
SHUT UP!
I CAN'T BELIEVE YOU DID THAT TO--

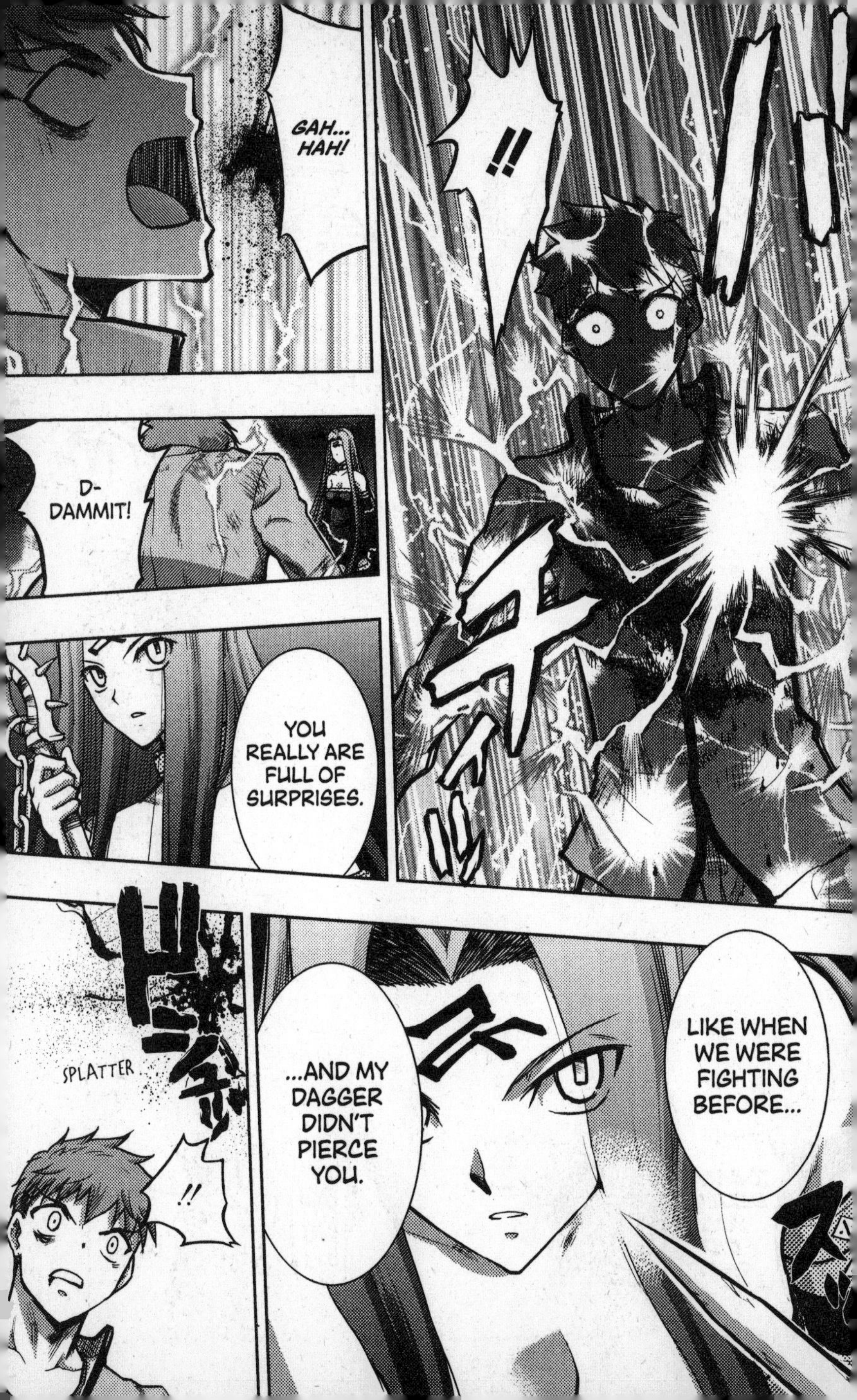
!!
GAH... HAH!
D-DAMMIT!
YOU REALLY ARE FULL OF SURPRISES.
LIKE WHEN WE WERE FIGHTING BEFORE...
...AND MY DAGGER DIDN'T PIERCE YOU.
SPLATTER
!!

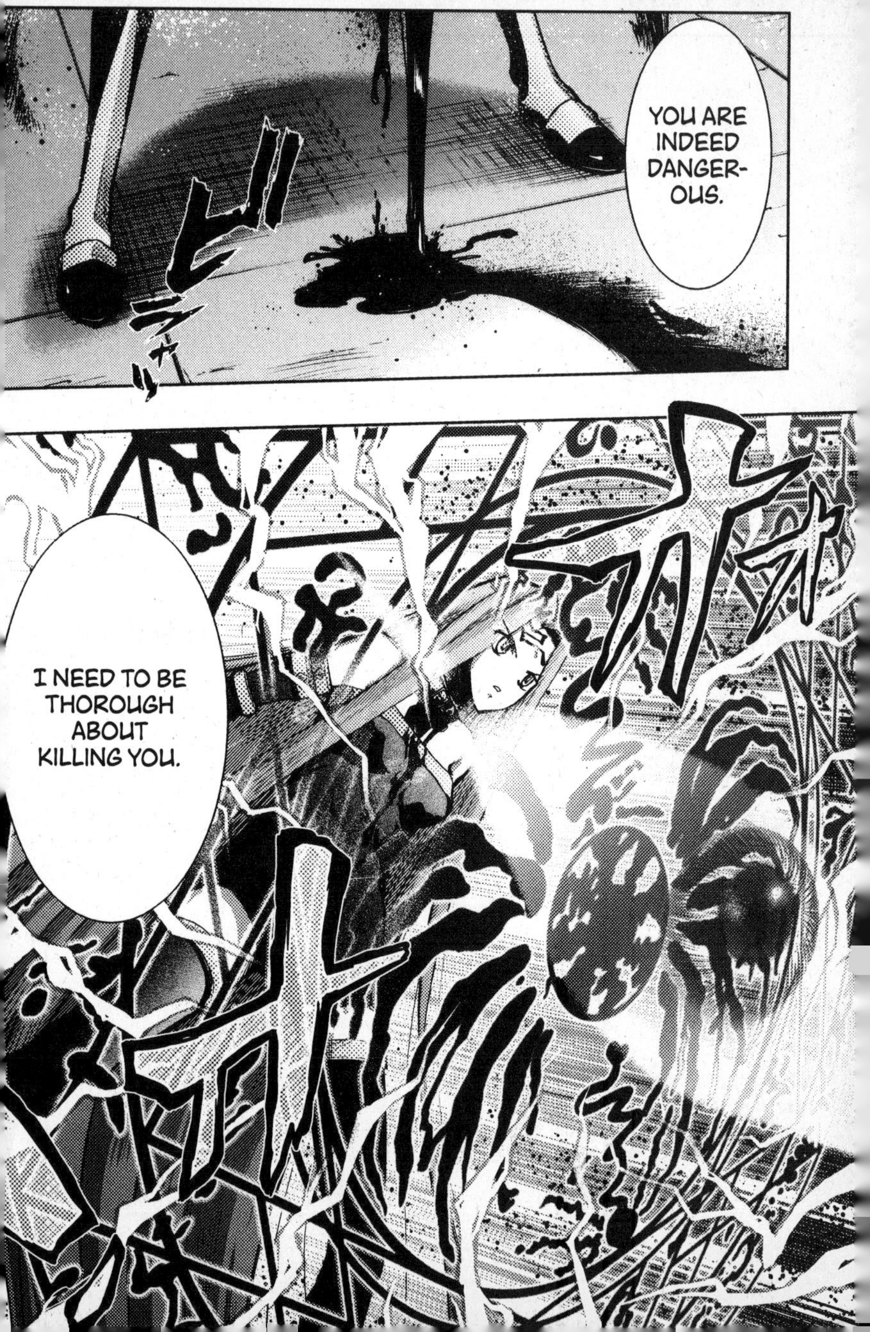
YOU ARE INDEED DANGER-OUS.
I NEED TO BE THOROUGH ABOUT KILLING YOU.

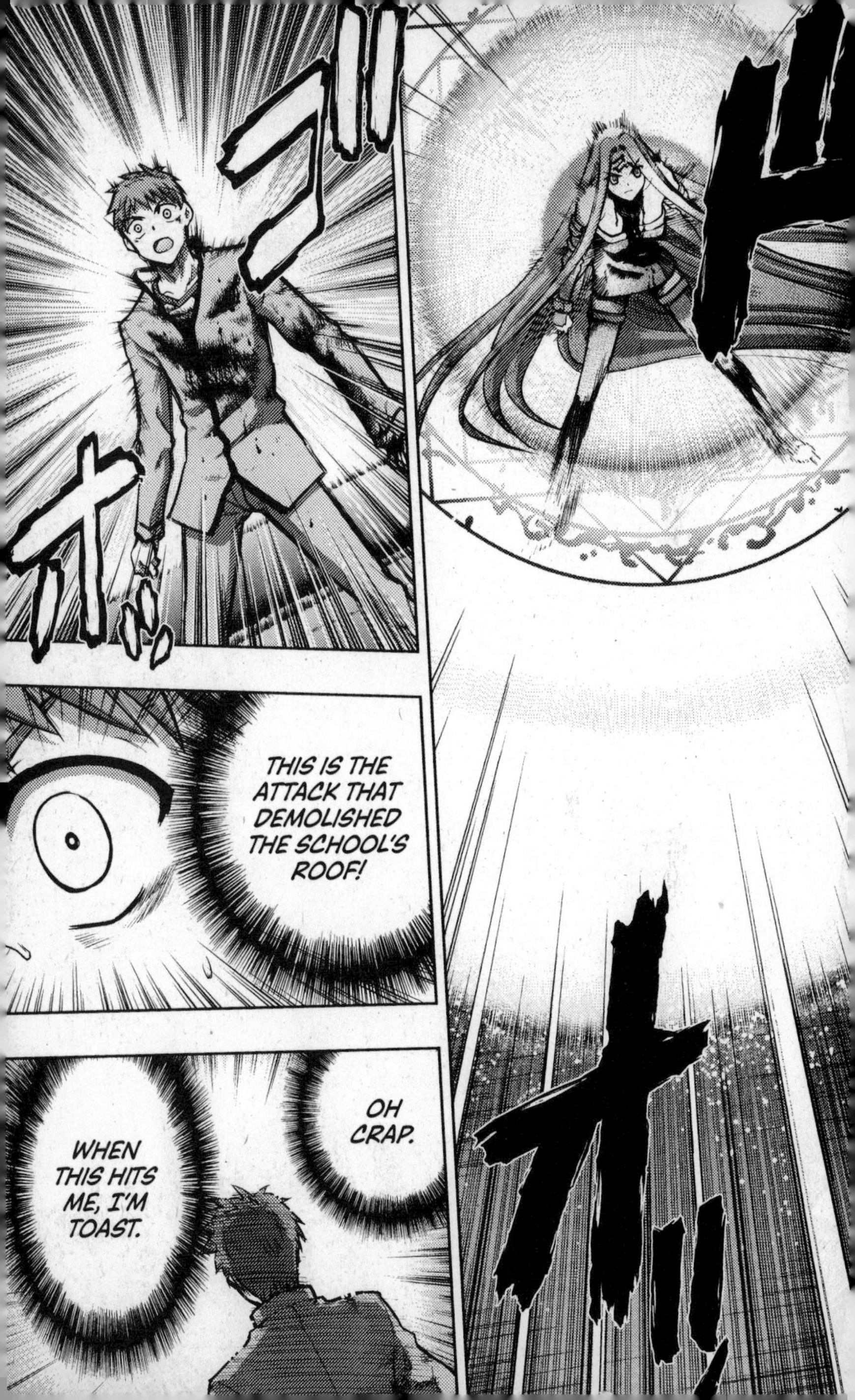
THIS IS THE ATTACK THAT DEMOLISHED THE SCHOOL'S ROOF!
OH CRAP.
WHEN THIS HITS ME, I'M TOAST.

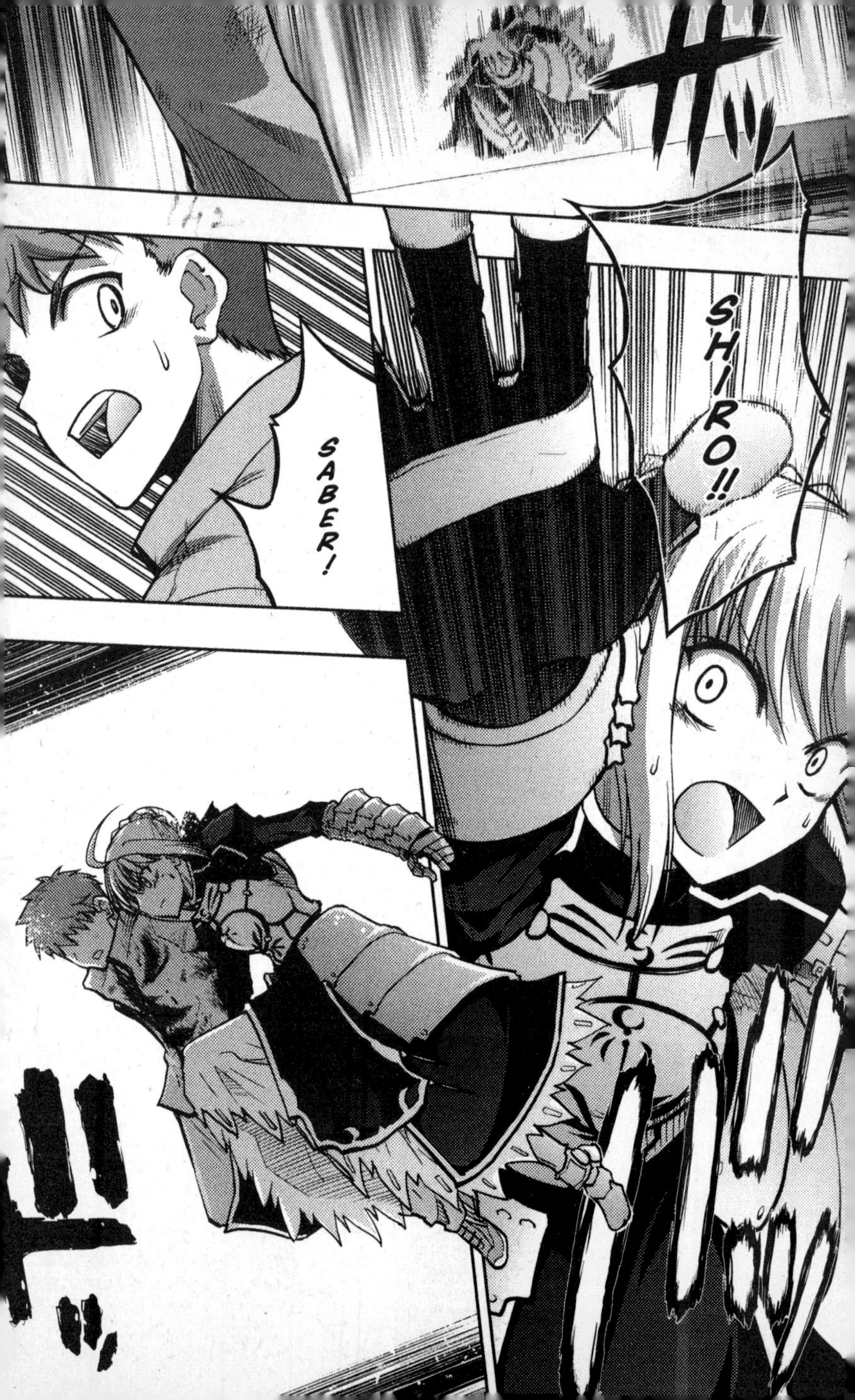
SHIRO!!
SABER!

I'M SORRY IT TOOK ME SO LONG, SHIRO!

THANK GOOD- NESS... YOU'RE ALIVE, SABER.

LEAVE THE REST TO ME!

I WILL KILL RIDER AT ONCE--

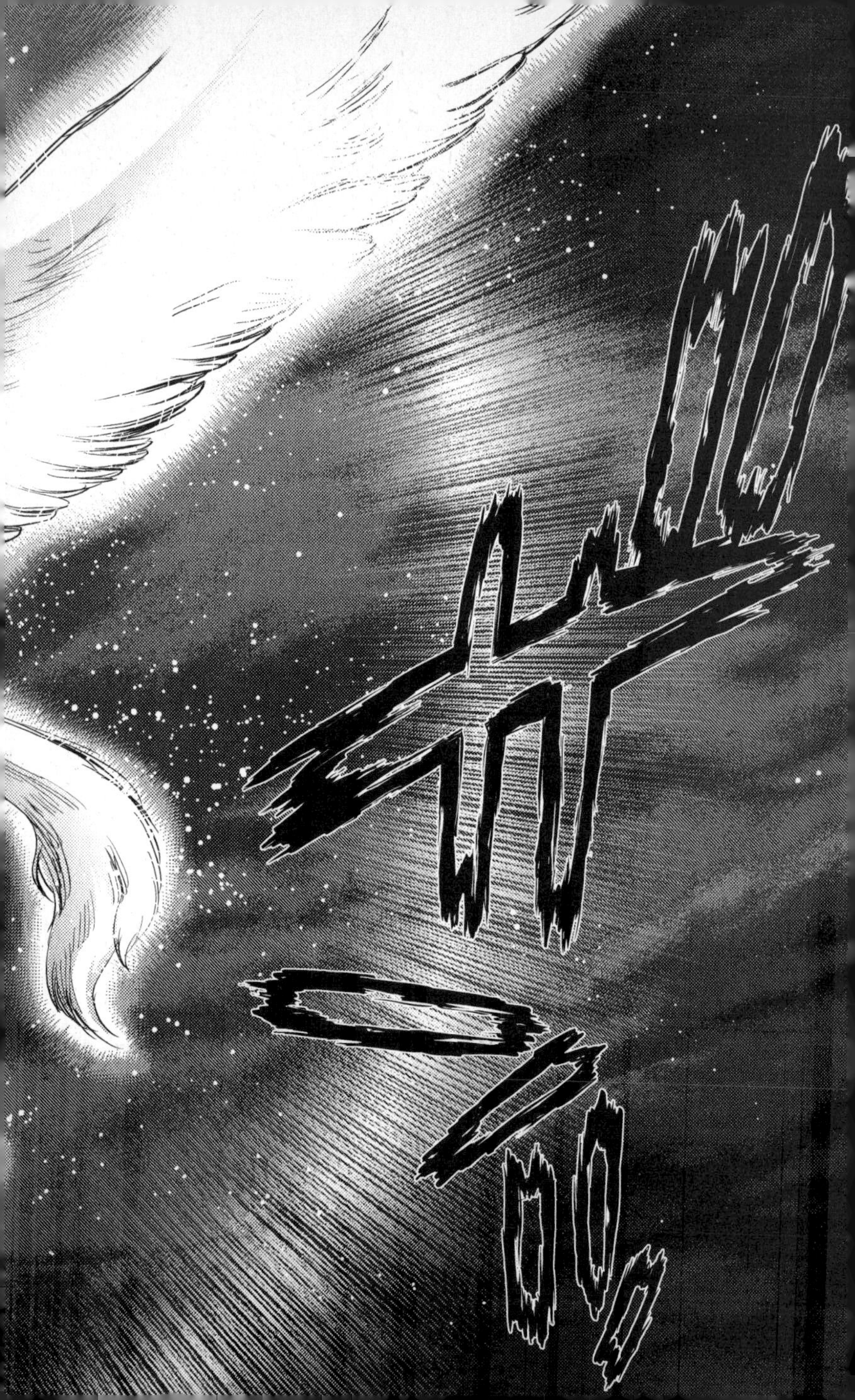

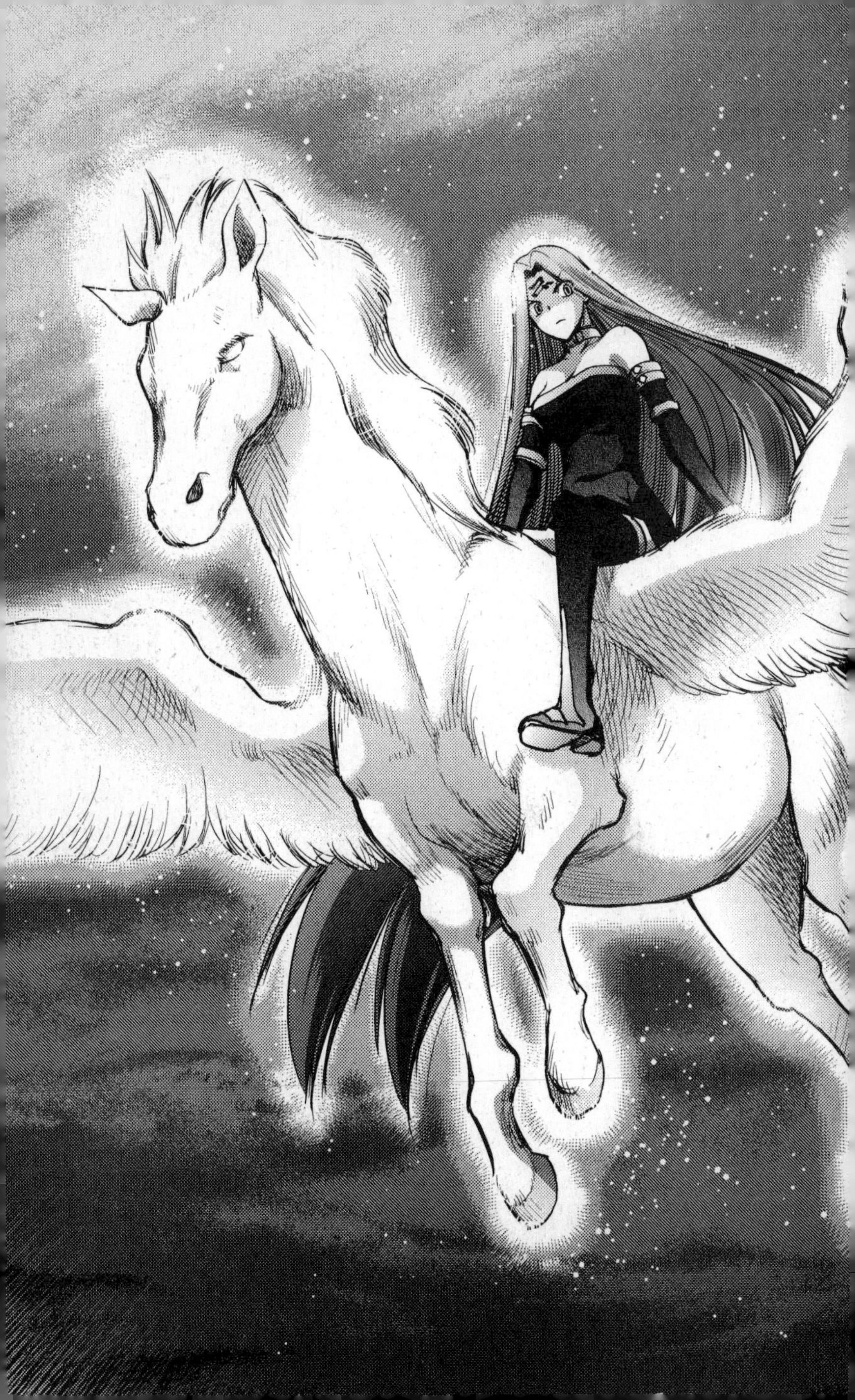

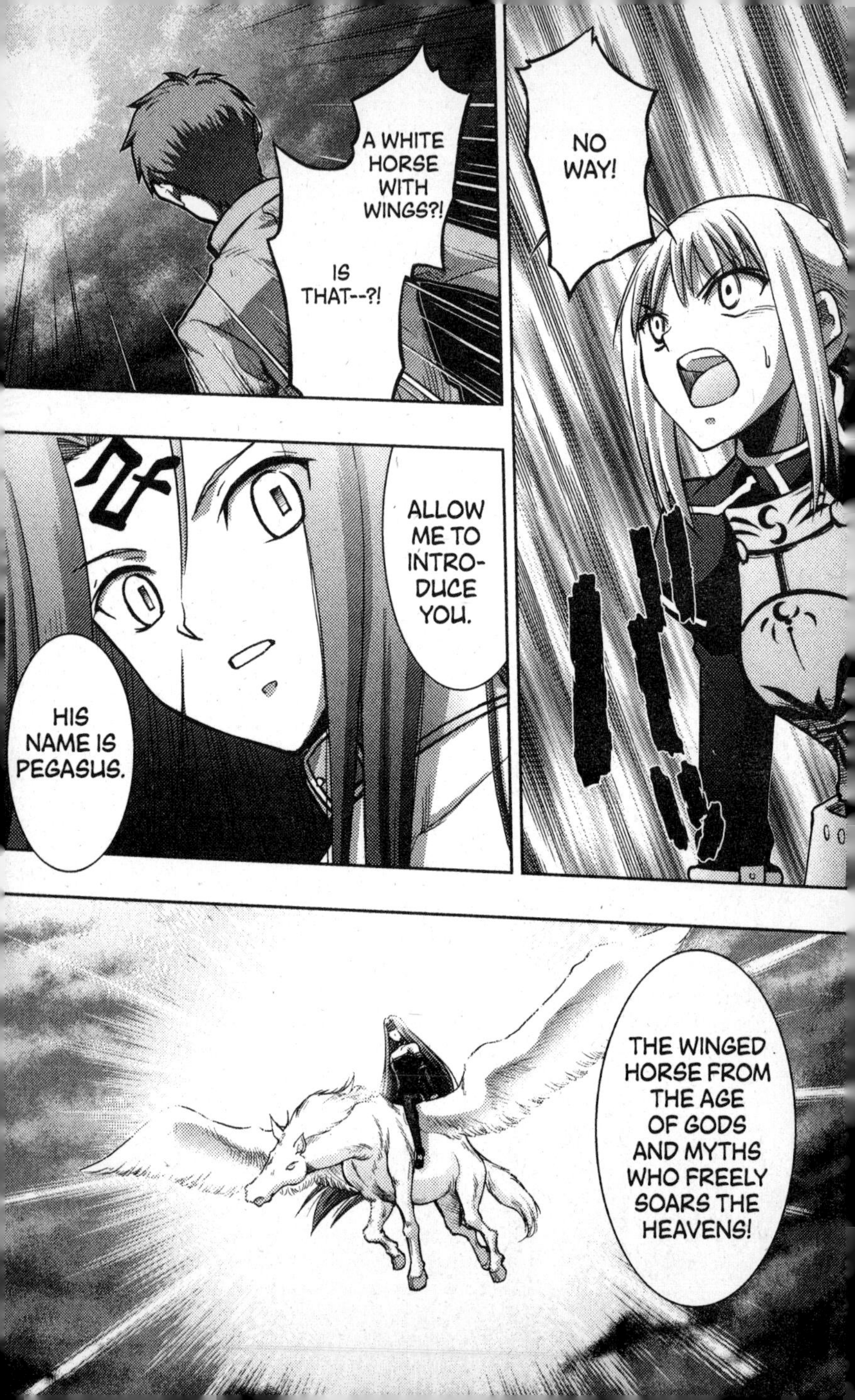
NO WAY!
A WHITE HORSE WITH WINGS?!
IS THAT--?!
ALLOW ME TO INTRODUCE YOU.
HIS NAME IS PEGASUS.
THE WINGED HORSE FROM THE AGE OF GODS AND MYTHS WHO FREELY SOARS THE HEAVENS!

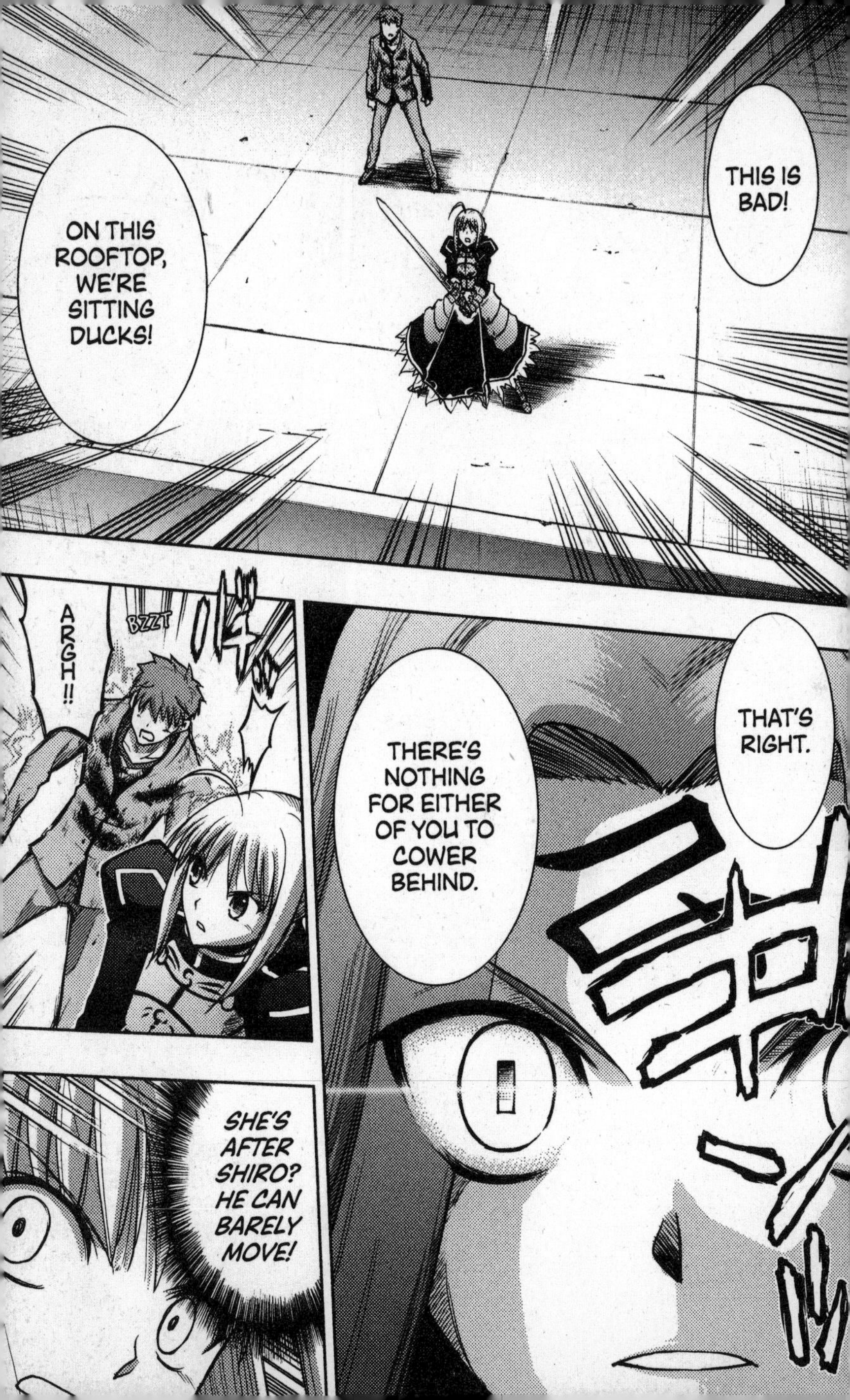
THIS IS BAD!
ON THIS ROOFTOP, WE'RE SITTING DUCKS!
THAT'S RIGHT.
THERE'S NOTHING FOR EITHER OF YOU TO COWER BEHIND.
BZZT
ARGH!!
SHE'S AFTER SHIRO? HE CAN BARELY MOVE!

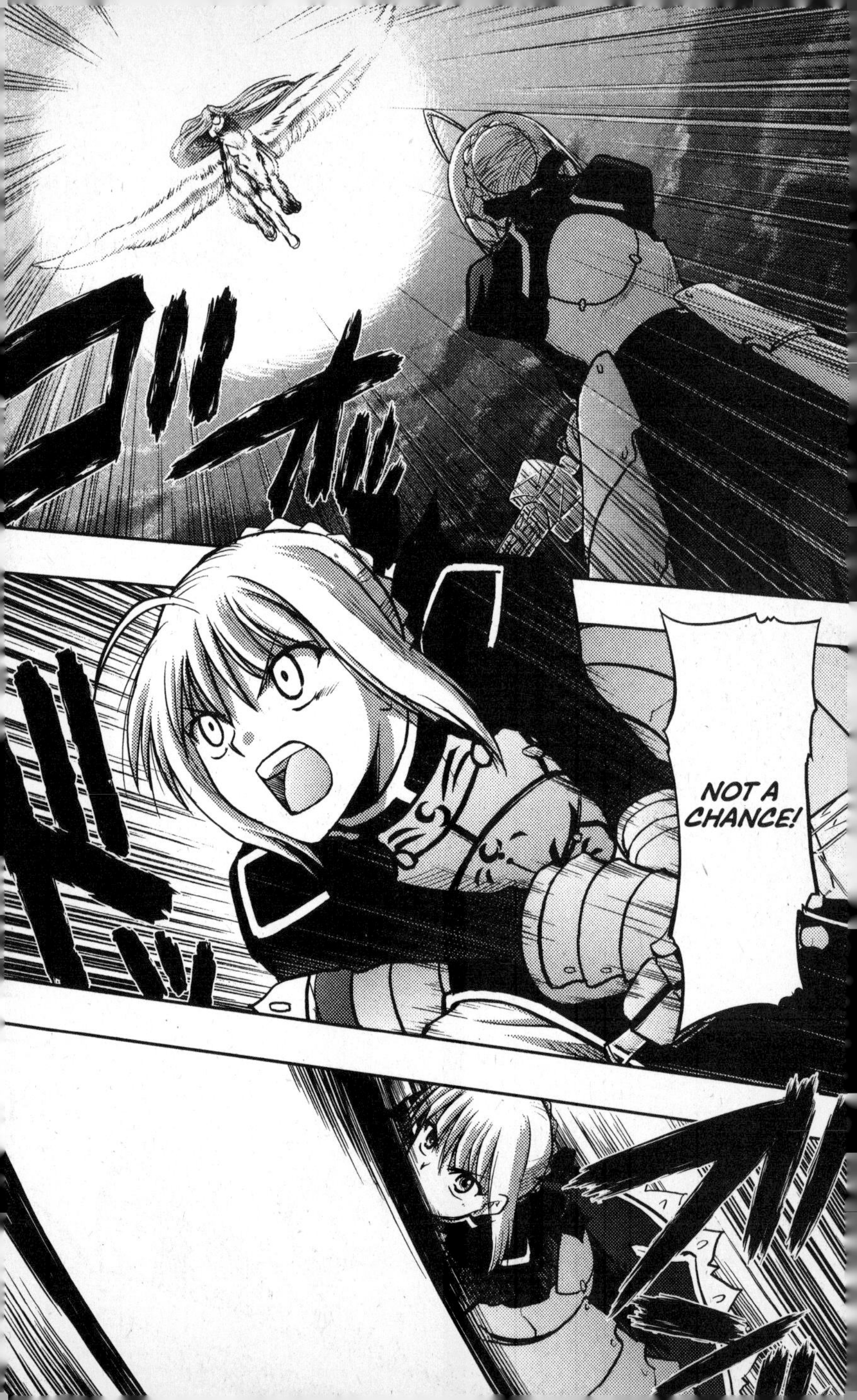
NOT A CHANCE!

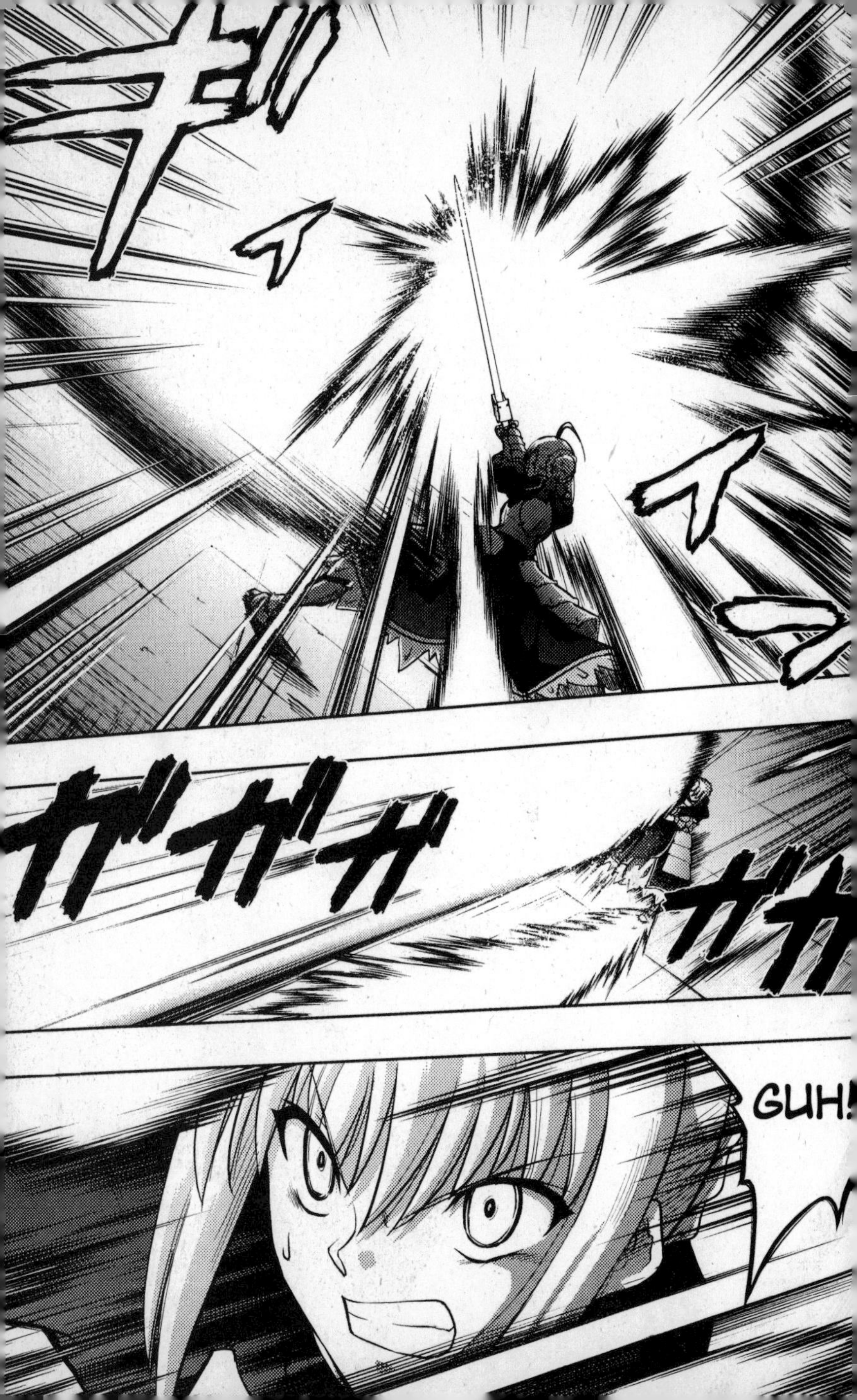
ギィィ
ガガガ
ガガ
GUH!

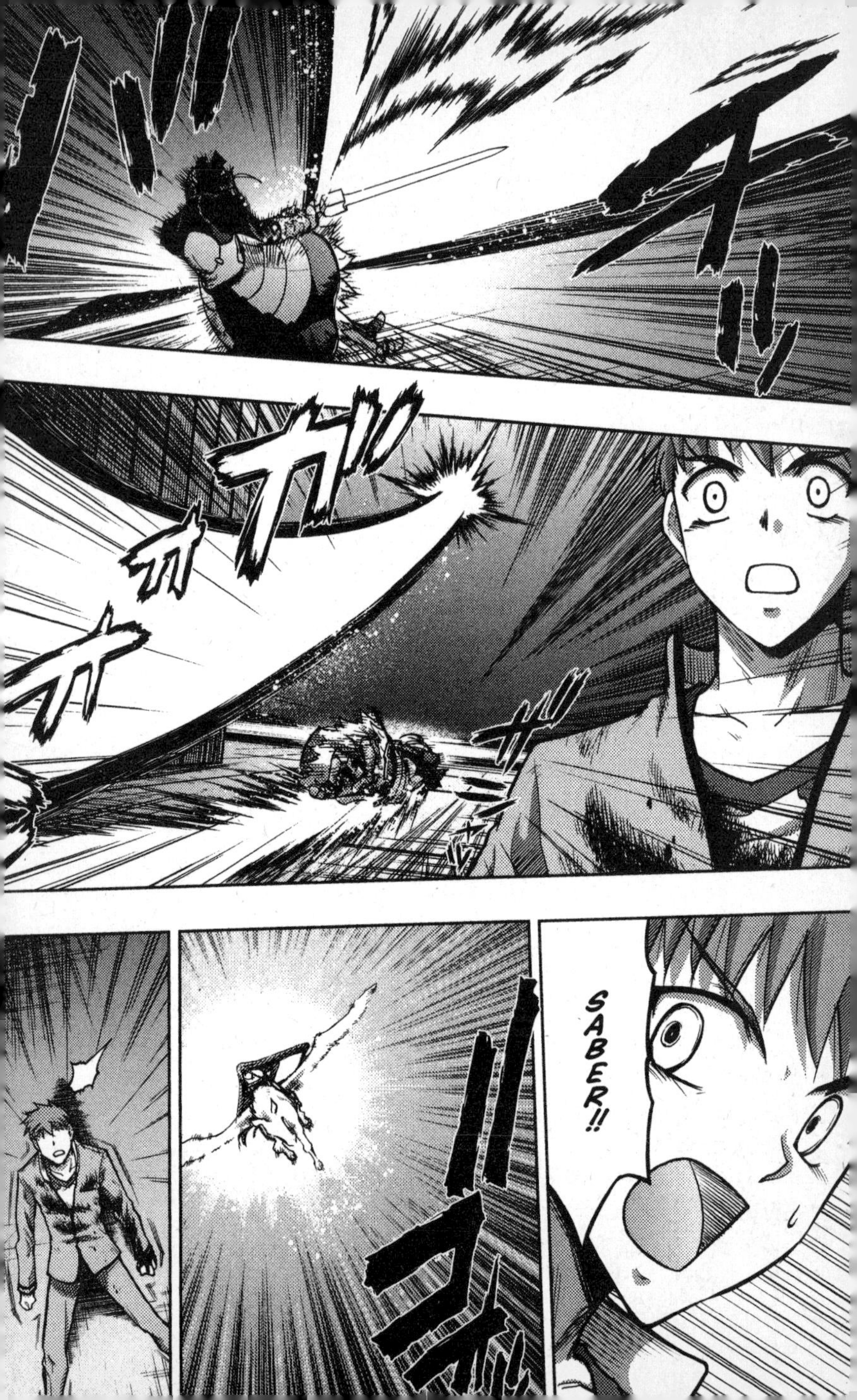
SABER!!

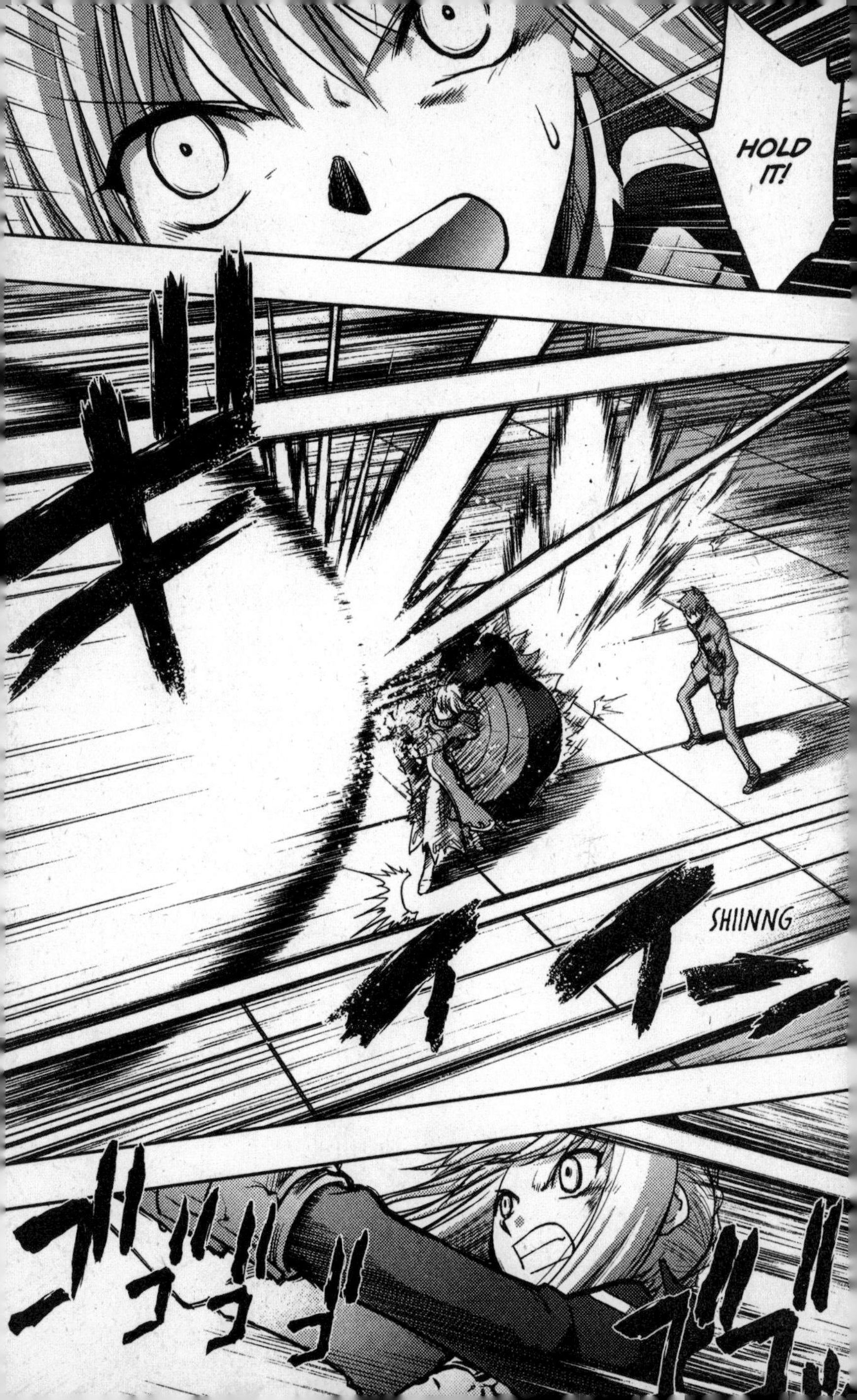
HOLD IT!
SHIINNG

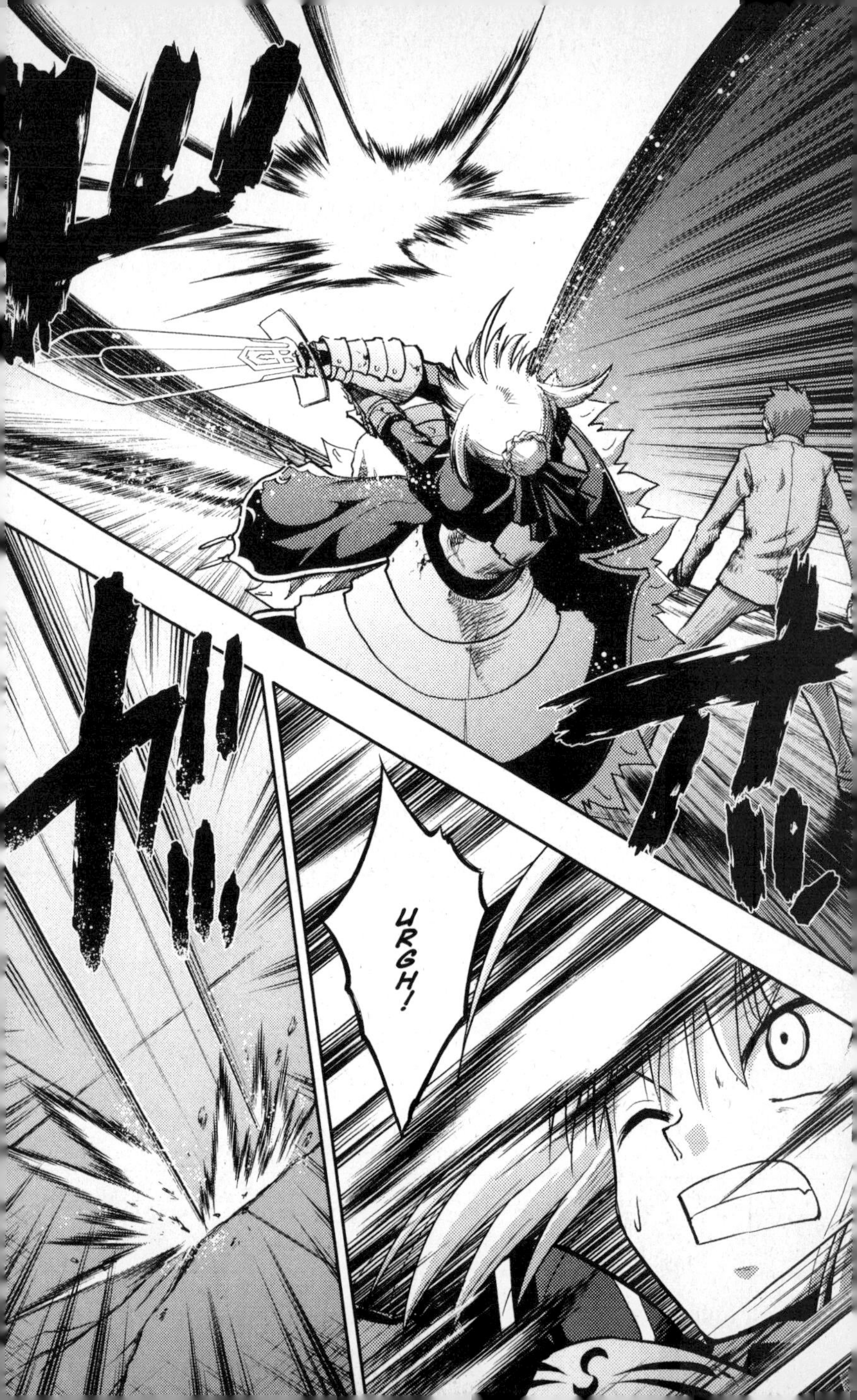
URGH!

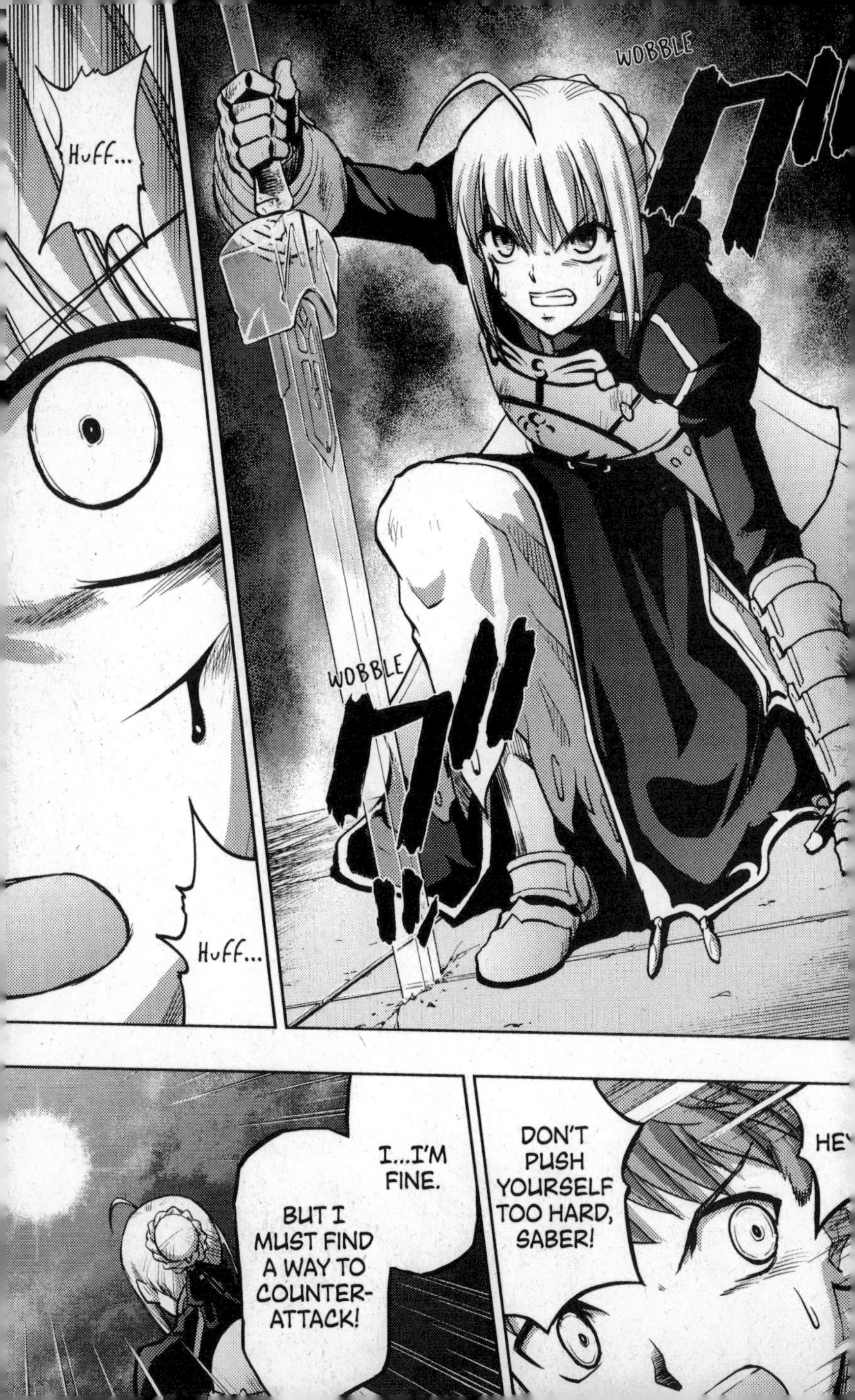
WOBBLE
WOBBLE
Huff...
Huff...
DON'T PUSH YOURSELF TOO HARD, SABER!
I...I'M FINE.
BUT I MUST FIND A WAY TO COUNTER-ATTACK!

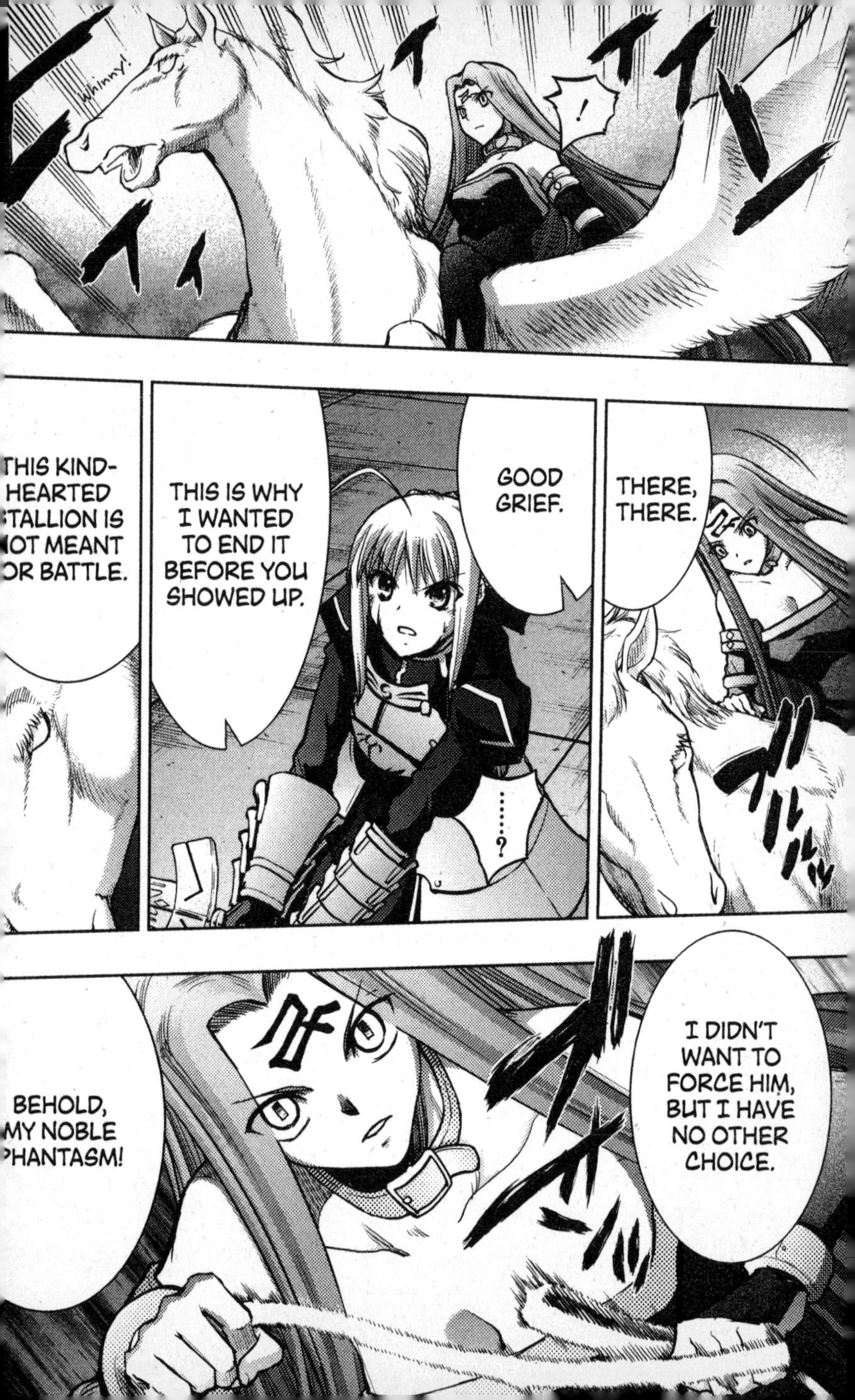
Whinny!
!
THERE, THERE.
GOOD GRIEF.
THIS IS WHY I WANTED TO END IT BEFORE YOU SHOWED UP.
......?
THIS KIND-HEARTED STALLION IS NOT MEANT FOR BATTLE.
I DIDN'T WANT TO FORCE HIM, BUT I HAVE NO OTHER CHOICE.
BEHOLD, MY NOBLE PHANTASM!

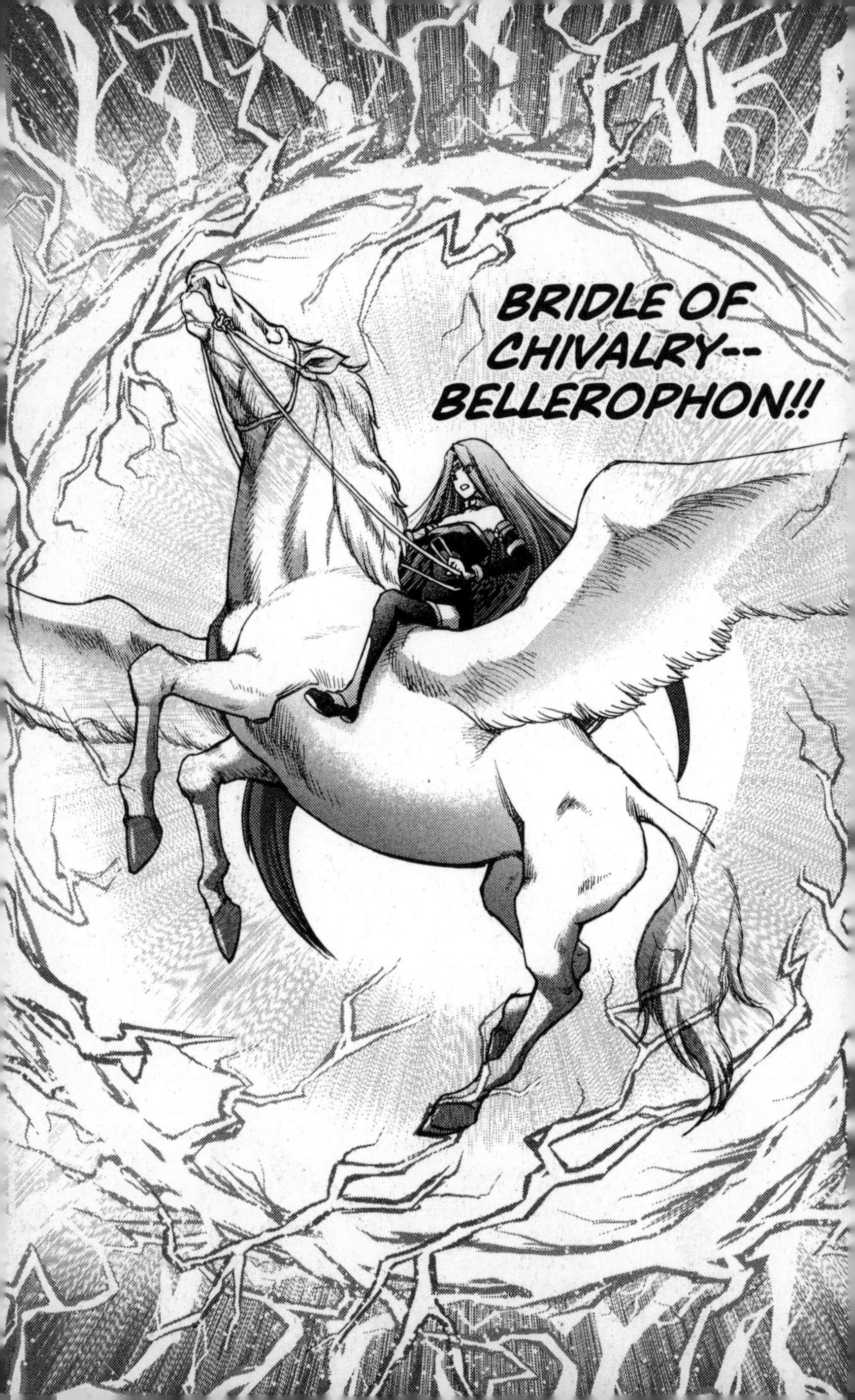
BRIDLE OF CHIVALRY--
BELLEROPHON!!

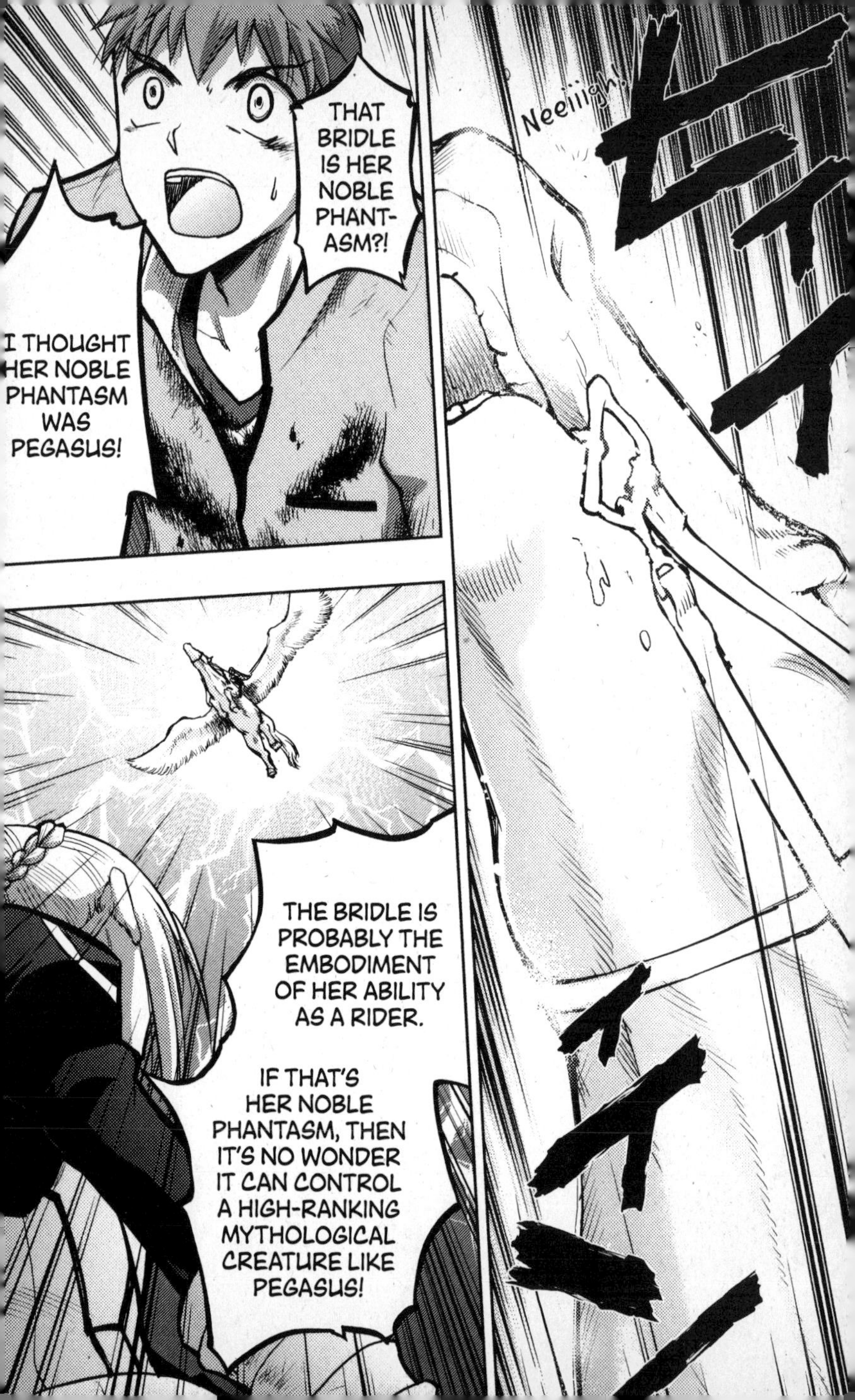
Neeiiigh!
THAT BRIDLE IS HER NOBLE PHANT-ASM?!
I THOUGHT HER NOBLE PHANTASM WAS PEGASUS!
THE BRIDLE IS PROBABLY THE EMBODIMENT OF HER ABILITY AS A RIDER.
IF THAT'S HER NOBLE PHANTASM, THEN IT'S NO WONDER IT CAN CONTROL A HIGH-RANKING MYTHOLOGICAL CREATURE LIKE PEGASUS!

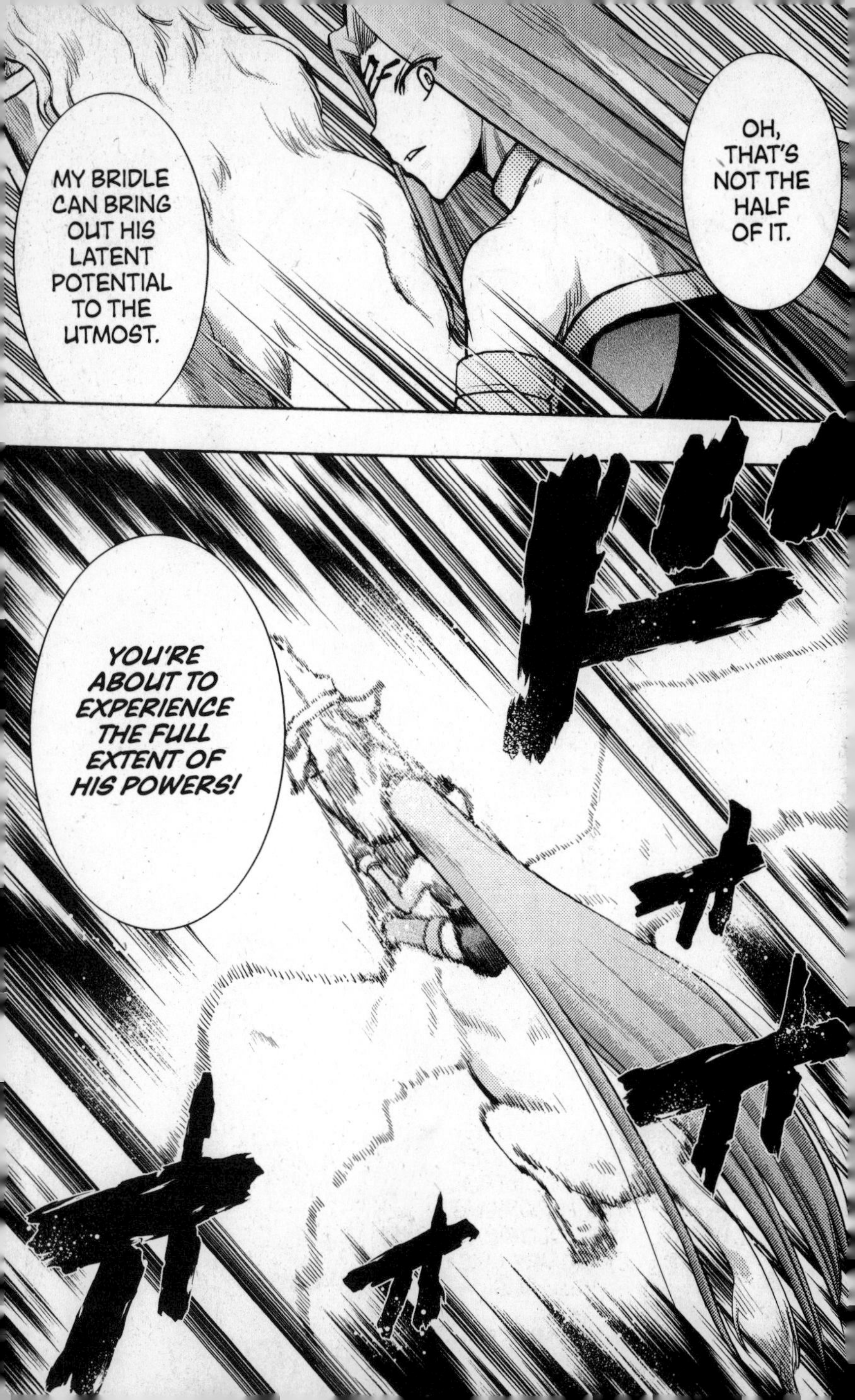
OH, THAT'S NOT THE HALF OF IT.
MY BRIDLE CAN BRING OUT HIS LATENT POTENTIAL TO THE UTMOST.
YOU'RE ABOUT TO EXPERIENCE THE FULL EXTENT OF HIS POWERS!

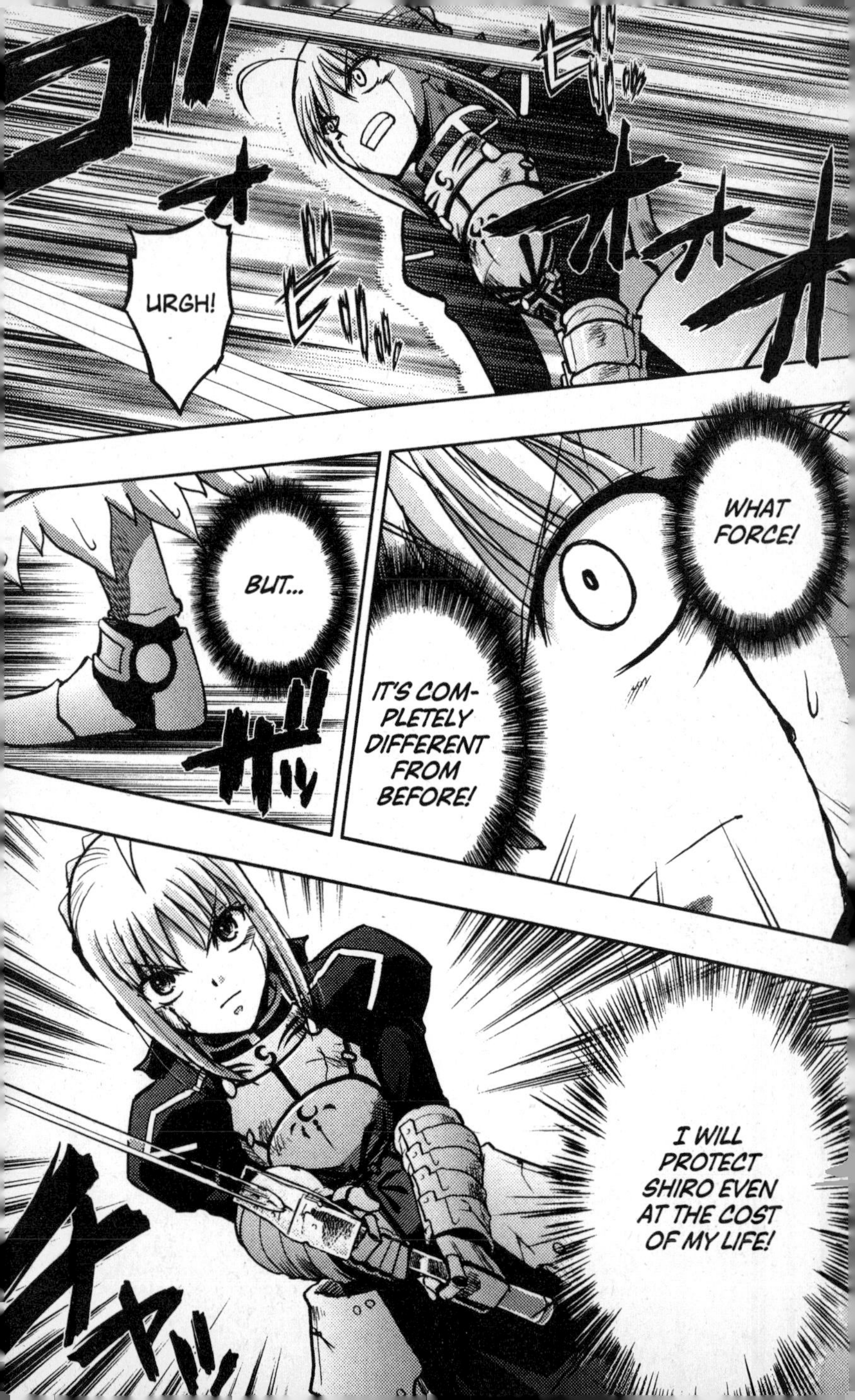
URGH!
WHAT FORCE!
IT'S COMPLETELY DIFFERENT FROM BEFORE!
BUT...
I WILL PROTECT SHIRO EVEN AT THE COST OF MY LIFE!

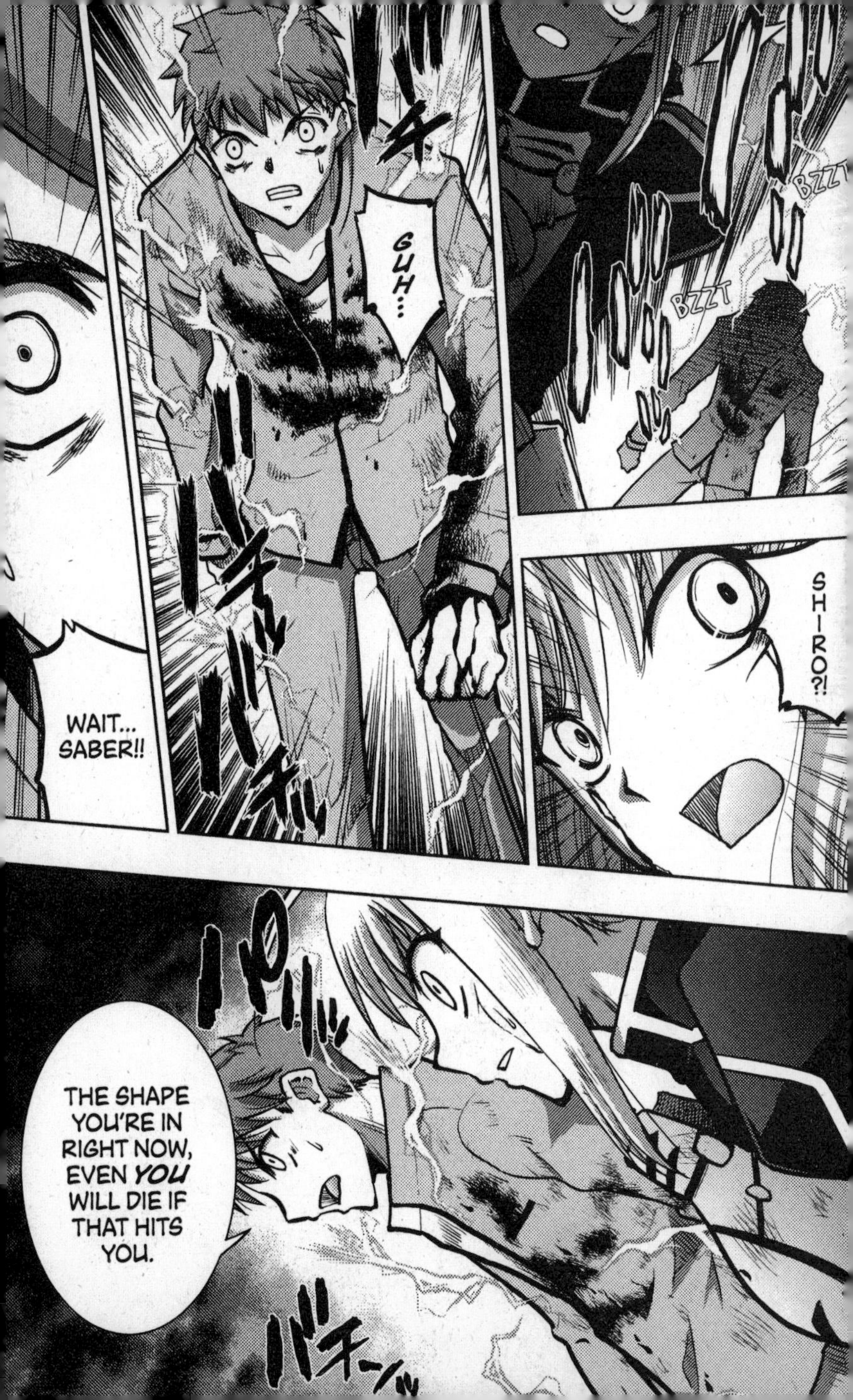
BZZT
BZZT
SHIRO?!
GUH...
WAIT... SABER!!
THE SHAPE YOU'RE IN RIGHT NOW, EVEN *YOU* WILL DIE IF THAT HITS YOU.

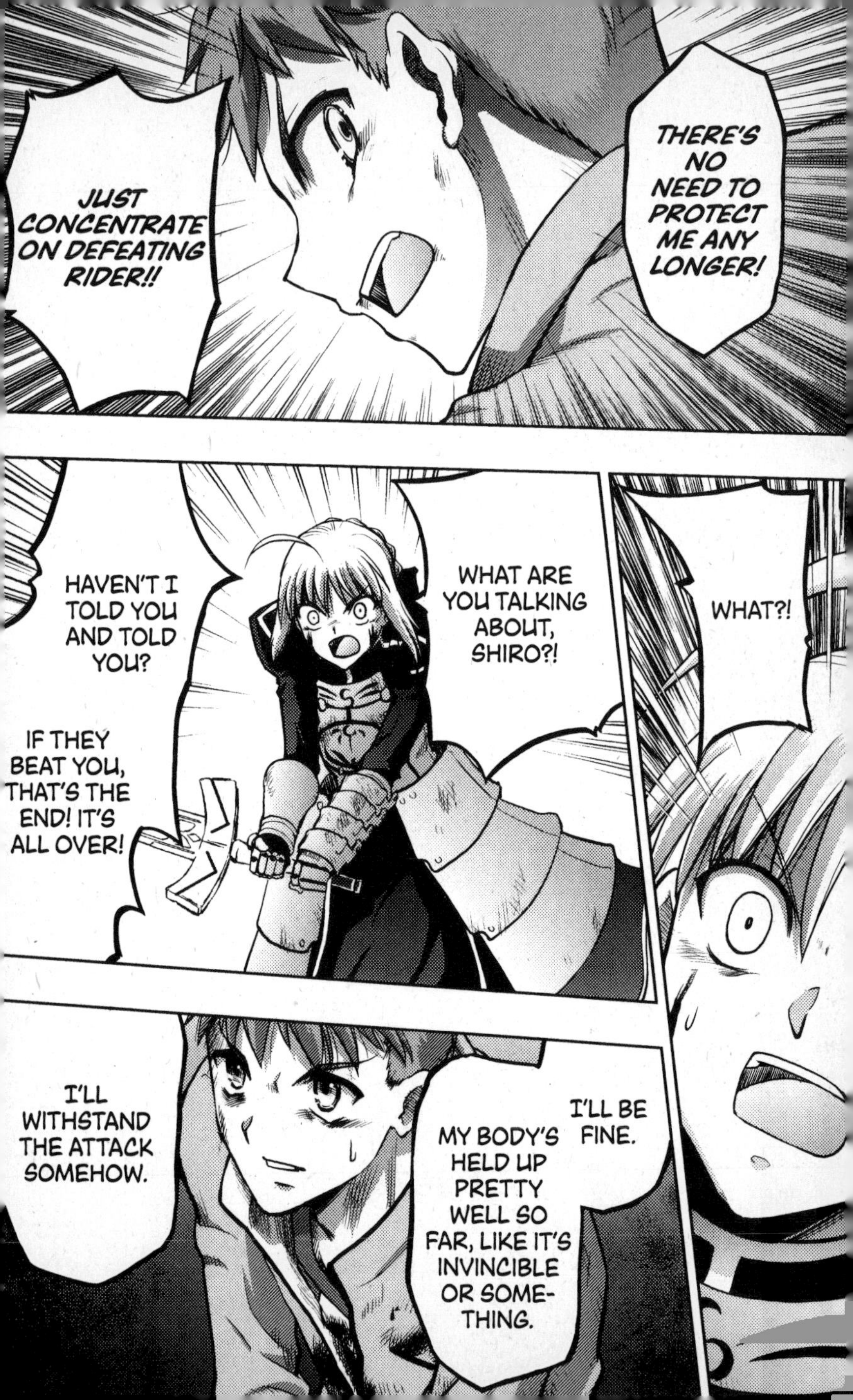
THERE'S NO NEED TO PROTECT ME ANY LONGER!
JUST CONCENTRATE ON DEFEATING RIDER!!
WHAT?!
WHAT ARE YOU TALKING ABOUT, SHIRO?!
HAVEN'T I TOLD YOU AND TOLD YOU?
IF THEY BEAT YOU, THAT'S THE END! IT'S ALL OVER!
I'LL BE FINE.
MY BODY'S HELD UP PRETTY WELL SO FAR, LIKE IT'S INVINCIBLE OR SOME-THING.
I'LL WITHSTAND THE ATTACK SOMEHOW.

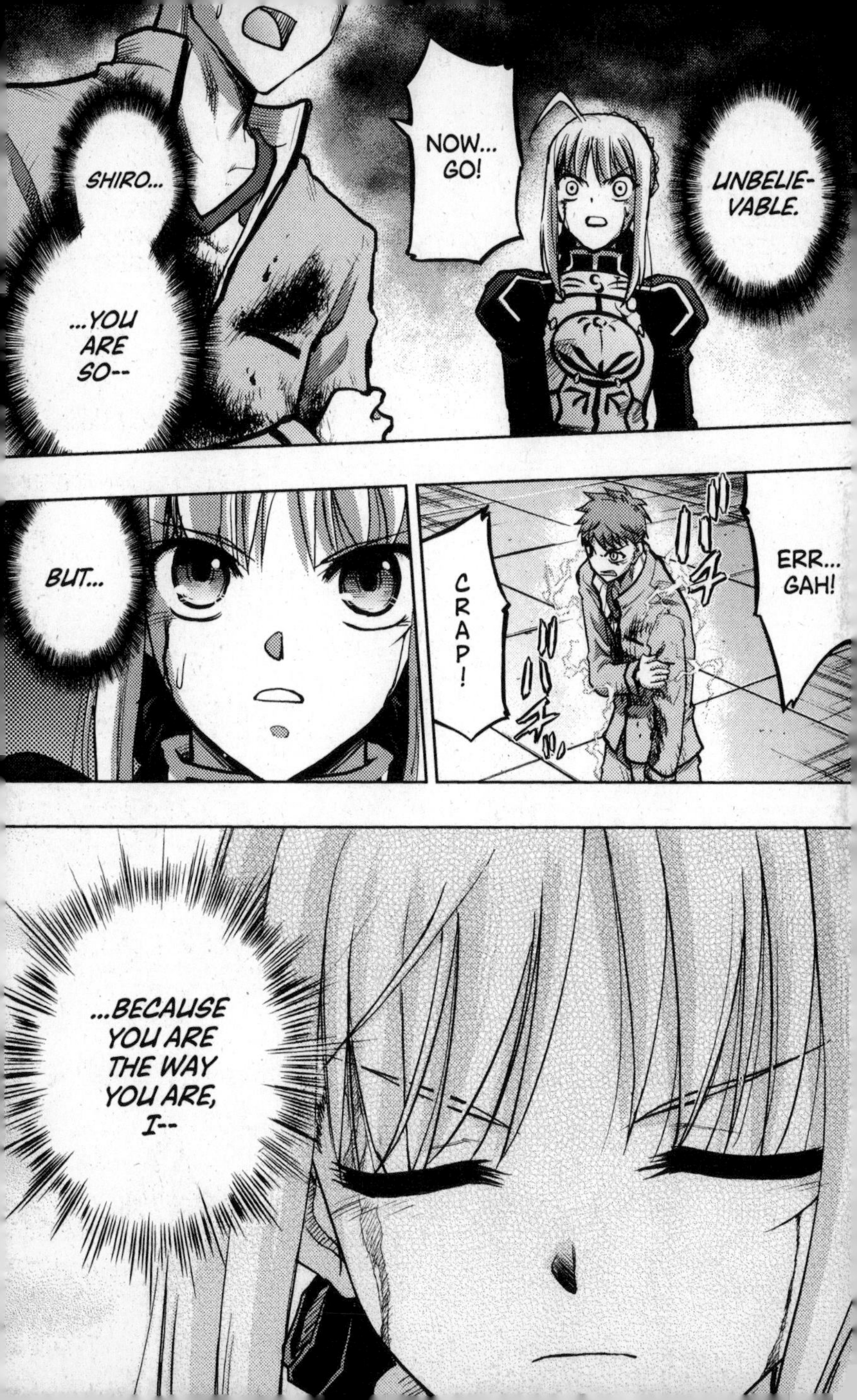
UNBELIE-VABLE.
NOW... GO!
SHIRO...
...YOU ARE SO--
ERR... GAH!
CRAP!
BUT...
...BECAUSE YOU ARE THE WAY YOU ARE, I--

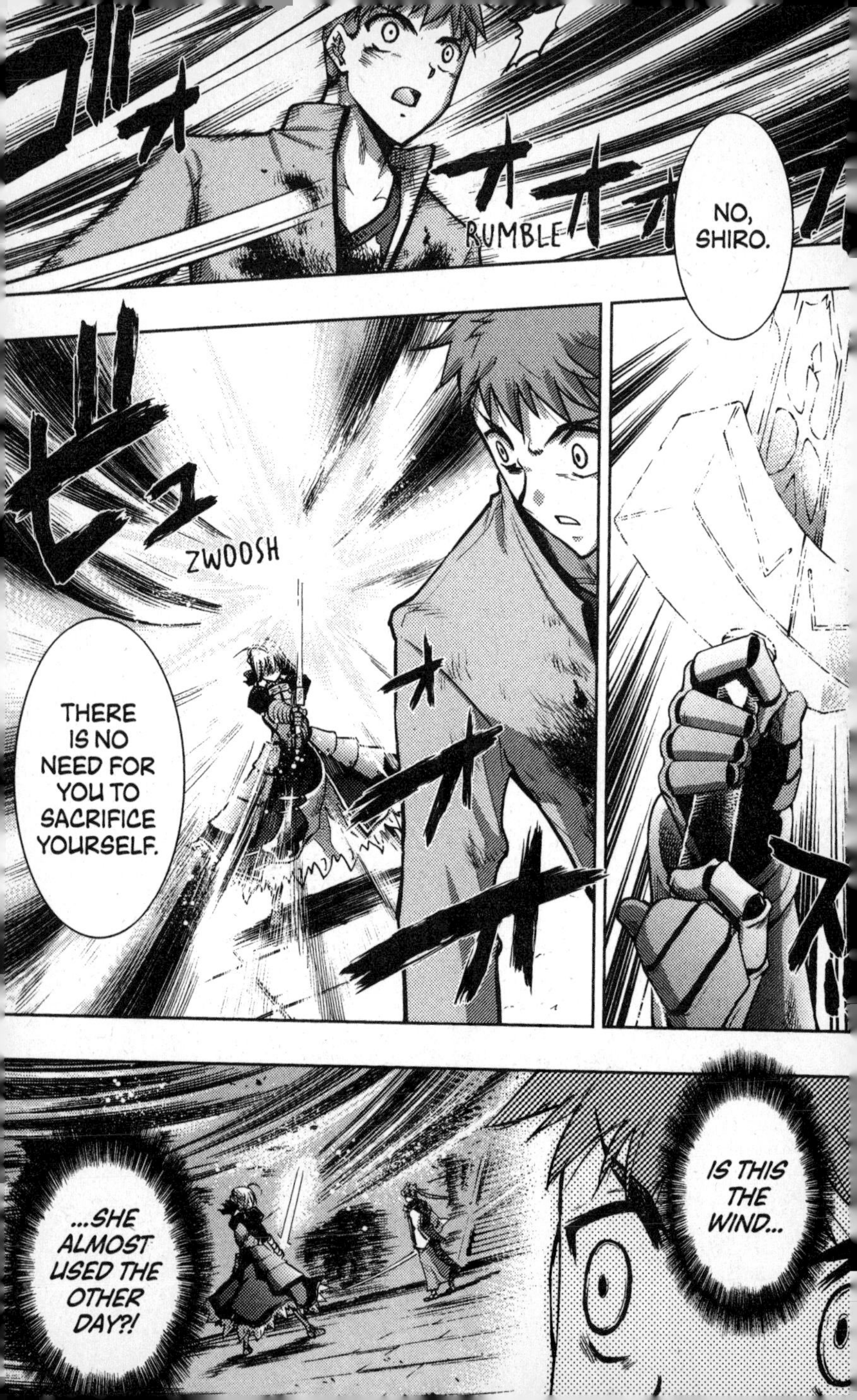
RUMBLE
NO, SHIRO.
ZWOOSH
THERE IS NO NEED FOR YOU TO SACRIFICE YOURSELF.
IS THIS THE WIND...
...SHE ALMOST USED THE OTHER DAY?!

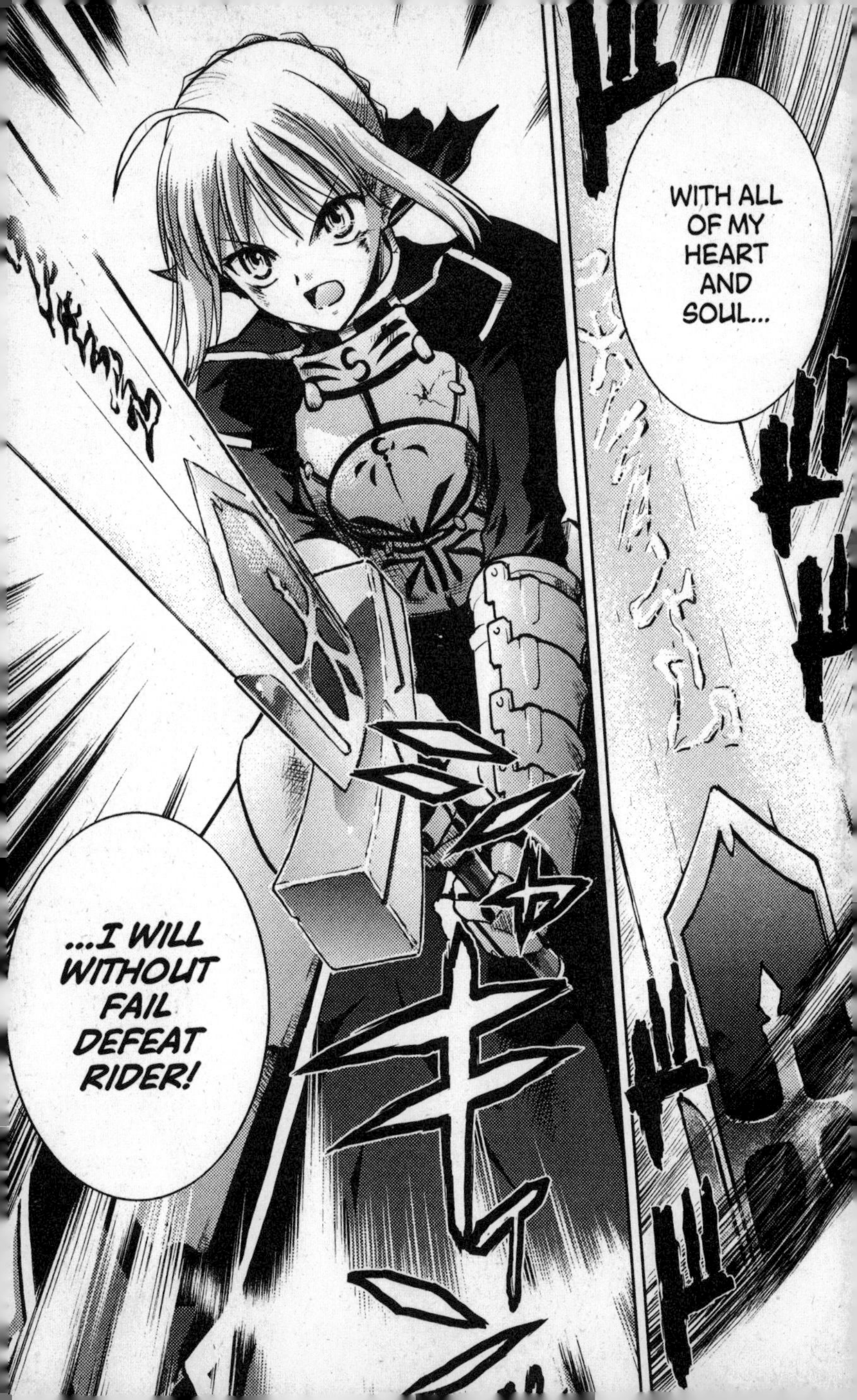
WITH ALL OF MY HEART AND SOUL...
...I WILL WITHOUT FAIL DEFEAT RIDER!

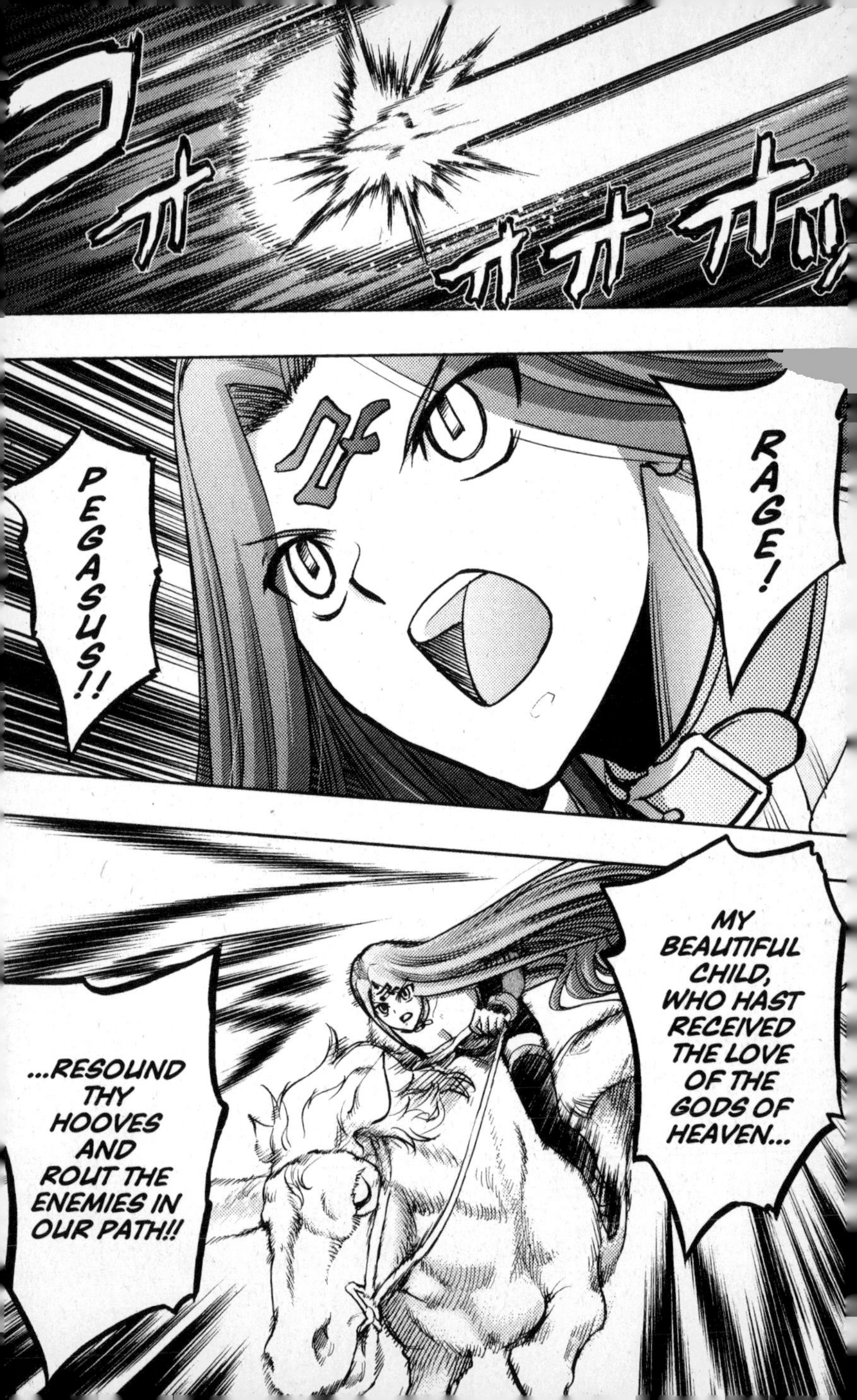
RAGE!
PEGASUS!!
MY BEAUTIFUL CHILD, WHO HAST RECEIVED THE LOVE OF THE GODS OF HEAVEN...
...RESOUND THY HOOVES AND ROUT THE ENEMIES IN OUR PATH!!

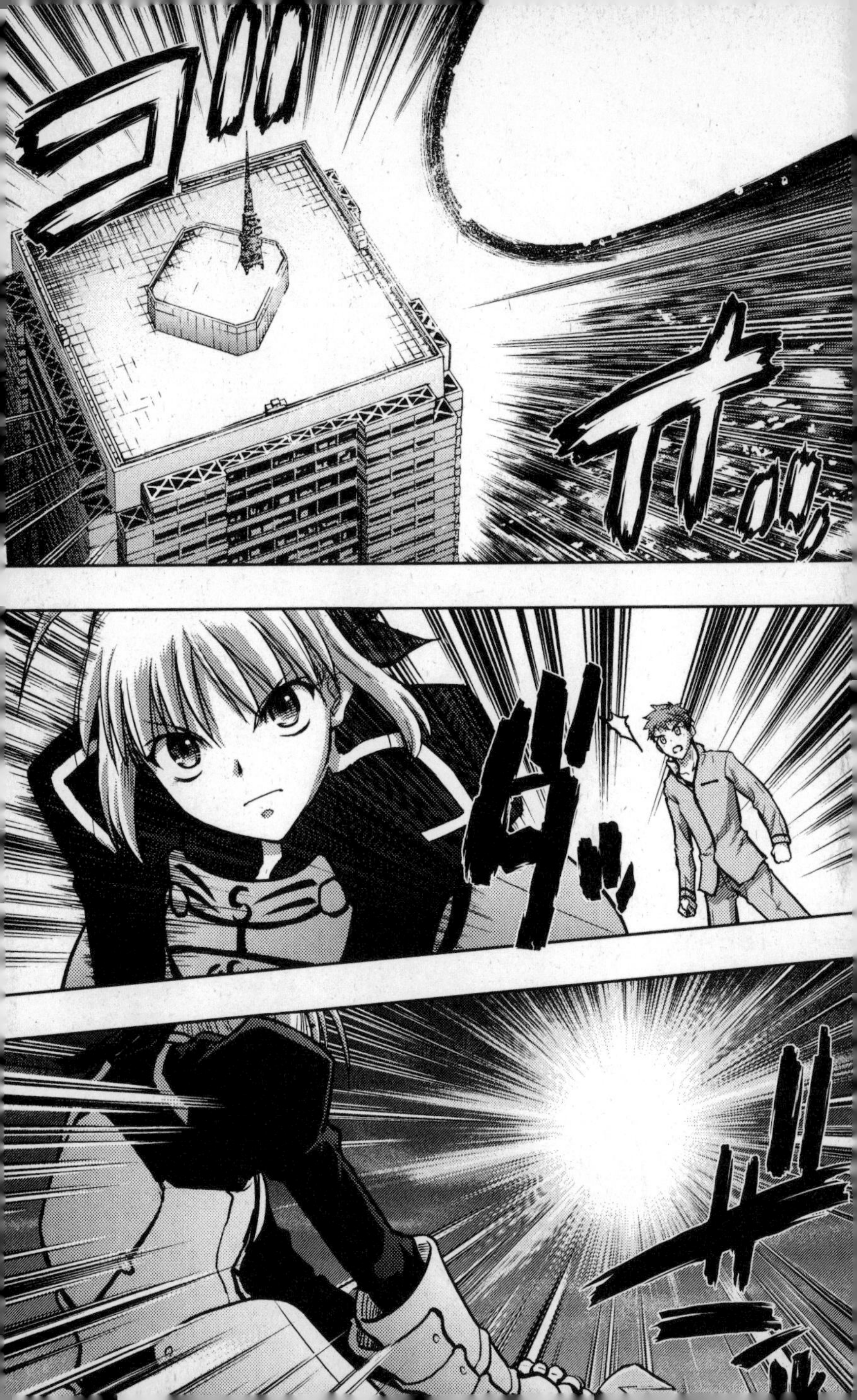

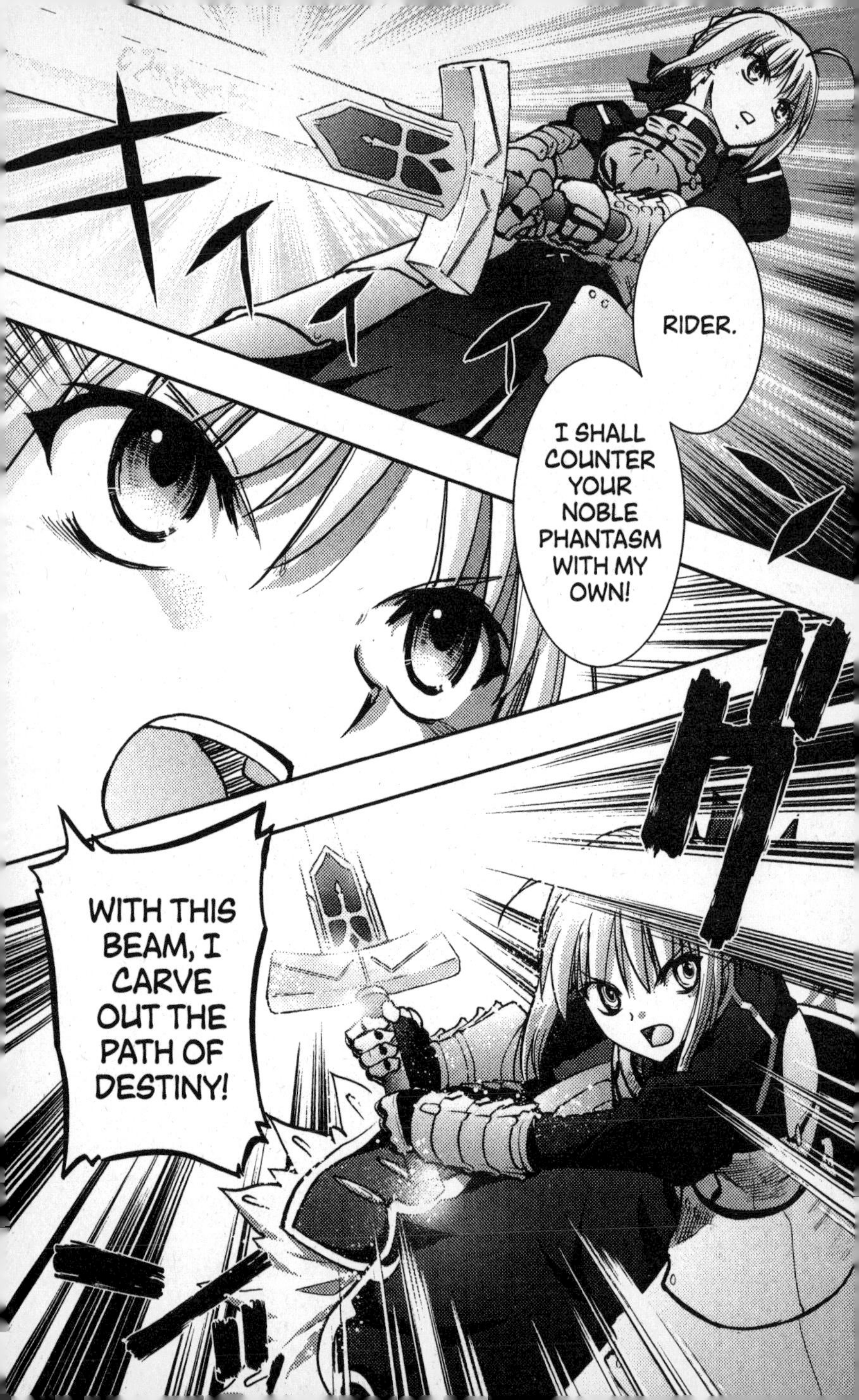
キイイ
RIDER.
I SHALL COUNTER YOUR NOBLE PHANTASM WITH MY OWN!
WITH THIS BEAM, I CARVE OUT THE PATH OF DESTINY!

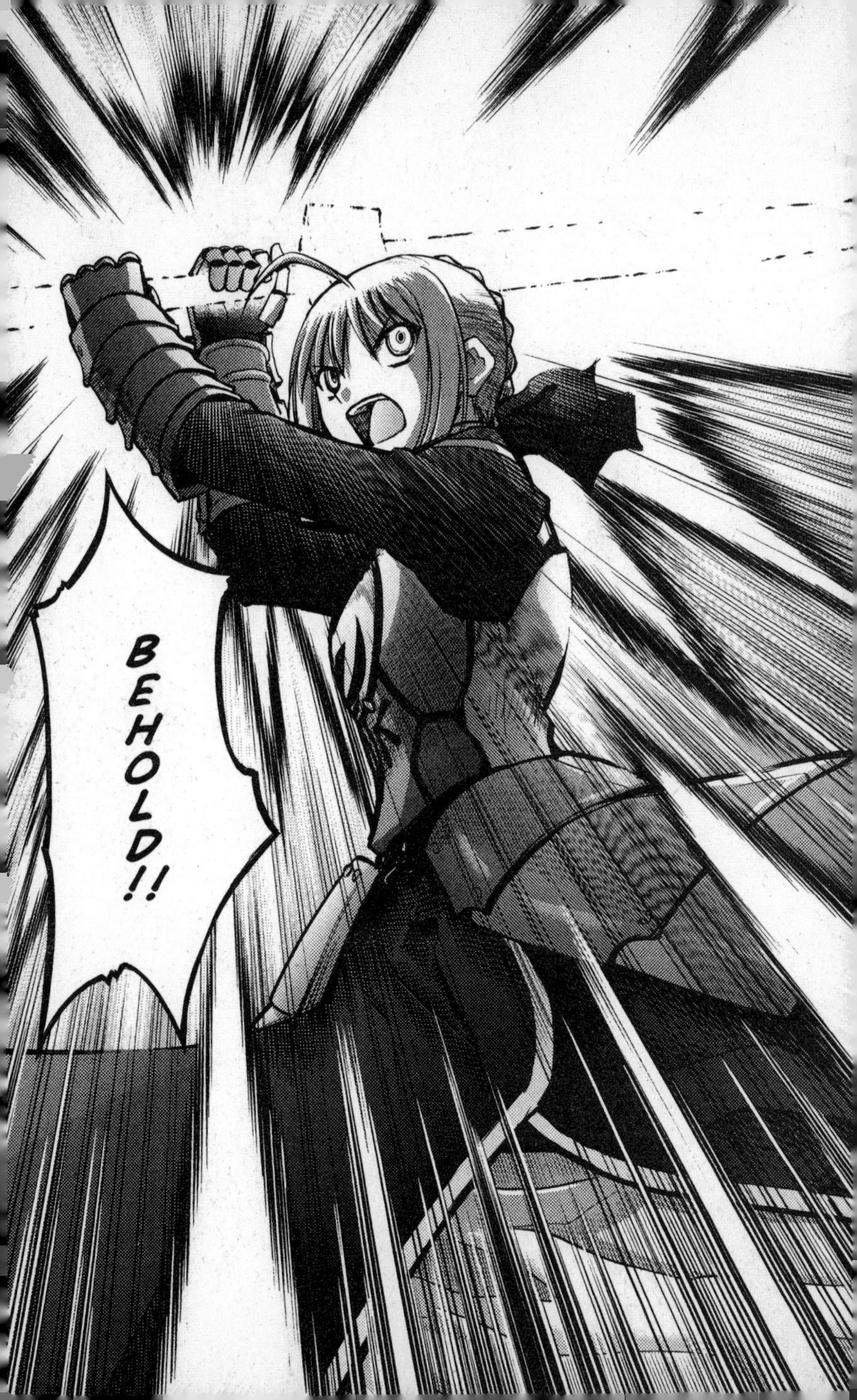
BEHOLD!!

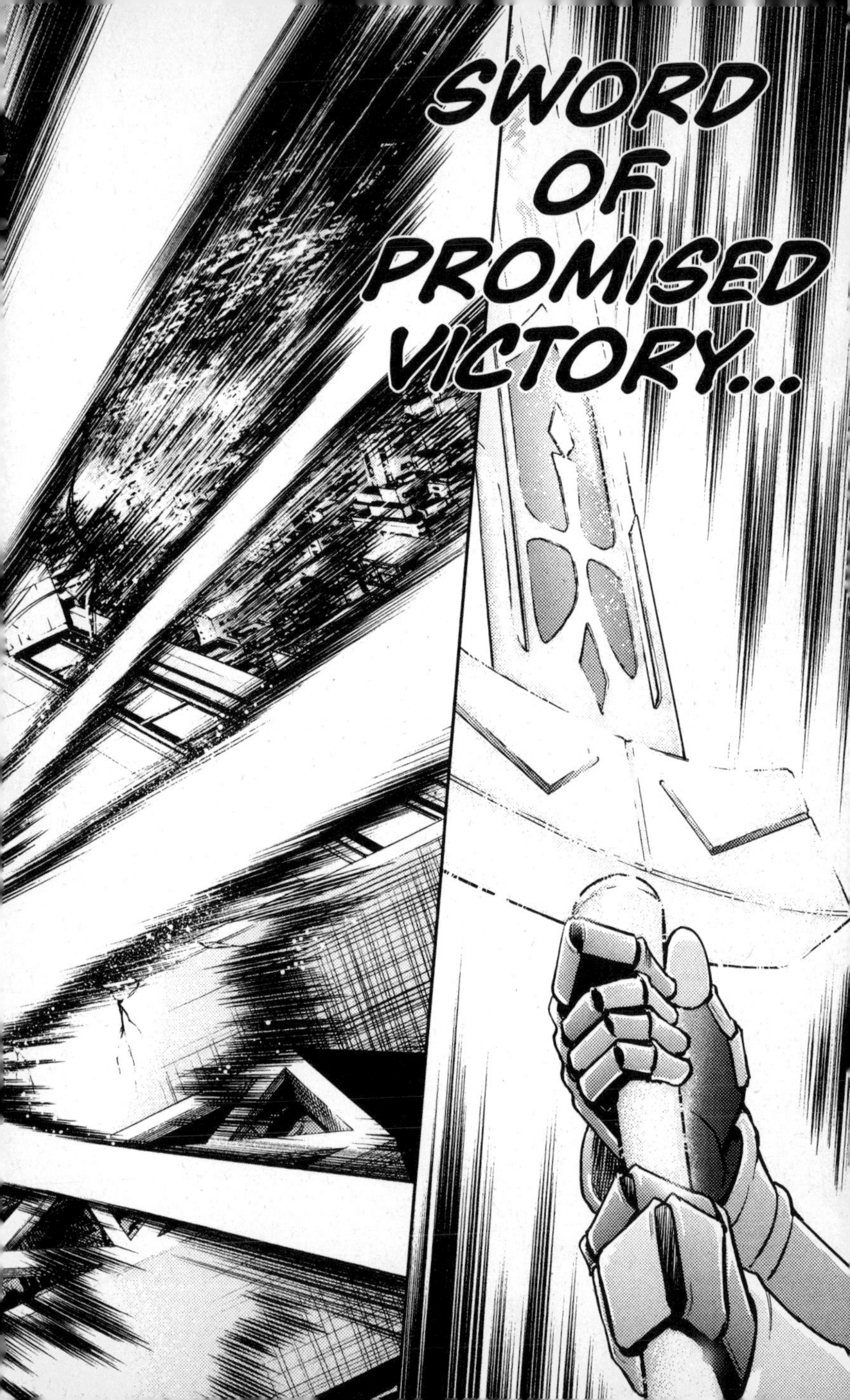
SWORD OF PROMISED VICTORY...

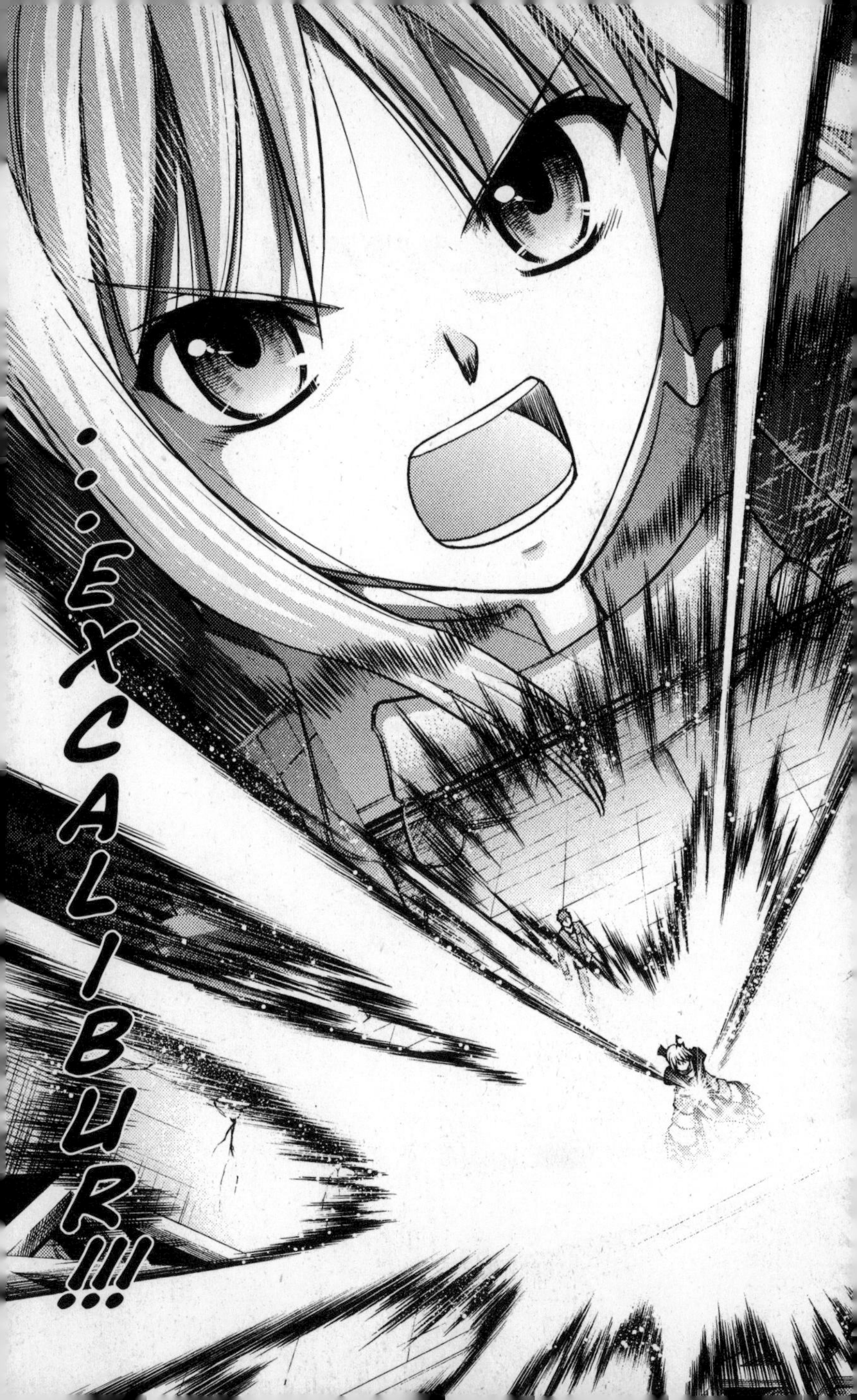
...EXCALIBUR!!!

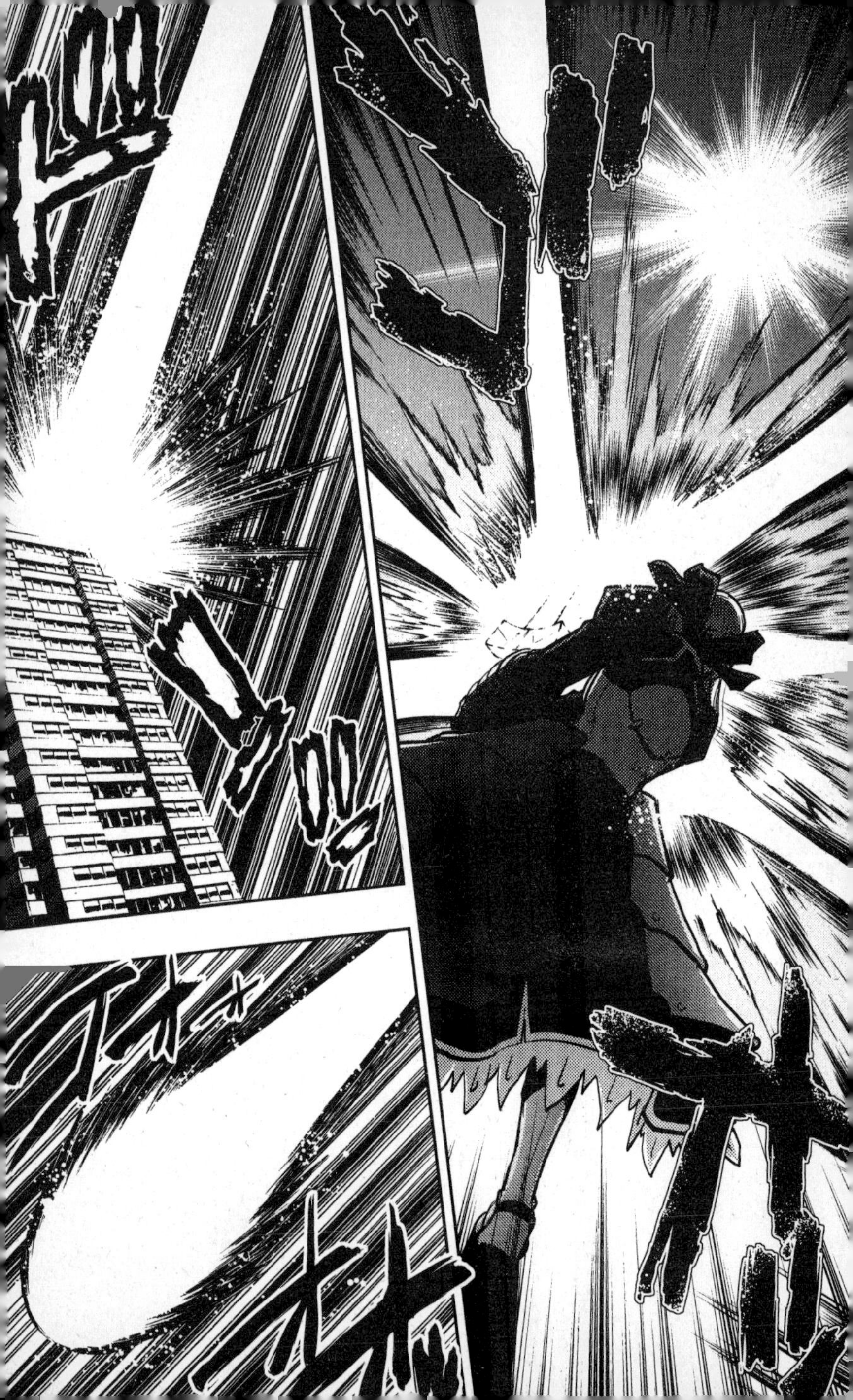

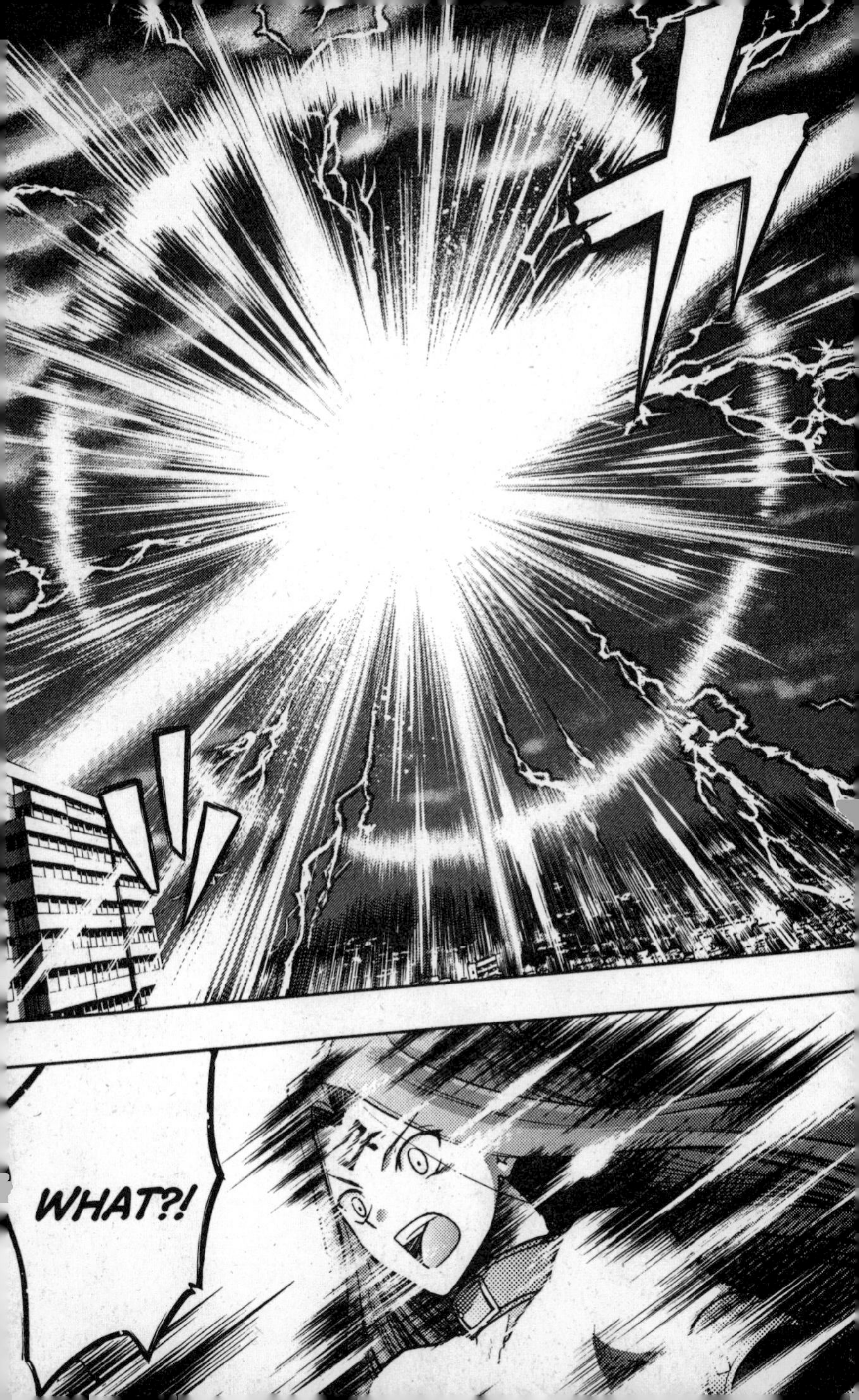
WHAT?!

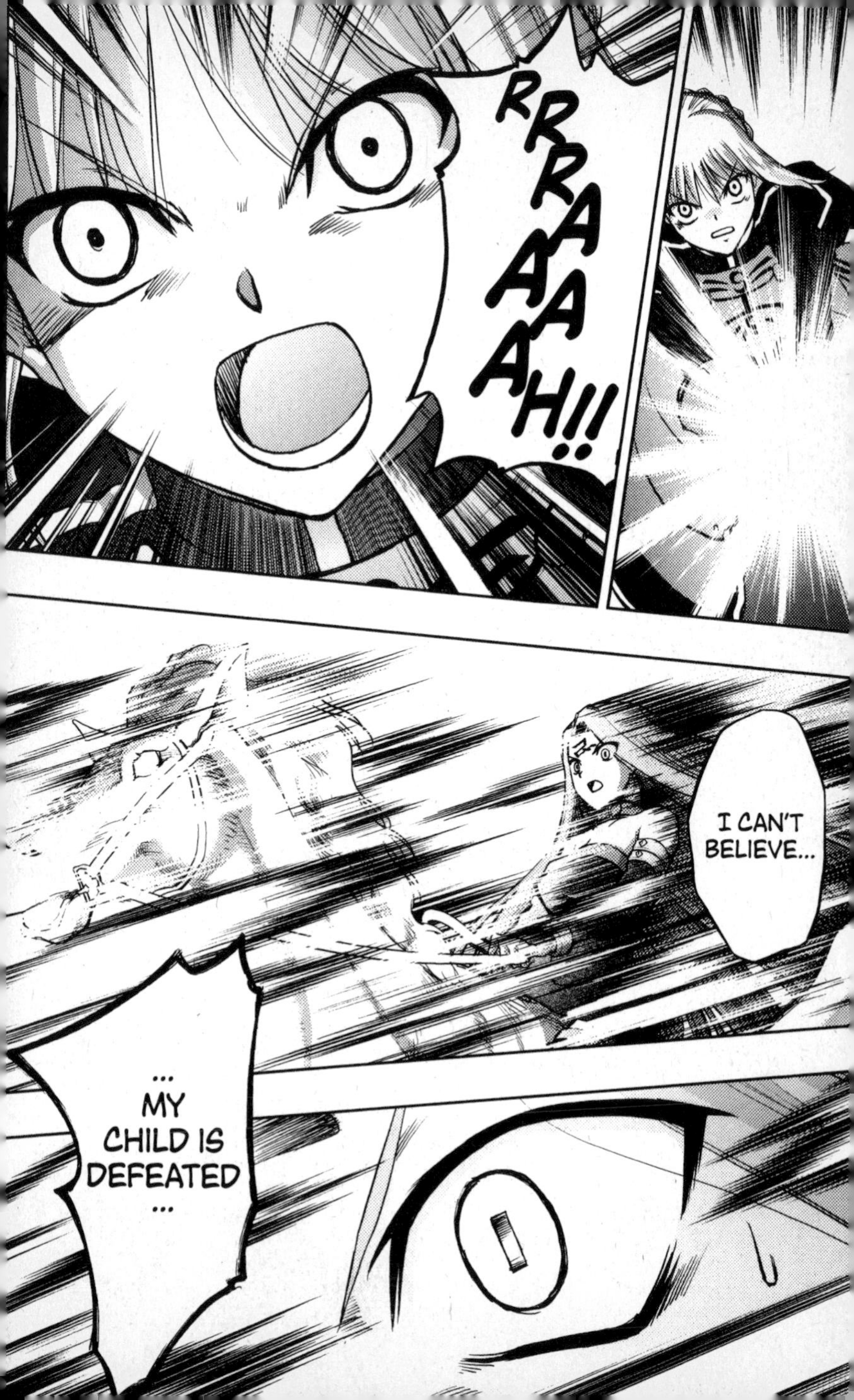
RRRAAAAH!!
I CAN'T BELIEVE...
... MY CHILD IS DEFEATED ...

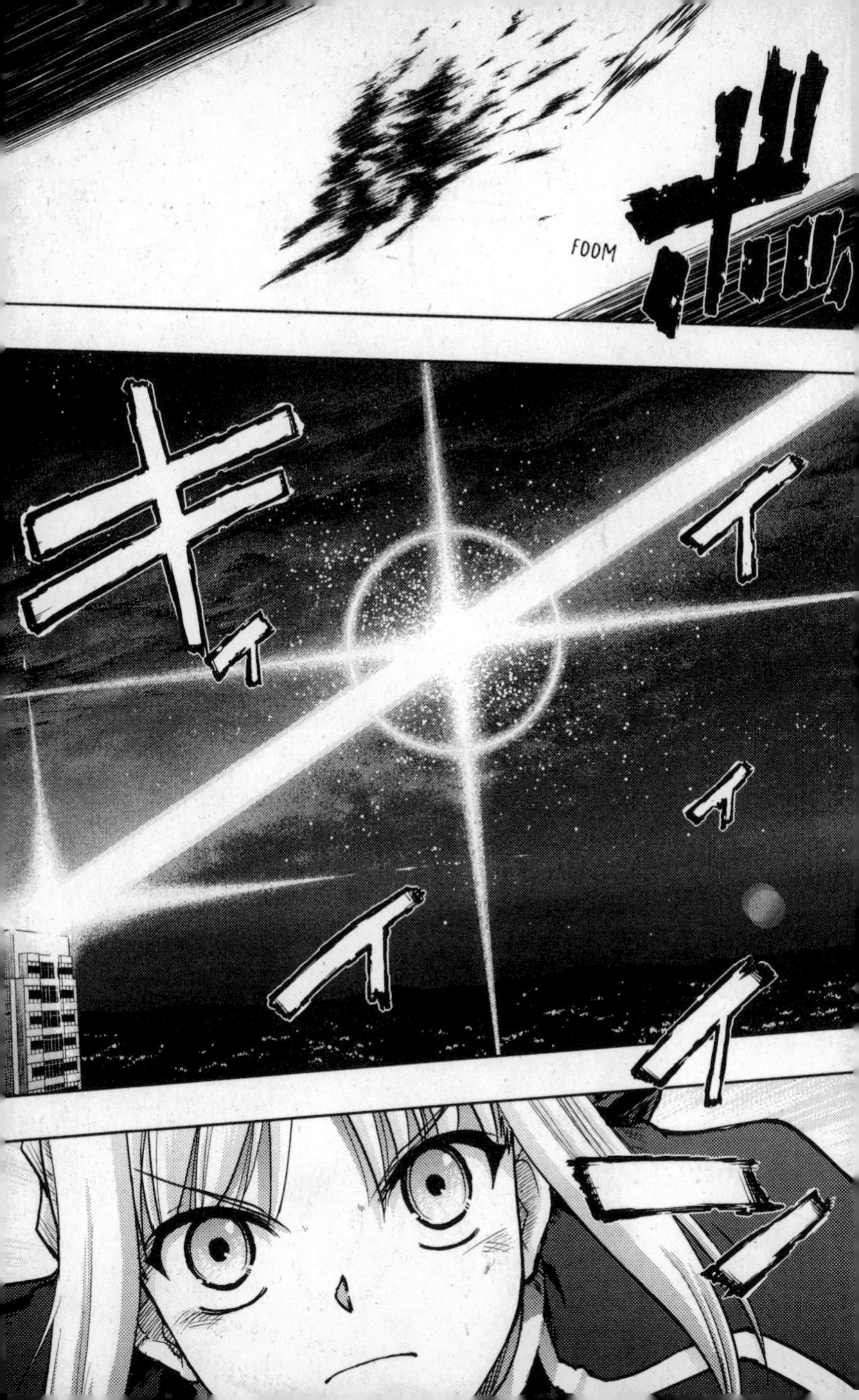
FOOM

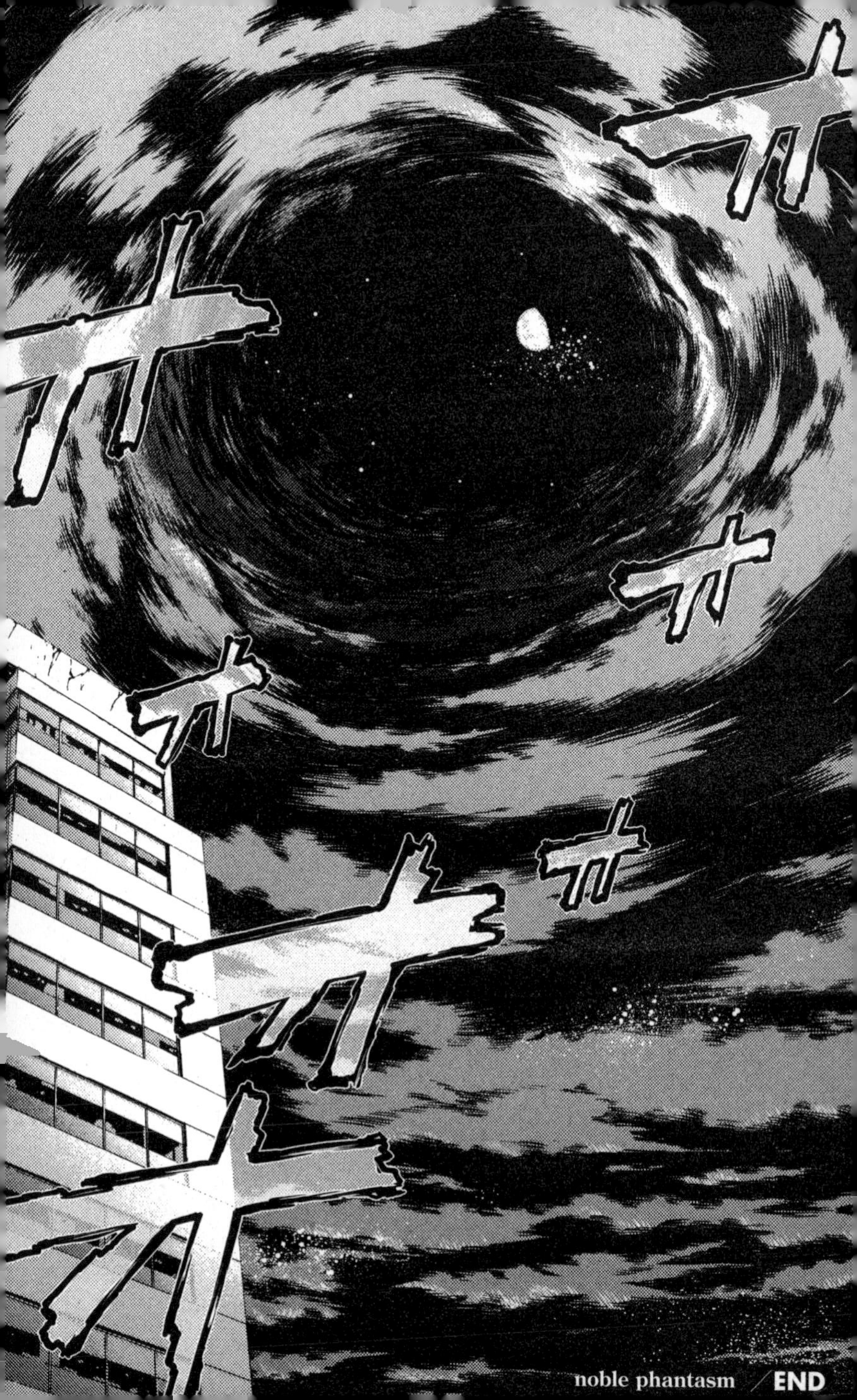
オオオオオオオ
noble phantasm ／END

To Be Continued...

Next Time In...

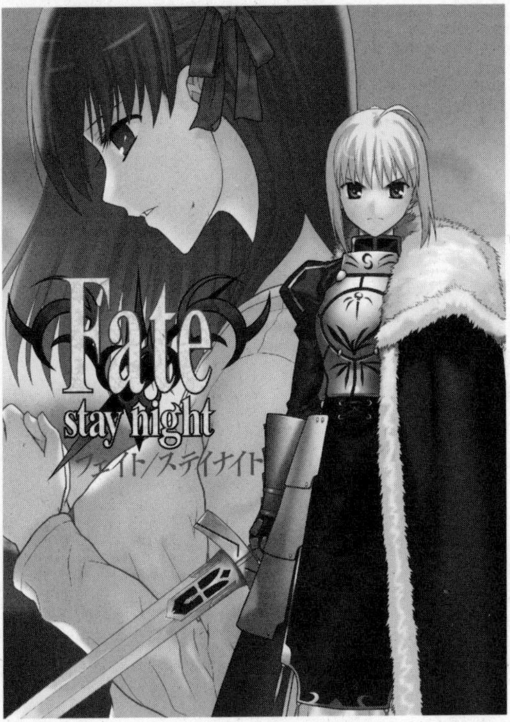
Fate
stay night
フェイト/ステイナイト

Shinji's defeat is at hand, but fate still has one twist in store! It turns out there's a lot more to the Mato family than meets the eye. Then, Shiro learns of Saber's true identity, and Caster takes advantage of the sudden power vacuum to step into the fray in a big way!

TOKYOPOP MANGA SUPPLEMENT

D·N·ANGEL

TOKYOPOP
D·N·ANGEL™
VOLUME 13 • YUKIRU SUGISAKI

The secret of the Hikari/Niwa curse is revealed!

The time has come for Satoshi to reveal to Daisuke the history behind the Hikari/Niwa curse. How will Daisuke respond when he finds out why Satoshi is destined to die so young? Meanwhile, another fight breaks out against Argentine, sending Daisuke spiraling toward death as he tries to rescue Risa...

FANTASY

T TEEN AGE 13+

BE SURE TO VISIT WWW.TOKYOPOP.COM/SHOP FOR EVERYTHING YOU COULD EVER WANT!

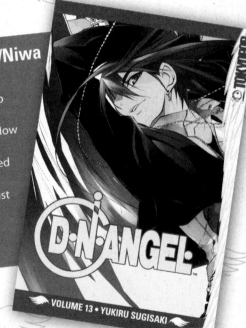

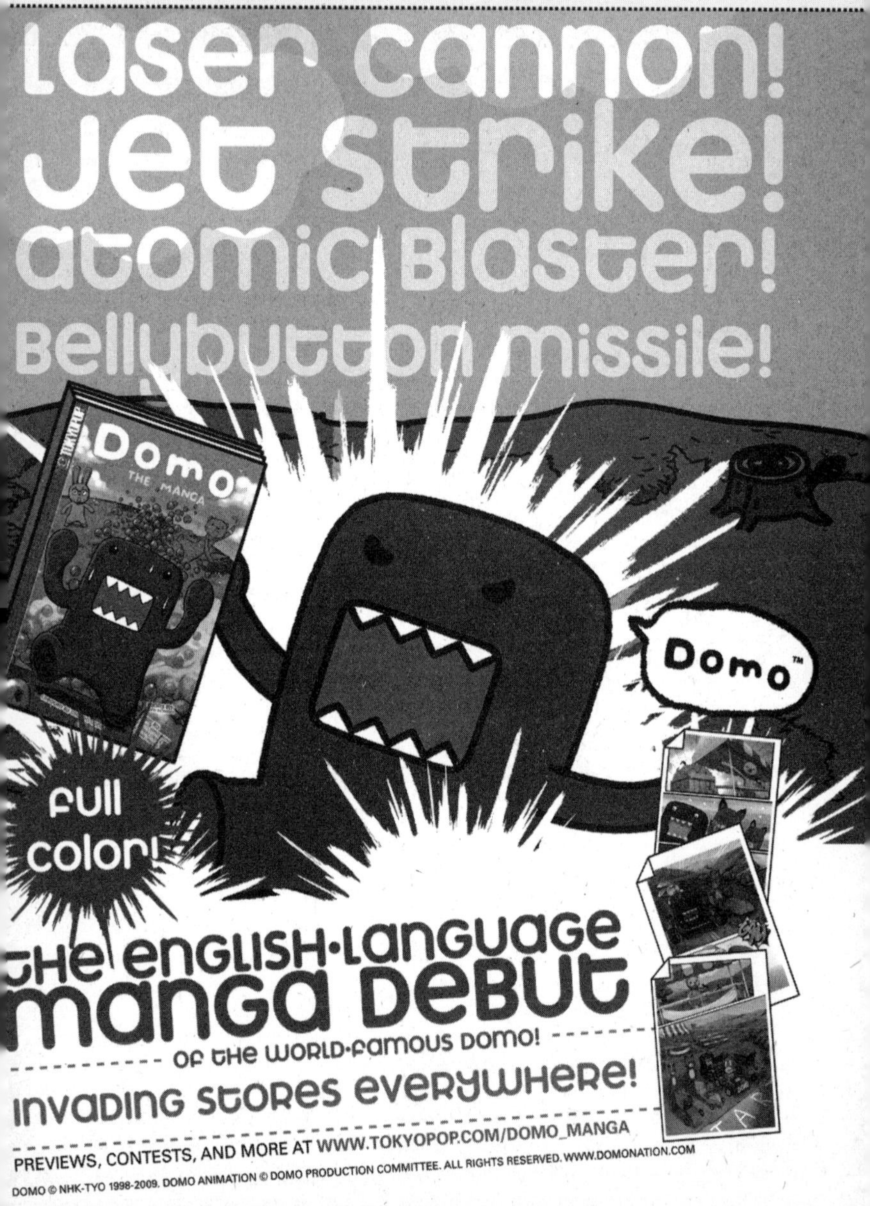
Laser Cannon!
Jet Strike!
Atomic Blaster!
Bellybutton Missile!
Domo THE MANGA
Domo™
full color!
THE ENGLISH-LANGUAGE
MANGA DEBUT
OF THE WORLD-FAMOUS DOMO!
INVADING STORES EVERYWHERE!
PREVIEWS, CONTESTS, AND MORE AT WWW.TOKYOPOP.COM/DOMO_MANGA
DOMO © NHK-TYO 1998-2009. DOMO ANIMATION © DOMO PRODUCTION COMMITTEE. ALL RIGHTS RESERVED. WWW.DOMONATION.COM

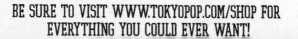

FEATURING THE CUTEST, MOST ORIGINAL CAST OF CHARACTERS SINCE +ANIMA!

CAN YOU PLEDGE SECRECY WHEN YOU ARE...A HUMAN BEING?

The fun never stops at Morimori High School! Fune and her friends are settling in to their classes and dorm life, but there are plenty of surprises in store as Fune learns more about the strange school rules, as well as some of its more mysterious students. And when it comes time to pick extra-curriculars—what will Fune do?!

STOP!

This is the back of the book.
You wouldn't want to spoil a great ending!

This book is printed "manga-style," in the authentic Japanese right-to-left format. Since none of the artwork has been flipped or altered, readers get to experience the story just as the creator intended. You've been asking for it, so TOKYOPOP® delivered: authentic, hot-off-the-press, and far more fun!

1
2
3
4
5
6
7
8
9
10

DIRECTIONS

If this is your first time reading manga-style, here's a quick guide to help you understand how it works.

It's easy... just start in the top right panel and follow the numbers. Have fun, and look for more 100% authentic manga from TOKYOPOP®!

THE MANGA REVOLUTION • LEADING THE MANGA REVOLUTION • LEADING

漫画革命